Liferay Portal Systems Development

Build dynamic, content-rich, and social systems on top of Liferay

Jonas X. Yuan

[PACKT] open source*

community experience distilled

PUBLISHING

BIRMINGHAM - MUMBAI

Liferay Portal Systems Development

First Edition: May 2009

Second Edition: January 2012

Production Reference: 1190112

Published by Packt Publishing Ltd.
Livery Place
35 Livery Street
Birmingham B3 2PB, UK.

ISBN 978-1-84951-598-6

www.packtpub.com

Cover Image by Rakesh Shejwal (shejwal.rakesh@gmail.com)

Credits

Author
Jonas X. Yuan

Reviewers
Piotr Filipowicz

Christianto Sahat Kurniawan

Szymon V. Gołębiewski

Acquisition Editor
Sarah Cullington

Lead Technical Editor
Hyacintha D'Souza

Technical Editors
Ankita Shashi

Manasi Poonthottam

Sakina Kaydawala

Azharuddin Sheikh

Copy Editors
Leonard D'Silva

Brandt D'Mello

Project Coordinator
Joel Goveya

Proofreaders
Lesley Harrison

Stephen Silk

Indexer
Tejal Daruwale

Graphics
Manu Joseph

Production Coordinator
Aparna Bhagat

Cover Work
Aparna Bhagat

About the Author

Dr. Jonas X. Yuan is an expert on Liferay Portal and Content Management Systems (CMS). As an open source community contributor, he published four Liferay books from 2008 to 2010. He is also an expert on Liferay integration with Ad Server OpenX, different search engines, enterprise contents including videos, audios, images, documents, records and web contents, social media, and other technologies, such as, BPM Intalio and Business Intelligence Pentaho, LDAP, and SSO. He holds a Ph.D. in Computer Science from the University of Zurich, where he focused on Integrity Control in Federated Database Systems. He earned his M.S. and B.S. degrees from China, where he conducted research on expert systems for predicting landslides. Previously, he worked as a Project Manager and a Technical Architect in Web GIS (Geographic Information System). He is experienced in Systems Development Lifecycle (SDLC) and has deep, hands on, skills in J2EE technologies. He developed a BPEL (Business Process Execution Language) Engine called BPELPower from scratch in the NASA data center. As the chief architect, Dr. Yuan led and successfully launched several large scale Liferay/Alfresco projects for millions of users each month.

He has worked on the following books: Liferay Portal Enterprise Intranets, 2008, ISBN 13: 978-1-847192-72-1; Liferay Portal 5.2 Systems Development, 2009, ISBN 13: 978-1-847194-70-1; Liferay Portal 6 Enterprise Intranets, 2010, ISBN 13: 978-1-849510-38-7; and Liferay Portal User Interface Development, 2010, ISBN 978-1-849512-62-6.

Acknowledgement

I would like to thank all team members at Liferay; especially Raymond Auge, Brian Chan, Jorge Ferrer, Michael Young, Bryan Cheung, Jerry Niu, Ed Shin, Craig Kaneko, Brian Kim, Bruno Farache, Thiago Moreira, Amos Fong, Scott Lee, David Truong, Alexander Chow, Mika Koivisto, Julio Camarero, Douglas Wong, Ryan Park, Eric Min, John Langkusch, Marco Abamonga, Ryan Park, Eric Min, John Langkusch, Marco Abamonga, Michael Han, Samuel Kong, Nate Cavanaugh, Arcko Duan, Richard Sezov, Joshua Asbury, Shuyang Zhou, Michael Saechang, Juan Fernández, James Falkner, Olaf Kock, Zsolt Berentey, Dennis Ju, Sergio Gonzalez, Zsolt Balogh, Jonathan Mak, Eduardo Lundgren, Iliyan Peychev, Bruno Basto, Jonathan Lee, Aaron Delani, and Angelo Jefferson of Liferay for providing all the support and valuable information. Much thanks to all my friends in the Liferay community.

I sincerely thank and appreciate Sarah Cullington and Hyacintha D'Souza, Acquisition Editor and Lead Technical Editor respectively at Packt Publishing for criticizing and fixing my writing style. Thanks to Joel Goveya, Sakina Kaydawala, Azharuddin Sheikh, Ankita Shashi, Manasi Poonthottam, and the entire team at Packt Publishing; it is really joyful to work with them.

Last but not least, I would like to thank my parents and my wife, Linda, for their love, understanding, and encouragement. My special thanks to my wonderful and understanding kid, Josua.

About the Reviewers

Piotr Filipowicz is a technical architect and software developer with eo Networks S.A., Poland. He is an expert in Content Management Systems (CMS). He currently holds the position of a team leader in a group tasked with developing Liferay-based software. His accomplishments in enhancing and creating various Liferay components are evident in the number of successful implementations. His experience and knowledge are supported by certifications as a Liferay Portal Administrator, Sun Certified Web Component Developer for the Java Platform, Sun Certified Programmer for the Java 2 Platform.

Since 2002 he has created various kinds of IT systems, from desktop applications through CMS applications supporting large banking and financial systems. His main interest lies in web applications. He uses Java and J2EE technologies on a daily basis, but his mind is open to other technologies and solutions. He holds a Master's in Software Systems from Politechnika Białostocka, Poland.

Christianto Sahat Kurniawan is a software engineer who has been using Java as his programming language since 2001, and using Liferay since 2007. After having experience implementing Liferay for a big global bank and few other companies while working in Singapore and Germany, he decided to start a company focusing on enterprise portal development and training. You can read his blog at www.javaenterpriseportal.com.

> I would like to thank the Liferay team, especially Jorge Ferrer, Olaf Kock, Amos Fong, and Ray Augé, who have contributed a lot in answering questions on Liferay's forum. And for the rest of Liferay team who have created a great open source software.

Szymon V. Gołębiewski is the Chief of Competence Center for Portals at eo Networks S.A. — a Poland-based company noted in Deloitte Technology Fast 50.

In his work, Szymon and his team focus on using Liferay as a tool for bringing best solutions for the company's clients. His team is responsible for commencing usability tests, preparing in-depth analysis of customer needs and delivering stable tools for company developers. One of his competences is managing product cycle of Liferay inside his company with all custom-made plugins and portlets. His vast knowledge of internet and usability standards gives him a useful advantage, when participating in Liferay programs like 100 PaperCuts program, Community Leadership, BugSquad.

His commitment to Liferay community development has resulted in participating at the East Coast Symposium 2011 as a speaker.

www.PacktPub.com

Support files, eBooks, discount offers, and more

You might want to visit www.PacktPub.com for support files and downloads related to your book.

Did you know that Packt offers eBook versions of every book published, with PDF and ePub files available? You can upgrade to the eBook version at www.PacktPub.com and as a print book customer, you are entitled to a discount on the eBook copy. Get in touch with us at service@packtpub.com for more details.

At www.PacktPub.com, you can also read a collection of free technical articles, sign up for a range of free newsletters and receive exclusive discounts and offers on Packt books and eBooks.

http://PacktLib.PacktPub.com

Do you need instant solutions to your IT questions? PacktLib is Packt's online digital book library. Here, you can access, read and search across Packt's entire library of books.

Why Subscribe?

- Fully searchable across every book published by Packt
- Copy and paste, print and bookmark content
- On demand and accessible via web browser

Free Access for Packt account holders

If you have an account with Packt at www.PacktPub.com, you can use this to access PacktLib today and view nine entirely free books. Simply use your login credentials for immediate access.

This book is dedicated to:

my wife Linda, my son Joshua, and my parents, Daxian and Zhengzi.

This book would not have been possible without your love and understanding.

Thank you from the bottom of my heart.

Table of Contents

Preface

Liferay portal is one of the most mature portal frameworks in the market, offering many key business benefits that involve personalization, customization, content management systems, web content management, collaboration, social networking, and workflow. Liferay delivers enterprise solutions for portals, publishing content, social and collaboration. Dynamic, content-rich, and social systems are built fast and easily on top of Liferay portal.

Liferay Portal Systems Development is a development cookbook explaining how to use Liferay kernel as a framework to develop custom web and WAP systems, which will help you to maximize your productivity gains. Get ready for a rich, friendly, intuitive, social and collaborative end-user experience! Its explicit instructions are accompanied by plenty of source code. If you are a Java developer who wants to build custom websites and WAP sites using Liferay portal, this book is all you need.

The book shows you exactly how to build dynamic, content-rich, and social systems in Liferay:

- Use Liferay tools (CMS, WCM, collaborative API, and social API) to create your own websites and WAP sites with hands-on examples
- Customize Liferay portal using the JSR-286 portlets, hooks, ext plugins, themes, layout templates, web plugins, and diverse portlet bridges
- Build your own websites with kernel features, such as indexing, workflow, staging, scheduling, publishing, messaging, polling, tracking, auditing, reporting, and more

The clear, practical examples in the sample application that runs throughout this book will enable professional Java developers to build custom websites, portals, intranet, and mobile applications using Liferay portal as a framework. You will learn how to make all of your organization's data and web content easily accessible by customizing Liferay into a single point of access. The book will also show you how to improve your inter-company communication by enhancing your websites and WAP sites, so that you can share content with colleagues.

By the end of this book, you will clearly understand shared documents, discussions, collaborative wikis, social activities, and more in a single, searchable portal. The portal is a great choice for intranets and Internets, easy-to-use, open source, extensible, integrated with other tools and standards. Service builder and Plugins SDK provide portal systems development and customization environments with plugins like ext, themes, layout templates, webs, portlets and hooks.

What this book covers

Chapter 1, Liferay Enterprise Portal, addresses what Liferay can offer your intranets and Internets. Liferay delivers enterprise solutions for portals, publishing content, social and collaboration. Dynamic, content-rich, and social systems will be built fast and easily on top of Liferay portal.

Chapter 2, Service-Builder and Development Environment, discusses how to set up, build, and deploy portal core and plugins in the Eclipse IDE. Then it discusses how to use service builder to generate services and models, and how to add new features on service builder. It also addresses how to populate default data, how to use default project creation and templates, and how to set up fast development of plugins with Tomcat.

Chapter 3, Generic MVC Portlets, first introduces how to develop a portlet project with default templates. Then it addresses how to construct basic MVC portlets by viewing the title and adding an action, and how to build advanced MVC portlets. Finally, it discusses how to build and re-build services, how to bring portlets into Control Panel, how to set security and permissions, dynamic query, and custom SQL.

Chapter 4, Ext Plugin and Hooks, addresses Ext plugin and project default templates, upgrading a legacy Ext environment, deploying processes and what it does, class loader proxy and how it works, hooks and project default templates, portal properties hooks, language properties hooks and multiple languages support, custom JSP hooks, indexer post processors, service wrappers hooks, servlet filters and servlet mappings hooks, and struts actions hooks.

Chapter 5, Enterprise Content Management, introduces video, audio, and image management. It also discusses document and media library and document management, WebDAV implementation, multiple repositories integration, CMIS consumers and producers, web scanning, OCR and record management, content relationship, content authoring, and content archiving.

Chapter 6, DDL and WCM, addresses how to customize web content models and services, to build web content structure and template, to publish web content via asset publisher, to integrate CKEditor and its plugins, to use Expando – custom attributes, to leverage DDL (Dynamic Data Lists) and DDM (Dynamic Data Mapping), to manage assets, asset links, tags and categories and to publish assets with asset query.

Chapter 7, Collaborative and Social API, first introduces how to use collaborative tools – wiki, blogs, calendar event, message boards, polls, bookmarks. Then it addresses how to manage more collaborative assets – both core assets and custom assets, and how to collaborate assets – both core assets and custom assets. Afterwards, it introduces how to use social networking, social coding, and social office. Finally, it addresses social activity, social equity capabilities, and OpenSocial API.

Chapter 8, Staging, Scheduling, Publishing, and Cache Clustering, introduces in depth: the Portal-Group-Page-Content (PGPC) pattern, LAR exporting and importing, local staging and publishing, remote staging and publishing, scheduling and messaging, caching and clustering.

Chapter 9, Indexing, Search, and Workflow, addresses web plugins and WAI first. Then it shows how to build web plugins using cas-web and solr-web plugins as examples, how to index and search assets – both portal core assets and plugins custom assets, how to set up solr-web plugin, and how to apply workflow on assets and employ kaleo-web plugin.

Chapter 10, Mobile Devices and Portlet Bridges, introduces layout template plugins, theme plugins, and WAP mobile themes first. The mobile devices detectors and WURFL get addressed, too. Then it addresses the portlet bridges, Struts 2 portlets, JSF 2 portlets, and Spring 3 MVC portlets.

Chapter 11, Common API, addresses user management, password policy, authentication and authorization, LDAP and SSO, tracking and auditing, rules engine and reporting engine, scripting engine, polling, web services, WSRP producers and consumers, and OSGi framework.

> Chapter 11 is not present in the book. You can download it from the Packt website at `https://www.packtpub.com/sites/default/files/downloads/5986_11.pdf`.

What you need for this book

This book uses Liferay portal version 6.1 with the following settings:

- MySQL database 5.1
- Java SE 6
- Liferay portal bundled with Tomcat 7

Although this book explores in depth the various technologies used in Liferay portal, it explains all the topics in an easy-to-understand way. This book is for any Java developers.

If you have some basic knowledge in web applications including servlets and portlets, you will understand better the discussions in this book.

Most importantly, if you like problem-solving and have an eye for perfection, this book is written for you.

We have opened our arms to welcome you to the Liferay world.

Who this book is for

This book is for Java developers who don't need any prior experience with Liferay portal. Although Liferay portal makes heavy use of open source frameworks, no prior experience of using these is assumed.

Conventions

In this book, you will find a number of styles of text that distinguish between different kinds of information. Here are some examples of these styles, and an explanation of their meaning.

Code words in text are shown as follows: "By the way, we use $JDK_MAJOR_VERSION to represent the major version of JDK."

A block of code is set as follows:

```
public interface AuditedModel
{
    public long getCompanyId();
    // see details in AuditedModel.java
    public void setUserUuid(String userUuid);
}
```

When we wish to draw your attention to a particular part of a code block, the relevant lines or items are set in bold:

```
public interface AuditedModel
{
    public long getCompanyId();
    // see details in AuditedModel.java
    public void setUserUuid(String userUuid);
}
```

Any command-line input or output is written as follows:

```
svn://svn.liferay.com/repos/public/portal/trunk/portal-impl/src/com/
liferay/portlet/documentlibrary/service.xml
```

New terms and important words are shown in bold. Words that you see on the screen, in menus or dialog boxes for example, appear in the text like this: "clicking the **Next** button moves you to the next screen".

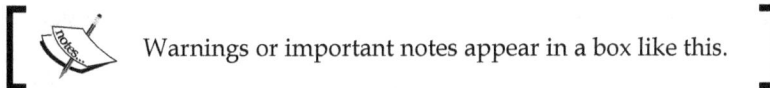

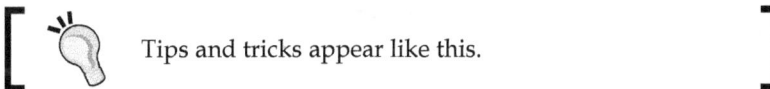

> Warnings or important notes appear in a box like this.

> Tips and tricks appear like this.

Reader feedback

Feedback from our readers is always welcome. Let us know what you think about this book—what you liked or may have disliked. Reader feedback is important for us to develop titles that you really get the most out of.

To send us general feedback, simply send an e-mail to feedback@packtpub.com, and mention the book title through the subject of your message.

If there is a topic that you have expertise in and you are interested in either writing or contributing to a book, see our author guide on www.packtpub.com/authors.

Customer support

Now that you are the proud owner of a Packt book, we have a number of things to help you to get the most from your purchase.

Downloading the example code

You can download the example code files for all Packt books you have purchased from your account at http://www.packtpub.com. If you purchased this book elsewhere, you can visit http://www.packtpub.com/support and register to have the files e-mailed directly to you.

Errata

Although we have taken every care to ensure the accuracy of our content, mistakes do happen. If you find a mistake in one of our books—maybe a mistake in the text or the code—we would be grateful if you would report this to us. By doing so, you can save other readers from frustration and help us improve subsequent versions of this book. If you find any errata, please report them by visiting http://www.packtpub.com/support, selecting your book, clicking on the **errata submission form** link, and entering the details of your errata. Once your errata are verified, your submission will be accepted and the errata will be uploaded to our website, or added to any list of existing errata, under the Errata section of that title.

Piracy

Piracy of copyright material on the Internet is an ongoing problem across all media. At Packt, we take the protection of our copyright and licenses very seriously. If you come across any illegal copies of our works, in any form, on the Internet, please provide us with the location address or website name immediately so that we can pursue a remedy.

Please contact us at copyright@packtpub.com with a link to the suspected pirated material.

We appreciate your help in protecting our authors, and our ability to bring you valuable content.

Questions

You can contact us at questions@packtpub.com if you are having a problem with any aspect of the book, and we will do our best to address it.

1
Liferay Enterprise Portal

As the world's leading open source portal platform, Liferay is the market's leading provider of open source portal, web publishing, content, social and collaboration enterprise solutions, providing a unified web interface to data and tools scattered across many sources. Within Liferay, a portal is composed of a number of portlets, which are self-contained interactive elements that are written to a particular standard. Dynamic, content-rich, social systems could be built quickly and easily on top of Liferay Portal.

Liferay was created in 2000 to provide an enterprise portal solution for non-profit organizations. In 2004, the company was incorporated under the name Liferay. In 2011/2012, Liferay was going to bring several enhancements and new features such as an improved document library (renamed as document and media library), **Dynamic Data Lists (DDL)**, **Dynamic Data Mapping (DDM)**, setup wizard, mobile device enhancements, multiple repository mounting and apps store (called **marketplace**).

This book will show you how to develop and/or customize portal systems with Liferay Portal. In this chapter, we will look at:

- The features that Liferay Portal has
- Why Liferay Portal is an excellent choice for building custom systems
- The Liferay Portal framework and architecture for customization
- What portal development strategies are and how they work
- Finding more technical information about what Liferay is and how it works

So let's begin by looking at exactly what Liferay Portal is and how to customize it.

Liferay functionalities

Liferay currently has the following four main functionalities:

- **Liferay Portal** – JSR-168/JSR-286 enterprise portal platform
- **Liferay CMS** and **WCM** – JSR-170 content management system and web content management
- **Liferay social collaboration** – Collaboration software such as blogs, calendar, web mail, message boards, polls, RSS feeds, Wiki, presence (AJAX chat client, dynamic friend list, activity wall, and activity tracker), alert and announcement, asset links, asset tagging and classification, social equity, social activities, OpenSocial, and more
- **Liferay social office** – A social collaboration on top of the portal; a dynamic team workspace solution – all you have to do is log in and work the way you want to, at your convenience

Generally speaking, a website built by Liferay might consist of a portal, CMS and WCM, collaboration, and/or social office.

Document and media library—CMS

Document and Media Library is a useful tool to manage any media such as basic documents, images, records, videos, and audios with built-in features, for example, dynamic data list, dynamic data mapping, dynamic document type and metadata runtime creation, authoring, versioning, imaging, check-in / check-out, archiving, access control, and indexing. In particular, **multiple repositories** are supported as well as **CMIS**. For example, in the document and media library, you can add document types and metadata sets as well as folders and subfolders to manage and publish documents. The document and media library make up the **Content Management Systems (CMS)** available to power both intranets and extranets. The CMS is equipped with customizable document types and folders, and acts as a web-based shared drive for all your team members, no matter where they are. As content is accessible only to those authorized by administrators, each individual file is as open or as secure as you need it to be.

Web content management—WCM

Your company may have a lot of HTML text, audio, videos, images, records, and documents using different structures and templates, and you may need to manage all of these as well. Therefore, you require the ability to manage a lot of web content, and then publish that web content to intranets or Internets.

We will see how to manage and publish web content within Liferay. **Liferay Journal** (renamed as **Web Content**) not only provides the ability to publish, manage, and maintain web content and documents, but it also separates content from layout. **WCM** allows us to create, edit, and publish web content (formerly called Journal articles) as well as article templates for one-click changes in layout. It has built-in workflow, article versioning, search and metadata.

The portal also provides dynamic data lists (DDL) and dynamic data mapping (DDM). Through DDL and DDM, we can define web forms, document types, metadata sets, and columns of various input styles, such as free form, drop-down lists, combo boxes, date, number, text, and pre-defined list values such as lists of users, order types, inventory types, and more.

Personalization and internalization

All users get a personal space that can be either made public (published as a website with a unique, friendly URL) or kept private. In fact, users can have both private and public pages at the same time. You can also customize how the space looks, what tools and applications are included, what goes into the document and media library, and who can view and access any of this content.

In addition, you can use your own language. Multilingual organizations get out-of-the-box support for up to 42 languages (such as Hindi, Hebrew, Ukrainian, and Romanian), and new languages can be added easily within the portal framework. Users can toggle between different language settings with just one click and produce/publish multilingual documents and web content. You can also easily add other languages in your public pages, private pages, or other organizations.

Workflow, staging, scheduling, and publishing

You can use workflows to manage definitions, instances, and tasks. There are many workflow engines such as **jBPM** workflow, **Kaleo** workflow, **Activiti** BPM, and **Intalio | BPMS**, and all of these can be integrated easily with Liferay. And then, with a workflow engine as the backend, a portal user can add workflow functionality to any activity such as CMS content approval and the like. In addition, Liferay Portal allows you to define publishing workflows that track changes to web content as well as the pages of the site in which they live.

Staging is a major feature of Liferay Portal. The staging environment allows us to make changes to the site in a specialized staging area, and then publish the whole site to **Live** when you are done, either locally or remotely. **Scheduling** is another major feature of Liferay Portal, using a built-in **Quartz** job scheduling engine. Before going live, you are able to schedule events to publish selected pages with all included content.

The **Site snapshot** feature means that branching and versioning of staged layouts are supported as well. Thus at the end of a workflow, you would be able to keep the current version of the layout as history; this is done in case the users want to use an old version of the layout at a later time.

Social network and social office

Liferay Portal supports social network—you can easily connect your accounts in Liferay with **Facebook**, **MySpace**, **Google+**, **Twitter**, and more. Of course, you can also manage your instant messenger accounts in Liferay Portal, such as **AIM**, **ICQ**, **Jabber**, **MSN**, **Skype**, and **YM**. In addition, you are able to track social activities and social equity as well.

Social office gives us social collaboration on top of the portal—a full virtual workspace that streamlines communication and builds up group cohesion. All components in social office are tied together seamlessly, getting everyone on the same page by sharing the same look-and-feel. More importantly, the dynamic activity tracking gives us a bird's-eye view of who has been doing what and when within each individual site.

Monitoring, auditing, and reporting

The portal provides abilities to monitor portlets and portal transactions. This includes—but is not limited to—average transaction time per portlet for each phase of the portlet life cycle, minimum and maximum transaction time for each portlet transaction, average time for portal requests (inclusive of all portlets), and minimum and maximum time for each portal request. By the way, statistics are exposed using JMX MBeans.

An audit trail of user actions is required by many organizations. Fortunately, the portal provides audit service, which is a method for storing the audit trail from the portal and plugins. Then the information processed by the audit service plugin can be stored in a log file or database. Note that audit services employ Liferay Lightweight Message Bus and Plugin architecture. The audit service itself is a plugin, handling the processing and logging of the audit messages sent through the Message Bus. Therefore, any plugin can produce audit messages to the audit Message Bus destination.

The Liferay **JasperReports** Report Engine provides an implementation of Liferay BI using Jasper. **JasperReports** is an open source Java reporting tool that can write to screen, a printer, or to PDF, HTML, Microsoft Excel, RTF, ODT, CSV (Comma Separated Value) formats, and XML files. The portal provides full integration of JasperReports with its reporting framework. The portal provides the ability to schedule reports and deliver them using document and media library and e-mail. In addition, the portal supports Jasper XLS data sources in its reporting framework.

Tagging

The portal tagging system allows us to tag web content, documents, message board threads, and more, as well as to dynamically publish assets by tags. Tags provide a way of organizing and aggregating content. **Folksonomies** are a user-driven approach to organizing content through tags, cooperative classification, and communication through shared metadata. The portal implements folksonomies through tags. **Taxonomies** are a hierarchical structure used in scientific classification schemes. The portal implements taxonomies as vocabularies and categories, which includes category hierarchy, in order to tag contents and classify them.

Integration

In particular, the portal provides a framework so that you can integrate external applications easily. For example, you could integrate external applications such as Alfresco, Documentum, SharePoint, OpenX, LDAP, SSO CAS, Facebook, NTLM, OpenSSO, SiteMinder, SAML 2.0, Orbeon Forms, KonaKart, PayPal, Solr, Coveo, Salesforce.com, SugarCRM, JasperForge, Drools, jBPM, and more. With the portal, integrating standalone Java web applications into the portal is not an easy task. However, Liferay makes it possible to achieve near-native integration with minimal effort using the **WAI (Web Application Integrator)** portlet or the IFrame portlet.

In addition, the portal uses the **OSGi** framework, that is, the portal supports a module system and service platform for the Java programming language that implements a complete and dynamic component model. Please refer to `http://www.osgi.org` for more information.

In a word, the portal offers compelling benefits to today's enterprises—reduced operational costs, improved customer satisfaction, and streamlined business processes.

Framework and architecture

Liferay Portal architecture supports high availability for mission-critical applications using clustering, as well as fully-distributed cache and replication support across multiple servers.

The following diagram depicts various architectural layers and portlet functionality:

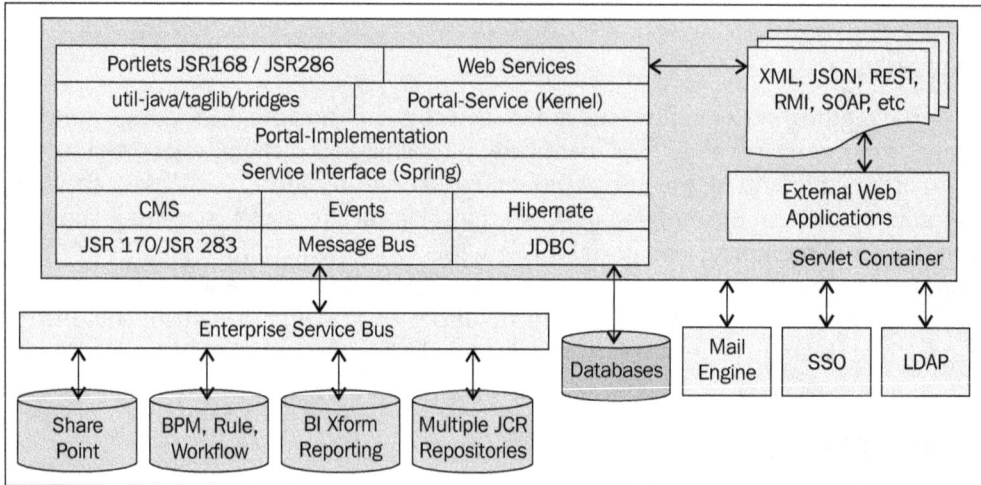

Service Oriented Architecture

Liferay Portal uses **Service Oriented Architecture (SOA)** design principles throughout, and provides the tools and framework to extend the SOA to other enterprise applications. Under the Liferay enterprise architecture, not only can the users access the portal from traditional and/or wireless devices, but the developers can also access it from the exposed APIs using REST, SOAP, RMI, XML-RPC, XML, JSON, Hessian, Burlap, and custom-tunnel classes.

In addition, Liferay Portal is designed to deploy portlets that adhere to the portlet API, which is compliant with both JSR-168 and JSR-286. A set of useful portlets built on top of **Struts 1.2.9** are bundled with the portal, such as document and media library, calendar, message boards, blogs, wikis, and so on. They can be used as examples for adding custom portlets.

> In a nutshell, the key features of Liferay include using SOA design principles throughout, reliable security, integrating with SSO and LDAP, multitier and limitless clustering, high availability, caching pages, and dynamic virtual hosting.

Enterprise Service Bus

The **Enterprise Service Bus** (**ESB**) is a central connection manager that allows applications and services to be added quickly to an enterprise infrastructure. When an application needs to be replaced, it can be easily disconnected from the bus at a single point. Liferay Portal can use either Mule or ServiceMix as the ESB.

Through the ESB, the portal can integrate with SharePoint, BPM (such as jBPM workflow engine, Intalio | BPMS engine), a rule engine (Drools), BI Xforms reporting, JCR repository, and so on. It adds another layer like JSR-170, where the repository can be abstracted. Furthermore, it supports events' system with asynchronous messaging and Lightweight Message Bus.

Liferay Portal uses Spring framework for its business and data services layers. It also uses Spring framework for its transaction management. Based on service interfaces (Spring framework), **portal-implementation** (`portal-impl`) is implemented and exposed only for internal use — for example, they are used for the extension environment or Ext plugins. Both **portal-kernel** and **portal-service** (these two packages are merged into one known as `portal-service`) are provided for both external and internal use — for example, they are used for the Plugins SDK environment. Custom portlets, both JSR-168 and JSR-286, and web services can be built based on portal-kernel and portal-service.

In addition, the Web 2.0 Mail portlet and Chat portlet are supported. More interestingly, scheduled staging and remote staging and publishing serve as a foundation via tunnel web for web content management and publishing.

Liferay Portal supports web services to make it easy for different applications in an enterprise to communicate with each other. Java, .NET, and proprietary applications can work together easily because its web services use XML standards. It also supports REST-style JSON web services for lightweight, maintainable code, and it also supports AJAX-based user interfaces.

Liferay Portal uses industry-standard, government-grade encryption technologies, including advanced algorithms such as DES, MD5, and RSA. Liferay was benchmarked as one of the most secure portal platforms using LogicLibrary's Logiscan suite. Liferay offers customizable single sign-on with Yale CAS, JAAS, LDAP, NTLM, Netegrity, Microsoft Exchange, Facebook, and more. Open ID, OpenAuth, Yale CAS, Facebook, Siteminder, and OpenSSO (renamed as OpenAM) integration are offered by the portal out-of-the-box.

In short, Liferay Portal uses the ESB in order to provide an abstraction layer on top of an implementation of an enterprise messaging system. It allows integration architects to exploit the value of messaging without having to write the code. As you can see, understanding the framework and architecture will be helpful if you want to customize the portal correctly.

Standards

Liferay Portal runs on existing application servers, databases, and operating systems to eliminate new expenses on infrastructure. Moreover, Liferay Portal is built based around common standards. This is a more technical benefit, however, a very useful one if you ever want to use Liferay in a more specialized way.

Liferay is developed based on standard technologies that are popular with developers and other IT experts. Liferay is standards compliant, namely, open standards for content, portlets, web services, and frontend technologies to reduce development cost. The main features are listed as follows:

- **Built using Java**: Java is a very popular programming language that can run on just about any computer. There are millions of Java programmers in the world, so it won't be too hard to find developers who can customize Liferay.

- **Based on tried and tested components**: With any tool, there's a danger of bugs. Liferay uses lots of well known, widely-tested components to minimize the likelihood of bugs creeping in. If you are interested, these are some of the well known components and technologies Liferay uses — Apache ServiceMix, Mule, ehcache, Hibernate, ICEfaces, Java J2EE/JEE, jBPM, Intalio | BPMS, JGroups, Alloy UI, Lucene, and Solr, Seam, Spring and AOP, Struts and Tiles, Tapestry, Vaadin, Velocity, and FreeMarker. Especially, Liferay runs PHP, Ruby, Python, Grails and other lightweight scripting technologies within a robust Java framework.

- **Uses standard methods to communicate with other software**: There are various standards established for sharing data between pieces of software. Liferay uses these so that you can easily get information from Liferay into other systems. The standards implemented by Liferay include AJAX, iCalendar, Microformat, JSR-168, JSR-127, JSR-170, JSR-286 (Portlet 2.0), and JSR-314 (JSF 2.0), OpenSearch, Open platform with support for web services (including JSON, Hessian, Burlap, REST, RMI, and WSRP), WebDAV, and CalDAV.

- **Makes publication and collaboration tools WCAG 2.0 (Web Content Accessibility Guidelines) compliant**: This is the new W3C recommendation to make web content accessible to a wide range of people with disabilities, including blindness and low vision, deafness and hearing loss, learning disabilities, cognitive limitations, limited movement, speech disabilities, photosensitivity, and combinations of these. For example, the portal is integrated with CKEditor, which supports standards W3C (WAI-AA and WCAG), 508 (Section 508).

- Supports **HTML 5**, **CSS 3**, and **YUI 3** (Yahoo! User Interface Library).

- **Supports Apache Ant 1.8 and Maven 2**: Liferay Portal could be run through Apache Ant by default, where you can build services, clean, compile, build JavaScript CMD, build language native to ASCII, deploy, fast deploy, and support most application servers such as Tomcat, JBoss, Websphere, Weblogic, and so on. Moreover, Liferay supports Maven 2 SDK, providing **Community Edition** (CE) releases through public Maven repositories as well as allowing **Enterprise Edition** (EE) customers to install Maven artifacts in their local Maven repository.

Many of these standards are things that you will never need to know much about, so don't worry if you've never heard of them. Liferay is better for using them, but mostly, you won't even know they are there.

Terminologies

Earlier, we have addressed many terminologies regarding Liferay Portal. So here we're going to introduce a pattern: **Portal-Group-Page-Content** (PGPC). As you would expect, we are trying to summarize the main features and behaviors of the portal in a simple pattern.

First of all, let's examine a high-level overview of terminologies, scope and hierarchy in the portal. As shown in the following diagram, the portal is implemented by Portal Instances. The portal can manage multiple portal instances in one installation. Of course, you can also install multiple portal instances in multiple installations, separately.

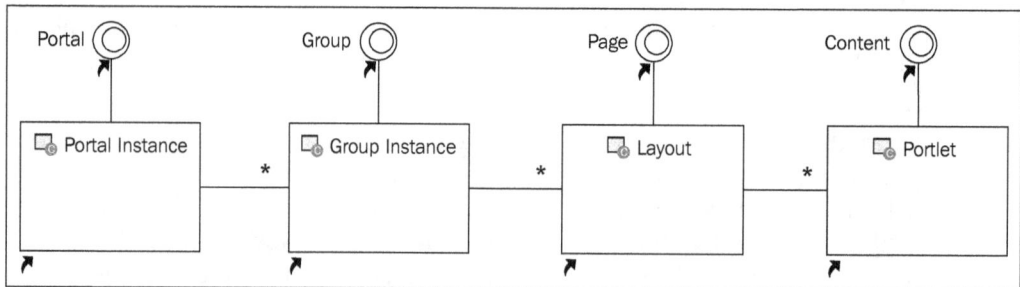

Each portal instance can have many groups, which are implemented as organizations, communities, user groups, and users. Note that each user can be represented as a group by itself, since if a user is a power user, they will get public pages and private page as any group does. Here we can use the term Group Instance to present organizations, locations, communities, user groups, and users (there is only one user in a group). Each portal instance has complete isolation of the users, organizations, locations, and user groups. In particular, organizations have a hierarchical, for example, parent organization, child organizations, and location. Note that one page can have only one parent organization and many child organizations.

Each group has two sets of pages (that is, public pages and private pages, called **layout-set**); each page is implemented as a **layout**. Most interestingly, there is a hierarchy in layouts too, such as parent pages and child pages. Note that a page can have one and only one parent page and many child pages.

Each page may contain different content, which would be implemented as portlets. Thus the content will have different scopes. For example, the content would be scoped into page, group, portal instance and portal. This pattern is known as Portal-Group-Page-Content. We will address these terminologies, scope and hierarchy in detail in the coming sections and chapters.

Multi-tenancy

Liferay Portal allows us to run more than one portal instance on a single installation. Data used for each portal instance is maintained separately from every other portal instance. Portal data, however, can be kept either in the same database or in different databases. This is called **database sharding**.

This feature should be useful for Multi-tenancy, which is a principle in software architecture where a single instance of the software serves multiple client organizations (called tenants). With a multi-tenant architecture, the portal is designed to virtually partition its data and configuration and each client organization works with a customized virtual portal instance.

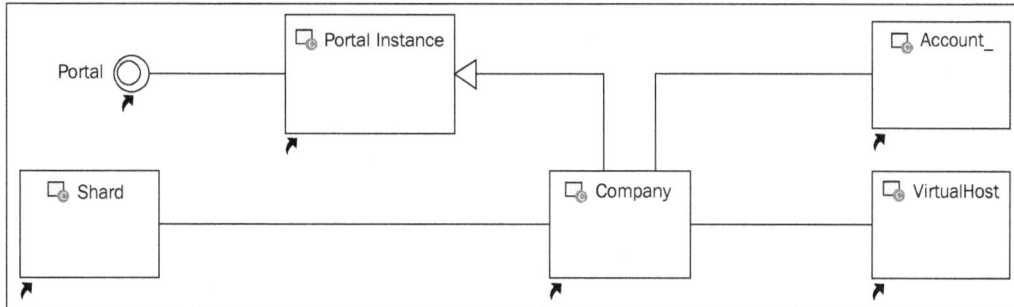

Let's have a brief look at multi-tenant capabilities. As shown in the previous diagram, a portal instance is implemented as a set of database tables such as Company, Account_, Shard, and VirtualHost. As you can see, portal instances are presented as different values of companyId; each portal instance has its own account information (presented as database table Account_), possible database (implemented as database table Shard_), and virtual host settings (presented as database table VirtualHost).

Role-based access control

Traditional membership security models address two basic criteria: authentication (who can access) and authorization (what they can do):

- Authentication is a process of determining whether someone or something is, in fact, who or what it is declared to be

- Authorization is a process of finding out if the person, once identified, is permitted to have access on a resource

The portal extends the security model by terminologies: resources, users, organizations, locations, user groups, communities, teams, roles, permissions, and so on. The portal provides a fine-grained, role-based permission security model (known as **RBAC**) – a full access control security model:

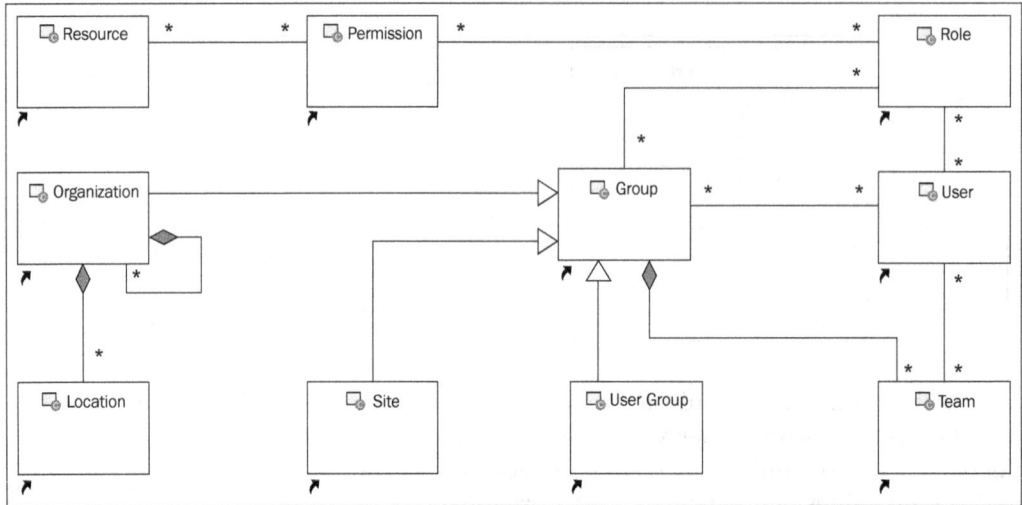

Resource, role, and permission

As shown in the preceding diagram, a **resource** is a base object. It can be a portlet (message boards, calendar, document and media library, and so on), an entity (message board topics, calendar event, document and media library folder, and so on), or a file (documents, images, applications, and so on). Resources are scoped into portal, group, page, and content – model-resource and application (or called portlet).

Permission is an action on a resource. Portal-level permissions can be assigned to the portal (users, user groups, communities, and organizations) using roles. Group-level permissions can be assigned to groups such as organization and communities. Page-level permissions can be assigned to page layouts. Model permissions can be assigned to model resource such as blog entries, web, and content. Portlet permissions can be assigned to portlets such as View and Configuration.

A **role** is a collection of permissions. Roles can be assigned to a user, user group, site, location, or organization. If a role is assigned to a user group, site, organization, or location, then all the users who are members of that entity receive the permissions of that role.

User

A **user** is an individual who performs tasks using the portal. Depending on what permissions have been assigned, the user either has the permission or doesn't have the permission to perform certain tasks.

Additionally, a registered user who has the permission can have public pages and private pages. More interestingly, a user's private pages and public pages have the ability to use page templates which can be used to customize a set of pages. The pages – private/public – are configurable in properties. You can turn on or turn off access to these pages. Also, only a power user can use a private/public page. A guest is also a user.

Group

A group is implemented as an organization, user, and user group. A user is a group with only one member, that is, the user itself. An organization could be a regular organization and location.

Organizations represent the enterprise-department-location hierarchy. Organizations can contain other organizations as sub-organizations. Moreover, an organization acting as a child of a top-level organization can also represent departments of a parent corporation.

A **location** is a special organization, having only one parent organization associated and having no child organization associated. Organizations can have any number of locations and sub organizations. Both roles and users can be assigned to organizations (locations or sub organizations). By default, locations and sub organizations inherit permissions from their parent organization using roles.

A **community** (renamed as **site**) is a special organization with a flat structure. It may hold a number of users who share common interests. Thus we can say a site is a collection of users who have a common interest. Both roles and users can be assigned to a site.

A **user group** is a special group with no context, which may hold a number of users. In other words, users can be gathered into user groups. Users can be assigned to user groups, and permissions can be assigned to user groups using roles. Therefore, every user that belongs to that user group will receive those role-based permissions.

A **team** is a group of users under a community or an organization. A community or organization can group a set of users and create a team. The notion of a team is somewhat similar to a role, but a role is a portal-wide entry, while a team is restricted to a particular site or organization. Therefore, you can manage the permissions of a team like a role. That is, a team is like a site or organization role, but specific to a certain site or organization. A team is different from a User Group too. A user group has the scope of a portal, while a team is always exclusive to a site or organization.

In addition, each group can have public pages and private pages. Thus users in a user group can share private and public pages. More interestingly, a group's private and public pages do have the ability to apply page templates or site templates in order to customize a set of pages in a fast way.

Systems development

Liferay is, first and foremost, a platform where you can build your applications with the tools you feel most comfortable using, such as JSF 2 - ICEfaces, Struts 2, Spring 3 MVC, Vaadin, jQuery, Wicket, Dojo and more.

When developing systems, the **Model–View–Controller** (**MVC**) pattern is followed throughout the book. The model manages the behavior and data of the portal domain, responds to requests for information about its state from the view, and responds to instructions to change its state from the controller. The view (like JSP, XHTML, JavaScript) renders the model into a form suitable for interaction, typically a user interface element; while the controller (such as actions, controllers) receives input and initiates a response by making calls on model objects.

In Liferay, there's a concept called a plugin, which is a WAR file that can be hot-deployed into the portal at runtime. Plugins can be categorized as portlets, themes, layout templates, hooks, and webs. These plugins can be developed using the **Plugins SDK**. Prior to Liferay 6, there used to be an ext environment, where the developer could customize the core portal module. Since Liferay 6, it has been replaced by the Ext plugins approach.

Service-Builder is a Liferay tool to generate persistence and service-layer code, by reading an XML file.

Of course, you're not required to write a lot of code yourself. You can use Service-Builder to generate a lot of the code for building the models and services. Generally speaking, the Service-Builder is a tool built by Liferay to automate the creation of interfaces and classes that are used by a given portal or portlet. The Service-Builder is used to build Java services that can be accessed in a variety of ways, including local access from Java code, as well as remote access using web services.

In general, the Service-Builder is a code generator. Using an XML descriptor, it generates:

- Java Beans
- SQL scripts for database tables creation
- Hibernate Configuration
- Spring Configuration
- Axis Web Services
- JSON JavaScript Interface

The Plugins SDK Environment is a simple environment for the development of Liferay plugins, such as ext, themes, layout templates, portlets, hooks, and webs (web applications). It is completely separated from the Liferay Portal core services by using external services only if required.

The portal supports six different types of plugins out-of-the-box. They are Portlets, Themes, Layout Templates, Webs, Hooks, and Ext:

- **Portlets**: Web applications that run in a portion of a web page
- **Themes**: Look-and-feel of pages
- **Layout Templates**: Ways of choosing how the portlets will be arranged on a page
- **Hooks**: Allow hooking into the portal core functionality
- **Webs**: Regular Java EE web modules designed to work with the portal such as ESB (Enterprise Service Bus), and SSO (Single Sign-On). Note that a web is a pure web application where a thin layer is added to provide checking for dependencies. A web also adds support for embedding hook definitions or Service Builder services within a plain old web application. And finally, you can deploy them using the auto-deploy mechanism the same way that you can with other plugins.
- **Ext**: ext environment as a plugin means you can use the extension environment as a plugin in the Plugins SDK environment.

As you can see, you can generate code for plugin Portlets, Webs, and Ext. Normally, you would have one project for each plugin, for example, theme, layout template, hook, ext, or web; you can have many portlets in one plugin project portlet. Hook plugins can be standalone, or they could be included with portlets and web. This means, in one plugin project portlet or web, you can have hooks and many portlets or a web as one WAR file. What are the advantages of aggregating many portlets into one WAR? We have shared database workspace with many portlets and can implement collaboration between each other.

Liferay IDE is used to provide best-of-breed Eclipse tooling for the Liferay Portal development platform for version 6 and greater. The availabilities of Liferay IDE cover, but are not limited to, the plugins SDK support, plugin projects support, project import and conversion, wizards, code assist such as portlet taglibs, customizable templates, and XML catalog (XSD) contributions.

Ext plugin

The Extension environment provides the capability to customize Liferay Portal completely. As it is an environment which extends Liferay Portal development environment, it has the name "Extension", (called "Ext"). With Ext, we could modify internal portlets which are also called by the out-of-the-box portlets. Moreover, we could override the JSP files of the portal and out-of-the-box portlets. This kind of customization is kept separate from the Liferay Portal source code. That is, the Liferay Portal source code does not have to be modified, and a clear upgrade path is available in the Ext.

Starting with version 6, Ext environment is available as a plugin called **Ext plugin**. As shown in the following diagram, custom code will override Liferay Portal source code in the Ext plugins only. In the deployment process, custom code is merged with Liferay Portal source code. That is, developers can override the Liferay Portal source code. Moreover, custom code and Liferay Portal source code will be constructed as a customized Liferay Portal first, and then the customized Liferay Portal will be deployed to an application server. In addition, both direct deploy (ant direct-deploy) and standard deploy (ant deploy) are available.

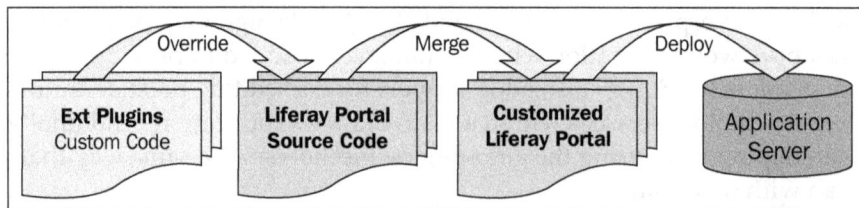

Hook plugin

Hooks are a feature to catch hold of the properties and JSP files into an instance of the portal, as if we were catching them with a hook. Hook plugins are more powerful plugins that complement portlets, themes, layout templates, and web modules. A hook plugin can, but does not have to, be combined with a portlet plugin or a web plugin. For instance, the portlet called so-portlet is a portlet plugin for social office with hooks; a hook plugin can simply provide translation or override a JSP page.

In general, hooks are a very helpful tool to customize the portal without touching the code of the portal, as shown in the following diagram. In addition, you could use hooks to provide patches for portal systems or social office products.

In general, there are several kinds of hook parameters:

- `portal-properties` (called portal properties hooks),
- `language-properties` (called language properties hooks),
- `custom-jsp-dir` (called custom JSPs hooks),
- `custom-jsp-global` (applying custom JSPs hooks globally or locally),
- `indexer post processors` (called indexer hook),
- `service` (called portal service hooks) – including model listeners and service wrappers,
- `servlet-filter` and `servlet-filter-mapping` (called servlet-filter hooks),
- `struts-action` (called portal struts action hooks)

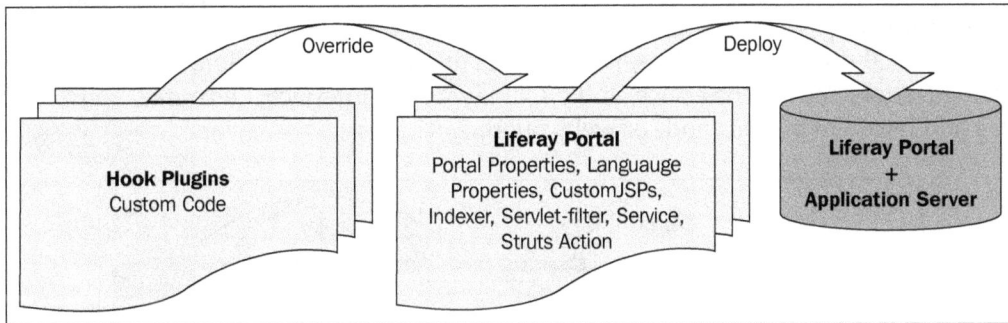

As you can see, JSPs hooks can set a `custom-jsp-dir` that will overwrite portal JSPs. You can also add `<custom-jsp-global>false</custom-jsp-global>` (default to `true`) so that JSPs hooks will not apply globally but only to the current scope. Each site (or organization) can choose to have that hook apply just for that site (or organization).

In addition, Liferay allows portal JSPs to be overloaded by theme templates – this pattern will require that within the theme's templates folder, the complete path to the original JSP be maintained with the file extension replaced to match that of the theme's chosen template language.

Portlet, layout template, and web plugins

As you can see, the Plugins SDK is a simple environment for the development of Liferay plugins, including portlets, layout templates, and webs (that is, web applications). It provides the capability to create hot-deployable hooks, themes, layout templates, portlets, and webs.

How does it work? As shown in the following diagram, the Plugins SDK provides an environment for developers to build portlets and webs. Later, it uses the Ant Target Deploy or Maven to form a WAR file and copy it to the Deploy directory. Then, Liferay Portal together with the application server will detect any WAR files in the Deploy (auto deploy, hot deploy, or sandbox deploy) folder, and automatically extract the WAR files into the application server deployment folder. Note that the portal is able to recognize the type of the plugin and enhance it appropriately before hot-deploying it. For example, for portlets it will modify web.xml by adding required listeners and filters.

During customization, you could use the Service-Builder to generate models and services in portlets and/or web plugins. In general, the Service-Builder is a code generator using an XML descriptor. For a given service.xml XML file, it will generate SQL for creating tables, Java Beans, Hibernate configuration, Spring configuration, Axis Web Service, and JSON JavaScript Interface. Of course, you can add hooks in portlets and/or webs plugins.

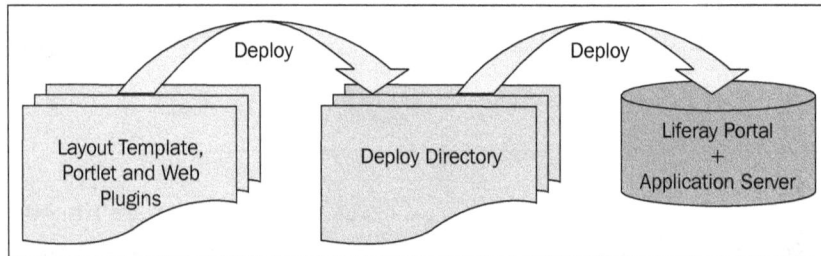

Theme plugin

A theme specifies the styles of all major global portlets and content; therefore, it controls the way the portal will look. In general, a theme uses CSS, images, JavaScript, and Velocity (or FreeMarker) templates to control the whole look-and-feel of the pages generated by the portal.

As shown in the following diagram, the theme plugin can use default themes as a basis, building differences on top.

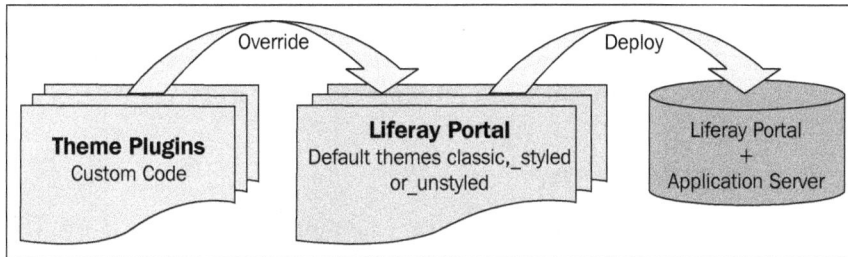

Development strategies

As mentioned earlier, there are at least three development environments: portal core source code, Ext plugin, and normal plugins. Thus, you may ask: Which kind of development environment is suitable for our requirements? When should we use the Ext plugin? And when should we use other plugins, or even Liferay Portal source code? Let's take a deep look at the development strategies.

As shown in the following diagram, Liferay Portal is extensible on at least three levels, for example the **Plugins SDK Environment (Level I)**, **Ext plugin (Level II)**, and **Liferay Portal source code (Level III)**. As you can see, each level of extensibility offers a different compromise of flexibility with different migration requirements to future versions. Thus we need to choose the appropriate level for the requirements at hand ; one which allows for the easiest future maintainability.

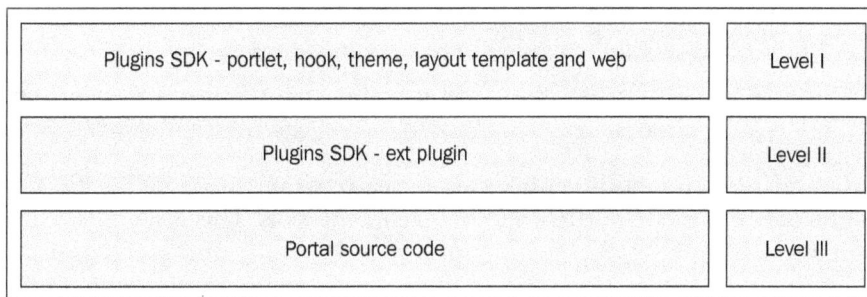

Level I development

In Level I, we can develop portlets, themes, layout templates, hooks, and webs as independent software components. Moreover, these plugins can be distributed and deployed as WAR files, and can be organized in plugin repositories. Liferay Portal provides the Plugins SDK to help us with the development of these plugins.

In addition, portlets developed in the Plugins SDK can only import classes from the portal API (`Portal-Service`), not `Portal-Impl`. This means, portlet development in the Plugins SDK does not touch portal properties, language properties, core services, and JSP files related to `Portal-Impl`. Fortunately, hooks provide the capability to access portal properties, language properties, struts actions, core services related to `Portal-Impl`, and custom JSP files.

Level II development

In Level II, we can manage configuration files, custom source code, custom JSP files, and modified JSP files related to the `Portal-Impl`. This means that the, Ext plugin provides different sublevels (for example, configuration files, custom source code, custom JSP files, and modified JSP files) of extensibility.

Among the configuration files, `portal-ext.properties` has the main configuration options: layouts, deployment, themes, Hibernate, cache, instance settings, users, groups, language, session, auth, integration, and events. Meanwhile, the `system-ext.properties` file is a convenient way to provide and extend the Java System properties used by Liferay Portal. We can also create custom classes for the most common extensibility, which need to be configured through the `portal.properties` file. Examples are authentication chain, upgrade and verification processes, deployment processes, database access and caching, user fields' generation and validation, session events, permissions, and model listeners.

For custom source code, we can use Spring-based dependency injection mechanisms configured in the `ext-spring.xml` file as follows:

1. Add the `Servlet` extended in the `web.xml` file.
2. Add the Struts action extended in the `struts-config.xml` file.
3. Moreover, create portlets that access `Portal-Impl`, or events extending its models and services.

For custom JSP files and modified JSP files, we can customize any of the JSP files used by the out-of-the-box portlets and management tools. This is a very flexible extension mechanism.

> Without a doubt, it is easier to develop portlets in Ext plugin, where you can easily access and use all of the Portal APIs, taglibs, JSP files, and almost everything else. This isn't the case with the other plugins.

Starting with version 6, the Extension environment becomes the Ext plugin. **Golden rule**: support for Service-Builder in Ext plugins will be deprecated in future versions. Ext plugins are designed to override the portal's core code in ways that can't be done with hooks, layout templates, portlets, or themes. Ext plugins aren't meant to contain new custom services. Thus any `5.x service.xml` in Ext environment should be migrated into a portlet plugin.

Level III development

In Level III, we can modify the Liferay Portal source code. This approach can only be used for sponsored development or providing patches for bug fixes, new features/improvements, and portal core contribution development. This means, you can develop specific features for specific projects first and then contribute back to Liferay Portal source code, or provide patches to override `Portal-Impl`, `Util-Java`, `Util-Taglib` and `Util-Bridges` partially.

In brief, if your requirements are related to customize and/or extend `Portal-Impl` (for example, UI changing, LDAP import algorithms, document and media library lock mechanism, forms for user registration or organization creation, integration, modifying the out of the box portlets, and so on.), you should use Ext plugin. Otherwise, it is better to use other Plugins. Note that with hooks, you can hook up portal properties, language properties, core services, and Struts actions related to `Portal-Impl`.

Keep in mind that Ext plugin is designed to override the portal's core code in ways that can't be done with hooks, layout templates, portlets, or themes; and Ext plugin shouldn't contain any custom services.

An example: Knowledge base management

What's a knowledge base? According to Business Dictionary (refer to `http://www.businessdictionary.com/definition/knowledge-base.html`), a knowledge base is defined as:

> "*Organized repository of knowledge (in a computer system or an organization) consisting of concepts, data, objectives, requirements, rules, and specifications. Its form depends on whether it supports an (1) artificial intelligence or expert system-based retrieval, or (2) human-based retrieval. In the first case, it takes the form of data, design constructs, couplings, and linkages incorporated in software. In the second case, it takes the form of physical documents and textual information.*"

How to implement a knowledge base in the portal? A knowledge base could be implemented as a set of portlets plus hooks with the following major requirements. Of course, you can add your specific requirements in **knowledge base** management (**KB**).

- Modeling knowledge base as articles plus article templates, article comments, private messages, contacts, and tasks

- Versioning and authoring articles, and organizing them in a hierarchy of navigable and scope-able articles

- Supporting multiple languages on title, content, and description of articles

- Ability to lock and unlock articles

- Supporting look-ahead typing in articles search

- Supporting caching, asynchronous threads, indexing, and advanced search

- Representing knowledge base management as a set of JSR-286 portlets, for example, **Admin**, **Private Messaging**, **Contacts**, **Tasks**, **Docs Viewer**, **Aggregator**, **Display**, **Search**, and **List**; and supporting inter-portlet communication (**IPC** – events and public render parameters) among portlets Aggregator, Display and List; and leveraging different portlet bridges such as Struts 2, JSF 2, Spring 3 MVC, Wicket, and so on

- Leveraging dynamic data list and dynamic data mapping to build dynamic document types and meta-data sets

- Leveraging dynamic query APIs and custom SQL

- Adding permission checker on articles

- Ability to add attachments and images to articles

- Ability to add asset links, asset ratings, and asset view counts

- Ability to add asset comments to articles and votes on comments

- Ability to add hierarchy of asset categories

- Ability to add asset tags to articles

- Ability to add RSS feeds and to subscribe to articles

- Ability to add polls on articles

- Exporting and converting articles to PDF and other formats

- Supporting configurable workflow

- Ability to add custom attributes (called custom fields)

- Ability to archive (import and export) and to remotely publish articles

- Allowing use of auditing, rule engine (**Drools**), and reporting engine (**JasperReports**)

- Ability to import a semantic mark-up language for technical documentation called DocBook, referring to http://www.docbook.org
- Providing web services for knowledge base articles
- Providing JSON services for knowledge base articles
- Providing RESTful services for knowledge base articles
- Integrating CAPTCHA or reCAPTCHA with knowledge base articles
- Applying JavaScript such as jQuery and mash-ups when building portlets
- Supporting asset rendering in the Asset Publisher portlet
- Integrating social activity and social equity
- Ability to apply portal core and other features to knowledge base articles

This book is going to show you how to develop portal systems via a real example – knowledge base management. By the end of this book, you will be familiar with major portal features, be able to apply them to knowledge base articles, and implement the aforementioned requirements as well. Of course, you will know the portal in-depth from a systems development viewpoint, and moreover, on top of Liferay Portal, you will be able to cook your own favorite dishes quickly and concisely.

More useful information

In this chapter, we have looked at what Liferay can do for your corporate intranet, and we have briefly seen why it's a good choice.

If you want more background information on Liferay, the best place to start is the Liferay corporate website (http://www.liferay.com) itself. You can find the latest news and events, various training programs offered worldwide, presentations, demonstrations, and hosted trials. More interestingly, Liferay eats its own dog food; corporate websites with forums (called message boards), blogs, and wikis are built by Liferay using its own products. It is a real demo for the Liferay Portal.

Liferay is 100 percent open source and all downloads are available from the Liferay Portal website (http://www.liferay.com/web/guest/downloads/portal) and the **SourceForge** website at http://sourceforge.net/projects/lportal/files. The source code repository is available at http://svn.liferay.com/repos/public (credentials—the username is Guest and no password) and Github (https://github.com/liferay), and source code can be explored at http://svn.liferay.com.

Liferay's website wiki (`http://www.liferay.com/web/guest/community/wiki`) contains documentation such as a tutorial, user guide, developer guide, administrator guide, roadmap, and more.

Liferay's website discussion forums can be accessed at `http://www.liferay.com/web/guest/community/forums` and the blogs at `http://www.liferay.com/web/guest/community/blogs`. The road map can be found at `http://www.liferay.com/web/guest/community/wiki/-/wiki/Main/RoadMap`. The official plugins are available from `http://www.liferay.com/web/guest/downloads/official_plugins`.

The community plugins are available from `http://www.liferay.com/web/guest/downloads/community_plugins`. They are the best places to share your thoughts, to get tips and tricks about Liferay implementation, to examine the road map, and to use and contribute community plugins.

If you would like to file a bug or know more about the fixes in a specific release, then you should visit the bug tracking system at `http://issues.liferay.com/`.

Alloy UI Forms is a set of taglibs built on top of the Alloy UI JavaScript + CSS framework. For more information about the framework, you can visit: `http://alloy.liferay.com`. CSS3, CSS level 3, is available from `http://www.w3.org/Style/CSS/current-work`. A detailed description of HTML5 is available from `http://dev.w3.org/html5/spec/Overview.html`. YUI 3 is Yahoo!'s next-generation JavaScript and CSS library at `http://developer.yahoo.com/yui/3/`.

Summary

In this chapter, we have looked at what Liferay can offer to your intranets and Internet. Particularly, we saw:

- The portal provides shared documents, videos, audios, images, and records, discussions, collaborative wikis, social activities, dynamic web content, web forms, and more in a single, searchable portal
- The portal is a great choice for intranets and Internets, easy-to-use, open source, extensible, integrated with other tools and standards
- Service-Builder and the Plugins SDK provide portal systems development and customization environments with plugins such as Ext, themes, layout templates, webs, portlets, and hooks

In the next chapter, we're going to introduce the Service-Builder and the development environment.

2
Service-Builder and Development Environment

Before moving on to develop JSR-286 portlets, we have to set up our development environment properly. Fortunately, Liferay provides a development environment, namely, the Plugins SDK environment (Plugins SDK) for developing Ext plugin, portlets, hooks, themes, layout templates, and webs. Liferay portal also provides **Service-Builder** as a tool to build Java services that can be accessed in a variety of ways. This chapter will first introduce how to set up Plugins SDK and how to build it. Then, it will address how to use Service-Builder and what happens when the portal starts from scratch.

By the end of this chapter, you will have learned how to:

- Set up a development environment
- Navigate through the portal and plugins structure
- Use Service-Builder
- Populate database schema and default data
- Use default project creation and templates
- Develop portlets within Tomcat in a fast way

Plugins SDK development environment

Plugins SDK is a simple environment for plugins development such as Ext (Ext stands for extension) plugins, themes, layout templates, portlets, hooks, and webs (web applications). It is completely different from the Liferay portal core services as it uses external services `portal-service` only if required.

In order to set up the development environment, Plugins SDK for development, customization, deployment, and debugging, we need to consider the following aspects: required tools, databases, application servers, IDE (Integrated Development Environment), portal runtime bundle, and portal source code. We will have a deeper look at these aspects.

Of course, you can use **Liferay Developer Studio**, where all aspects are packaged as one simple bundle or **Liferay IDE**. Liferay IDE is an extension of the Eclipse platform that supports development of plugins projects such as portlets, hooks, layout templates, themes, and Ext plugins — as you can see, webs are not involved. Liferay Developer Studio is a shrink-wrapped productized version of Eclipse, pre-installed with Liferay IDE and also bundled with Portal EE (**Enterprise Edition**) and Plugins SDK along with several example projects.

Here we will not show you how to use the out-of-the-box Liferay Developer Studio and Liferay IDE; instead, we will show you how to build your own development environment — getting the same or similar functions as that of Liferay Developer Studio and Liferay IDE.

Required tools

Liferay portal is a Java-based portal application that uses the Ant build tool. Thus the required tools are **JDK** and **Ant**; **Maven** would be an alternative to Ant. For these tools, we recommend you use the latest version.

JDK

First, you need to download the latest version of JDK. It is available at `http://www.oracle.com/technetwork/java/javase/downloads/index.html` for every OS. The installation instructions can also be found there. When you install it, make a note of the location as you will need it when you set the `JAVA_HOME` variable. Note that Liferay supports **JDK 1.5** or above.

Next, you need to set the `JAVA_HOME` variable. You should set up the `JAVA_HOME` variable in Windows, Linux, Unix, or Mac operating systems as you can run Liferay portal on any OS.

You can check whether your OS recognizes Java, and also if it is the correct version, by typing the command `java -version`. By the way, we use `$JDK_MAJOR_VERSION` to represent the major version of JDK. For example, the value of `$JDK_MAJOR_VERSION` could be `1.5`, `1.6`, or `1.7`.

Ant

Apache Ant is a Java library and command-line tool to drive processes described in build files as **targets** and extension points that depend on each other. You need to download the latest version of Apache Ant. It is available at `http://ant.apache.org` for every OS. The installation instructions can also be found there. When you install it, make a note of the location as you will need it when you set up the `ANT_HOME` variable.

Then, you need to set the `ANT_HOME` variable in a similar manner as the `JAVA_HOME` variable was set. You can check whether your OS recognizes `Ant`, and also if it is the correct version by running the command `ant -version`.

Maven

Based on the concept of a **project object model (POM)**, **Maven** can manage a project's build, reporting, and documentation from a central piece of information. You need to download the latest version of Apache Maven. It is available at `http://maven.apache.org` for every OS. The installation instructions can also be found there. When you install it, make a note of the location as you will need it when you set up the `MAVEN_HOME` variable.

Databases

Liferay portal supports many databases. Databases which the Liferay portal can run on include Apache Derby, IBM DB2, Firebird, Hypersonic, Informix, InterBase, JDataStore, Oracle, PostgreSQL, SAP, SQL Server, Sybase, MySQL, and almost any database. Eventually, you can use any one of them. For demo purposes, here we will use MySQL.

MySQL

You need to download the latest version of **MySQL**. It is available at `http://www.mysql.com` for every OS. The installation instructions can also be found there. When you install it, make a note of the location as you will need it when you set up the `MYSQL_HOME` variable. Then, you need to set the `MYSQL_HOME` variable in a similar manner as the `JAVA_HOME` variable was set. Similarly, you can check whether your OS recognizes MySQL, and also if it is the correct version, by running the command `mysql --version`.

In addition, we need to prepare a database bookpub and
username/password lportal/lportal, which has full access
to the database bookpub. Of course, you can have a different
database name, username, and password. We use bookpub as the
value of database, and lportal/lportal as the values of the
username/password for demo purposes.

Application servers

Liferay portal supports almost any application server. The application servers (or
the servlet containers) that the Liferay portal can run on include Borland ES, Apache
Geronimo, GlassFish, JBoss AS, JOnAS, JRun, Oracle AS, Orion, JSAS, WebLogic,
WebSphere, Jetty, Resin, Tomcat, and almost any application server.

Of course, it is up to you to choose one of them. However, for demo purposes, we
will use Tomcat for testing, debugging, and developing. Optionally, there are a
set of Liferay portal bundles, available at http://www.liferay.com/downloads/
liferay-portal/available-releases, bundled with application servers. You
can use one of them for the servlet container or the full Java EE application server.
It is easy to use Liferay portal bundles—simply downloads one bundle from the
preceding URL and unzips it to the specific folder on your local machine.

Why use Tomcat, and not Liferay portal bundled with Tomcat? Naturally, it is better
to use Liferay portal bundled with Tomcat as it is preconfigured. However, you will
lose an opportunity to learn how to configure Tomcat with Liferay portal from a
new installation. We will here choose Tomcat and will show you how to configure
Tomcat to support the Liferay portal.

Tomcat

Before installing Tomcat, we need to set the working folder $LIFERAY_PORTAL
variable. Logically, you can have a different folder name. However, in order to be
referred to simply and easily, we use a folder named Liferay-Portal, that is, the
folder $LIFERAY_PORTAL setting has a value, Liferay-Portal. More specifically,
you will have a value for $LIFERAY_PORTAL—C:\Liferay-Portal in Windows,
or /opt/Liferay-Portal in Linux, Unix, and MacOS. You will see some specific
examples and diagrams in this book with these values related to a specific
OS—Windows.

First of all, you need to download the most recent version of Tomcat. It is available at http://tomcat.apache.org for every OS. It is a ZIP file named $TOMCAT_ZIP_FILENAME.zip (you can download a ZIP file named $TOMCAT_ZIP_FILENAME.tar.gz also). Here, the TOMCAT_ZIP_FILENAME is the actual ZIP filename, for example, apache-tomcat-version. The version is made up of a major version named $TOMCAT_MAJOR_VERSION and a minor version named $TOMCAT_MINOR_VERSION.

In order to install Tomcat, we need to unzip the ZIP file into the folder, $LIFERAY_PORTAL, and set the value of the variable $CATALINA_HOME to $LIFERAY_PORTAL/$TOMCAT_ZIP_FILENAME.

Why do we need to install Tomcat under the $LIFERAY_PORTAL folder?

In the runtime, Liferay portal will create two folders, data and deploy, under the $LIFERAY_PORTAL folder sharing the same parent folder $LIFERAY_PORTAL, with the folder $TOMCAT_ZIP_FILENAME. Thus, if we install Tomcat in the folder, $LIFERAY_PORTAL, it would be easy to refer to the data and deploy folders as $LIFERAY_PORTAL/data and $LIFERAY_PORTAL/deploy, respectively.

IDE

Why do we need an IDE? An IDE or Integrated Development Environment provides comprehensive facilities for software development. An IDE normally consists of a source code editor, a compiler, an interpreter, build automation tools, and a debugger. Of course, you can develop portlets in Liferay portal without using any IDE. An IDE is designed to maximize the programmer's productivity by providing tightly knit components with similar user interfaces. Thus we plan to use an IDE.

There are a set of IDEs you may choose from—Eclipse IDE, NetBeans IDE, and IntelliJ. We will use Eclipse IDE for development, customization, deployment, and debugging custom code based on the Liferay portal.

Eclipse IDE

You can download the most recent version for every OS available at http://www.eclipse.org. There are still a lot of download choices—Eclipse Classic, Eclipse IDE for Java EE Developers, Eclipse IDE for Java Developers, and so on. For demo purposes, we will choose Eclipse Classic.

You can install Eclipse IDE anywhere. When you install it, make a note of the location, as you will need it when you set up ECLIPSE_IDE_HOME. For convenience, we prefer to install Eclipse IDE under the folder $LIFERAY_PORTAL. Thus the $ECLIPSE_IDE_HOME setting has the value $LIFERAY_PORTAL/eclipse.

Workspace

Before starting the Eclipse IDE, we need to build a workspace and a folder to store projects. Logically, you could create the folder for the workspace anywhere and give it any name. For the sake of convenience, we use the name workspace as the folder for the workspace. Moreover, place the folder workspace under the folder $LIFERAY_PORTAL. Thus we can refer to the folder for the workspace simply as $LIFERAY_PORTAL/workspace.

When starting Eclipse IDE, you are asked to provide the workspace path — enter it as $LIFERAY_PORTAL/workspace. After that, you will have your own Eclipse IDE.

Subclipse

In order to get Liferay portal source code, we have to use **Subclipse** in the Eclipse IDE. Subclipse is an Eclipse Team Provider plugin providing support for Subversion (an open source version control system) within the Eclipse IDE. You may refer to http://subclipse.tigris.org for more information.

As you can see, there are a set of version control systems for source management, for example, Fast Version Control System (**Git**, refer to http://git-scm.com), Concurrent Versions System (CVS), Perforce, Subversion (SVN), IBM Rational ClearCase, and so on. Why do we need SVN or GIT? As the Liferay portal source code is managed through Subversion and **GitHub** (refer to https://github.com/liferay), we have to use SVN or Git. Let's install the Subclipse plugin in the Eclipse IDE.

Portal and plugins structure

Before navigating to the portal runtime structure, portal source code structure, plugins runtime structure, and plugins SDK source code structure, let's first build a portal source code Java project named portal-trunk (represented as a variable $PORTAL_SRC_HOME) and a plugins SDK source code Java project named plugins-trunk (represented as a variable $PLUGINS_SDK_HOME).

- Check out svn://svn.liferay.com/repos/public/portal/trunk as the Java project portal-trunk in Eclipse IDE; of course, you can use any name for this project. We are using this name only for ease-of-reference.

- Check out `svn://svn.liferay.com/repos/public/plugins/trunk` as the Java project `plugins-trunk` in Eclipse IDE; again, you can use any name for this project. This name is used for ease-of-reference.

Using the IDE, you will see the portal source code Java project `portal-trunk` and the plugins source code Java project `plugins-trunk`.

In addition, you may be interested in Alloy UI source code. Therefore, check out `svn://svn.liferay.com/repos/public/alloy/trunk` as the Java project `alloy-ui-trunk` in Eclipse IDE or a different project name.

Portal source code

Where do we get the source code for the portal? In general, there are four kinds of portal sources: the officially released version, the tag version, the branch version, and the trunk version. Let's take a deeper look at these options. The officially released version has only one version (either the major version, for example 6.1, or the minor version, for example 2). If you need the new version, say 6.1.3 or 6.1.4, then you have to download the latest version and install it again.

The tag version is functionally the same as the officially released version. You can check this out on a specific tag at `svn://svn.liferay.com/repos/public/portal/tags`.

The branch version provides the portal source code with a fixed major version. You can check out the latest branch at `svn://svn.liferay.com/repos/public/portal/branches`. Note that there is only one major version (for example, 6.1), but you can get the latest minor version from the SVN update. However, if you need a new major version, say 6.2 or 7, you have to get another branch and install it again.

The trunk version provides the portal source code with the latest version—both major and minor. For demo purposes, we will use the trunk version. Note that the trunk version is not recommended for production because it is still under development, and not stable. Moreover, it is better to use the branch version because it is the latest stable release with a bug fix.

Portal source code structure

The portal source code has the following folder structure:

Folder name	Description
benchmarks	Covers benchmarks.properties, build.xml, grinder. properties, the folder scripts, and the file login.py.
Definitions	Covers DTD files and XSD files, such as hibernate-mapping-3.0.dtd, liferay-service-builder_6_1_0.xsd, liferay-workflow-definition_6_1_0.xsd, and so on.
Lib	Lib JAR files are grouped into three folders: development, global, and portal; dependent JAR versions are specified in version. html, versions.xml. For example, ROME JAR /portal/rome.jar is used to generate and convert all of the popular RSS and Atom formats
portal-client	Generates an Axis web service client, covering buil.xml, namespace-mapping.properties, and portal-client.jar.
portal-impl	Contains implementation of portal kernels, models, and services; generates JAR portal-impl.jar, including build.xml, folders src, and test. In particular, it covers portal.properties and system.properties.
portal-service	Contains portal interfaces of kernels, models, and services; generates JAR portal-service.jar, including build.xml, folders src and test
portal-web	Contains the web application root; generates WAR portal-web. war, including build.xml and the folders docroot, test, test-ant-templates, and third-party; as a normal web application, the WAR portal-web.war is deployable in application servers.
Sql	Contains SQL build files, such as build.xml and build-parents. xml, and SQL files, such as indexs.sql, portal-tables.sql, sql.properties, indexes.properties, sequence.sql, update-*.sql, and so on.
support-maven	Contains Maven support, including pom.xml and the folders archetypes and plugins
support-tomcat	Contains Tomcat support libraries; including build.xml and the source code folder src, more specifically, com.liferay.support. tomcat;

Folder name	Description
Tools	Contains a set of tools folders such as db-upgrade, maven, putty, selenium, servers, and zip_tmpl, for example, the default settings of setenv.bat and setenv.sh are specified at /tools/servers/tomcat/bin; similarly, you can find the default settings for Geronimo, jetty, and resin.
tunnel-web	Contains tunnel web, including build.xml and the web application folder docroot/WEB-INF; generates the WAR tunnel-web.war
util-bridges	Contains bridges, utilities, libraries, including build.xml and the source code folder src – it covers the folder com.liferay.util.bridges; generates the JAR util-bridges.jar
util-java	Contains Java utilities libraries, including build.xml and the source code folder src – it covers the folder com.liferay.util and the WSDD file client-config.wsdd; generates the JAR util-java.jar
util-taglib	Contains tag libraries, including build.xml, the source code folder – it covers the folders com.liferay.taglib and META-INF; under the folder META-INF, there are a set of XML files, such as faces-config.xml and liferay-faces.taglib.xml and TLD files, such as liferay-aui.tld and liferay-faces.tld; generates the JAR util-taglib.jar

In addition, you will find a set of XML files and properties files under the folder $PORTAL_SRC_HOME. The following are some of these files:

File name	Description	Comments
app.server.properties	Specifies application server info, for example, app.server.type could be geronimo, glassfish, jboss, jetty, jonas, oc4j, resin, tomcat, and so on. By default, it is specified as Tomcat. It also specifies Clean processes, such as clean.log.dir, clean.temp.dir, and clean.work.dir.	Do not update the properties of this file. Instead, create a separate properties file named app.server.${user.name}.properties with the properties to overwrite.
build-common-java.xml	Ant build; specifies the Ant common Java targets	Ant targets: compile, clean, deploy, jar, jar-javadoc, jar-source, javadoc, manifest, and so on.
build-common-web.xml	Ant build; specifies the Ant common web targets	Ant targets: clean, compile, deploy, war

File name	Description	Comments
`build-common.xml`	Ant build; specifies the Ant common targets	Ant targets: compile, format-javadoc, print-current-time, setproxy, test,
`build.xml`	Ant build; specifies the Ant targets	Import file build-common-build.xml; ant targets: clean, start, deploy.
`release.properties`	Specifies release information, such as `lp.version`, `lp.version.dtd`, `lp.version.major`.	`com.liferay.portal.tools.ReleaseInfoBuilder;`

In the same folder, you will find a set of `build-test` XML files such as `build-test-cluster.xml`, `build-test-db-*.xml`, `build-test-glassfish.xml`, `build-test-jboss.xml`, `build-test-ldap.xml`, and so on. You may use these `build-test` XML files to test different scenarios.

Plugins SDK source code

Plugins SDK is a simple environment for the development of Liferay plugins, such as themes, layout templates, portlets, hooks, Ext plugins, and webs (web applications). It is completely different from the Liferay portal core services as it uses external services only if required.

How do we set up Plugins SDK? First, let's see where we would find the source code of Plugins SDK. In general, there are three kinds of source code for Plugins SDK: the specific version package, the branch version, and the trunk version. The specific version package is released with the portal.

The branch version provides the source code of Plugins SDK with a fixed major version. You can check out the latest branch at `svn://svn.liferay.com/repos/public/plugins/branches`.

The trunk version provides the source code of Plugins SDK with the latest versions, both the major and minor versions. By the way, both the branch version and the trunk version contain a lot of sample themes, layout templates, portlets, hooks, Ext plugins, and webs.

Plugins SDK structure

The plugins SDK has the following folder structure:

Folder name	Description
clients	Covers `build-common-client.xml`, `build.xml`, and folders for clients projects, for example, the sample clients project `ip-geocoder-client`.
ext	Covers `build-common-ext.xml`, `build.xml`, `create.bat`, `create.sh` and, possibly, folders for Ext plugins projects.
hooks	Covers `build-common-hook.xml`, `build.xml`, `create.bat`, `create.sh`, and folders for hooks plugins projects, for example, `mongodb-hook`, `antisamy-hook`, and so on.
layouttpl	Covers `build-common-layouttpl.xml`, `build.xml`, `create.bat`, `create.sh`, and folders for layout templates plugins projects, for example, `3-2-3-columns-layouttpl`.
lib	Includes global library JAR files, such as `activation.jar`, `jsp-api.jar`, `log4j.jar`, `mail.jar`, `servlet-api.jar`, and so on.
portlets	Covers `build-common-portlet.xml`, `build.xml`, `create.bat`, `create.sh`, and folders for portlets plugins projects, for example, `knowledge-base-portlet`, `sample-service-builder-portlet`, and so on.
theme	Covers `build-common-theme.xml`, `build.xml`, `create.bat`, `create.sh`, and folders for themes plugins projects, for example, `so-theme`, `igoogle-theme`, and so on.
tools	Contains a set of plugins templates folders, such as `ext_tmpl`, `hook_tmpl`, `layouttpl_tmpl`, `portlet_jsf_tmpl`, `portlet_tmpl`, `portlet_vaadin_tmpl`, and `theme_tmpl`.
webs	Including `build-common-web.xml`, `build.xml` and folders for webs plugins projects, for example, `kaleo-web`, `solr-web`, and so on.

In addition, you would find a set of XML files and property files under the folder $PLUGINS_SDK_HOME. The following are some of these files:

File name	Description	Comments
build. properties	Specifies the application server info, for example, app.server.type could be geronimo, glassfish, jboss, jetty, jonas, oc4j, resin, tomcat, and so on. By default, it is specified as tomcat. It also specifies a version, such as lp.version, and compilers, such as javac.compiler, ant.build.javac.source, ant.build.javac.target, and so on.	Do not update the properties of this file. Instead, create a separate properties file named build.${user.name}.properties with the properties to overwrite.
build-common-plugin.xml	Ant build; specifies Ant common plugin targets	Ant targets: clean, deploy, build-client, build-db, build-lang-cmd, build-service, build-wsdd, and so on.
build-common-plugins.xml	Ant build; specifies Ant common plugins targets	Ant targets: build-service, clean, clean-module, compile, compile-module, deploy, deploy-module, jar, and so on.
build-common.xml	Ant build; specifies Ant common targets	Ant targets: compile-java, format-javadoc, format-source, print-current-time, and so on.
build.xml	Ant build; specifies Ant targets	Import file build-common.xml; Ant targets: clean, deploy, build-service, build-summary, compile, and so on.

Portal runtime structure

Portal has its own runtime structure. You could simply download a bundle, unzip it, and take a deeper look at the portal runtime structure. However, here we will show you how to build the portal runtime. Generally, using the following steps, you can build a runtime bundle.

1. Create a file named `app.server.${env.name}.properties` in `$PORTAL_SRC_HOME` and add the following lines to it:

   ```
   app.server.parent.dir=$LIFERAY_PORTAL
   app.server.tomcat.dir=${app.server.parent.dir}/$CATALINA_HOME
   ```

2. Run `ant clean start deploy`

As shown in the preceding steps, you clean and start building the portal, and finally deploy the portal to your local Tomcat server. In general, `${env.name}` could be one of the pre-defined variables such as `${user.name}`, `${env.COMPUTERNAME}`, `${env.HOST}`, `${env.HOSTNAME}`. Here we use `${user.name}`. Of course, you can build the portal runtime against other application servers such as Geronimo, Glassfish, JBoss, jetty, Jonas, OC4J, resin, and so on.

Ant target clean

The Ant `target clean` command processes the following tasks:

- Cleaning Java classes under the `classes` folder
- Cleaning Java classes under the `portal-client` and `portal-service` folders
- Cleaning Java classes under the `util-bridges`, `util-java`, and `util-taglib` folders
- Cleaning Java classes under the `portal-impl` folder
- Cleaning Java classes under the `portal-web` and `tunnel-web` folders

There are more tasks which exist, such as cleaning the folder `/data/sql`, Tomcat `work` folder, Tomcat `temp` folder, Tomcat `logs` folder, and so on. You can find more details in `$PORTAL_SRC_HOME/build.xml`.

Ant target start

The Ant `target start` command processes the following tasks:

- Compiling the Java code under the `portal-service` folder
- Compiling the Java code under the `util-bridges`, `util-java`, and `util-taglib` folders
- Building the database `sql` and rebuilding the default embedded database `hypersonic`
- Compiling the Java code under the `portal-impl` folder

Ant target deploy

The Ant `target start` command processes the following tasks, mapping the portal source code to the portal runtime:

Source $PORTAL_SRC_HOME	Runtime $CATALINA_HOME	Description
/portal-service/portal-service.jar	/lib/ext/portal-service.jar	Portal service interfaces and models
/lib/global/portlet.jar	/lib/ext/portlet.jar	JSR-286 portlets
/lib/development/hsql.jar, jtds.jar, mysql.jar, postgresql.jar	/lib/ext/ hsql. jar,jtds.jar, mysql. jar,postgresql.jar	You may add other JDBC drivers, such as `ojdbc6.jar` for Oracle 11g
/lib/developmen/ccpp.jar, activation.jar, jms.jar, jta.jar, mail.jar, persistence.jar	/lib/ext/ccpp. jar,activation.jar,jms. jar,jta.jar,mail. jar,persistence.jar	Global dependencies
/support-tomcat/support-tomcat.jar	/lib/ext/support-tomcat.jar	Tomcat support only
/portal-impl/portal-impl.jar	/webapps/ROOT/WEB-INF/ lib/portal-impl.jar	Portal service and model implementation
/definitions/*	/webapps/ROOT/dtd/*	DTD, XSD, XML
/sql/*	/portal-impl.jar /com/ liferay/portal/tools/ sql/dependencies/*	Packaged as a part of `portal-impl.jar`
/util-bridges/util-bridges.jar	/webapps/ROOT/WEB-INF/ lib/util-bridges.jar	Bridge utilities
/util-java/util-java.jar	/webapps/ROOT/WEB-INF/ lib/util-java.jar	Java utilities
/util-taglib/util-taglib.jar	/webapps/ROOT/WEB-INF/ lib/util-taglib.jar	Taglib utilities
/lib/development/*.jar	/webapps/ROOT/WEB-INF/ lib/*.jar	Dependencies
/portal-web/docroot/*	/webapps/ROOT/*	ROOT
/sql/lportal.properties, lportal.script	$LIFEARY_PORTAL/ data/hsql/ lportal. properties, lportal. script	Sample Hypersonic data and properties
/portal-impl/classes /com/ liferay/portal/jcr/jackrabit. dependencies/repository.xml	$LIFEARY_HOME/data/ jackrabbit/repository. xml	JCR Jackrabbit repository settings

Source $PORTAL_SRC_HOME	Runtime $CATALINA_HOME	Description
/tunnel-web/tunnel-web.war	`/webapps/tunnel-web/*`	Tunnel web
/tools/servers/tomcat/bin/setenv.sh,setenv.bat	`/bin/setenv.sh,setenv.bat`	JVM settings
/tools/servers/tomcat/conf/Catalina/localhost/ROOT.xml	`/conf/Catalina/localhost/ROOT.xml`	Context path and cross context settings

In addition, as you have seen in the preceding table, the portal runtime covers the following main folders under $LIFERAY_HOME:

- `deploy`: A folder for hot deploy
- `data`: A folder for runtime data, such as, `document_library`, `hsql`, `jackrabbit`, and `lucene`
- `data/ee`: A folder for license information, **Enterprise Edition (EE)**
- `license`: A folder for license information, **Community Edition (CE)**
- $APPLICATION_SERVER_DIR: A folder for the application server directory, for example, Tomcat $CATALINA_HOME

What is happening?

As mentioned earlier, ${env.name} could be one of the pre-defined variables such as ${user.name}, ${env.COMPUTERNAME}, ${env.HOST}, and ${env.HOSTNAME}. Why? The file build-common.xml has the following definitions:

```
<property file="${project.dir}/app.server.${user.name}.properties" />
// see details in build-common.xml
<property file="${project.dir}/app.server.properties" />
```

Similar specifications would be found at com.liferay.portal.util.PortalImpl as the following lines.

```
_computerName = System.getProperty("env.COMPUTERNAME");
if (Validator.isNull(_computerName)) {
  _computerName = System.getProperty("env.HOST");
}
if (Validator.isNull(_computerName)) {
  _computerName = System.getProperty("env.HOSTNAME");
}
```

Plugins runtime structure

Each plugin has its own runtime structure. You could simply download a plugin WAR, deploy it to `$LIFERAY_HOME/deploy` and take a deeper look at the plugin runtime structure. However, here we are going to show you how to build a plugin's runtime, using `knowledge-base-portlet` as an example. Generally, using the following steps, you can build a plugin runtime:

1. Create a file named `build.${env.name}.properties` in `$PLUGINS_SDK_HOME` and the add following lines to it:

   ```
   app.server.parent.dir=$LIFERAY_PORTAL
   app.server.dir=${app.server.parent.dir}/$CATALINA_HOME
   ```

2. Run `ant clean deploy` under the folder `$PLUGINS_SDKP_HOME/portlets/knowledge-base-portlet`.

Ant target clean

The Ant `target clean` command processes the following tasks:

- Cleaning Java classes under the `$PLUGINS_SDK_HOME/portlets/knowledge-base-portlet/docroot/WEB-INF/classes` folder
- Removing the existing WAR under the `$PLUGINS_SDK_HOME/dist` folder

Ant target deploy

The Ant `target deploy` command processes the following tasks:

- Compiling Java classes, `$PLUGINS_SDK_HOME/portlets/knowledge-base-portlet/docroot/WEB-INF/src`
- Packaging all files as a WAR in the `$PLUGINS_SDK_HOME/dist` folder
- Copying the WAR file to the folder `$LIFEARY_HOME/deploy`

After deploying, all folders and files under the folder `$PLUGINS_SDK_HOME/portlets/knowledge-base-portlet/docroot` have been packaged to `$CATALINA_HOME/webapps/knowledge-base-portlet`. In particular, a few JAR files have been added at `$CATALINA_HOME/webapps/knowledge-base-portlet/WEB-INF/lib`, such as, `commons-logging.jar`, `util-bridges.jar`, `util-java.jar`, and `util-taglib.jar`. In addition, `web.xml` at `$CATALINA_HOME/webapps/knowledge-base-portlet/WEB-INF` was overridden in the deployment process. Why? We will show the details in the next chapter.

Portal service and implementation

As you can see, portal core services and models interfaces are specified in `portal-service.jar`, which is accessible to all plugins. When you develop your plugins, you can leverage all the core services and models interfaces in `portal-service.jar`. Of course, you can also leverage the JSR-286 portlets services and models interfaces specified in `portlet.jar`. Note that both `portal-service.jar` and `portlet.jar` should be specified as global libraries (libraries that can be read by all web applications deployed into an application server). Thus, you should not include these JAR files in your plugins `/WEB-INF/lib` folder; instead, you can use these JAR files explicitly.

In addition, portal deployment processes will add JAR files such as `commons-logging.jar`, `util-bridges.jar`, `util-java.jar`, and `util-taglib.jar` to the plugin runtime folder `/WEB-INF/lib`. Thus, you would be able to use these utilities in your plugins, but you won't need to include these JAR files in the folder `/WEB-INF/lib` explicitly.

Most importantly, plugins that use Ant target compile will detect the inclusion of `portal-impl.jar` in `/WEB-INF/lib`. The JAR `portal-impl.jar` is designed with a large number of singleton classes which are instantiated on the basis that they will exist alone in the application server. While compile-time issues may be resolved, plugins, such as portlets, cannot be made to work by simply adding `portal-impl.jar`, because doing so violates the assumption and the resulting problems will be extremely difficult to debug. Thus, you need to find a solution that does not require `portal-impl.jar`.

In `$PLUGINS_SDK_HOME/build-common-plugin.xml`, you will find the following code:

```
<if>
  <available file="docroot/WEB-INF/lib/portal-impl.jar" />
  <then>
    <fail>
      Detected inclusion of portal-impl.jar in WEB-INF/lib.
    </fail>
  </then>
</if>
```

Interface and implementation

As you can see, portal service and model interfaces are specified in `portal-service.jar`, which is accessible globally, while utilities such as `util-bridges.jar`, `util-java.jar`, and `util-taglib.jar` exist at `/webapps/ROOT/WEB-INF/lib/`, and when deploying a plugin, get added. In particular, implementation of the portal service and model interfaces are specified in `portal-impl.jar`.

The following table shows the portal service and model interfaces and their implementation with a few examples:

	Portal Service - `portal-service.jar`	**Portal Implementation** `portal-impl.jar`	**Description**
Properties keys	`com.liferay.portal.kernel.util.PropsKeys`	`com.liferay.portal.util.PropsValues`	`PropsKeys` should be available in plugins
Web keys	`com.liferay.portal.kernel.util.Webkeys`	`com.liferay.portal.util.Webkeys`	Use kernel `WebKeys` in plugins
Browser support	`com.liferay.portal.kernel.servlet.BrowserSniffer`	`com.liferay.portal.servlet.BrowserSnifferImpl`	Use interface `BrowserSniffer` in plugins
Counter model	`com.liferay.counter.model.Counter`	`com.liferay.counter.model.impl.CounterImpl`	Use model `Counter` in plugins
Counter service	`com.liferay.counter.service.CounterLocalServiceUtil`	`com.liferay.counter.service.impl.CounterLocalServiceImpl`	Use `CounterLocalServiceUtil` in plugins
String Utility	`com.liferay.portal.kernel.util.StringUtil`	N/P	String utilities
Minifier filter	`com.liferay.portal.kernel.servlet.BaseFilter,LiferayFilter`	`com.liferay.portal.servlet.filters.minifier.MinifierFilter`	Filters
Dynamic CSS Filter	`com.liferay.portal.kernel.servlet.BaseFilter,LiferayFilter`	`com.liferay.portal.servlet.filters.dynamiccss.DynamicCSSFilter`	Filters for dynamic CSS and **Sass** - an extension of CSS3
Virtual Host Filter	`com.liferay.portal.kernel.servlet.BaseFilter,LiferayFilter`	`com.liferay.portal.servlet.filters.virtualhost.VirtualHostFilter`	Filters

As shown in the preceding table, the portal provides a central service interface to detect different browsers, either web or WAP. In general, the Liferay portal supports almost any browser. In `BrowserSniffer`, it provides a set of interfaces to detect browsers as follows:

```
public static final String BROWSER_ID_FIREFOX = "firefox";
// more interfaces
```

In particular, `BrowserSnifferImpl` implements `BrowserSniffer`. For example, it pre-defines the following aliases:

```
private static final String[] _FIREFOX_ALIASES = {
"firefox", "minefield", "granparadiso", "bonecho", "firebird",
"phoenix", "camino" };
// see details in BrowserSnifferImpl.java
```

Liferay introduces a minifying-filter named `MinifierFilter` to minify JavaScript files, JSP files, and CSS files in runtime. Using minifying-filter `MinifierUtil` consumed by `MinifierFilter`, the portal will remove unnecessary characters from the code to reduce its size, thereby improving load time. More specifically, when files are minified, all comments are removed, as well as unneeded white space characters such as space, newline, and tab. In the case of JavaScript files, this improves the response time performance as the size of the downloaded file is reduced.

Note that the minifying-filter `MinifierFilter` does not only minify JavaScript files, CSS files, and JSP files from portal core, but also it minifies JavaScript files, CSS files, and JSP files from any plugins.

JAR-based fix patch

When should you use source code `portal-service`, `portal-impl`, `util-bridges`, and `util-java`, `util-taglib`? In the following use cases, you may need to override the source code and generate a JAR-based fix patch:

- Customize service and model interfaces in `portal-service`

- Fix bugs or add new features in `portal-impl`

- Change default behaviors in `util-bridges`, `util-java`, `util-taglib`

How to generate a JAR-based fix patch? Let's have a look at a real example. Let's say that there is a custom model—each **brand** can have many destinations, while each **destination** can have many **hotels**; each brand, destination, or hotel will have its own public and private pages.

Each brand will have a public virtual host—domain name and SEO friendly URL as follows.

- Use case A) for brand:

  `http://www.${brand.name}.com[/${locale}]`

  Where `${brand.name}` should be a brand (it could be presented as a root-level organization) friendly URL. Destination and hotel don't need virtual host, but they do need SEO-friendly URLs.

- Use case B) for destination:

  `http://www.${brand.name}.com[/${locale}]/${destination.name}`

- Use case C) for hotel:

  `http://www.${brand.name}.com[/${locale}]/${destination.name}/${hotel.name}`

Where `${destination.name}` should be the destination (it could be presented as a first-level organization) SEO-friendly URL. `${hotel.name}` should be the hotel (it is presented as a second-level organization) SEO-friendly URL.

The preceding use cases could be implemented as a JAR-based fix patch. More precisely, customize the group-friendly URL and the virtual host in `VirtualHostFilter` and generate a JAR-based fix patch. As `VirtualHostFilter` is packaged inside `portal-impl.jar`, the patch should be packaged into a JAR file, and this JAR file must be loaded before `portal-impl.jar`. One way to realize that is by using a naming convention, where the app server would load JAR files alphabetically. For example, `portal-impl.jar` starts with the letter p, then the name for patch should be prefixed with a letter between a-o, which alphabetically precedes the letter p.

Note that the JAR-based fix patch for `portal-service` should be copied into the folder `$CATALINA_HOME/lib/ext`. The JAR-based fix patch for `portal-impl`, `util-bridges`, `util-java`, and `util-taglib` should be copied into the folder `$CATALINA_HOME/webapps/ROOT/WEB-INF/lib`.

Service-Builder

Liferay portal provides a tool named Service-Builder, which could automate the creation of interfaces and classes for database persistence, local and remote services. In brief, Service-Builder will generate most of the common code needed to implement, find, create, update, and delete operations on the database, allowing developers to focus on the higher-level aspects of the service design directly.

The term **service** is a class or set of classes designed to handle retrieving and storing data classes. A service could be local or remote. A local service is used in the local Liferay instance, while a remote service is accessible from anywhere. By default, remote services support SOAP, JSON, and Java RMI. This section is going to discuss Service-Builder in the portal core, and the next chapter is going to focus on Service-Builder in plugins.

Ant target build-service

Ant target `build-service` is specified in `$PORTAL_SRC_HOME/portal-impl/build.xml` as follows. Liferay eats its own dog food—almost all services and models in portal core were generated by the Ant target, `build-service`. Similarly, the Ant target `build-service` was specified in `$PLUGINS_SDK_HOME/build-common-plugin.xml`, where it can generate, automatically, models and services for custom plugins.

```
<target name="build-service">
<java classname="com.liferay.portal.tools.servicebuilder.
ServiceBuilder"
classpathref="project.classpath">
<arg value="-Dexternal-properties=com/liferay/portal/tools/
dependencies/portal-tools.properties" />
<!-- see details in build-common-plugin.xml --></java>
<delete file="ServiceBuilder.temp" />
<ant dir="../portal-service" target="compile" inheritAll="false" />
</target>
```

As shown in the preceding code, `com.liferay.portal.tools.servicebuilder.ServiceBuilder` is the main entry to build services and models. The available arguments include `/portal-impl/src/META-INF/portal-hbm.xml`, `portal-orm.xml`, `portal-model-hints.xml`, `portal-spring.xml`, `${service.file}` and so on.

In portal core, `${service.file}` could be one of following possible values under the folder `/portal-impl/src/`:

```
com/liferay/counter/service.xml - counter services
com/liferay/portal/service.xml - portal core services
// ignore details
com/liferay/portlet/wiki/service.xml - wiki services
```

As shown in the preceding code, model classes and their attributes are defined in a `service.xml` file.

Database structure definition

The Liferay portal provides counter services, which are used to autogenerate the database entity primary key. As you know, Liferay can support different databases as it does not use the sequences of any databases. Instead, Liferay has its own default counter for specific database. Optimizing this counter can increase performance. Here we use `com/liferay/counter/service.xml` to show how to define the database structure through Service-Builder. Counter service has the following definition, where additional comments were added for demo purposes:

```
<service-builder package-path="com.liferay.counter">
<namespace>Counter</namespace>
```

```
<entity name="Counter" local-service="true" remote-service="false"
cache-enabled="false">
<!-- PK fields -->
<column name="name" type="String" primary="true" />
<!-- Other fields -->
<column name="currentId" type="long" />
<!-- Relationships -->
<!-- Order -->
<!-- Finder methods -->
<!-- References -->
</entity>
</service-builder>
```

The element `service-builder` is the root of the deployment descriptor for a Service-Builder descriptor that is used to generate services available to portlets. Service-Builder saves the developer time by generating Spring utilities, SOAP utilities, and Hibernate persistence classes to ease the development of services. Service-Builder has the following attribute list declarations:

```
<!ATTLIST service-builder
  package-path CDATA #REQUIRED
  auto-namespace-tables CDATA #IMPLIED
>
```

The `package-path` value specifies the package of the generated code. The `auto-namespace-tables` value specifies whether or not to automatically use namespace tables. The default value is `false` for portal core services or `true` for plugin services.

As shown in the following element type declarations, the element `service-builder` can have no more than one `author` (this item is optional), one `namespace`, one or more `entity`, and no more than one `exceptions` (this item is optional)

```
<!ELEMENT service-builder (author?, namespace, entity+, exceptions?)>
```

Author, namespace, and exceptions

The `author` element is the name of a user that is associated with the generated code. The `namespace` element must be a unique namespace, as table names will be prefixed with this namespace, and generated JSON JavaScript will be scoped to this namespace as well. For example, it will be `Liferay.Service.Counter.*` if the namespace is `Counter`.

The `exceptions` element contains a list of generated `exceptions`. This does not save a lot of typing, but can still be helpful. In addition, you can refer to Service-Builder DTD details at `svn://svn.liferay.com/repos/public/portal/trunk/definitions/liferay-service-builder_6_1_0.dtd`.

Entity

An **entity** usually represents a business facade and a table in the database. If an entity does not have any columns, then it only represents a business facade. As shown in the following element type declarations, the element `entity` can have one or more `column`, no more than one `order` (this item is optional), one or more `finder`, one or more `reference`, and one or more `tx-required`:

```
<!ELEMENT entity (column*, order?, finder*, reference*, tx-required*)>
```

Service-Builder will always generate an empty business facade **POJO** (**Plain Old Java Object**) if it does not exist. Moreover, Service-Builder will check to see if the business facade already exists. If it exists and has additional methods, then Service-Builder will also update the **SOAP** (**Simple Object Access Protocol**) wrappers. If an entity does have columns, then the value object, the POJO class that is mapped to the database, and other persistence utilities are also generated based on the `order` and `finder` elements.

Attribute list declarations

The following DTD shows the element `entity` attribute list declarations:

```
<!ATTLIST entity
  name CDATA #REQUIRED
  human-name CDATA #IMPLIED
  table CDATA #IMPLIED
  // see details in liferay-service-builder_6_1_0.dtd
  tx-manager CDATA #IMPLIED
  cache-enabled CDATA #IMPLIED
>
```

The `name` value specifies the name of the entity, for example, `Counter`. This is the required attribute and the rest of the attributes are optional. The `human-name` value specifies the readable name to use when generating documentation for this entity. If none is specified, then one will be generated from the name.

The `table` value specifies the name of the table that this `entity` maps to in the database. If this value is not set, then the name of the table is the same as that of the entity. If the `uuid` value is `true`, then the service will generate a **UUID** column for the service. This column will automatically be populated with a **UUID**. The default value is `false`.

If the `local-service` value is `true`, then the service will generate local interfaces for the service. The default value is `false`. If the `remote-service` value is `true`, then the service will generate remote interfaces for the service. The default value is `true`.

The `persistence-class` value specifies the name of your custom persistence class. This class must implement the generated persistence interface or extend the generated persistence class. This allows developers to override the default behavior without modifying the generated persistence class.

The `data-source` value specifies the data source target that is set to the persistence class. The default value is the **Liferay data source**. The `session-factory` value specifies the session factory that is set to the persistence class. The default value is the **Liferay session factory**.

The `tx-manager` value specifies the transaction manager that Spring uses. The default value is the **Spring Hibernate transaction manager** that wraps the Liferay data source and session factory.

The `cache-enabled` value specifies whether or not to cache queries for this entity. You can set this to `false` if the data in the table will be updated by other programs. The default value is `true`.

In particular, `portal-impl com.liferay.portal.tools.servicebuilder.Entity` specifies the element `entity` and its attribute list declarations. The default data source, session factory, and TX-manager are defined as follows in the `Entity`:

```
public static final String DEFAULT_DATA_SOURCE = "liferayDataSource";
// see details in Entity.java
public static final String DEFAULT_TX_MANAGER =
"liferayTransactionManager";
```

Column

The `column` element represents a **column** in the database. The following DTD shows the element `entity` attribute list declarations. As you can see, only the attributes `name` and `type` are required; the rest of the attributes are optional.

```
<!ATTLIST column
  name CDATA #REQUIRED

  // see details in liferay-service-builder_6_1_0.dtd
  convert-null CDATA #IMPLIED
  localized CDATA #IMPLIED
>
```

The `name` value specifies the getter and setter name in the entity. The `type` value specifies whether the column is a primitive type such as `boolean`, `int`, `short`, `long`, `float`, `double`, or a data type `Integer`, `String`, or `Date`. For example, the column `name` of the entity `Counter` has the type value `String`; and the column `currentId` has the type value `long`.

The `db-name` value maps the field to a physical database column that is different to the column name. If the `primary` value is set to `true`, then this column is part of the Primary Key of the entity. If multiple columns have the primary value set to `true`, then a compound key will be created. For instance, the column `name` is the Primary Key of the entity `Counter`.

If the `entity` and `mapping-key` attributes are specified and `mapping-table` is not, then Service-Builder will assume that you are specifying a **one-to-many relationship**. If the `entity` and `mapping-table` attributes are specified and `mapping-key` is not, then Service-Builder will assume that you are specifying a **many-to-many** relationship. For example, the following column specifies that there will be a getter named `getUsers` that will return a collection. It will use a mapping table named `Users_Groups` to give a many-to-many relationship between groups and users:

```
<column name="users" type="Collection" entity="User" mapping-
table="Users_Groups" />
```

If you are creating a mapping table for an entity defined in another `service.xml`, then you need to specify the full package path, such as `com.liferay.portal.User`.

The `id-type` and `id-param` values are used in order to create an auto-generated, auto-incrementing Primary Key when inserting records into a table. This can be implemented in four different ways, depending on the type of database being used. In all cases, the Primary Key of the model object should be assigned a value of `null`, and Hibernate will know to replace the `null` value with an auto-generated and auto-incremented value.

Most importantly, if no `id-type` value is used, it is assumed that a non-auto-generated Primary Key will be assigned.

The attribute `id-type` can have the following values to create an auto-generated, auto-incrementing Primary Key:

- **Class**: The class specified in the `id-param` value, for example, `com.liferay. counter.service.persistence.IDGenerator`, will be called to retrieve a unique identifier that will be used as the Primary Key for the new record. Note that this implementation works for all supported databases.

- **Increment**: Generate identifiers that are unique only when no other process is inserting data into the same table. This implementation should not be used in a clustered environment, but it does work for all supported databases.

- **Identity**: Using an identity column to generate a Primary Key; the create table SQL generated for this entity will create an identity column that natively auto-generates a Primary Key whenever an insert occurs. Note that this implementation is only supported by DB2, MySQL, and MS SQL Server.

- **Sequence**: Using a sequence to generate a Primary Key, a create sequence SQL statement is generated based on the `id-param` value stored in `/sql/sequences.sql`. This sequence is then accessed to generate a unique identifier whenever an insert occurs. Note that this implementation is only supported by DB2, Oracle, PostgreSQL, and SAP DB.

- The `filter-primary` value specifies the column to use as the Primary Key column when using filter finders. Only one column should ever have this value set to `true`. If no column has this set to `true`, then the default primary column is to be used.

The `convert-null` value specifies whether or not the column value is automatically converted to a `non-null` value if it is `null`. This only applies if the type value is `String`. This is particularly useful if your entity is referencing a read only table or a database view, so that Hibernate does not try to issue unnecessary updates. The default value is `true`.

The `localized` value specifies whether or not the value of the column can have different values for different locales. The default value is `false`. In particular, `portal-impl com.liferay.portal.tools.servicebuilder.EntityColumn` specifies the element `column` and its attribute list declarations.

Finder

The `finder` element represents a generated finder method. Each `finder` element can have one or more elements, such as `finder-column`, and the following attributes list declarations where the attributes' `name` and `return-type` are required and the rest of the attributes are optional:

```
<!ATTLIST finder
  name CDATA #REQUIRED
  // see details in liferay-service-builder_6_1_0.dtd
  db-index CDATA #IMPLIED
>
```

The `name` value specifies the name of the finder method. The `return-type` value specifies the return type of the finder. Valid values are **Collection** or the name of the entity. If the value is `Collection`, then this finder returns a list of entities. If the value is the name of the entity, then this finder returns, at most, one entity.

If the `unique` value is `true`, then the finder must return a unique entity. If the `db-index` value is `true`, then the service will automatically generate a SQL index for this finder. The default value is `true`.

The `finder-column` element specifies the columns to 'find' by. It has the following attribute list declarations, where the attribute `name` is required and the other attributes are optional:

```
<!ATTLIST finder-column
  name CDATA #REQUIRED
  // see details in liferay-service-builder_6_1_0.dtd
  arrayable-operator CDATA #IMPLIED
>
```

The `name` value specifies the name of the finder method. For example:

```
<finder name="UserId" return-type="Collection">
  <finder-column name="userId" />
</finder>
```

The preceding settings will create a finder with the name `findByUserId` that will return `Collection` and require a given `userId`. It will also generate several more `findByUserId` methods that take in pagination fields and more sorting options. Service-Builder will also generate `removeByUserId` and `countByUserId`.

The attribute `case-sensitive` is a `boolean` value and it is only used if the column is a String value. The attribute `comparator` takes in the values =, !=, <, <=, >, >=, or `LIKE` and it is used to compare columns.

The attribute `arrayable-operator` takes in the values `AND` or `OR` and it will generate an additional finder where this column's parameter takes an array instead of a single value. Every value in this array will be compared with the column using the comparator, and the conditions will be combined with either an `AND` or `OR` operator. In addition, `portal-impl com.liferay.portal.tools.servicebuilder. EntityFinder` specifies the element `Finder` and its attribute list declarations.

Reference

The `reference` element allows you to inject services from another `service.xml` within the same class loader. For example, if you inject the `Group` entity, then you would be able to reference the `Group` services from your service implementation through the `getGroupLocalService` and `getGroupService` methods. You would also be able to reference the `Group` services through the `GroupLocalService` and `GroupService` variables.

The `reference` element can take two optional attributes, namely, `package-path` and `entity` as follows:

```
<!ATTLIST reference
  package-path CDATA #IMPLIED
  entity CDATA #IMPLIED
>
```

For example, if you inject the `Group` entity, then you could have the following settings:

```
<reference package-path="com.liferay.portal" entity="Group" />
```

The `package-path` attribute has the value `com.liferay.portal`, while the `entity` attribute has the value `com.liferay.portal`. In addition, the entity-mapping model is specified through the class `portal-impl com.liferay.portal.tools.servicebuilder.EntityMapping`.

Order and tx-required

The `order` element specifies a default ordering and sorting of the entities when they are retrieved from the database. As shown in the following example, each order element can have one or more elements `order-column` and one attribute `by`:

```
<order by="asc">
  <order-column name="name" />
</order>
```

The attribute `by` is set to `asc` or `desc` to order by ascending or descending. The `order-column` element allows you to order the entities by specific columns. The element has the following attribute list declarations, where the attribute name is required and the rest of the attributes are optional. The attributes of the `order-column` element allow you to fine-tune the ordering of the entity, such as `Counter`.

```
<!ATTLIST order-column
  name CDATA #REQUIRED
  case-sensitive CDATA #IMPLIED
  order-by CDATA #IMPLIED
>
```

The attribute `order-by` is set to `asc` or `desc` to order by ascending or descending, respectively. Moreover, the attribute `case-sensitive` is set to `true` or `false` to order in a case-sensitive manner or non-case-sensitive manner, respectively. The default value is `true`.

```
<order>
  <order-column name="articleId" order-by="asc" />
  <order-column name="version" order-by="desc" />
</order>
```

The preceding settings will order by `articleId` in an ascending manner and then by `version` in a descending manner. The element `order` and its attribute declarations are defined in the class, `portal-impl com.liferay.portal.tools.servicebuilder.EntityOrder`.

The `tx-required` element has a text value that will be used to match method names that require transactions. By default, the methods: `add*`, `check*`, `clear*`, `delete*`, `set*`, and `update*` require propagation of transactions. All other methods support transactions, but are assumed to be read only. If you want additional methods to fall under transactions, then you can add the method name to this element.

Reserved names

The `name` value of an `entity` specifies the name of the entity; the `table` value of an entity specifies the name of the table that this `entity` maps to in the database. Some names or aliases for the `name` and `table` values should be reserved. Similarly, the `name` value of a column specifies the getter and setter name in the entity. Some names or aliases for the `name` value of a column should be reserved too.

Reserved alias names

Reserved entity alias names are specified in `com.liferay.portal.tools.servicebuilder.dependencies.bad_alias_names.txt`.

```
all
and
and more
```

If the `name` value of an entity is one of the above list, then the table name will be overridden with a postfix `_`. Why? In `ServiceBuilder`, it has the following code:

```
if (_badAliasNames.contains(alias.toLowerCase())) {
  alias += StringPool.UNDERLINE;
}
```

If you need to add a new reserved alias name, such as `Entity`, you can by adding the reserved alias name `Entity` at the last newline of `com.liferay.portal.tools.servicebuilder.dependencies.bad_alias_names.txt`. Therefore, if the `name` value is `Entity`, the table name will be overridden as `Entity_`.

Reserved table names

The following table names are reserved after being specified in `com.liferay.portal.tools.servicebuilder.dependencies.bad_table_names.txt`.

```
Account
Action
and more
```

If the `table` value is one of the above list, the table name will be overridden with a postfix UNDERLINE (that is, _). Why? In `ServiceBuilder`, it has the following code:

```
if (_badTableNames.contains(mappingTable)) {
  mappingTable += StringPool.UNDERLINE;
}
```

In case you need to add a new reserved table name, such as `Table`, you can by adding the reserved table name, `Table`, after the last newline of `com.liferay.portal.tools.servicebuilder.dependencies.bad_table_name.txt`. Therefore, if the `table` value is `Table`, the table name will be overridden as `Table_`.

Reserved column names

Reserved column names are specified in `com.liferay.portal.tools.servicebuilder.dependencies.bad_column_names.txt` as follows:

```
abstract
access
active
and more
```

If the `name` value of a column is one of the reserved column names, the `name` value will be overridden with a postfix UNDERLINE (that is, _), because, in `ServiceBuilder`, it has the following modification:

```
if (_badColumnNames.contains(columnName)) {
  columnDBName += StringPool.UNDERLINE;
}
```

You can add your own reserved column names to `com.liferay.portal.tools.servicebuilder.dependencies.bad_column_names.txt`. For example, `Trigger` is a reserved word in MySQL, and this word should not be used as a column when MySQL is in use. Therefore, you can add the word `Trigger` as one of the reserved column names. When the `name` value of a column is `trigger`, then the table name will be overridden as `trigger_`.

Reserved JSON types

The following are a few JSON types marked as reserved. They are called bad JSON types:

```
byte[]
com.liferay.portal.kernel.io.FileCacheOutputStream
and more
```

As shown in the preceding list, reserved JSON types are specified in `com.liferay.portal.tools.servicebuilder.dependencies.bad_json_types.txt`.

> **Downloading the example code**
>
> You can download the example code files for all Packt books you have purchased from your account at `http://www.packtpub.com`. If you purchased this book elsewhere, you can visit `http://www.packtpub.com/support` and register to have the files e-mailed directly to you.

Mappings

Mappings of Service-Builder covert Java data types to SQL data types, service XML to models and services, SQL scripts generation, properties creation, JSON JavaScript generation, and Spring and Hibernate configuration.

Data types

Service-Builder provides flexibility to map Java data types into SQL data types as follows:

Java data type	SQL data type	Description
boolean, Boolean	BOOLEAN	Boolean type
Double, Double	DOUBLE	Double type
float, Float	FLOAT	Float type
int, Integer	INTEGER	Integer type
long, Long	BIGINT	Long type
short, Short	INTEGER	Short type
Date	TIMESTAMP	Date type
String	CLOB	Max-Length = 2000000
	TEXT	Max-Length > 4000
	STRING	Max-Length = 4000
	VARCHAR	Max-Length < 4000

Models and services

Service-Builder will generate most of the services and models for each entity, presented as ${entity.name}. Here we will use the example entity Asset (that is, ${entity.name} = Asset) to show how Service-Builder generates services and models.

The following table shows models, extended models, and their implementation:

Models and services	FTL com.liferay. portal.tools. servicebuilder. dependencies	Service-Builder Method	Sample
${entity.name}Model	model.ftl	_createModel(entity)	AssetModel
${entity.name}	extended_model.ftl	_createExtended ModelImpl(entity)	Asset
${entity.name} Wrapper	model_wrapper.ftl	_createModel Wrapper(entity)	AssetWrapper
${entity.name}Clp	model_clp.ftl	_createModelClp (entity)	AssetClp
${entity.name}Soap	model_soap.ftl	_createModelSoap (entity)	AssetSoap
${entity.name} ModelImpl	model_impl.ftl	_createModelImpl (entity)	AssetModelImpl
${entity.name}Impl	extended_model.ftl	_createExtended ModelImpl (entity)	AssetImpl

The following table shows exception, finder, and its implementation, using the entity Group as an example. Note that you could write your ${entity.name}FinderImpl class in /service/persistence/, service-builder methods _createFinder(entity) and _createFinderUtil(entity) will get ${entity.name}FinderImpl and generate interfaces. That is, you can have your own Finder implementation; Service-Builder will generate the interfaces.

Models and services	FTL com.liferay. portal.tools. servicebuilder. dependencies	Service-Builder Method	Sample
${exception}Exception	exception.ftl	_createExceptions (exceptionList)	GroupName Exception
${entity.name}Finder	finder.ftl	_createFinder(entity)	GroupFinder, GroupFinderImpl
${entity.name} FinderUtil	finder_util.ftl	_createFinderUtil (entity)	GroupFinderUtil

The following table shows persistence services, using the entity Group as an example. Similarly, you could write your own ${entity.name}PersistenceImpl class at /service/persistence/, service-builder methods _createPersistence(entity) and _createPersistenceUtil(entity) will get ${entity.name} PersistenceImpl and generate interfaces. In brief, you can have your own Persistence implementation; the Service-Builder will generate the interfaces.

Models and services	FTL com.liferay. portal.tools. servicebuilder. dependencies	Service-Builder Method	Sample
${entity.name} Persistence	persistence.ftl	_createPersistence (entity)	GroupPersistence
${entity.name} PersistenceImpl	persistence_impl.ftl	_createPersistenceImpl (entity)	GroupPersistence Impl
${entity.name}Util	persistence_util.ftl	_createPersistenceUtil (entity)	GroupUtil

The following table shows local and remote services, using the entity Group as an example:

Models and services	FTL com.liferay. portal.tools. servicebuilder. dependencies	Service-Builder Method	Sample
${entity.name} LocalService	service.ftl	_createService	GroupLocalService
${entity.name}Service	service.ftl	_createService	GroupService
${entity.name} LocalServiceImpl	Service_impl.ftl	_createServiceImpl	GroupLocalService Impl
${entity.name} ServiceImpl	Service_impl.ftl	_createServiceImpl	GroupServiceImpl
${entity.name} ServiceBaseImpl	service_base_impl.ftl	_createService BaseImpl	GroupLocalService BaseImpl
${entity.name} LocalServiceUtil	service_util.ftl	_createServiceUtil	GroupLocal ServiceUtil
${entity.name} ServiceUtil	service_util.ftl	_createServiceUtil	GroupServiceUtil
${entity.name} LocalServiceWrapper	service_wrapper.ftl	_createService Wrapper	GroupLocalService Wrapper

Models and services	FTL com.liferay. portal.tools. servicebuilder. dependencies	Service-Builder Method	Sample
${entity.name} ServiceWrapper	service_wrapper.ftl	_createService Wrapper	GroupService Wrapper
${entity.name} LocalServiceClp	service_clp.ftl	_createServiceClp	
${entity.name} ServiceClp	service_clp.ftl	_createServiceClp	
ClpSerializer	service_clp_ serializer.ftl	_createServiceClp Serializer()	ClpSerializer
ClpMessageListener	service_clp_ message_listener.ftl	_createServiceClp MessageListener()	ClpMessageListene
${entity.name} ServiceSoap	service_soap.ftl	_createServiceSoap	GroupServiceSoap
${entity.name} JSONSerializer	service_json_ serializer.ftl	_createServiceJson Serializer(entity)	

As shown in the preceding overview, you will see that GroupLocalService is the interface for the local service. It contains the signatures of every method in GroupLocalServiceBaseImpl and GroupLocalServiceImpl. GroupLocalServiceBaseImpl contains a few automatically-generated methods providing common functionality. The GroupLocalServiceImpl class is auto-generated, but you still have a chance to add your own custom code. Running Service-Builder again will generate services based on your custom code.

Why have the Service tier and the Persistence tier separate? The **Persistence** tier is meant to go directly to the database and may expose many more methods than should ever be used by anyone except the **Service** tier that encapsulates the business logic. Therefore, the Service tier is the business tier that packages up many low-level calls.

SQL scripts, properties, and JSON JavaScript

Service-Builder will generate a set of SQL scripts, properties, and JSON JavaScript. The following table shows the generated SQL scripts, properties, and JSON JavaScript, FTL templates, service-builder method, and mapping description:

SQL scripts or properties	FTL com.liferay.portal.tools.servicebuilder.dependencies	Service-Builder Method	Description
indexes.sql	N/P	`_createSQLIndexes()`	SQL indexes
sequences.sql	N/P	`_createSQLSequences`	SQL sequences
tables.sql	N/P	`_createSQLTables()`	SQL tables
indexes.properties	N/P	`createSQLIndexes()`	Indexes properties
service.properties	props.ftl	`_createProps()`	Service properties
service.js	json_js.ftl, json_js_method.ftl	`_createJsonJs()`	JSON JavaScript

Spring and Hibernate

Service-Builder will generate a set of Spring and Hibernate configurations. The following table shows the generated XML configuration, FTL templates, service-builder method, and mapping description:

XML in META-INF	FTL com.liferay.portal.tools.servicebuilder.dependencies	Service-Builder Method	Description
base-spring.xml	spring_base_xml.ftl	`_createSpringBaseXml()`	Spring base
cluster-spring.xml	spring_cluster_xml.ftl	`_createSpringClusterXml()`	Spring cluster
dynamic-data-source-spring.xml	spring_dynamic_data_source_xml.ftl	`_createSpringDynamicDataSourceXml()`	Dynamic data source
hibernate-spring.xml	spring_hibernate_xml.ftl	`_createSpringHibernateXml()`	Spring Hibernate
Infrastructure-spring.xml	spring_infrastructure_xml.ftl	`_createSpringInfrastructureXml()`	Spring infrastructure
portlet-hbm.xml	hbm_xml.ftl	`_createHbmXml()`	HBM

XML in META-INF	FTL com.liferay.portal.tools.servicebuilder.dependencies	Service-Builder Method	Description
portlet-model-hints.xml	model_hints_xml.ftl	_createModelHintsXml()	Model hints
portlet-orm.xml	orm_xml.ftl	_createOrmXml()	ORM
portlet-spring.xml	spring_xml.ftl	_createSpringXml()	Spring
shard-data-source-spring.xml	spring_dynamic_data_source_xml.ftl	_createSpringShardDataSourceXml()	Database sharding data source
remoting-servlet.xml	Remoting_xml.ftl	_createRemotingXml()	Remote servlet

Element convert-null

Service-Builder supports primitive types, including `boolean`, `int`, `short`, `long`, `float`, and `double`, and the data types, `String` and `Date`. As the default value of the above data types could be `NULL` or a specific value, Service-Builder introduced the **convert-null** element. The convert-null value specifies whether or not the column value is automatically converted into a `non-null` value if it is null. Currently, this feature only applies if the type value is `String`. This is particularly useful if your entity is referencing a read only table or a database view, so that **Hibernate** does not try to issue unnecessary updates. The default setting of this `convert-null` attribute is `true`.

Here we will address how to apply the `convert-null` element to other data types, for example primitive types such as `boolean`, `int`, `short`, `long`, `float`, and `double`. For example, you may expect `long` values and `Integer` values to have a `null` value to a table, rather than the value `0`. Most importantly, you may need the option to save the `long` value and the `Integer` value as either `null` or `0`.

In general, this feature can be implemented as a fix patch. The following steps show a possible solution:

1. Map the `covert-null` value into the database SQL. For example, in `service.xml`, a column is listed as follows:

   ```
   <column name="salary" type="Integer" convert-null="false" />
   ```

2. It will be mapped into the following database SQL:

   ```
   field0 INTEGER null
   ```

3. How to implement this? You can simply add the following code in the
   method `_getCreateTableSQL` of `ServiceBuilder.java`:

```
else if ( (
   colType.equalsIgnoreCase("boolean") ||
   // see details in ServiceBuilder.java
   colType.equalsIgnoreCase("float") ) &&
   !col.isConvertNull() ) {
   sb.append(" null");
}
```

4. The preceding code shows that it will append NULL for primitive types
   such as `boolean, int, short, long, float, and double`.

5. Map column types with `convert-null="false"` into different **ORM** object
   types with the default value NULL.

By default, Liferay provides the following object types for ORM mappings with the
default value:

- `com.liferay.portal.dao.orm.hibernate.ShortType`: Mapped into the
  data type `short` with the default value 0

- `IntegerType`: Mapped into the data type `int` with the default value 0

- `LongType`: Mapped into the data type `long` with the default value 0

- `BooleanType`: Mapped into the data type `boolean` with the default
  value `false`

- `FloatType`: Mapped into the data type `float` with the default value `0.0f`

- `DoubleType`: Mapped into the data type `double` with the default value `0.0d`

So how do you map column types with `convert-null="false"` into different
ORM object types with the default value NULL? You can do so by modifying ORM
mappings in `com.liferay.portal.tools.servicebuilder.dependencies.hbm_
xml.ftl` as follows:

```
<#if column.isConvertNull()>
type="com.liferay.portal.dao.orm.hibernate.${serviceBuilder.
getPrimitiveObj("${column.type}")}Type"
<#else>
type="org.hibernate.type.${serviceBuilder.getPrimitiveObj("${column.
type}")}Type"
</#if>
```

As shown in the preceding code, it adds a condition along with different object-type mappings for ORM mappings. If the value of the element convert-null is false, map type into **Hibernate** object type, where the default value is set to NULL; otherwise, map type into Liferay default object type, where the default value is set to 0 (0.0f for float and 0.0d for double).

Service-Builder improvement

Besides the feature — applying convert-null element to the service generator — it would be nice if the Service-Builder would be able to support the following features:

- NOT NULL constraint support
- foreign key support
- field length constraint support explicitly
- default value constraint support explicitly
- data type BigDecimal support

Any application or portlet dealing with currencies and monetary values should really use the Java BigDecimal class. Thus it would be nice for Service-Builder to support the data type BigDecimal.

The following are the proposed steps to support the data type BigDecimal in Service-Builder:

1. Add two constraint elements for the data type BigDecimal in Service-Builder DTD. constraint-precision M is the maximum number of digits (the precision) while constraint-scale D is the number of digits to the right of the decimal point (the scale).

2. The SQL standard requires that the precision of NUMERIC(M,D) be exactly M digits. For DECIMAL(M,D), the standard requires a precision of at least M digits but permits more. In MySQL, DECIMAL(M,D) and NUMERIC(M,D) are the same, and both have a precision of exactly M digits. For example, the column salary could be presented in the database SQL as follows:

   ```
   salary NUMERIC(5,2)
   ```

3. As shown in the preceding code, constraint-precision has the value 5 (M=5) and constraint-scale has the value 2 (D=2).

4. Add a data type named BigDecimal in the service-builder DTD. For example, the column salary could be specified in service.xml as follows:

   ```
   <column name="salary" type="BigDecimal" constraint-precision="5"
   constraint-scale="2" convert-null="false" />
   ```

5. Add an object type in the Liferay portal core named `com.liferay.portal.dao.orm.hibernate.BigDecimalType`, which specifies the default value.

6. Map `BigDecimal` into `NUMERIC(M,D)` as part of the SQL scripts

7. Map `BigDecimal` into the object type `com.liferay.portal.dao.orm.hibernate.BigDecimalType` if `convert-null` is set to `true`; or map `BigDecimal` into the object type `org.hibernate.type.BigDecimalType` if `convert-null` is set to `false`.

8. Map `BigDecimal` into the Java class `java.math.BigDecimal` when generating models and services.

In the preceding steps, we could make the data type `BigDecimal` available in Service-Builder.

In order to support NOT NULL constraints in Service Builder, we should add a new element named `constraint-not-null` for the entity column. For example, the column `salary` as the type `Integer` and NOT NULL could be presented as follows:

```
<column name="salary" type="Integer" constraint-not-null="true" />
```

For foreign key support in Service-Builder, we could add elements named `foreign-key`, `on-delete`, and `on-update`. Afterwards, the foreign key of column `userId` could be represented as follows:

```
<column name="userId" type="long" foreign-key="true" entity="User" on-delete="action-Value" on-update="action-Value" />
```

As shown in the preceding code, `action-Value` could be one of these values: `restrict`, `cascade`, `set-null`, or `no-action`. Note that if you are creating a foreign key for an entity defined in another `service.xml`, you need to specify the full package path, for example, `com.liferay.portal.User`.

For `field length` support in Service-Builder explicitly, we could add a new element named `constraint-max-length` for the entity column. For example, the column `title` is defined as the type `String` and the constraint max length is `150`. It can be presented in `service.xml` as follows:

```
<column name="title" type="String" constraint-max-length="150" />
```

For `default value` support in Service-Builder explicitly, we could add an element named `constraint-default-value` for the entity column. For example, the column `number` is defined as the type `Integer` and the constraint's default value is `1`. It can be presented in `service.xml` as follows:

```
<column name="number" type="Integer" constraint-default-value="1" />
```

More services

Besides the Ant target build-service, the portal provides capabilities to build web services **wsdd**, web service clients, database SQL scripts, different language properties, javadoc, and so on. The Ant target javadoc is very useful for generating Java API docs. Besides javadoc, both the portal core and plugins SDK support the rest of the services. This section is going to introduce these services in detail. In the coming chapters, we will address these services in plugins SDK in detail.

Ant target build-db

As mentioned earlier, the Liferay portal supports almost any database system such as Apache Derby, IBM DB2, Firebird, Hypersonic, Informix, InterBase, JDataStore, Oracle, PostgreSQL, SAP, SQL Server, Sybase, MySQL, and so on. The Ant target build-db provides the capability to build database SQL scripts for these databases in $PORTAL_SRC_HOME/sql/build-parent.xml as follows:

```
<target name="build-db">
  <java classname="com.liferay.portal.tools.DBBuilder"
    classpathref="project.classpath" >
  <!-- see details in build-parent.xml   -->
  </java>
</target>
```

As shown in the preceding code, database-SQL-scripts-building is specified in com.liferay.portal.tools.DBBuilder, which builds SQL files based on generic SQL scripts such as portal.sql, portal-minimal.sql, indexes.sql, sequences. sql, portal-tables.sql, and update-*.sql. The database SQL scripts are generated for different databases such as db2, derby, firebird, informaix, mysql, oracle, postgresql, sql server, and sybase.

Ant target build-lang

As mentioned earlier, the Liferay portal supports up to 42 languages.

Of course, new languages can be added easily in the current portal framework. In addition, you can leverage the online auto-translation feature to build the new language properties file. In general, language properties could be translated manually. However, the Liferay portal provides a way to build and translate text using online auto-translators. More precisely, Ant targets build-lang and build-lang-cmd provide the capability to build language property files using the online auto-translation feature in $PORTAL_SRC_HOME/portal-impl/build.xml as follows:

```
<target name="build-lang">
  <antcall target="build-lang-cmd">
```

```
      <!-- see details in build.xml --></antcall>
  </target>
  <target name="build-lang-cmd">
    <java classname="com.liferay.portal.tools.LangBuilder"
      classpathref="project.classpath"
      fork="true" newenvironment="true">
    <!-- see details in build.xml -->
    </java>
    <copy file="${lang.dir}/${lang.file}.properties"
      tofile="${lang.dir}/${lang.file}_en.properties" />
  </target>
```

As shown in the preceding code, both language-building and online auto-translation are specified in `portal-impl com.liferay.portal.tools.LangBuilder`.

Note that the automatic translator doesn't support Arabic, Basque, Bulgarian, Catalan, Czech, Finnish, Galician, Hebrew, Hindi, Hungarian, Indonesian, Norwegian Bokmål, Persian, Polish, Romanian, Russian, Slovak, Swedish, Turkish, Ukrainian, or Vietnamese. You can find detailed info at `portal-impl com.liferay.portal.tools.TranslationWebCacheItem`, which implements `portal-service com.liferay.portal.kernel.webcache.WebCacheItem`.

As you can see, **Yahoo! Babel Fish** is used as the default online translator. In `TranslationWebCacheItem`, you will find the following code snippet.

```
StringBundler sb = new StringBundler(6);
sb.append("http://babelfish.yahoo.com/translate_txt?");
// see details in TranslationWebCacheItem.java
String text = HttpUtil.URLtoString(new URL(sb.toString()));
```

In addition, Liferay integrates with **Pootle** (an online translation management tool with a translation interface – `http://translate.sourceforge.net/wiki/pootle/index`).

Ant target build-wsdd

In general, web services are resources called over the HTTP protocol to return data. Web services are platform-independent, allowing communication between applications on different operating systems and application servers. When database entries are generated by Service-Builder, web services can be generated as well based on Apache Axis, deployed into an Axis message processing node using an XML-based deployment descriptor file known as a **Web Service Deployment Descriptor (wsdd)**.

In particular, the Ant target `build-wsdd` provides the capability to build `wsdd` in `$PORTAL_SRC_HOME/portal-impl/build.xml` as follows:

```
<target name="build-wsdd" depends="compile">
<java classname="com.liferay.portal.tools.WSDDBuilder"
classpathref="project.classpath" fork="true"
maxmemory="512m" newenvironment="true" >
<!—see details in build.xml -->
</java>
</target>
```

As shown in the preceding code, the Ant target `build-wsdd` is specified in `portal-impl com.liferay.portal.tools.WSDDBuilder`. In addition, `WSDDMerger` provides the method `merge(String source, String destination)` for `WSDDBuilder`. Moreover, `service-config.wsdd` will be generated and stored in the folder `/$PORTAL_SRC_HOME/tunnel-web/docroot/WEB-INF/`.

In the preceding code, the Ant target `build-wsdd` is a basis, using an argument `${service.file}`. For example, in order to build WSDD against the portal core `service.xml`, the Ant target `build-wsdd-portal` can be defined as follows:

```
<target name="build-wsdd-portal">
  <antcall target="build-wsdd">
    <param name="service.file"
      value="${basedir}/src/com/liferay/portal/service.xml" />
  </antcall>
</target>
```

Note that the service name may have the prefix `Portal_` if web services are portal core services. Alternatively, the service name may have the prefix `Plugin_` / `Portlet_` if web services are plugins/portlets services. You can find the code details in `WSDDBuilder` as follows:

```
String serviceName = StringUtil.replace(_portletShortName, " ", "_");
if (!_portalWsdd) {
  serviceName = "Plugin_" + serviceName;
}
else {
  if (!_portletShortName.equals("Portal")) {
    serviceName = "Portlet_" + serviceName;
  }
}
```

Ant target build-client

The Liferay portal provides the capability to generate an Axis web service client—Java Stubs for SOAP services and Spring Remote services. This will give you the JAR files you need to access these services. Of course, you can also use these JAR files to create a very simple web application.

As you can see, the Ant target `build-client` provides the capability to build SOAP client in `$PORTAL_SRC_HOME/portal-client/build.xml` as follows:

```
<target name="build-client" depends="clean">
<java
classname="com.liferay.portal.tools.PortalClientBuilder"
classpathref="project.classpath" failonerror="true"
fork="true" newenvironment="true" >
<!-- see details in build.xml -->
</java>
</target>
```

As shown in the preceding code, the Ant target `build-client` is specified in portal-impl `com.liferay.portal.tools.PortalClientBuilder`. Namespace mappings are specified in `$PORTAL_SRC_HOME/portal-client/namespace-mapping.properties`. In particular, `PortalClientBuilder` calls util-java `com.liferay.util.ant.Wsdl2JavaTask` to generate the Java code from the `wsdd` file.

Default data population

Now you can start the portal. As you have noticed, the default database, Hypersonic, and the default data are in use. As shown in the following settings, Liferay is configured to use Hypersonic as its database. Do not use Hypersonic in production. Hypersonic is an embedded database useful only for development and demo purposes. The default database settings are defined in `portal.properties`, which can be overridden by creating `portal-ext.properties`.

```
# Hypersonic
jdbc.default.driverClassName=org.hsqldb.jdbcDriver
jdbc.default.url=jdbc:hsqldb:${liferay.home}/data/hsql/lportal
jdbc.default.username=sa
jdbc.default.password=password
```

As shown in the preceding code, the default data is stored at $LIFERAY_PORTAL/ data/hsql/lportal.script. Moreover, the portal provides a **dialect detector** in com.liferay.portal.spring.hibernate.DialectDetector. This dialect detector will check dialects such as HSQL (Hypersonic), ASE (SybaseASE15Dialect), DB2 (DB2Dialect), Microsoft (SQLServer2008Dialect), Oracle (Oracle10gDialect), and others such as MySQL. If no dialect was specified, DB2400Dialect is dynamically chosen as the Hibernate dialect for DB2.

Of course, you should have your own database information such as the driver class name, URL, username, and password. The question then is: why portal-ext. properties? When the portal started, it took roughly the following sequence:

1. Deploying the configuration descriptor ROOT.xml from the folder /conf/Catalina/localhost.
2. Loading JAR for system.properties.
3. Loading jar for portal.properties.
4. Loading the file /webapps/ROOT/WEB-INF/classes/portal-ext. properties.
5. // ignore details.
6. AutoDeployDir: The auto deploy scanner started for /deploy.

As you can see, portal-ext.properties gets loaded after portal.properties; and if you have it, system-ext.properties gets loaded after system.properties.

Release information

As you can see, the Liferay portal adopts the Spring-Hibernate framework (for example, com.liferay.portal.spring.hibernate. PortletHibernateConfiguration), and supports almost any database. As shown in the preceding sequence, the portal will detect the dialect and JDBC driver by calling com.liferay.portal.spring.hibernate.DialectDetector, after loading properties. In the preceding case, it determined the dialect for MySQL and the found dialect org.hibernate.dialect.MySQLDialect.

Then the portal loaded the global libraries /lib/ext/and the portal libraries / webapps/ROOT/WEB-INF/lib/ through PortalImpl. Portal-reserved parameter names including p_auth, p_auth_secret, p_l_id, p_l_reset, p_p_auth, p_p_id, p_p_lifecycle, and so on.

After `PortalImpl`, you would see release information , such as "Starting Liferay Portal ... ", specified in `com.liferay.portal.kernel.util.ReleaseInfo`. `ReleaseInfo` covers `name`, `version`, `versionDisplayName`, `codeName`, `build`, `buildNumber`, and `date`.

Finally, the portal detects the database setting and populates it with data. In general, there are three use cases as follows:

1. The database schema and default data are not ready, that is, the database instance is empty and there is no database schema — you run the portal for the first time with the newly created database, and no database schema is involved.

2. The database schema and default data are ready, but portal version in the database is different from that of `ReleaseInfo` — you run the old portal version, and now it is ready to upgrade to the current version, specified in `ReleaseInfo`.

3. The database schema and default data are ready and the portal version in the database is exactly the same as that of `ReleaseInfo` — you run the same portal version for a while.

Let's have a closer look at the first use case — the portal is running for the first time with the newly created database and no database schema is involved.

Data population

When the portal is run for the first time with a newly created database and no database schema is involved, it will check if the database table `lock_` exists, which is reported by `JDBCExceptionReporter`.

Then, it will test the first database table, `release_`, reported by `com.liferay. portal.service.impl.ReleaseLocalServiceImpl`. If the database table `release_` does not exist, then it will create tables and populate them with default data.

The method `createTablesAndPopulate()` is defined in `ReleaseLocalServiceImpl` as follows.

```
public void createTablesAndPopulate() throws SystemException
{
  DB db = DBFactoryUtil.getDB();
  db.runSQLTemplate("portal-tables.sql", false);
  // see details in ReleaseLocalServiceImpl.java
}
```

As shown in the preceding code, SQL scripts such as `portal-tables.sql`, `portal-data-common.sql`, `portal-data-counter.sql`, `portal-data-release.sql`, `indexes.sql` and `sequences.sql` are included in the method `createTablesAndPopulate()` in the full package `com.liferay.portal.tools.sql`. Similarly, you could find other methods such as `addRelease()`, `updateRelease()`. Once the tables are ready, the portal will populate them with default data.

Default data population is specified in the method `checkCompany` of `com.liferay.portal.service.impl.CompanyLocalServiceImpl`. Default data population covers the following steps:

```
Add default company info (table company), account info
   (table account_) and sharding (table shard);
Add virtual host (table virtualhost);
// see details in CompanyLocalServiceImpl.java
Add portlets
```

Of course, you can find more methods from `CompanyLocalServiceImpl` such as `add*`, `check*`, `delete*`, `update*`, `search*`. The entry point is specified at the `init()` method from `com.liferay.portal.servlet.MainServlet`. As you can see, the following processes are defined in the `init` method:

```
Process startup events
Initialize servlet context pool
// see details in MainServlet.java
Initialize companies
Initialize message resources
Initialize plugins
```

Database case-sensitive queries

After creating tables and populating with default data, the portal will check the database **case-sensitive queries**. What is happening here? The first test-string "You take ..." is stored in the table `release_`. Then `ReleaseLocalServiceImpl` runs the following query:

```
private static final String _TEST_DATABASE_STRING_CASE_SENSITIVITY =
"select count(*) from Release_ where releaseId = ? and testString =
?";
```

As shown in the preceding code, if the count is 0, it means that the database supports case-sensitive queries; otherwise, it says that the database does not support case-sensitive queries.

Verifying processes

Then, it runs `VerifyProcess` to verify processes, such as `com.liferay.portal.verify.VerifyProcessSuite`, extending `VerifyProcess`. For example, in the method `doVerify()`,`VerifyProcessSuite`, specify the following processes:

```
verify(new VerifyProperties());
// and more
verify(new VerifyUser());
verify(new VerifyWiki());
```

As shown in the preceding code, it will verify the properties, user, Wiki, and so on. Of course, you can add more verifying processes, such as `VerifyBlogsTrackbacks` and `VerifyImage`.

Default project creation and templates

Plugins SDK provides default plugins project creation and templates, which are used in Liferay IDE. This section is going to show you the default creation scripts and default templates.

Plugins default project creation—Ant targets

Plugins SDK provides default plugins project creation Ant targets, where you can build your own plugins simply. For example, Ext plugins could be created with the following Ant command line at `$PLUGINS_SDK_HOME/ext/`:

```
create.sh: ant -Dext.name=$1 -Dext.display.name=\"$2\" create
```

```
create.bat: call ant -Dext.name=%1 -Dext.display.name=%2 create
```

The first parameter is your extension plugin name. A new directory will be created based on the extension plugin name. The second parameter is the extension plugin's display name.

The hook plugins could be created in the following Ant command line at `$PLUGINS_SDK_HOME/hooks/`:

```
create.sh: ant -Dhook.name=$1 -Dhook.display.name=\"$2\" create
```

```
create.bat: call ant -Dhook.name=%1 -Dhook.display.name=%2 create
```

The first parameter is your hook plugin name. A new directory will be created based on the hook plugin name. The second parameter is the hook plugin's display name.

Similarly, the layout templates plugins could be created in the following Ant command line at $PLUGINS_SDK_HOME/layouttpl/:

```
create.sh: ant -Dlayouttpl.name=$1 -Dlayouttpl.display.name=\"$2\" create
create.bat: call ant -Dlayouttpl.name=%1 -Dlayouttpl.display.name=%2 create
```

As shown in the preceding code, the first parameter is your layout template plugin name. A new directory will be created based on the layout templates plugin name. The second parameter is the layout templates plugin's display name.

In the same way, you could create new portlet plugins and theme plugins from scratch as well. The following lines show how to create a new portlet plugin at $PLUGINS_SDK_HOME/portlets/:

```
create.sh: ant -Dportlet.name=$1 -Dportlet.display.name=\"$2\" -Dportlet.framework=$3 create
create.bat: call ant -Dportlet.name=%1 -Dportlet.display.name=%2 -Dportlet.framework=%PORTLET_FRAMEWORK% create
```

As shown in the preceding code, the first parameter is your portlet plugin name. A new directory will be created based on the portlet plugin name. The second parameter is the portlet plugin's display name. A third value can be passed to specify the portlet framework to use. Valid values are MVC, JSF, or Vaadin.

The theme plugins could be created in the following Ant command line at $PLUGINS_SDK_HOME/themes/:

```
create.sh: ant -Dtheme.name=$1 -Dtheme.display.name=\"$2\" create
create.bat: call ant -Dtheme.name=%1 -Dtheme.display.name=%2 create
```

As shown in the preceding code, the first parameter is your theme plugin name. A new directory will be created based on the theme plugin name. The second parameter is the theme plugin's display name.

As you can see, Plugins SDK provides the default creation and templates for plugins such as ext, hook, layout template, portlet, and theme. Unfortunately, the plugin webs are not involved. That is, if you want to build your own webs, then you need to create them manually.

Plugins default project templates

Plugins SDK provides a set of default templates for the creation of new plugins. These templates cover the **EAR** template, Ext template, hook, layout templates, **JSF** portlet, **Vaadin** portlet, and theme. You can find details on this at `$PLUGINS_SDK_HOME/tools/`.

For example, in `/portlet_vaadin_tmpl`, it adds support for making portlet plugin projects that use the Vaadin framework. The following is the code snippet for `/docroot/WEB-INF/src/Application.java`:

```
package @portlet.java.package.name@;
public class @portlet.java.class.name@Application extends Application
{
public void init() {
// initial
}
}
```

Plugins SDK also added a new hook plugin project template and modified build scripts to create shortcut support in `/hook_tmpl`. The hook plugin project template includes `build.xml`, `/docroot/WEB-INF/liferay-hook.xml`, and `liferay-plugin-package.properties`. The following is the code snippet for `/build.xml`.

```
<?xml version="1.0"?>
<project name="@hook.name@-hook" basedir="." default="deploy">
 <import file="../build-common-hook.xml" />
</project>
```

Similarly, you will find the JSF portlet template in `/portlet_jsf_tmpl`, the portlet template in `/portlet_tmpl`, theme template in `/theme_tmpl`, layout templates at `/layouttpl_tmpl`, Ext plugin template in `/portlet_jsf_tmpl`, and the EAR template in `/ear_tmpl`.

Fast development

What is fast development of plugins? Fast development allows developers to work with exploded plugin WARs instead of having to package them for deployment. For example, if you change JSP files in a plugin, these JSP files will be modified when you refresh the page in your browser. Furthermore, if you update other files (for example, JSF pages, Java beans, servlets, and so on) besides JSP files, these files will automatically be reloaded by the class loader of Tomcat. Obviously, this will save a lot of development time.

How do we make it happen? Firstly, you need to add a new Ant target deploy-exploded inside the file $PLUGINS_SDK_HOME/build-common-plugin.xml as follows:

```
// after <target name="deploy" depends="war">
// <copy file="${plugin.file}" todir="${auto.deploy.dir}" />
// </target>, add following lines:
<antelope:stringutil string="${basedir}/${plugin.name}.xml"
property="plugin.context.file">
  <antelope:replace regex="\\" replacement="/" />
</antelope:stringutil>
<target name="deploy-exploded" depends="compile">
  <copy file="${plugin.context.file}" todir="${auto.deploy.dir}" />
</target>
```

Then, you need to create a plugin context file for that specific plugin, pointing to the exploded plugin WAR. The plugin context file is an XML file, which is called in a manner similar to how a plugin is called. For example, if the plugin is a portlet named knowledge-based-portlet, then the plugin context file must be called knowledge-based-portlet.xml, and the content will look like this:

```
<Context
path="${plugin.name}"
docBase="$PLUGINS_SDK_HOME/portlets/${plugin.name}-portlet/docroot"
/>
```

The preceding code shows the content of the plugin context file. ${plugin.name} represents the plugin name, for example, knowledge-base. $PLUGINS_SDK_HOME represents the home of Plugins SDK.

By default, the property auto.deploy.tomcat.conf.dir is used to set the path to Tomcat's configuration directory, $CATALINA_HOME/conf/Catalina/localhost. This property is used to auto deploy **exploded** WARs. The Tomcat context XML file, found in the auto deploy directory, will be copied to Tomcat's configuration directory. The context XML file must have a docBase attribute that points to a valid WAR directory.

When you are ready, you can run the Ant target ant deploy-exploded from build.xml. From now on, if you change JSP files, they are modified when you refresh the page in your browser. For Java classes and XML files, you need to run the Ant target compile from the plugin build.xml first, and then run the Ant target ant deploy-exploded.

Generally, you can now update JSP files, JSF pages, Java beans, servlets, and so on, and they will automatically be reloaded by the class loader of Tomcat.

What is happening?

Once you run the Ant target `deploy-exploded`, the plugin context file will be copied into the auto-deploy directory first. Then, the Liferay portal will copy the plugin context file to the folder, `$CATALINA_HOME/conf/Catalina/localhost`. Later, the plugin will be registered. If the WAR was previously deployed, a new copy of the context file to the auto-deploy directory will cause a re-deploy of the exploded plugin.

Note that if you had deployed your plugin before, it will be better to remove the old deployed application and restart Tomcat. The solution just mentioned is used for Tomcat only. Of course, you would get similar solutions for other application servers.

The Ant target `deploy-exploded` is useful for plugins: hook, layout template, portlet, and theme. Why? The portal provides following settings by default in `portal.properties`.

```
auto.deploy.listeners=\
    com.liferay.portal.deploy.auto.ExtAutoDeployListener,\
    // see details in the portal.properties
com.liferay.portal.deploy.auto.exploded.tomcat.
ThemeExplodedTomcatListener
```

As shown in the preceding code, you would be able to find all exploded Tomcat **Deployers** and **Listeners** within a package named `com.liferay.portal.deploy.auto.exploded.tomcat`. For example, you can find the following listeners: `HookExplodedTomcatListener`, `LayoutTemplateExplodedTomcatListener`, `PortletExplodedTomcatListener`, and `ThemeExplodedTomcatListener`. In addition, Deployers and Listeners-related dependencies are specified at `com.liferay.portal.deploy.dependencies`.

Summary

This chapter discussed how to set up, build, and deploy the portal core and plugins in the Eclipse IDE. Then it discussed how to use Service-Builder to generate services and models, and how to add new features to the Service-Builder. It also addressed how to populate the default data, how to use the default project creation and templates, and how to set up fast development of plugins with Tomcat.

In the next chapter, we are going to use Plugins SDK for building generic MVC portlets.

3
Generic MVC Portlets

We discussed the Service-Builder and the development environment in the previous chapter. It is time to develop JSR-286 portlets for the intranet or Internet website, or WAP site. First of all, let's have a closer look at generic portlets with the **Model-View-Controller** (**MVC**) architecture. The **Model** represents the business or database code, the **View** represents the page design code, and the **Controller** represents the navigational code. Normally, JSP files are used to build the view for portlets.

This chapter first introduces how to develop a portlet project with the default templates, focusing on the view part and the portlet structure. It then addresses how to construct basic MVC portlets by viewing the title and adding an action, as well as how to build advanced MVC portlets. Finally, it discusses how to build and re-build services, to bring portlets into the Control Panel, to set security and permissions, use dynamic queries, to use custom queries, and to deploy portlets.

By the end of this chapter, you will have learned how to:

- Set up a portlet project with the default templates
- Build a basic MVC portlet
- Build an advanced MVC portlet
- Use the Service-Builder
- Bring portlets into the Control Panel
- Set up security and permissions
- Use a dynamic query
- Leverage custom SQL

Plugin portlet project

Liferay plugins SDK provides a set of default templates such as EAR, Ext, hook, layout template, portlet, theme, and so on. Using these templates, you can build your own plugin projects easily. This section is going to introduce the portlet project's default template.

Naming conventions and filter mappings

Liferay has standardized file naming conventions and filter mappings for plugins. The following are the standardized rules for naming conventions and filter mappings:

- All stylesheet assets are placed in a css subfolder, including stylesheets written in JSP. The main stylesheet asset is named main.css. When any stylesheet is written with the jsp functionality, a css_init.jsp is included in the docroot directory. If no stylesheets require the jsp functionality, then css_init.jsp is not included.

- Portlets are wrapped with a CSS class that will be injected into the DIV that wraps the viewable content. This class name will be based on the name of the plugin package. For example, the knowledge base portlet would use a knowledge-base-portlet class name.

- Stylesheets will use the CSS class to style the portlet-specific content. For example, a knowledge base portlet would style paragraphs used in the portlet with .knowledge-base-portlet p, and the knowledge base portlet would style images used in the portlet with .knowledge-base-portlet img.

- Stylesheets will use a .portlet-configuration CSS class to style any elements within the portlet's configuration page. For example, the knowledge base portlet would style paragraphs within the portlet's configuration page with .portlet-configuration p and images within the portlet's configuration page with .portlet-configuration img.

- All JavaScript assets are placed in a js subfolder. The main JavaScript asset is named service.js.

Portlet project default template

Liferay plugins SDK provides the portlet project with a default template. This default template has the following structure. The portlet project folder name is represented as @portlet.name@-portlet (folder name pattern: ${plugin.name}-${plugin.type}). For example, @portlet.name@ has the value, knowledge-base, for the knowledge base portlet. Under the folder @portlet.name@-portlet, there is a folder named docroot and an XML file named build.xml. As you can see, build.xml has the following code:

```xml
<?xml version="1.0"?>
<project name="@portlet.name@-portlet" basedir="." default="deploy">
  <import file="../build-common-portlet.xml" />
</project>
```

As shown in the preceding code, `@portlet.name@` represents the real portlet name. When using Ant `target create`, it will create a new portlet project. Under the folder `docroot`, it includes a `css` folder with a CSS file `main.css`, a `js` folder with a JavaScript file `main.js`, and a folder `WEB-INF`.

The subfolder `WEB-INF` covers XML files, such as `portlet.xml`, `liferay-portlet.xml`, `liferay-plugin-package.properties`, and `liferay-display.xml`. Inside these XML files, you will find that the template variables, `@portlet.name@` and `@portlet.display.name@`, are in use.

As mentioned earlier, Ant `target create` will create a new portlet project based on three parameters: `portlet.name`, `portlet.display.name`, and `portlet.framework`. Note that the parameters `portlet.name` and `portlet.display.name` are required and `portlet.framework` is optional — the valid values are `mvc`, `jsf`, or `vaadin`, while the default value is `mvc`.

What's happening when you use Ant `target create`? Ant `target create` was specified in `$PLUGINS_SDK_HOME/portlets/build.xml`. This Ant target does roughly the following tasks:

- Checks `portlet.dir` and copies `${project.dir}/tools/portlet_tmpl`
- Builds `portlet.xml`, `liferay-portlet.xml`, `liferay-plugin-package.properties`, and `liferay-display.xml` with the real names `portlet.name` and `portlet.display.name`
- Copies TLD files to `${portlet.dir}/docroot/WEB-INF/tld`, such as `liferay-portlet.tld`, `liferay-portlet-ext.tld`, `liferay-security.tld`, `liferay-theme.tld`, `liferay-ui.tld`, and `liferay-util.tld`

Knowledge base portlet project

Following the portlet project default template, the knowledge base portlet project named `knowledge-base-portlet` can be generated against the `portlet.name=knowledge-base` and `portlet.display.name="Knowledge Base"` parameters as well.

In detail, the generated portlet project includes a folder `docroot` and the `build.xml` file. Under the folder `docroot`, it includes a `css` folder with the CSS file `main.css`, a `js` folder with the JavaScript file `main.js`, and a `WEB-INF` folder.

In particular, the subfolder `WEB-INF` covers the XML files `portlet.xml`, `liferay-portlet.xml`, `liferay-plugin-package.properties`, and `liferay-display.xml`. Inside these XML files, you would see that the parameter values `knowledge-base` and `Knowledge Base Admin` are in use.

Under the folder `${portlet.dir}/docroot/WEB-INF/tld`, you would see TLD files `liferay-portlet.tld`, `liferay-portlet-ext.tld`, `liferay-security.tld`, `liferay-theme.tld`, `liferay-ui.tld`, and `liferay-util.tld`.

Basic MVC portlet

First of all, let's use the knowledge base admin portlet as an example that requires portlet development in the Plugins SDK. This section will use the knowledge base project, as mentioned in the previous section.

Project structure

As mentioned earlier, we will first create the folder, either by executing the Ant target or by manually using `knowledge-base-portlet` under the folder `$PLUGINS-SDK-HOME/portlets`. Under the folder, you will see the `docroot` folder and the `build.xml` file. For fast development, you can add the XML file `knowledge-base-portlet.xml` with the following lines.

```
<Context path="knowledge-base" docBase="$PLUGINS_SDK_HOME/portlets/
knowledge-base-portlet/docroot"
/>
```

Under the folder `docroot`, you will see the subfolders `css`, `js`, and `WEB-INF`. In addition to the default folders and files generated by the default template, we're going to create a folder named `icons` and a file under the folder `icons` named `kb-admin.png` for the knowledge base admin portlet icon. Add the JSP file, `init.jsp`, and the folder `admin` under the folder `docroot` and a JSP file `view.jsp` under the folder `admin` for the knowledge base admin portlet view.

Portlet definition

First, we need to set up the portlet in the `portlet.xml` file. You can simply create an XML file `portlet.xml` in `$PLUGINS_SDK_HOME/portlets/knowledge-base-portlet/docroot/WEB-INF`. Add the following lines of code at the beginning of `portlet.xml`:

```
<portlet-name>kb-admin-portlet</portlet-name>
<display-name>Knowledge Base (Admin)</display-name>
```

```
<portlet-class>com.liferay.util.bridges.mvc.MVCPortlet</portlet-class>
<init-param>
<name>view-jsp</name>
<value>/admin/view.jsp</value>
<!-- see details in portlet.xml -->
```

The preceding code shows the definition of the kb-admin-portlet portlet and the display name, Knowledge Base Admin. Also, most importantly, the default view name init-param must be view-jsp. Incidentally, you can find the portlet app **XSD (XML Schema Definition)** in portlet-app_2_0.xsd.

Liferay portlet registration

Next, we need to register the portlets. To do so, create the XML file liferay-portlet.xml in $PLUGINS_SDK_HOME/portlets/${portlet.name}/docroot/WEB-INF. Add the following lines at the beginning of liferay-portlet.xml:

```
<liferay-portlet-app>
<portlet>
  <portlet-name>kb-admin-portlet</portlet-name>
  <icon>/icons/kb-admin.png</icon>
  <instanceable>true</instanceable>
  <!—see details in Liferay-portlet.xml
</portlet>
</liferay-portlet-app>
```

The preceding code shows the registration of the portlet kb-admin-portlet. It specifies the portlet name kb-admin-portlet by the tag portlet-name. It also specifies the icon with the value /icons/kb-admin.png, instanceable with the value true, the header portlet CSS with the value /admin/css/main.css, and the header portlet-JavaScript with the value /js/service.js. Also, the order of the tags is important, referring to the portlet **DTD** in liferay-portlet_6_1_0.dtd.

Liferay portlet display

Additionally, we expect to put the portlets in the category Knowledge Base. To do so, create an XML file liferay-display.xml in $PLUGINS_SDK_HOME/portlets/${portlet.name}/docroot/WEB-INF and open it. Add the following lines at the beginning of liferay-display.xml and save it:

```
<display>
  <category name="Knowledge Base">
    <portlet id="kb-admin-portlet"/>
  </category>
</display>
```

As shown in the preceding code, the portlet `kb-admin-portlet` is displayed in the category `Knowledge Base`. Parenthetically, you can find the details of the Liferay display DTD in `liferay-display_6_1_0.dtd`.

Liferay plugin package

Most importantly, you need to add a plugin properties file called `liferay-plugin-package.properties` under the folder `WEB-INF`. This file lists the plugin `knowledge-base-portlet` with the following properties available in a plugin repository:

```
// see details in liferay-plugin-package.properties
portal-dependency-jars=\=\
    jstl-api.jar,\
    jstl-impl.jar
portal-dependency-tlds=\
    c.tld
```

As shown in the preceding code, the Liferay plugin package covers a set of properties, for example, `name`, `module-group-id`, `module-incremental-version`, `tags`, `short-description`, `change-log`, `page-url`, `author`, `licenses`, `portal-dependency-jars`, `portal-dependency-tlds`, and so on. Note that we can't include `portal-impl.jar`.

When deploying the plugin, the deploying process will generate the Liferay plugin package XML file `liferay-plugin-package.xml` in the folder `/webapps/${plugin.name}/WEB-INF`. You can find the details of the Liferay plugins package DTD in `liferay-plugin-package_6_1_0.dtd`.

View specification

As seen in `portlet.xml`, a tag element `init-param` has been specified with the attribute name `view-jsp` and the value `/admin/view.jsp`. Thus, we need to create a JSP file named `view.jsp` at `$PLUGINS_SDK_HOME/portlets/${portlet.name}/docroot/admin/`.

First of all, let's bring the tags and predefined objects into the view. To do so, create a JSP file named `init.jsp` in the folder `$PLUGINS_SDK_HOME/portlets/${portlet.name}/docroot/` and add the following lines:

```
<%@ taglib uri="http://java.sun.com/jsp/jstl/core" prefix="c" %>
<%@ taglib uri="http://java.sun.com/portlet_2_0" prefix="portlet" %>
<%@ taglib uri="http://liferay.com/tld/aui" prefix="aui" %>
<%@ taglib uri="http://liferay.com/tld/portlet" prefix="liferay-portlet" %>
```

```
<%@ taglib uri="http://liferay.com/tld/security" prefix="liferay-
security" %>
<%@ taglib uri="http://liferay.com/tld/theme" prefix="liferay-theme"
%>
<%@ taglib uri="http://liferay.com/tld/ui" prefix="liferay-ui" %>
<%@ taglib uri="http://liferay.com/tld/util" prefix="liferay-util" %>
<portlet:defineObjects />
<liferay-theme:defineObjects />
```

As shown in the preceding code, it first imports the **JSTL** taglib with the prefix c, where you would have sample code such as `<c:if>`, `<c:choose>`, `<c:when>`, and `<c:otherwise>`. Then, it brings in Portlet 2.0 with the prefix `portlet` and a Liferay portlet with the prefix `liferay-portlet`. Then, it brings the Liferay taglibs — security (prefix `liferay-security`), theme (prefix `liferay-theme`), UI (prefix `liferay-ui`), and utility (prefix `liferay-util`). Finally, it includes two sets of defined objects: `portlet:defineObjects` and `liferay-theme:defineObjects`. For more details about these taglibs, refer to the book *Liferay User Interface Development*.

Next, add your custom code to `view.jsp`. The following is the sample code. You should have your own logic and view.

```
<%@ include file="/init.jsp" %>
<%
PortletPreferences preferences = renderRequest.getPreferences();
%>
```

Portlet XSD and DTD

As you can see, there are at least four kinds of XML files and properties involved: `portlet.xml`, `liferay-portlet.xml`, `liferay-display.xml` and `liferay-plugin-package.properties`. The DTD of these XML files and properties files are defined in `$PORTAL_SRC_HOME/definitions`. In addition, the XML file `liferay-plugin-package.xml` will be generated during the deployment process in `/webapps/${plugin.name}/WEB-INF`.

Portlet app XSD

The portlet app XSD is the XML schema for the Portlet 2.0 deployment descriptor. The `portlet-app` element is the root of the deployment descriptor for a portlet application. This element has a required attribute version that specifies which version of the schema the deployment descriptor conforms to. In order to be a valid JSR 286 portlet application, the version must have the value 2.0.

The portlet element contains the name of a portlet such as `portlet-name`. This name must be unique within the portlet application. At the same time, you should have a display name such as `display-name` and a portlet class such as `portlet-class`. If you are interested in more details, refer to the XSD file at the following link:

`svn://svn.liferay.com/repos/public/portal/trunk/definitions/portlet-app_2_0.xsd`.

Additionally, JSR-286 specifies that the portlet preferences should be unique per user, by default. Liferay assumes that they are owned by a group (that is, a site or an organization), by default.

Liferay portlet app DTD

The `liferay-portlet-app` element is the root of the deployment descriptor for a Liferay portlet application. It can have zero or many elements, such as `portlet`, `role-mapper`, and `custom-user-attribute`.

The `custom-user-attribute` contains a list of names that are retrieved using a custom class that extends `com.liferay.portlet.CustomUserAttributes`. This element can have one or many `name`, and only one `custom-class`.

The `role-mapper` contains two names specified by `role-name` and `role-link`. The `role-name` value must be a role specified in `portlet.xml`. The `role-link` value must be the name of a Liferay role that exists in the database. The `role-mapper` element pairs up these two values to map roles from `portlet.xml` to roles in the Liferay database.

The `portlet` element contains the declarative data of a portlet as follows:

```
<!ELEMENT portlet (portlet-name, icon?, virtual-path?, struts-path?,
// see details in liferay-portlet-app_6_1_0.dtd
footer-portlet-javascript*, css-class-wrapper?, facebook-integration?,
add-default-resource?, system?, active?, include?)>
```

As shown in the preceding code, the element `portlet` can have many child elements, such as `portlet-name`, `icon`, `instanceable`, `header-portlet-css`, `header-portlet-javascript`, `css-class-wrapper`, `add-default-resource`, and so on.

The child element, such as `portlet-name`, must occur once, and only once inside the `portlet` element.

The + sign declares that the child element must occur one or more times inside the root element.

The * sign in the preceding example declares that the child element `header-portlet-css` can occur zero or more times inside the `portlet` element.

And the ? sign in the preceding example declares that the child element `icon` can occur zero times or once inside the `portlet` element.

The `portlet-name` element contains the unique name of the portlet. This name must match the portlet name specified in `portlet.xml`, while the `icon` element specifies an image that represents the portlet.

You can set the value of the child element `instanceable` to `true`, if the portlet can appear multiple times on a page. If set to `false`, the portlet can only appear once on a page. The default value is `false`. Within the child element `css-class-wrapper`, you can also set the name of the CSS class that will be injected in the DIV that wraps this portlet.

If the value of `add-default-resource` is set to `false`, and the portlet does not belong to the page but has been dynamically added, then the user will see that he/she doesn't have the permissions to view the portlet. If the element is set to `true`, the default portlet resources and permissions are added to the page. The user can then view the portlet. The default value is `false`.

All other elements will be discussed in detail in the coming sections and chapters. Refer to the following link for the full definition:

svn://svn.liferay.com/repos/public/portal/trunk/definitions/liferay-portlet-app_6_1_0.dtd.

Liferay display DTD

The `display` element is the root of the deployment descriptor that describes how portlets are categorized and displayed for users to choose when personalizing a page in the Liferay Portal. It can have many categories and portlets of elements.

The `category` element organizes a set of portlets. A `portlet` can exist in more than one category. The required `name` of a category is mapped to the portal's `Language properties`. If the category name is `kb`, then the required `key` attribute in the portal's resource bundle will be `category.kb`. The `portlet` element represents a portlet. The `id` attribute must match the unique `portlet-name` specified in `portlet.xml`.

> Note that there is a special category name called `category.hidden`, where the portlets specified in this category will be invisible in the **Application** panel. This means you can't search and find these portlets in the **Application** panel; these portlets, under the category `category.hidden`, will only be in use by the system or the Control Panel only.

The portal has the following CSS specification at `svn://svn.liferay.com/repos/public/portal/trunk/portal-web/docroot/html/portal/css/portal/add_content.jspf`.

```
.lfr-content-category.hidden {
  display: none;
}
```

As shown in the preceding code, when it has the category `category.hidden`, the CSS attribute `display` had the value `none` — that is, it hid related content.

In particular, in the portlet category constants, `com.liferay.portal.model.PortletCategoryConstants`, it specifies the following constant:

```
public static final String NAME_HIDDEN = "category.hidden";
```

And in the portlet category, `com.liferay.portal.model.PortletCategory`, it specifies the following method:

```
public boolean isHidden() {
if (_name.equals(PortletCategoryConstants.NAME_HIDDEN)) {
  return true;
} else { return false; }
}
```

As shown in the preceding code, it uses the category name `category.hidden` and specifies the method `isHidden`. Moreover, this method has been used in `svn://svn.liferay.com/repos/public/portal/trunk/portal-web/docroot/html/portlet/layout_configuration/view.jsp` as follows:

```
if (curPortletCategory.isHidden()) {
  continue;
}
```

The Liferay plugin package DTD

The `plugin-package` element contains the declarative data of a plugin. It has the required attributes, such as name, `module-id`, types, `short-description`, `change-log`, author, licenses, `liferay-versions`, and optional attributes, such as `recommended-deployment-context`, tags, `long-description`, `page-url`, screenshots, and `deployment-settings`.

The name element contains the name of the plugin package that will be shown to the users. The `module-id` element contains the full identifier of the plugin using the Maven-based syntax: `groupId/artifactId/version/file-type`. The `recommended-deployment-context` element determines the context to which this plugin should be deployed and the types element contains a list of plugin types included in the package. The type element contains the type of the plugin. Note that valid values for the type are portlets, `layout-templates`, and themes.

The tags element contains a list of tags to categorize the plugin, while the tag element contains a tag that categorizes the plugin. These tags would be useful for search. The `short-description` element contains a short description of the plugin and the `long-description` element contains a detailed description of the plugin. The `change-log` element contains an explanation of the changes made in the latest release, while the `page-url` element contains the URL of the home page of the plugin.

The screenshots element contains a list of screenshots for the plugin, while the screenshot element contains two URLs for the thumbnail and large images versions of the screenshot. The `thumbnail-url` element contains the URL of a thumbnail screenshot of the plugin, while the `large-image-url` element contains the URL of a large image screenshot of the plugin.

The author element contains the name of the author of the plugin. The licenses element contains a list of licenses under which the plugin is provided, while the license element contains the name of a license under which the plugin is provided. The `osi-approved` attribute specifies if the license is open source and approved by the **Open Source Initiative (OSI)**, and the url attribute specifies the URL of a page that describes the license.

The `liferay-versions` element contains a list of Liferay Portal versions that are supported by the plugin. The `liferay-version` element contains a version of the Liferay Portal that is supported by the plugin. The `deployment-settings` element contains a list of parameters that specifies how the package should be deployed. The setting element specify a `name-value` pair that provides information on how the package should be deployed, while the name attribute specifies the name of the setting and the value attribute specifies the value of the setting.

The properties (portal dependency JARs: `portal-dependency-jars` and portal dependency TLDs: `portal-dependency-tlds`) are specified in the plugins deploying process, `com.liferay.portal.tools.deploy.BaseDeployer`, and the plugins environment building process, `PluginsEnvironmentBuilder`. More specifically, portal dependency JARs are copied from the portal `lib` to the plugin `lib`, and portal dependency TLDs are copied from portal TLDs such as `$PORTAL_ROOT_HOME/WEB-INF/tld` to plugin TLDs such as `${plugin.name}/WEB-INF/tld`.

Note that JARs, such as `commons-logging.jar`, `log4j.jar`, `util-bridges.jar`, `util-java.jar`, and `util-taglib.jar`, are copied by default. These JARs are not required to be explicitly specified in the property `portal-dependency-jars`.

In addition, TLDs such as `Liferay-aui.tld`, `Liferay-portlet.tld`, `Liferay-portlet-ext.tld`, `Liferay-security.tld`, `liferay-theme.tld`, `liferay-ui.tld`, and `liferay-util.tld` are copied by default. These TLDs are not required to be explicitly specified in the property `portal-dependency-tld`.

As mentioned earlier, when deploying the plugin, the deploying process will generate the Liferay plugin package XML file `liferay-plugin-package.xml` in the folder `/webapps/${plugin.name}/WEB-INF`.

What's happening?

In `BaseDeployer`, it defines a method called `copyDependencyXml` as follows:

```
public void copyDependencyXml(String fileName, String targetDir,
Map<String, String> filterMap,boolean overwrite) throws Exception {
  // see details in BaseDeployer.java
}
```

As shown in the preceding code, `BaseDeployer` uses the default template file, `com/liferay/portal/deploy/dependencies/liferay-plugin-package.xml`, in the Liferay plugin package and the properties settings, `liferay-plugin-package.properties`, first and then generates the Liferay plugin package, `liferay-plugin-package.xml`.

MVC portlet bridge

As you know, JSP files are HTML files with special tags containing Java source code that provide dynamic content. It is easy to learn and allows developers to quickly produce websites and applications in an open and standard way.

Moreover, an MVC portlet is made up of the following typical MVC components:

- Model—Java objects put in as request attributes
- View—Template, for example, `init.jsp` and `view.jsp`
- Controller—Portlet process action

The controller specifies the JSP portlet actions. The view provides a JSP template, which will generate the content of the portlet by pulling out dynamic model information from the request attributes. The standard JSP variables involve request, response, session, and so on. The model is made up of Java objects, put in as request attributes. For example, the variable UID (the unique identity of assets) is available in the model. It can be retrieved from the request attribute, as shown in the following example:

```
String uid = (String) request.getAttribute("uid");
```

An MVC portlet is a good starting point, if you are new to Liferay Portal. On one hand, JSP portlets help you to learn the basic file and directory structure that you will need to know in order to develop the MVC portlets using `portlet.xml` and `liferay-portlet.xml`. They further allow you to develop generic portlets within the Liferay Portal. On the other hand, the MVC portlets show how to add a title and category using `Language.properties` and `liferay-display.xml`.

In short, the following are the main steps to build MVC portlets on top of the Liferay Portal:

1. Define portlets (JSR-286 attributes) in `portlet.xml`.
2. Register portlets (Liferay portlet attributes) in `liferay-portlet.xml`.
3. Create JSP pages: `view.jsp` and `init.jsp`.
4. Map the title and a category in `Language_en.properties`.
5. Add the portlets to a category in `liferay-display.xml`.

MVC portlet extension

In `portlet.xml`, the `portlet-class` is specified as an MVC portlet bridge `com.liferay.util.bridges.mvc.MVCPortlet`. In particular, `MVCPortlet` is specified in `util-bridges.jar`.

As you can see, `MVCPortlet` extends `LiferayPortlet`, and `LiferayPortlet` extends `GenericPortlet`. In `MVCPortlet`, the following `init-param` names get defined:

```
aboutJSP = getInitParameter("about-jsp");
// see details in MVCPortlet.java
viewJSP = getInitParameter("view-jsp");
```

As shown in the preceding code, a set of init parameters gets defined, such as about-jsp, config-jsp, edit-jsp, view-jsp, and so on. In the previous example, view-jsp was in use. That is, if you used the default MVCPortlet, you had to reuse the same name such as view-jsp—all characters are case-sensitive. Of course, you can leverage other init parameters as well.

In addition, the methods init, processAction, and serveResource get specified in LiferayPortlet. In MVCPortlet, these methods and others such as doAbout, doConfig, doEdit, doView, and so on, get re-defined. Of course, you can also extend and override MVCPortlet yourself, which will be discussed in the coming sections.

Portlet JSP/JavaScript/CSS loading

We discussed the JSP view-jsp in the portlet.xml file and JavaScript and CSS in the liferay-portlet.xml file. This section will introduce the portlet JSP, JavaScript, and CSS loading.

AJAX and render weight

The element ajaxable declares whether a portlet is AJAX-enabled or not. The default value of ajaxable is true. If set to false, then this portlet can never be displayed via AJAX. When a portlet is ajaxable, the portal will load the page first and then load the portlet using AJAX. This ajaxable property has an added advantages when an ajaxable portlet takes a long time to load.

The element render-weight declares whether the portlet is rendered in parallel or in sequence. The default value of render-weight is 1. If set to a value less than 1, the portlet is rendered in parallel. If set to a value of 1 or greater, then the portlet is rendered serially. In particular, portlets with a greater render weight have greater priority and will be rendered before portlets with a lower render weight.

If the ajaxable value is set to false, then render-weight is always set to 1, if it is set to a value less than 1. This means ajaxable can override render-weight if ajaxable is set to false.

Header JavaScript/CSS and footer JavaScript/CSS

It would be a normal use case that you would like to include your own JavaScript and CSS in the custom portlet. In liferay-portlet.xml, you will be able to set the path to the header and footer JS/CSS as follows:

Tag name	Description	Comments
`header-portal-css`	Sets the CSS path that will be referenced in the page's header, relative to the portal's context path	Header CSS
`header-portlet-css`	Sets the CSS path that will be referenced in the page's header, relative to the portlet's context path	Header CSS
`header-portal-javascript`	Sets the JavaScript path that will be referenced in the page's header, relative to the portal's context path	Header JavaScript
`header-portlet-javascript`	Sets the JavaScript path that will be referenced in the page's header, relative to the portlet's context path.	Header JavaScript
`footer-portal-css`	Sets the CSS path that will be referenced in the page's footer, relative to the portal's context path	Footer CSS
`footer-portlet-css`	Sets the CSS path that will be referenced in the page's footer, relative to the portlet's context path	Footer CSS
`footer-portal-javascript`	Sets the JavaScript path that will be referenced in the page's footer, relative to the portal's context path	Footer JavaScript
`footer-portlet-javascript`	Sets the JavaScript path that will be referenced in the page's footer, relative to the portlet's context path	Footer JavaScript

Predefined objects

As shown in the JSP file `init.jsp`, a set of taglibs are in use such as `jstl` (prefix c), portlet 2.0 (prefix `portlet`), alloy ui (prefix `aui`), `liferay-portlet`, `liferay-security`. `liferay-theme`, `liferay-ui`, `liferay-util`, and so on. Taglib is defined in the folder `$PORTAL_SRC_HOME/util-taglib`. In particular, two sets of defined objects are specified—`portlet:defineObjects` and `liferay-theme:defineObjects`.

The following table shows the attribute name, class name, and portlet phase for `portlet:defineObjects`. You can refer to the code detailed in `com.liferay.taglib.portlet.DefineObjectsTag`. Ideally, you can use these attribute names directly in the JSP file, `view.jsp`, or in your own JSP file.

Attribute name	Class name	Phase	Comments
portletConfig	PortletConfig	LIFECYCLE_PHASE	Portlet request
portletName	String	LIFECYCLE_PHASE	Portlet request
actionRequest	PortletRequest	ACTION_PHASE	Action request
eventRequest	PortletRequest	EVENT_PHASE	Event request
renderRequest	PortletRequest	RENDER_PHASE	Render request
resourceRequest	PortletRequest	RESOURCE_PHASE	Resource request
portletPreferences	PortletPreferences	LIFECYCLE_PHASE	Portlet preference
portletPreferencesValues	Map	LIFECYCLE_PHASE	Portlet preference
portletSession	PortletSession	LIFECYCLE_PHASE	Portlet session
portletSessionScope	Map	LIFECYCLE_PHASE	Portlet session
actionResponse	PortletResponse	ACTION_PHASE	Action response
eventResponse	PortletResponse	EVENT_PHASE	Event response
renderResponse	PortletResponse	RENDER_PHASE	Render response
resourceResponse	PortletResponse	RESOURCE_PHASE	Resource response

The following table shows the attribute name and class name for `liferay-theme:defineObjects`. You can refer to the code detailed in `com.liferay.taglib.theme.DefineObjectsTag`. Similarly, you can leverage these attribute names in the JSP file, `view.jsp`, or in your own JSP file, such as `themeDisplay`, `company`, `user`, `scopeGroupId`, and so on.

Attribute name	Class name	Description
themeDisplay	ThemeDisplay	Theme display object
Company	Company	Company — table `Company`
Account	Account	Company account info — table `Account_`

Attribute name	Class name	Description
User	User	User info – table `User_`
realUser	User	User info
Contact	Contact	User contact info – table `Contact_`
Layout	Layout	Page layout – table `Layout_`
Layouts	List<layout>	A list of page layouts
Plid	Long	Page layout ID
layoutTypePortlet	LayoutTypePortlet	Layout type portlet
scopeGroupId	Long	Scoped group ID
permissionChecker	PermissionChecker	Permission checker
Locale	Locale	Current locale
timeZone	TimeZone	Current time zone
Theme	Theme	Current theme
colorScheme	ColorScheme	Theme color scheme
portletDisplay	PortletDisplay	Portlet display object

Direct JSP servlet

As mentioned earlier, a lot of taglibs use JSP files to present their content. `com.liferay.taglib.util.IncludeTag` and all of its sub tag classes require JSP dispatching and depends heavily on the app-server's resource lookup and dispatch. The dispatching involves a complex checking and `FilterChain`, which is not needed for taglib.

Direct JSP servlets provide a direct way of invoking the taglib without asking for help from the application server. The portal provides the following properties to configure **Direct-Servlet-Context**.

```
direct.servlet.context.enabled=true
direct.servlet.context.reload=true
```

The preceding code shows that you can set the property `direct.servlet.context.enabled` to `true` to enable dispatching to a servlet directly to speed up request dispatching. You can also set the property `direct.servlet.context.reload` to `true` to refresh the servlet associated with a JSP when the JSP has been modified. This property is not used unless the property `direct.servlet.context.enabled` is set to `true`.

What's happening?

First, direct-servlet-context was defined as `com.liferay.portal.kernel.servlet.DirectServletContext`, when implementing the interface `javax.servlet.ServletContext`. Then, the direct servlet registry was specified as a single object called `DirectServletRegistry`, the direct request dispatcher was specified as `DirectRequestDispatcher`, and `IncludeTag` uses `DirectServletContext`.

Finally, `JspFactoryWrapper` extending `JspFactory` uses `DirectServletRegistry`.

Advanced MVC portlet

We have discussed the basic MVC portlet in the previous section. In this section, we will discuss the advanced MVC portlet features, such as portlet bridge extension, bringing portlets into the Control Panel, portlet configuration and preferences, redirecting, more actions, and interacting with the database.

Portlet bridge extension

As mentioned earlier, `MVCPortlet` extends `LiferayPortlet` and `LiferayPortlet` extends `GenericPortlet`. `MVCPortlet` is useful, since it specifies a set of JSP views such as `about-jsp`, `config-jsp`, `view-jsp`, and so on. In the real world, `MVCPortlet` may not be sufficient. Thus you should extend it.

For example, for the knowledge base admin, `MVCPortlet` got extended as `com.liferay.knowledgebase.admin.portlet.AdminPortlet`. In the `portlet.xml` file, the `portlet-class` element contains the fully-qualified class name of the portlet. Thus, to extend the MVC portlet bridge, the `portlet-class` element could be specified as follows:

```
<portlet-class>com.liferay.knowledgebase.admin.portlet.AdminPortlet</
portlet-class>
```

To do so, first we need to create a portlet `AdminPortlet.java` at the package path `com.liferay.knowledgebase.admin.portlet`. Of course, you can have a different name and package path. Let `AdminPortlet` extend `MVCPortlet` as follows:

```
public class AdminPortlet extends MVCPortlet {
// actions details
}
```

Then, add methods as shown in the following table, where method names, examples, and descriptions are specified:

Method name	Example	Description
addAttachment	addAttachment(ActionRequest req, ActionResponse res);	Adds attachments
deleteArticle	deleteArticle(ActionRequest req, ActionResponse res);	Deletes articles
deleteAttachment	deleteArticle(ActionRequest req, ActionResponse res);	Deletes attachments
deleteComment	deleteComment(ActionRequest req, ActionResponse res);	Deletes comments
deleteTemplate	deleteTemplate(ActionRequest req, ActionResponse res);	Deletes templates
render	render(RenderRequest req, RenderResponse res)	Renders function
serveArticleRSS	serveArticleRSS(ResourceRequest req, ResourceResponse res)	Serves article RSS
serve Attachment	serveAttachment(ResourceRequest req, ResourceResponse res)	Serves attachments
serveGroup ArticleRSS	serveGroupArticleRSS(ResourceReq uest req, ResourceResponse res)	Serves group article RSS
serveResource	serveResource(ResourceRequest req, ResourceResponse res)	Serves resource: attachment, article RSS, or group article RSS
subscribeArticle	subscribeArticle(ActionRequest req, ActionResponse res);	Subscribes articles
unsubscribe Article	unsubscribeArticle(ActionRequest req, ActionResponse res);	Unsubscribes articles
unsubscribeGroup Article	unsubscribeGroupArticle(ActionRe quest req, ActionResponse res);	Unsubscribes group articles
updateArticle	updateArticle(ActionRequest req, ActionResponse res);	Adds / Updates an article
updateAttachments	updateAttachments(ActionRequest req, ActionResponse res);	Updates attachments
updateComment	updateComment(ActionRequest req, ActionResponse res);	Adds / Updates a comment
updateTemplate	updateTemplate(ActionRequest req, ActionResponse res);	Adds / Updates a template

Bringing portlets into the Control Panel

In some use cases, you may want to hide the portlet `knowledge-base-admin` in the Application Panel and bring it into the Control Panel. How to implement these requirements? To hide a portlet in the Application Panel, you leverage a special category name called `category.hidden` in `liferay-display.xml`, as shown in the following code. Portlets under the category `category.hidden` will be usable by the system or the Control Panel only.

```
<category name="category.hidden">
 <portlet id="knowledge-base-admin"></portlet>
</category>
```

If you want a portlet available to the system, you can set the following line in `liferay-portlet.xml` for that portlet.

```
<system>true</system>
```

As shown in the preceding code, you should set the `system` value to `true`, if the portlet is a **system portlet** that a user can't manually add to their page. The default value is `false`.

To bring a portlet into the Control Panel, you can add the following lines for that portlet in `liferay-portlet.xml`:

```
<control-panel-entry-category>content</control-panel-entry-category>
<control-panel-entry-weight>7.5</control-panel-entry-weight>
```

As shown in the preceding code, you can set the `control-panel-entry-category` value to `my`, `content`, `portal`, or `server` to make this portlet available in the Control Panel under that category. You can also set the `control-panel-entry-weight` value to a double number to control the position of the entry within its Control Panel category. Higher values mean that the entry will appear further down the Control Panel menu. In addition, the `control-panel-entry-class` value must be a class that implements `com.liferay.portlet.ControlPanelEntry`, called by the Control Panel to decide whether the portlet should be shown to a specific user in a specific context or not. The default value is set as `DefaultControlPanelEntry`.

Actually, in `DefaultControlPanelEntryFactory.java`, it loads the Control Panel default entry class, `CONTROL_PANEL_DEFAULT_ENTRY_CLASS`. In `PortalImpl.java`, it provides a method called `filterControlPanelPortlets` to filter the Control Panel portlets by checking the Control Panel entry instance and portlets' visibility.

Portlet configuration and preferences

Portlets can have a set of preferences, which could be defined in `portlet.xml` for each portlet. The Liferay portlets are 100 percent compliant with the portlet preferences. In addition, Liferay adds the ability to configure the portlets at runtime.

Portlet configuration

The portlet `knowledge-base-admin` requires a few items should be configurable at runtime, such as, `Email From`, `Article Added Email`, `Article Updated Email`, `Display Settings`, `RSS`, and so on. How do we make it?

In three steps, you can make your portlet configurable at runtime:

1. Create a class named `ConfigurationActionImpl` under the package `com.liferay.knowledgebase.admin.action` as follows:

    ```
    public class ConfigurationActionImpl extends
    DefaultConfigurationAction {
      public void processAction( PortletConfig portletConfig,
        ActionRequest actionRequest, ActionResponse actionResponse)
      throws Exception {
        // add custom logic
    }
    ```

    As shown in the preceding code, `ConfigurationActionImpl` extends the portal service `DefaultConfigurationAction`, and `DefaultConfigurationAction` implements the interfaces `ConfigurationAction` and `ResourceServingConfigurationAction`. The following table shows implementation details:

Class name	Methods	Reference	Description
Configuration ActionImpl	processAction	PortletConfig, ActionRequest, ActionResponse	Configuration action implementation
DefaultConfiguration Action	getLocalized Parameter, getParameter, processAction, render, serveResource, setPreference	PortletRequest, PortletConfig, ActionRequest, ActionResponse, RenderRequest, RenderResponse, ResourceRequest, ResourceResponse	Default configuration action class

Class name	Methods	Reference	Description
ConfigurationAction	processAction, render	PortletConfig, ActionRequest, ActionResponse, RenderRequest, RenderResponse	Configuration action interface
ResourceServing ConfigurationAction	serveResource	PortletConfig, ResourceRequest, ResourceResponse	Resource serving configuration action interface

Note that all configurations are saved as portlet preferences. In `DefaultConfigurationAction.java`, you will see the following code snippet:

```
PortletPreferences portletPreferences =
  PortletPreferencesFactoryUtil.getPortletSetup(
    actionRequest, portletResource);
// see details in DefaultConfigurationAction.java
portletPreferences.store();
```

As shown in the preceding code, it first gets all portlet preferences and then sets name-value pairs. Finally, it stores the portlet preferences in the database.

2. Prepare the configuration JSP as `configuration.jsp`—create a JSP `configuration.jsp` in the folder `/admin` and configure it in `portlet.xml`.

You can add an `init-param` with the name `config-jsp` and the value `/admin/configuration.jsp` as follows in `portlet.xml`:

```
<init-param>
  <name>config-jsp</name>
  <value>/admin/configuration.jsp</value>
</init-param>
```

Note that the name of `init-param` must be `config-jsp`. In `DefaultConfigurationAction.java`, the `render` method has defined the following logic.

```
String configJSP = selPortletConfig.getInitParameter("config-jsp");
if (Validator.isNotNull(configJSP)) {
  return configJSP;
}
return "/configuration.jsp";
```

The preceding code says, if `config-jsp` is not null, then it returns the configuration JSP page; otherwise, it returns the default configuration JSP page, that is, `/configuration.jsp`.

3. Add the configuration class in `liferay-portlet.xml` as follows:

```
<configuration-action-class>com.liferay.knowledgebase.admin.
action.ConfigurationActionImpl</configuration-action-class>
```

As shown in the preceding code, the `configuration-action-class` value must be a class that implements `com.liferay.portal.kernel.portlet.ConfigurationAction` and is called to allow users to configure the portlet at runtime.

Portlet preferences

Liferay Portal stores the portlet preferences in the database as a table called `PortletPreferences`, which has a set of columns such as `portletPreferencesId`, `ownerId`, `ownerType`, `plid`, `portletId`, and `preferences`. In particular, the column `preferences` is defined as a long text, where the specific portlet preferences are stored in an XML format.

```
<portlet-preferences>
  <preference>
    <name>enable-article-description</name>
    <value>true</value>
  </preference>
</portlet-preferences>
```

As shown in the preceding code, the `preferences` element contains many preference elements. For a given portlet specification, there is one and only one `preferences` element. The `preference` element contains the name of the preference. This `name` must be unique within the portlet. Obviously, you can add your own portlet preferences to custom portlets.

In brief, there are two options that you can add in the portlet preferences, namely, static-value preferences in `portlet.xml` and dynamic-value preferences through portlet configuration in `liferay-portlet.xml`.

Portlet keys, title, and description

By default, the portlet title and description have been specified in `portlet.xml`. As you can see, the portlet title and description could be specified in one language only. In real cases, the portlet title and description should support multiple languages, for example, up to 37 languages as the portal did. How to implement the same in plugins? You can add the portlet title and description message as follows to `Language_en.properties` in the folder `$PLUGINS_SDK_HOME/portlets/${plugin.name}/docroot/WEB-INF/src/content`:

```
// see details in Language_en.properties
javax.portlet.title.knowledge-base-search_WAR_
knowledgebaseportlet=Knowledge Base Search
javax.portlet.title.knowledge-base-section_WAR_
knowledgebaseportlet=Knowledge Base Section
```

As shown in the preceding code, the description of a portlet is specified with the prefix `javax.portlet.description`, while the title of a portlet is defined with the prefix `javax.portlet.title`. Let's say that the language is presented as `${locale}`, while different language properties could be presented as `Language_${locale}.properties`. In order to support different languages, you can add the properties file `Language_${locale}.properties` and provide the portlet title and description in that language.

The portal's core portlets keys are specified in `com.liferay.portal.util.PortletKeys`. For example, `ACTIVITIES` has a value of `116`, `ALERTS` has a value of `83`, and so on. You can refer to the portal core portlet via `PortletKeys` in plugins. Of course, `PortletKeys` could get extended as well. For instance, `com.liferay.knowledgebase.util.PortletKeys` extends `PortletKeys` and defines the static strings as follows:

```
public static final String KNOWLEDGE_BASE_ADMIN =
  "knowledge-base-admin_WAR_knowledgebaseportlet";
// see details in PortletKeys.java ;
```

The web key `com.liferay.portal.kernel.util.WebKeys` provides a set of interfaces for keys, such as `ASSET_RENDERER`, `ASSET_RENDERER_FACTORY`, and so on. You can leverage these in your plugins. In such cases, you may need to add more custom web keys in plugins. Thus you can add a new class that implements `WebKeys`. For the plugin `knowledge-base-portlet`, the following static strings have been defined in `com.liferay.knowledgebase.util.WebKeys`, which implement the preceding `WebKeys`.

```
// see details in WebKeys.java
public static final String KNOWLEDGE_BASE_TEMPLATE =
  "KNOWLEDGE_BASE_TEMPLATE";
```

Message

The tag `liferay-ui:message` displays a localized message for a key. The key can be one of the predefined keys from the language properties such as `Language_${locale}.properties`, where a set of keys and values has been specified in different languages. Note that the translation doesn't support formatting. Thus you can't add HTML into the language properties file.

Render URL is defined in the `com.liferay.taglib.ui.MessageTag` tag class. It can have optional attributes such as `translateArguments` and `arguments`, and required attributes such as `key`. The following is an example of a message:

```
<liferay-ui:message key="was-this-information-helpful" />
<liferay-ui:message key="yes" /
<liferay-ui:message key="no" />
```

The preceding code shows three message keys: `yes`, `no`, and `was-this-information-helpful`. These keys are predefined in the language properties such as `Language_xx.properties`. For details, refer to the book *Liferay User Interface Development*.

The following are the sample key-value pairs in `Language_en.properties`. It specifically provides key-value pairs for models and action keys in English.

```
model.resource.com.liferay.knowledgebase.admin=Knowledge Base Admin
// see details in Language_en.properties
action.VIEW_TEMPLATES=View Templates
```

Of course, you can add your own key-value pairs in `Language_${locale}.properties` in order to support multiple languages, where `${locale}` presents the locale code.

Redirect

The view of `MVCPortlet` was specified using JSP files. There are sets of JSP files for different views. The following table shows a set of JSP files for the portlet `knowledge-base-admin`:

JSP filename	Sample code	Description
`view.jsp`	`<liferay-ui:search-container>`	Default view, including `top_tabs.jsp`, `article_action.jsp`, `article_search.jsp`, `article_search_results.jspf`, and `edit_article.jsp`

JSP filename	Sample code	Description
view_article. jsp	`<liferay-util:include page="/admin/ top_tabs.jsp" servletContext="<%= application %>" />`	View articles, including `top_tabs.jsp`, `article_ breadcrumbs.jsp`, `article_ tools.jsp`, `article_icons. jsp`, `article_attachments. jsp`, `article_assets.jsp`, `article_ratings.jsp`, `article_siblings.jsp`, and `article_comments.jsp`
view_ template.jsp	`<%@ include file="/ admin/init.jsp" %>`	View template, including `top_tabs.jsp`, `template_tools.jsp`, `template_icons.jsp`, and `template_comments.jsp`
View_ templates.jsp	`<portlet:renderURL var="searchURL">`	

In most cases, views of the portlet need to be redirected from one view to another view, such as search view, search results view, updating article view, and so on. In general, redirect would be implemented via the render URL, the action URL, or the resource URL.

Render URL

A render URL can be generated via the tags `<liferay-portlet>` or `<portlet>`. A render URL is defined in the `tag` class `com.liferay.taglib.portlet. RenderURLTag` and the `Tei` class `RenderURLTei`. It can have optional attributes such as `copyCurrentRenderParamaters`, `escapeXml`, `portletMode`, `secure`, `var`, and `windowState`. The following is an example of a render URL:

```
<portlet:renderURL var="historyURL">
    <portlet:param name="jspPage" value='<%= jspPath + "history.jsp"
%>' />
    <portlet:param name="resourcePrimKey" value="<%= String.
valueOf(article.getResourcePrimKey()) %>" />
</portlet:renderURL>
<liferay-ui:icon image="recent_changes" url="<%= historyURL %>"/>
```

As shown in the preceding code, the render URL gets specified, while the attribute `var` has the value `historyURL`. The render URL includes two portlet parameters, namely, `jspPage` and `resourcePrimKey`. Note that the parameter `jspPage` points to a JSP file, while the parameter `resourcePrimKey` points to the article ID.

Similarly, the render URL searchURL can be presented as follows. It includes the parameter jspPage.

```
<portlet:renderURL var="searchURL">
  <portlet:param name="jspPage" value="/admin/search.jsp" />
</liferay-portlet:renderURL>
```

As shown in the preceding code, the portlet parameter can have different names such as topLink, redirect, and so on. The name value of the portlet parameter is available to be used in the JSP file.

The tag portlet:param is defined in com.liferay.taglib.util.ParamTag. It can have required attributes such as name and value. You can refer to the UI taglib details in $PORTAL_ROOT_HOME/WEB-INF/tld/liferay-portlet.tld.

Action URL

The tag portlet:actionURL is defined in the tag class ActionURLTag and the Tei class ActionURLTei. It can have optional attributes such as copyCurrentRenderParamaters, name, escapeXml, portletMode, secure, var, and windowState. The following is an example of an action URL:

```
<portlet:actionURL name="deleteArticle" var="deleteURL">
    <portlet:param name="redirect" value="<%= currentURL %>" />
    <portlet:param name="resourcePrimKey" value="<%= String.
valueOf(article.getResourcePrimKey()) %>" />
</portlet:actionURL>
<liferay-ui:icon-delete url="<%= deleteURL %>" />
```

As shown in the preceding code, an action URL gets specified, while the attribute name has the value deleteArticle and the attribute var has the value deleteURL. The render URL includes two portlet parameters: redirect and resourcePrimKey. The value of the attribute var is used in the tag liferay-ui:icon-delete.

Note that the preceding attribute named deleteArticle will be mapped into the method deleteArticle in AdminPortlet.java. In the same way, you can define other action URL names, such as deleteComment, updateComment, subscribeArticle, unsubscribeArticle, updateAttachments, updateArticle, and so on.

In addition, you can leverage the resource URL called ResourceURL:

```
<portlet:resourceURL id="attachment" var="clipURL">
    <portlet:param name="companyId" value="<%= String.valueOf(company.
getCompanyId()) %>" />
    <portlet:param name="fileName" value="<%= fileName %>" />
</portlet:resourceURL>
```

The preceding tag, `portlet:resourceURL`, is defined in the `tag` class `ResourceURLTag` and the `Tei` class `ResourceURLTei`. It can have optional attributes such as `cacheability`, `escapeXml`, `id`, and `secure`.

Interacting with the database

The following diagram shows the main models for the knowledge base. They are **Template**, **Article**, and **Comment**. An article can have many child articles. Each article can have many comments. A template can be applied to articles. Each article can have many discussions, tags, categories, attachments, subscriptions, addresses, asset links, documents, dynamic data lists (DDL), and so on.

The entries `Article`, `Comment`, and `Template` are specified in `service.xml`.

The entry `Article` includes the following columns:

- `article Id` as primary key
- `resource Prim Key`, `group Id`
- `company Id`
- `user Id`
- `user Name`
- `create Date`
- `modified Date`
- `parent resource Prim Key`, `version`
- `title`
- `content`
- `description`
- `priority`
- `latest`
- `status`
- `status by user Id`
- `status by user name`
- `status date`

The entry `Template` includes the following columns:

- `template Id` as primary key
- `group Id`

- company Id
- user Id
- user Name
- create Date
- modified Date
- title
- content
- description

The entry Comment includes the following columns:

- comment Id as primary key
- group Id
- company Id
- user Id
- user Name
- create Date
- modified Date
- class name Id
- class PK
- content
- helpful

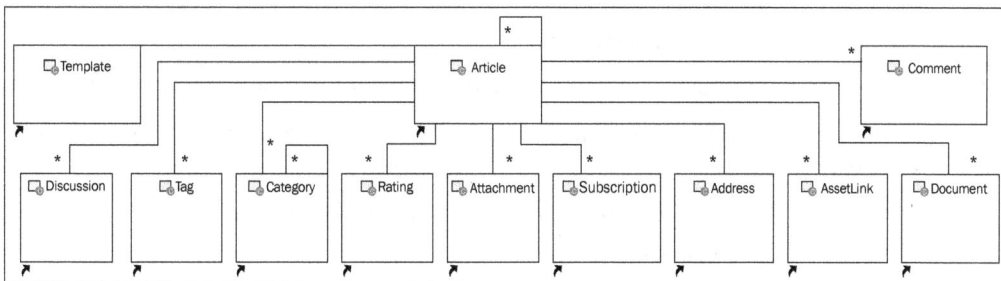

The following table shows the details of the entity `Article`.

Category	Values	Description
Package path	`com.liferay.knowledgebase`	Package name
Namespace	`KB`	Database table prefix
PK fields	`articleId`	Primary key fields
Resource	`resourcePrimKey`	Filter primary key
Group instance	`groupId`	Group instance as scopes
Audit fields	`company Id, user Id, user Name, create Date, modified Date`	Auditing columns
Relationship	`parentResourcePrimKey`	Hierarchy
Versioning	`Version`	Different versions
Other fields	`title, content, description`	Main content
Additional fields	`priority, latest`	Additional columns
Status	`status, status by user Id, status by user name, status date`	Workflow status

When ready, you can run the Ant target `build-service` to generate models, services, XML configuration files, query files, and so on. The following set of bullets shows the folder structure of generated services, models, XML configuration files, and query files under `$PLUGIN_SDK_HOME/${plugin.name}/docroot/WEB-INF`:

- `/src/${package.path}`: Implementation code
- `/src/content`: Language properties files
- `/src/META-INF`: XML configuration files
- `/src/custom-sql`: Custom query
- `/src/resource-actions`: XML-based permission actions
- `/src/portal.properties, portlet.properties, services.properties`: Property files
- `/js/service.js`: JSON JavaScript under the folder `docroot`
- `/client`: Web service SOAP client
- `/lib`: Service JAR files
- `/service`: Interface code
- `/sql`: Query files

Rebuilding services

Service-Builder provides the ability to build services and models automatically. However, there are a few scenarios where you need to rebuild services against `service.xml`. The following is a list of possible use cases:

- Use case 1: Change `package-path` to a different value such as `com.bookpub.knowledgebase` and / or change `name-space` to another value such as `KBM`

- Use case 2: Change the entity name to a different value such as `KBArticle`

- Use case 3: Update the columns, finders, orders, relationship, references, and exceptions

- Use case 4: Update signatures (and add new methods) in `local-service-impl` and / or `finder-impl` and / or update constraint `hint` in `portlet-model-hints.xml`

- Use case 5: Use other databases in plugins

In use cases 1 and 2, you should clean up the database and plugin source code and rebuild the services. In use cases 3 and 4, you could simply run the Ant target `build-service`. In use case 5, you have to use a database other than the default portal database.

What's happening?

First, when deploying the plugin with services and models, the portal will do the following tasks:

- Register a class name such as `com.liferay.knowledgebase.model.Article` in the table `ClassName_`

- Register the SQL script with a namespace such as `KB` in the table `ServiceComponent`

- Create database tables with table name `${namespace}_${entity.name}`, for example, `KB_Article`

Therefore, in use cases 1 and 2, cleaning up of source code and database tables is required. Before doing so, it is better to back up your custom code such as `*LocalServiceImpl`, `*FinderImpl`, and so on. The clean-up process should cover:

1. Removing the subfolders `/src`, `/service`, and `/sql` from the folder `$PLUGIN_SDK_HOME/${plugin.name}/docroot/WEB-INF`.

2. Optionally, drop the plugin data and tables from the database.

`PortalImpl.java` provides the method `getClassNameId(String value)`, where it calls `ClassNameLocalServiceUtil.getClassNameId(value)`. The method `getClassNameId` is implemented in `ClassNameLocalServiceImpl` as follows:

```
public ClassName getClassName(String value) throws SystemException {
   if (Validator.isNull(value)) {
      return _nullClassName;
   }
   // Always cache the class name. This table exists to improve
   // performance. Create the class name if one does not exist.
   ClassName className = _classNames.get(value);
   if (className == null) {
     className = classNameLocalService.addClassName(value);

     _classNames.put(value, className);
   }
   return className;
}
```

As you can see, `ClassNameLocalServiceImpl` always caches the class name. This table `ClassName_` exists to improve performance. It will create the class name, if one does not exist. Therefore, when first calling `getClassNameId` with a class name such as `com.liferay.knowledgebase.model.Article`, it will create the class name in the table, `ClassName_`.

Actually, `BaseHotDeployListener` implements `HotDeployListener` as follows:

```
public void invokeDeploy(HotDeployEvent event) throws
HotDeployException;
public void invokeUndeploy(HotDeployEvent event) throws
HotDeployException;
```

`PluginPackageHotDeployListener` extends `BaseHotDeployListener` and provides detailed implementation such as invoking deploy and invoking undeploy.

Model hints

The XML file `portlet-model-hints.xml` was generated by the Service-Builder through the template `model_hints_xml.ftl`. Once `portlet-model-hints.xml` is created, you can update model hints and rebuild services.

The model hint interface was specified in `ModelHints.java` as follows, and implemented as `ModelHintsImpl.java`:

```
public Map<String, String> getDefaultHints(String model);
// see details in ModelHintsImpl.java
public String trimString(String model, String field, String value);
```

Model hints configurations are defined in `portal.properties` as follows:

```
model.hints.configs=\
  META-INF/portal-model-hints.xml,\
  META-INF/ext-model-hints.xml,\
  META-INF/portlet-model-hints.xml
```

`ModelHintsImpl.java` will load the preceding property `PropsKeys.MODEL_HINTS_`
`CONFIGS` in the method `afterPropertiesSet`. The `portlet-model-hints.xml`
primarily controls how the fields appear when a `Bean` object is being displayed
using the tag `liferay-ui:*`. The following is a sample:

```
// see details in portlet-model-hints.xml
<field name="description" type="String">
  <hint-collection name="TEXTAREA" />
</field>
```

The model `hint-collection` is used to apply the same series of hints to multiple
fields. The attribute name can be `TEXTAREA`, `CLOB`, `max-length`, and so on. The
attribute's name, `max-length`, is used to set the maximum size of the column for SQL
file generation. The following is a sample abstracted from `portal-model-hints.xml`:

```
// see details in portlet-model-hints.xml
<hint-collection name="SEARCHABLE-DATE">
  <hint name="month-nullable">true</hint>
  <hint name="day-nullable">true</hint>
  <hint name="year-nullable">true</hint>
  <hint name="show-time">false</hint>
</hint-collection>
<field name="birthday" type="Date">
  <hint name="year-range-delta">70</hint>
  <hint name="year-range-future">false</hint>
  <hint name="show-time">false</hint>
</field>
```

As shown in the preceding example, model hints are a few default names and types.
The following table shows the details:

Model hint name	Data Type	Sample	Description
auto-escape	boolean	`<hint name="auto-escape">false</hint>`	Whether the text values should be escaped or not
check-tab	boolean	`<hint name="check-tab">true</hint>`	Checks for the tab

Model hint name	Data Type	Sample	Description
display-height	Integer	`<hint name="display-width">150</hint>`	Displays height
display-width	Integer	`<hint name="display-height">40</hint>`	Displays width
show-time	boolean	`<hint name="show-time">false</hint>`	Shows the date and time or only the date
upper-case	boolean	`<hint name="upper-case">true</hint>`	Whether all characters should be uppercase or not
day-nullable	boolean	`<hint name="day-nullable">true</hint>`	Allows the day to be null
month-nullable	boolean	`<hint name="month-nullable">true</hint>`	Allows the month to be null
year-nullable	boolean	`<hint name="year-nullable">true</hint>`	Allows the year to be null
year-range-delta	Integer	`<hint name="year-range-delta">70</hint>`	The number of years to display from today's date
year-range-future	boolean	`<hint name="year-range-future">false</hint>`	Shows the year range whether it is future or not
validator	boolean	`<validator name="required" />`	validation or not

Model hint constants are specified in `ModelHintsConstants` as follows:

```
public static final String TEXT_DISPLAY_HEIGHT = "15";
// see details in ModelHintsConstants.java
public static final String TEXTAREA_MAX_LENGTH = "4000";
```

Other databases in plugins

As you can see, the Service-Builder generated the services and models plus the Spring-Hibernate configuration. The plugins (portlets) will share the same database with the portal. However, in some cases, you may need other databases for plugins (portlets).

How does this work? The portlet should define services and models in `service.xml` as follows:

```
<service-builder package-path="com.liferay.knowledgebase">
  <namespace>KB</namespace>
  <entity name="Article" uuid="true" local-service="true"
remote-service="true" data-source="kbDataSource" session-
factory="kbSessionFactory" tx-manager="kbTransactionManager">
<!-- see details in service.xml -->
  </entity>
<!-- see details in service.xml -->
</service-builder>
```

As shown in the preceding code, the `data-source` value specifies the data source target that is set to the persistence class. The default value is `Liferay data source`. This is used in conjunction with `session-factory`. The `session-factory` value specifies the session factory that is set to the persistence class. The default value is `Liferay session factory`. This is used in conjunction with `data-source`. The `tx-manager` value specifies the transaction manager that Spring uses. The default value is `Spring Hibernate transaction manager` that wraps the `Liferay data source` and `session factory`.

In the following four steps, you can use other databases in your own plugins:

1. First create the other database—suppose that you are going to create a database in MySQL `bookpubstreet` using the account `lportal/lportal`, you can run the SQL query.

2. Next, create a file named `ext-spring.xml` in the folder `$PLUGINS_SDK_HOME/portlets/${plugin.name}/docroot/WEB-INF/src/META-INF` and add `jndiName`, `kbDataSource`, `kbSessionFactory`, and `kbTransactionManager` as follows. Of course, you can use a name other than `kb`:

    ```
    <bean id="kbDataSourceTarget" class="com.liferay.portal.spring.
    jndi.JndiObjectFactoryBean" lazy-init="true">
      <property name="jndiName">
        <value>jdbc/kbPool</value>
      </property>
    </bean>
    <!-- see more details in ext-spring.xml -->
    ```

3. Then set the JNDI name in `$CATALINA/conf/content.xml` as follows. Note that the setting of the JNDI name is different from application server to application server:

    ```
    <!-- MySQL -->
    <Resource
    ```

```
name="jdbc/kbPool"
auth="Container" type="javax.sql.DataSource"
driverClassName="com.mysql.jdbc.Driver"
url="jdbc:mysql://localhost/ bookpubstreet?useUnicode=true&amp;cha
racterEncoding=UTF-8&amp;useFastDateParsing=false"
username="lportal"
password="lportal"
maxActive="20"
/>
```

4. Finally, copy the WAR file into the folder `$LIFERAY_HOME/deploy`.

What's happening?

After running the Ant target build service, you should see the following changes
in `portlet-spring.xml` for both `${entity.name}PersistenceImpl` and
`${entity.name}FinderImpl`:

```
<bean id="com.liferay.knowledgebase.service.persistence.
ArticlePersistence" class="com.liferay.knowledgebase.service.
persistence.ArticlePersistenceImpl" parent="basePersistence">
    <property name="dataSource" ref="kbDataSource" />
    <property name="sessionFactory" ref="kbSessionFactory" />
</bean>
```

First, the template `spring_xml.ftl` is in use to generate the data source and session
factory for `${entity.name}FinderImpl` and `${entity.name}Persistence`.
Secondly, `ServiceBuilder.java` provides the following method to create the
XML file `portlet-spring.xml`:

```
_createSpringXml();
```

Note that the other database tables didn't get created automatically. You need to create
these tables manually. The other database tables should get created automatically. By
the way, `ext-spring.xml` didn't get generated by the Service-Builder. However, in a
real case, the Service-Builder should be able to generate the file `ext-spring.xml`.

Dynamic query API

The **dynamic query API** provides an elegant way to define complex queries without
a complex setup, or a stiff and abstract learning curve. This API allows us to leverage
the existing mapping definitions through access to the Hibernate session. This
section is going to show the dynamic query against one table in a plugin, to join
tables inside a plugin, to join tables among the plugins, and to join tables among the
plugins and the portal core.

The interface of the API is specified in the `com.liferay.portal.kernel.dao.orm.` `DynamicQuery` class under the folder `/portal-service/src`. The following is the interface:

```
public DynamicQuery add(Criterion criterion);
// see details in DynamicQuery.java
public DynamicQuery setProjection(Projection projection);
```

As shown in the preceding code, you can add a criterion in your custom dynamic queries. You can also add order, set limits, and set projection in your custom queries. In addition, the method `setProjection` implements the `SELECT` statement. The `SELECT` statement is used to select data from a database and the result is stored in a result table, called the result set.

In brief, subqueries, associations, projections, and aliases are the features available in the dynamic query API.

Queries in plugins

First of all, you can set up a dynamic query against one table in a plugin. For example, to query knowledge base articles with `companyId` and `groupId`, and ordered by created date—a descending order, of course. This query can be presented as one table in the plugin `knowledge-base-portlet` as follows:

```
DynamicQuery query =
  DynamicQueryFactoryUtil.forClass(Article.class,"article")
    .add(PropertyFactoryUtil.forName("article.companyId")
      .eq(new Long(companyId)))
    .add(PropertyFactoryUtil.forName("article.groupId")
      .eq(new Long(groupId)))
    .addOrder(OrderFactoryUtil.desc("article.createDate"));
List results = ArticleLocalServiceUtil.dynamicQuery(query);
```

As shown in the preceding code, it first uses the `DynamicQueryFactoryUti.` `forClass` method with the following parameters:

- The class `Article.class`
- The alias name `article`

It then adds the `companyId` and the `groupId` properties and sets the results ordered by the property `createDate` in a descending order.

The Service-Builder generates the following dynamic query-related methods in `service_base_impl.ftl` and `service_util.ftl` as follows. For example, for `knowledge-base-portlet`, the dynamic query-related methods are `ArticleServiceBaseImpl` and `ArticleLocalServiceUtil`, respectively.

```
public List dynamicQuery(DynamicQuery dynamicQuery);
// see details in DynamicQuery.java
public long dynamicQueryCount(DynamicQuery dynamicQuery);
```

Dynamic query factory

The interface for the method `forClass` is defined in `DynamicQueryFactory` as follows:

```
public DynamicQuery forClass(Class<?> clazz);
// see details in DynamicQueryFactory.java
public DynamicQuery forClass(Class<?> clazz, String alias, ClassLoader
classLoader);
```

The interfaces for the methods `asc` and `desc` are defined in `OrderFactory` as follows:

```
public Order asc(String propertyName);
public Order desc(String propertyName);
```

The interface for the method `forName` is defined as follows in `PropertyFactory`:

```
public Property forName(String propertyName);
```

Dynamic query operations

More specifically, the interface `Property` extends the interface `Projection`. The interface `Property` defines all the methods, such as `eq`, as follows:

```
public Order asc();
// see details in Property.java
public Criterion eq(Object value);
```

As shown in the preceding code, methods such as `asc`, `avg`, `between`, `count`, `desc`, and `eq` are defined. Other methods, which are not listed in the preceding code, are shown in the following table:

Names	Methods	Description

eq*	`eq(DynamicQuery subselect);`
	`eq(Object value);`
	`eqAll(DynamicQuery subselect);`
	`eqProperty(Property other);`
	`eqProperty(String other);`
	`eqSome(DynamicQuery subselect);`
		Equal to another property.

ge*	`ge(DynamicQuery subselect);`
	`ge(Object value);`
	`geAll(DynamicQuery subselect);`
	`geProperty(Property other);`
	`geProperty(String other);`
	`geSome(DynamicQuery subselect);`
		Greater than or equal to a value or another property.

group	`group();`	GROUP BY clause

gt*	`gt(DynamicQuery subselect);`
	`gt(Object value);`
	`gtAll(DynamicQuery subselect);`
	`gtProperty(Property other);`
	`gtProperty(String other);`
	`tSome(DynamicQuery subselect);`
		Greater than or equal to a value or another property.

in
 	
not in
	`in(Collection<Object> values);`
	`in(DynamicQuery subselect);`
	`in(Object[] values);`
	`notIn(DynamicQuery subselect);`
		Multiple values in or not in a WHERE clause.

is*	`isEmpty();`
	`isNotEmpty();`
	`isNotNull();`
	`isNull();`
		Empty, not empty, not null, or null.

Names	Methods	Description

le*	le(DynamicQuery subselect);
	 le(Object value);
	 leAll(DynamicQuery subselect);
	 leProperty(Property other);
	 leProperty(String other);
	 leSome(DynamicQuery subselect);
		Less than or equal to a value or another property.

like	like(Object value);	Searches for a specified pattern; % for one character, * for many characters.

lt*	lt(DynamicQuery subselect);
	 lt(Object value);
	 ltAll(DynamicQuery subselect);
	 ltProperty(Property other);
	 ltProperty(String other);
	 ltSome(DynamicQuery subselect);
		Less than a value or another property.

max
 	
 min
	max();
	
	 min();
		The largest / smallest value.

ne*	ne(DynamicQuery subselect);
	 ne(Object value);
	 neAll(DynamicQuery subselect);
	 neProperty(Property other);
	 neProperty(String other);
	 neSome(DynamicQuery subselect);
		Not equal to another property

SQL joins

In the previous section, we discussed using dynamic query for one table in a plugin. This section deals with SQL joins. **SQL joins** are used to query data from two or more tables, based on a relationship between certain columns in these tables.

Joining tables inside a plugin

With dynamic query API, you can join tables in a plugin. For example, the plugin knowledge-base-portlet has the tables Article and Comment. A query says "find me all articles with specific companyId and groupId, and helpful comments, ordered by createDate". Using dynamic query, this query can be presented as follows:

```
DynamicQuery qd0 =
   // ignore details
DynamicQuery query =
   DynamicQueryFactoryUtil.forClass(Article.class,"article")
     .add(PropertyFactoryUtil.forName("article.companyId")
       .eq(new Long(companyId)))
     .add(PropertyFactoryUtil.forName("article.groupId")
       .eq(new Long(groupId)))
     .add(PropertyFactoryUtil.forName("article.resourcePrimKey")
       .in(qd0))
     .addOrder(OrderFactoryUtil.desc("article.createDate"));
List results = ArticleLocalServiceUtil.dynamicQuery(query);
```

The preceding code shows a way to get articles by company ID, group ID, and helpful comments. The dynamic query API allows us to leverage the existing mapping definitions through access to the Hibernate session. For example, `DynamicQuery dq0` selects the comments by `companyId`, `groupId`, and `helpful` comments; `DynamicQuery query` selects articles by `companyId`, `groupId`, and `resourcePrimKey`, which exists in `DynamicQuery dq0`. Note that `resourcePrimKey` is used to present a relationship between `Article` and `Comment`, and not `articleId`, since `articleId` should be used for versioning.

Joining tables from different plugins

Using the dynamic query API, you can join tables from different plugins. For example, the plugin `knowledge-base-portlet` has the tables `Article` and `Comment`, while the plugin `chat-portlet` has the tables `Entry` and `Status`. A query says "find all articles with specific `companyId` and `groupId`, and `online` users ordered by `createDate`".

How to join tables between the plugin `knowledge-base-portlet` and the plugin `chat-portlet`? First, you need to make the third-party service JAR global, that is, you should move the service JAR `chat-service-portlet.jar` from the folder `/webapps/${plugin.name}/WEB-INF/lib` to the folder `/lib/ext`. Then, using dynamic query, you can present this query as follows:

```
DynamicQuery qd0 =
   // ignore details
DynamicQuery query =
   DynamicQueryFactoryUtil.forClass(Article.class,"article")
     .add(PropertyFactoryUtil.forName("article.companyId")
       .eq(new Long(companyId)))
     .add(PropertyFactoryUtil.forName("article.groupId")
       .eq(new Long(groupId)))
```

```
    .add(PropertyFactoryUtil.forName("article.userId")
      .in(qd0))
    .addOrder(OrderFactoryUtil.desc("article.createDate"));
List results = ArticleLocalServiceUtil.dynamicQuery(query);
```

The preceding code shows a way to get articles by company ID, group ID, and online users. For example, `DynamicQuery dq0` selects the comments by `companyId`, `groupId`, and `online` users. `DynamicQuery query` selects articles by `companyId`, `groupId`, and `userId`, which exist in `DynamicQuery dq0`.

Similarly, you can join multiple tables. If you expect that the service JAR `knowledge-base-service-portlet.jar` is available to other plugins, you can move the service JAR from the folder `/webapps/${plugin.name}/WEB-INF/lib` to the folder `/lib/ext`. Then, both chat service and knowledge base service are global, available, and accessible to others plugins.

Joining tables from plugins and portal core

Using the dynamic query API, you can join tables from plugins and portal core. The portal core provides a set of tables, such as `Address`, `AssetEntry`, `Subscription`, and so on. With the dynamic query API, you are able to join portal core tables in your own plugins. For example, if a query says "find me the 10 most popular articles for the knowledge base with their specific `companyId` and `groupId`", you can present the following query:

```
DynamicQuery dq0 =
  // ignore details
DynamicQuery query =
  DynamicQueryFactoryUtil.forClass(AssetEntry.class, "asset")
    .add(PropertyFactoryUtil.forName("asset.companyId")
      .eq(new Long(companyId)))
    .add(PropertyFactoryUtil.forName("asset.groupId")
      .eq(new Long(groupId)))
    .add(PropertyFactoryUtil.forName("asset.classPK").in(dq0))
    .addOrder(OrderFactoryUtil.desc("asset.viewCount"));
List assets = AssetEntryLocalServiceUtil.dynamicQuery(query);
```

The preceding code shows a way to get the most popular articles by company ID, group ID, and limited most popular articles. For example, `DynamicQuery dq0` selects the journal articles by `companyID` and `groupId`. `DynamicQuery query` selects the asset entries by `companyID`, `groupId`, and `classPK`, which exists in `DynamicQuery dq0` and ordering asset entries by `viewCount` as well.

Liferay provides several ways to define complex queries used in retrieving database data. For example, each service `Entity`, such as portal core `Address`, `AssetEntry`, `Subscription`, and custom `Article` and `Comment`, typically defines several `finder` methods. Why do you need dynamic query API? There are several use cases that require a dynamic query API:

- Query complexity, such as joining tables from plugins and joining tables from plugins and portal core
- Queries which implement aggregate SQL operations, such as, maximum (`max`), minimum (`min`), average (`avg`), `between`, and so on
- Query optimization
- Complex data access, like reporting

To summarize, the dynamic query API provides a flexible way to define complex queries without any complex setup. This abstracts away the SQL grammar and making it database agnostic. In particular, there are no configuration files and no embedded SQL strings. Moreover, the queries could be assembled through business logic, for the queries are created without the immediate need of a database session.

Custom query

A **custom query** allows creating dynamic criteria, like dynamic query API. In many situations, this avoids the need to create a custom query completely. However, in some cases, a custom query, called **custom-sql**, could be useful. For instance, there is a complex **JOIN** query and it is hard to do in the dynamic query API. In this case, custom query would be very helpful.

Let's consider a real example. A query says "find me all the articles with a specific `companyId` and `groupId`, subscribed to by a specific user, ordered by `createDate`". Of course, you could use the dynamic query API. Here, we are using this request as an example to show how to build a custom query in the Plugins SDK.

In general, you should be able to build a custom query in the Plugins SDK in five steps:

1. Create a folder named `custom-sql` under `$PLUGINS_SDK_HOME/portlets/${portlet.name}/docroot/WEB-INF/src` and create a file named `default.xml` under `custom-sql` with the following lines:

```
<?xml version="1.0"?>
<custom-sql>
  <sql id="com.liferay.knowledgebase.service.persistence.
ArticleFinder.findBySubscription">
    <![CDATA[
```

```
      // see details in default.xml
    ]]>
    </sql>
</custom-sql>
```

Note that the preceding code is just sample code. In the real world, you would write your own custom query and logic. In addition, you would see that the table name of the portal core, such as `Subscription`, doesn't have any prefix, while the table name of the plugins is made up of `${namespace}` plus an underscore `_` and `${entity.name}` such as `KB_Article`. All the table names are case-sensitive.

2. In `portlet.properties`, add the following line:

```
custom.sql.configs=custom-sql/default.xml
```

As shown in the preceding code, the property `custom.sql.configs` specifies custom SQL configurations. You would be able to input a list of comma-delimited custom SQL configurations.

3. Create a file named `com.liferay.knowledgebase.service.persistence.ArticleFinderImpl.java` under the folder `$PLUGINS_SDK_HOME/portlets/${portlet.name}/docroot/WEB-INF/src` as follows:

```
public class ArticleFinderImpl
    extends BasePersistenceImpl<Article> implements ArticleFinder {
}
```

As shown in the preceding code, `ArticleFinderImpl` extends `BasePersistenceImpl` generated by the Service-Builder and implements `ArticleFinder`, which doesn't exist at the moment.

4. Run the Ant target `build-service`.

As you can see, the Service-Builder will generate a service interface such as `ArticleFinder` and a service utility such as `ArticleFinderUtil`.

5. Write the logic to access the custom query in `ArticleFinderImpl.java`. The following is the code snippet. Run the Ant target `build-service` again:

```
public List<Article> findBySubscription(
    long groupId, long userId, int start, int end)
    throws SystemException {// see details in ArticleFinderImpl.java
}
```

As shown in the preceding code, a new session is open and three parameters, `className Id`, `groupId`, and `userId`, get added. Obviously, the search results limit gets added by `start` and `end`. In addition, after running the Ant target `build-service`, the Service-Builder adds the signature `findBySubscription` in both `ArticleFinder.java` and `ArticleFinderUtil.java`.

> Note that you shouldn't use custom query when dynamic query API will do. That is, sometimes the dynamic query API still isn't enough and thus you need a custom query.

What's happening?

As mentioned earlier, in order to generate a custom query, we run the Ant target `build-service` twice. In the first instance, `ArticleFinderImpl` extends `BasePersistenceImpl` and implements `ArticleFinder`, which doesn't exist at the moment.

After running the Ant target `build-service` the first time, `ArticleFinder` and `ArticleFinderUtil` were generated. However, the custom signature, `findBySubscription`, is not generated yet. After running the Ant target `build-service` the second time, the custom signature `findBySubscription` is added in both `ArticleFinder` and `ArticleFinderUtil`.

First, the two templates `finder.ftl` and `find_util.ftl` were were used to generate `${entity.name}Finder` and `${entity.name}FinderUtil`, respectively. For example, both `ArticleFinder` and `ArticleFinderUtil` were generated when `${entity.name}` was equal to the entity `Article`. This is the reason that `${entity. name}Finder` and `${entity.name}FinderUtil` were generated separately.

Second, `ServiceBuilder.java` provides the following two methods to create Finder and FinderUtil.

```
_createFinder(Entity entity);
_createFinderUtil(Entity entity);
```

As shown in the preceding code, `ServiceBuilder.java` first loads `${entity.name}FinderImpl`. It then prepares the content with templates such as `finder.ftl` or `find_util.ftl`. Finally, it writes the files `${entity.name}Finder` and `${entity. name}FinderUtil`.

Security and permissions

Liferay implements a fine-grained permissions system, used to implement access security in custom plugins. The portal extends the security model by the following terminologies: resources, users, organizations, locations, user groups, communities, roles, permissions, and so on. That is, this is a role-based, fine-grained permission security model.

In order to add permissions in the custom portlets, generally, you would carry out the following four steps:

1. Defining all resources and their permissions — defining resources and permissions.

2. Registering all the resources in the permission system — registering resources.

3. Associating the permissions with resources — assigning permission.

4. Checking the permissions before returning the resources — checking permission.

Adding resources

First of all, define your resources and permissions in the custom plugin, for example, `knowledge-base-portlet`. You can create a folder named `resource-actions` in the folder `$PLUGINS_SDK_HOME/portlets/${portlet.name}/docroot/WEB-INF/src` and then add an XML file named `default.xml` inside that folder.

```
<?xml version="1.0"?>
<resource-action-mapping>
  <portlet-resource>
    <portlet-name>knowledge-base-admin</portlet-name>
    <permissions>
      <supports>
        <action-key>ACCESS_IN_CONTROL_PANEL</action-key>
        <action-key>CONFIGURATION</action-key>
        <action-key>VIEW</action-key>
      </supports>
      <community-defaults />
      <guest-defaults />
      //<!-- see details in default.xml -->
</resource-action-mapping>
```

As shown in the preceding code, there are three-level permission action definitions, namely, `portlet-level`, `portlet-instance-level`, and `model-level`. The tag `portlet-resource` defines actions and default permissions at the portlet-level, such as `knowledge-base-admin`. Changes to the `portlet-level` permissions are performed on a group (like community) basis. The settings state whether the users can add the portlet to the Control Panel, edit its configuration, or view the portlet. All these actions are defined inside the tag `supports`.

The default `portlet-level` permissions for members of the community are defined inside the tag `community-defaults`. Likewise, the default guest permissions are defined in the tag `guest-defaults`. The tag `guest-unsupported` contains permissions that a guest may never be granted, even by an administrator. For the portlet, `knowledge-base-admin`, guests can never be given permission to configure the portlet or access it in the Control Panel.

The `portlet-instance-level` permissions are defined based on the scope of an individual instance of the portlet. These permissions are defined in the tag `model-resource`. Note that the tag `model-name` isn't the name of an actual Java class, but simply that of the package.

The `model-level` permissions are defined based on the scope of an individual instance of the model. These permissions are defined in the tag `model-resource`, too. Within this tag, it defines the model name. Note that the model name must be the fully-qualified Java class name of the model.

Furthermore, in `portlet.properties`, add the following line of code:

```
resource.actions.configs=resource-actions/default.xml
```

As shown in the preceding code, it shows where the resource action configurations can be located. Note that the resource action configurations will be read from the class path.

What's happening?

In `PortletHotDeployListener.java`, the following code is specified:

```
String[] resourceActionConfigs = StringUtil.split(
  portletProperties.getProperty(PropsKeys.RESOURCE_ACTIONS_CONFIGS));
for (String resourceActionConfig : resourceActionConfigs)
  ResourceActionsUtil.read(
    servletContextName, portletClassLoader, resourceActionConfig);
}
```

As shown in the preceding code, it first gets the property `RESOURCE_ACTIONS_` `CONFIGS`. It then uses `ResourceActionsUtil.java` to read the action's keys and permission settings.

In fact, `ResourceActionsImpl.java` provides a detailed implementation as follows:

```
public List<String> getPortletNames();
// see details in ResourceActionsUtil.java
public List<String> getResourceActions(String name);
```

Registering permission

The portal includes a pretty flexible permission system based on the concepts of roles, permissions, and resources, providing several different implementations for the algorithm used to check whether a given user has permissions to perform certain actions.

Permission algorithm

RBAC stands for **Role Based Access Control**. It is a permissions system in which permissions are always assigned through roles. RBAC implementation was started in portal 5.1, as a way to improve the existing system, especially in terms of ease-of-use and performance. There are two algorithms for RBAC: 5 and 6. Algorithm 5 was introduced for portal 5.1 and above. It uses a regular, normalized implementation. Algorithm 6 was introduced in portal 6. Algorithm 6 is an improved version of Algorithm 5. It provides the exact functionality as that of Algorithm 5, but it uses bitwise operations for even greater speed.

The legacy algorithms 1-4 were used in portal 5 and below. They all offer the same functionality and more flexibility to assign permissions to users. By the way, algorithms 1-4 are changeable; algorithms 5-6 are changeable, too. Data migration of algorithms 1-4 to 5-6 (RBAC) is available, but the data migration of algorithms 5-6 (RBAC) to 1-4 is unavailable.

Permission actions registration

In fact, there are two new tables involved for permissions in algorithm 6: `ResourceAction` and `ResourcePermission`.

`ResourceAction` maps the permission names (such as `VIEW` and `UPDATE`) to a long number. This is done automatically on startup and it is cached for greater efficiency. Hot deployed portlets are given unique numbers too — this can only be initialized serially before the portal or portlets are available — so that the retrieval is thread-safe and very fast. In addition, the most logical as `VIEW` is a common `ResourceAction` among all the resources.

`ResourcePermission` stores the permission in one long number and the portal will do bitwise operations to check if a user has the appropriate permission actions.

By the way, the `View` permission on an object must be checked if the user has view permission on the parent container. Fortunately, the portal has specified the following property in `portal.properties`:

```
permissions.view.dynamic.inheritance=true
```

As shown in the preceding code, the portal sets the property `permissions.view. dynamic.inheritance` to `true` to automatically check the view permission on the parent categories or folders when checking the permission on a specific item. For example, if the property was set to `true` to be able to have access to a document, a user must have the view permission on the document's folder and all its parent folders.

In brief, the portal uses `ResourceLocalService*` for adding and removing resources when creating and / or removing the model and portlet resources.

Assigning permissions

Permissions can be added by the `liferay-security:permissionsURL` tag as follows. In addition, the `liferay-ui:icon` tag shows a permission icon to the user:

```
<liferay-security:permissionsURL
  modelResource="<%= Article.class.getName() %>"
  modelResourceDescription="<%= article.getTitle() %>"
  resourcePrimKey="<%= String.valueOf(article.getResourcePrimKey())
%>"
  var="permissionsURL"
/>
<liferay-ui:icon   image="permissions"   url="<%= permissionsURL %>"
/>
```

The preceding code shows how to expose the permission interface to the user. The tag `liferay-security:permissionsURL` is specified in the tag class `com.liferay. taglib.security.PermissionsURLTag` and the Tei class `PermissionsURLTei`. It has the required attributes such as `modelResource`, `modelResourceDescription`, and `resourcePrimKey`, and optional attributes such as `redirect`, `var`, `roleTypes`, and `windowState`.

The `modelResource` attribute is the fully-qualified Java object class name, while the `modelResourceDescription` attribute describes this model instance. The `resourcePrimKey` attribute represents the primary key of the model instance. The `var` attribute is the variable name—passed to the `liferay-ui:icon` tag so that the permission icon will have the proper URL link.

In fact, `EditRolePermissionsAction.java` defines the following code:

```
if (PropsValues.PERMISSIONS_USER_CHECK_ALGORITHM == 6) {
    ResourcePermissionServiceUtil.removeResourcePermission(
      themeDisplay.getScopeGroupId(), themeDisplay.getCompanyId(),
      name, scope, primKey, roleId, actionId);
}
// see details in EditRolePermissionsAction.java
if (scope == ResourceConstants.SCOPE_COMPANY) {
  ResourcePermissionServiceUtil.addResourcePermission(
  groupId, companyId, selResource, scope,
  String.valueOf(role.getCompanyId()), roleId, actionId);
}
```

As shown in the preceding code, it removes resource permission when `PERMISSIONS_USER_CHECK_ALGORITHM` is equal to 6. It adds resource permission when the scope is `SCOPE_COMPANY`. Of course, you can refer to the details in `ResourcePermissionServiceUtil.java`.

Checking permission

By default, the portal provides the interface `PermissionChecker` as follows:

```
public boolean hasOwnerPermission(long companyId, String name,
  long primKey, long ownerId, String actionId);
// see details in PermissionChecker.java
public boolean hasUserPermission(long groupId, String name,
  String primKey, String actionId, boolean checkAdmin);
```

In plugins, it would be better to implement their own permission checker. For example, `com.liferay.knowledgebase.service.permission.ArticlePermission` uses the above interface `PermissionChecker` with the following methods:

```
public static void check(PermissionChecker permissionChecker,
  Article article, String actionId)
// see details in ArticlePermission.java
public static boolean contains(PermissionChecker permissionChecker,
  long resourcePrimKey,  String actionId)
```

In JSP files, you can add the permission checker using `ArticlePermission` as follows:

```
<c:if test="<%= ArticlePermission.contains(permissionChecker, article,
ActionKeys.VIEW) %>">
<c:if test="<%= ArticlePermission.contains(permissionChecker, article,
ActionKeys.UPDATE) %>">
```

The preceding code checks the action keys VIEW and UPDATE. Similarly, you can check the other action keys, such as PERMISSIONS and DELETE.

What's happening?

There are two new tables involved for permissions in Algorithm 6: ResourceAction and ResourcePermission.

ResourceAction maps the permission action names to a long number. For example, when deploying the portlet knowledge-based-admin, you would see following data in the table ResourceAction. Note that this table only shows the sample data; the resourceAction ID values will vary.

resourceActionId (Long)	name (String)	actionId (String)	bitwiseValue (Long)
716	knowledge-base-admin_WAR_ knowledgebaseportlet	ACCESS_IN_ CONTROL_PANEL	2 (0000 0000 0000 0010)
717	knowledge-base-admin_WAR_ knowledgebaseportlet	CONFIGURATION	4 (0000 0000 0000 0100)
718	knowledge-base-admin_WAR_ knowledgebaseportlet	VIEW	1 (0000 0000 0000 0001)
729	com.liferay. knowledgebase.model. Article	UPDATE	64 (0000 0000 0100 0000)

As shown in the preceding table, the column resourceActionId shows a long resource action ID, which is generated automatically, that is, the number shown in this column is just a sample. The column name shows the string portlet name or the model name. If it was a portal core portlet, it would show the portlet name; if it was a plugin WAR, it would show the portlet name plus string _WAR_, and the plugin name such as knowledgebaseportlet. If it was a model name, it would show the model name such as com.liferay.knowledgebase.model.Article.

The column shows string action Id, that is, action keys specified in /resource-actions/default.xml, such as ACCESS_IN_CONTROL_PANEL, CONFIGURATION, VIEW, and UPDATE. The column, bitwiseValue, shows long the bitwise value is for each action key.

`ResourcePermission` stores the permission actions in one long number, and the portal will do bitwise operations to check if a user has proper permission actions. The following table shows an example:

resource PermissionId (Long)	companyId (Long)	name (String)	Scope (Integer)	primKey (String)	roleId (Long)	actionIds (Long)
4872	10132	knowledge-base-admin_WAR_knowledge baseportlet	4	10152_LAYOUT_knowledge-base-admin_WAR_knowledge baseportlet	10140	7

As shown in the preceding table, the column `resourcePermissionId` shows long resource permission IDs, generated automatically, that is, the number shown in this column is just a sample. The column `companyId` shows the long company ID (portal instance ID). The column `name` shows the string portlet name or the model name, which is the same as that in the table `ResourceAction`.

The column `scope` shows the integer scope of the resource constants. The full scope values are defined in `ResourceConstants.java` as follows:

```
public static final long PRIMKEY_DNE = -1;
// see details in ResourceConstants.java
public static final int SCOPE_COMPANY = 1;
```

As you can see, there are a set of scopes, such as `SCOPE_INDIVIDUAL`, `SCOPE_GROUP`, `SCOPE_GROUP_TEMPLATE`, and `SCOPE_COMPANY`.

The column `primKey` shows the string primary key and the column `roleId` shows the long associated role ID. More importantly, the column `actionId` shows the long actions IDs.

Similarly, the resource permission constants are specified in `ResourcePermissionConstants.java` as follows:

```
public static final int OPERATOR_ADD = 1;
public static final int OPERATOR_REMOVE = 2;
public static final int OPERATOR_SET = 3;
```

The preceding code shows operators such as `OPERATOR_ADD`, `OPERATOR_REMOVE`, and `OPERATOR_SET`.

In brief, when checking permission, only two tables get involved and memory costs are much lower. In addition, bitwise operations are of the lowest level, and the fastest operations you can perform.

For example, reconsidering the preceding tables, checking for the UPDATE permission is as simple as follows:

```
if ((actionIds & 64) == 64) { has permission }
```

As you can see, & is bitwise AND and | is bitwise OR. Generally speaking, checking for any permission can be presented as follows:

```
if ((actionIds & ACTION-KEY) == ACTION-KEY) { has permission }
```

As shown in the preceding code, ACTION-KEY could be VIEW, ACCESS_IN_CONTROL_PANEL, CONFIGURATION, and so on. As shown in the preceding table ResourcePermission, the role with the ID 10140 has the actions ID 7. It means that the role has the permission actions VIEW, ACCESS_IN_CONTROL_PANEL, and CONFIGURATION, since the following expressions are true:

```
(7 & 1 == 1)
(7 & 2 == 2)
(7 & 4 == 4)
```

JSR-286 defines a simple security scheme using portlet roles and their mapping to portal roles. On top of that, Liferay implements a fine-grained role-based permissions system with bitwise operations. Everything in the portal is secure, such as, portlet, portlet instance, and model.

Summary

This chapter first introduced how to develop a portlet project with the default templates. Then, it addressed how to construct basic MVC portlets by viewing the title and adding an action only, and how to build advanced MVC portlets. Finally, we discussed how to build and rebuild services, how to bring portlets into the Control Panel, how to set security and permissions, dynamic query, and custom SQL.

In the next chapter, we will discuss Ext plugin and hooks plugins.

4
Ext Plugin and Hooks

Ext plugin is a powerful tool to extend the Liferay portal core. There are almost no limits to what can be customized. Thus, the Ext plugin has to be used carefully. Ext plugin is designed to be used only in special scenarios where all other plugin types such as portlets, hooks, themes, layout templates, and webs cannot meet the needs.

Hooks can fill a wide variety of common needs for overriding the portal core functionality. Whenever possible, hooks should be used in place of the Ext plugin, as hooks are hot deployable and more forward compatible. There are common scenarios which require the use of a hook, for example, performing custom actions on portal startup or user login, overwriting or extending portal JSPs, modifying portal properties, replacing a portal service with custom implementation, modifying indexer post processors, and updating struts actions, servlet filters, and servlet filters mappings.

This chapter will first introduce the Ext plugin. Then, it will address the deployment process, especially for Ext plugins. Multiple languages will be addressed and class loader processes will be introduced afterwards. Finally, hooks will be addressed in detail.

By the end of this chapter, you will have learned how to:

- Use the Ext plugin
- Upgrade a legacy Ext environment
- Deploy processes
- Leverage class loader proxy
- Hook portal properties
- Hook language properties and multiple languages
- Hook custom JSP
- Hook indexer post processors

- Hook service wrappers
- Hook servlet filters and servlet mappings
- Hook struts actions

Ext plugin

The Extension environment (called **Ext environment**) provides the capability to customize the Liferay portal completely. As it is an environment which extends the Liferay portal development environment, it has the name Extension; its short form is Ext. By **Ext**, you would modify internal portlets (also called out-of-the-box portlets). Moreover, we would override the JSP files of the portal and out-of-the-box portlets.

Starting from Version 6, the Ext environment is available as a plugin called **Ext plugin**. Custom code will override the Liferay portal source code in the Ext plugin. In the deployment process, custom code is merged with the Liferay portal source code (that is, it will override files of the portal core). Ext plugins provide the most powerful methods of extending the Liferay portal core, designed to be used only in special scenarios in which all other plugin types cannot meet the needs.

Ext plugin project default template

In the previous chapter, we have discussed a set of default templates such as EAR, layout template, portlet, theme, and so on. Obviously, by using these templates you could build your own plugins projects easily. This section is going to introduce the Ext (**Ext** stands for **Extension**) plugin project default template.

Liferay plugins SDK provides the Ext plugin project default template, ext_tmpl. This default template has the following structure. The Ext plugin project folder name is represented as @ext.name@-ext. For example, @ext.name@ has a value hello-world for the plugin Hello World Ext. Under the folder @ext.name@-ext, there is a folder named docroot and the XML file build.xml. As you can see, build.xml has the following code:

```xml
<?xml version="1.0"?>
<!DOCTYPE project>
<project name="@ext.name@-ext" basedir="." default="deploy">
  <import file="../build-common-ext.xml" />
</project>
```

As shown in the preceding code, `@ext.name@` represents the real plugin name. When using the Ant target `create`, it will create a new Ext plugin project. Under the folder `docroot`, it includes a folder named `WEB-IBF`. The folder `WEB-INF` contains a set of subfolders and files, which are shown in the following table:

Folder name	Subfolders	Files	Description
ext-impl	src	portlal-ext. properties	Portal implementation extension
ext-lib	global portal	None	Portal and global dependencies extension
ext-service	src	None	Portal service extension
ext-util-bridge	src	None	Utility bridge extension
ext-util-java	src	None	Utility Java extension
ext-util-taglib	Src	None	Utility taglib extension
ext-web	docroot/ WEB-INF	liferay-portlet-ext.xml portlet-ext.xml strus-config-ext.xml tiles-defs-ext.xml web.xml	Portal web extension – including folder html/ common, /portal, / portlet, /icons, /js, /taglibs, / themes, and so on
sql	none	None	SQL scripts extension

Creating an Ext plugin project

Ant target `create` will create a new Ext plugin project based on two parameters (`ext.name` and `ext.display.name`) as follows:

```
ant -Dext.name=$1 -Dext.display.name=\"$2\" create
```

The first, `$1`, for `ext.name` is the Ext plugin name such as `hello-world`. A new directory will be created based on the Ext plugin name. The second, `$2`, for `ext.display.name` is the Ext plugin's display name such as `Hello World`. The quotation marks are only needed as there is a space in the display name.

In fact, you can refer to the Ant target `create` in `build.xml` as follows:

```
<target name="create">
<if>
<!-- see details in build.xml -->
<else>
```

```
<!-- see details in build.xml -->
<replace dir="${ext.parent.dir}/${ext.name}-ext">
<replacefilter token="@ext.name@" value="${ext.name}" />
<replacefilter token="@ext.display.name@" value="${ext.display.name}"
/>
</replace>
</else>
</if>
</target>
```

Advanced customization

As you can see, you would be able to change almost everything within Liferay when using the Ext plugin, therefore, be careful when using such a powerful tool, as implementation classes of new version may have changed. Thus if you have changed the Liferay source code directly, you may have to merge your changes into the newer version. An alternative approach to minimize these conflicts is that you don't change anything, but only extend the class you want to change and override the methods needed.

An Ext plugin will make changes to the Liferay portal itself, instead of staying as a separate component that can be removed at any time, for example, hooks and portlets. Once an Ext plugin has been deployed, some files are copied inside the Liferay portal installation, so that the only way to remove its changes is by redeploying an unmodified Liferay application. What is happening? Let's first have a look at the Ext plugin project structure by using the "Hello World" example.

The following table shows the Ext plugin folders, sample code, and portal core mapping:

Ext plugin folder	Sample	Portal core mapping	Description
ext-impl/src	com.liferay. portal.action. LoginAction portal-ext. properties	portal-impl.jar	It contains portal-ext. properties, configuration files, and custom implementation classes that override portal core classes within portal-impl.jar.
ext-lib/ global	ojdbc14.jar	lib/ext/*	It contains any library that should be copied to the global class loader of the application server.

Ext plugin folder	Sample	Portal core mapping	Description
`ext-lib/ portal`	`commons- configuration.jar`	`$PORTAL_ ROOT_HOME/ WEB-INF/ lib`	It contains any library that should be copied to `$PORTAL_ ROOT_HOME/WEB-INF/lib`.
`ext- service/ src`	`com.liferay. counter.service. CounterLocal ServiceUtil`	`portal- service. jar`	It contains classes that overwrite the classes of `portal-service.jar`.
`ext- util- bridges/ src`	`com.liferay.util. bridges.mvc. MVCPortlet`	`util- bridges. jar`	It contains classes that overwrite the classes of `util- bridges.jar`.
`ext- util- java/src`	`com.liferay.util. CookieUtil`	`util-java. jar`	It contains classes that overwrite the classes of `util- java.jar`.
`ext- util- taglib/ src`	`com.liferay. taglib.util. IncludeTag`	`util- taglib.jar`	It contains classes that overwrite the classes of `util- taglib.jar`.

As mentioned earlier, several files are added to the Ext plugin by default. The following table shows these files:

File name	Location	Portal core Reference	Description
`portal-ext. properties`	`ext-impl/ src`	`portal. properties` in the folder `$PORTAL_ SRC_HOME/ portal-impl/ src`	It overwrites any configuration property of Liferay, even those that cannot be overridden by a hook plugin. If this file is included, it will be read instead of any other `portal- ext.properties` in the application server.
`liferay- display.xml`	`ext-web/ docroot/ WEB-INF`	`liferay- display.xml`	It overwrites the portlets that will be shown in the "Add application" pop-up panel and the categories in which they are organized. This is done to change the categorization, hide portlets, or make Control Panel portlets available to be added to a page.

File name	Location	Portal core Reference	Description
`liferay-portlet-ext.xml`	`ext-web/ docroot/ WEB-INF`	`liferay-portlet.xml`	It overwrites the definition of a Liferay portlet. To do so, copy the complete definition of the desired portlet from `liferay-portlet.xml` within the portal core source code and then apply the necessary changes.
`portlet-ext.xml`	`ext-web/ docroot/ WEB-INF`	`portlet-custom.xml`	It overwrites the additional definition elements of a Liferay portlet. To do so, copy the complete definition of the desired `portlet` `from` `portlet-custom.xml` within the portal core source code and then apply the necessary changes.
`liferay-layout-templates-ext.xml`	`ext-web/ docroot/ WEB-INF`	`liferay-layout-templates.xml`	It specifies custom template files for each of the layout templates provided by default with Liferay.
`liferay-look-and-feel-ext. xml`	`ext-web/ docroot/ WEB-INF`	`liferay-look-and-feel.xml`	It changes the properties of the default themes provided by default with Liferay.
`strus-config-ext. xml`	`ext-web/ docroot/ WEB-INF`	`strus-config. xml`	It customizes the struts actions used by Liferay's core portlets.
`tiles-defs-ext.xml`	`ext-web/ docroot/ WEB-INF`	`tiles-defs.xml`	It customizes the struts tiles definition used by Liferay's core portlets.
`web.xml`	`ext-web/ docroot/ WEB-INF`	`web.xml`	It customizes `web.xml`.

Similar to the preceding files, you can overwrite other files in the folder `$PORTAL_SRC_HOME/portal-web/docroot/WEB-INF` such as `liferay-plugin-package.xml`, `liferay-web.xml`, `urlrewrite.xml`, and so on. That is, `ext-web` contains `/WEB-INF/*-ext.xml` files that are used to override what is in `portal-web`.

Note that if you modify `ext-web/docroot/WEB-INF/web.xml`, then these changes are merged into `portal-web/WEB-INF/web.xml`.

Advanced configuration

Liferay portal uses several internal configuration files for easier maintenance, and to configure the libraries and frameworks it depends on, such as Struts and Spring. Thus it may be useful to override the configuration specified in these files; this is a clean way to do so from an Ext plugin without modifying the original files.

The following table shows these configuration files and the original file — the portal core reference in `$PORTAL_SRC_HOME/portal-impl/src/META-INF/`:

Ext configuration file	Location	Portal core reference	Description
`ext-model-hints.xml`	`ext-impl/src/META-INF`	`portal-model-hints.xml`	It overwrites the default properties of the fields of data models used by Liferay's core portlets. These properties determine how the form to create or edit each model is rendered.
`ext-spring.xml`	`ext-impl/src/META-INF`	`*-spring.xml`	It overwrites the Spring configuration used by Liferay and its core portlets, for example, it configures specific datasources or swaps the implementation of a given service with a custom one.
`portal-log4j-ext.xml`	`ext-impl/src/META-INF`	`portal-log4j.xml`	It overwritesthe the log4j configuration to increase or decrease the log level of a given package or class to obtain more information or hide unneeded information from the logs, respectively.
`Language-ext_*.properties`	`ext-impl/src/content`	`Language_*.properties`	It overwritesthe value of any key to support I18N.
`repository-ext.xml`	`ext-impl/src/com/liferay/portal/jcr/jackrabbit/dependencies/`	`repository.xml`	It overwrites the configuration of the Jackrabbit repository

Advanced portal core API overwriting

In the Ext plugin, you can overwrite the portal core API. In some scenarios, you may need to change the API of a method provided by Liferay's services, for example, `UserLocalService`, `GroupLocalService`, and so on. In brief, you would be able to overwrite `portal-impl`, `portal-service`, `util-bridges`, `util-java`, and `util-taglib`, as shown in the following table:

Sample	Package path	Ext location	Portal core location	Description
LoginAction.java	com. liferay. portal. action	ext- impl/src	portal- impl/src	Overwrite `portal-impl`; Package path must be exactly the same as that of the portal core
CounterLocal ServiceUtil.java	com. liferay. counter. service	ext- service/ src	portal- service/ src	Overwrite `portal-service` The class name must be exactly the same as that of the portal core
MVCPortlet.java	com. liferay. util. bridges. mvc	ext- util- bridges/ src	util- bridges/ src	Overwrite `util-bridges`
CookieUtil.java	com. liferay. util	ext- util- java/src	util- java/src	Overwrite `util-java`
IncludeTag.java	com. liferay. taglib. util	ext- util- taglib/ src	util- taglib/ src	Overwrite `util-taglib`

> As you can see, you would be able to overwrite anything in the portal core API. To do so, keep in mind that package path in the Ext plugin must be exactly the same as that of the portal core; and class case-sensitive name must be exactly the same as that of the portal core. Note that you should not add a new field to a model class or not use the Service-Builder to generate new models and services in Ext plugins.

Generally speaking, the best way to extend an existing service is by creating a complementary custom service. It will invoke this custom service instead of the default service. For example, you desire to change the implementation of the original service, such as `UserLocalServiceImpl`, to call your custom one `ExtUserLocalServiceImpl`, you can leverage the Ext plugin. To achieve this, override the Spring definition for `UserLocalServiceUtil` in `ext-spring.xml` and point it to your implementation `ExtUserLocalServiceImpl`, instead of the default `UserLocalServiceImpl`. Thus, both `ExtUserLocalServiceUtil` and `UserLocalServiceUtil` will use the same Spring bean, that is, `ExtUserLocalServiceImpl`.

Advanced portal web overwriting

Similarly, you can overwrite any files of portal web in the Ext plugin. `ext-web/docroot/html` contains the code that will override the code in `portal-web/docroot/html`. It covers JSP files, JavaScript files, HTML files, image files, CSS files, and so on. The following table shows these files and their mappings to that of `portal-web`:

Folder	Sample	Ext location	Portal web location	Description
common	bottom-ext. jsp	/common/ themes	/common/ themes	Overwrites common JSP files and common themes JSP files
icons	calendar. png	/icons	/icons	Overwrites image files
js	browser.css	/js/editor/ ckeditor/ editor/ filemanager/ browser/ liferay	/js/editor/ ckeditor/ editor/ filemanager/ browser/ liferay	Overwrites CSS files
js	ckconfig.js	/js/editor/ ckeditor	/js/editor/ ckeditor	Overwrites JavaScript files
js	frmfolders. html	/js/editor/ ckeditor/ editor/ filemanager/ browser/ liferay	/js/editor/ ckeditor/ editor/ filemanager/ browser/ liferay	Overwrites HTML files
portal	j_login.jsp	/portal	/portal	Overwrite the UI in the portal level like aui, CSS, layout

Folder	Sample	Ext location	Portal web location	Description
portlet	login.jsp	/portlet/login	/portlet/login	Overwrite out-of-the-box portlets UI: JSP and CSS
taglib	init-ext.jsp	/taglib	/taglib	Overwrite taglib UI: aui, portlet, theme, ui tag
themes	portal_normal.ftl	/themes/classic/templates	/themes/classic/templates	Overwrite default themes: classic and control panel
VAADIN	styles.css	/VAADIN/themes/liferay	/VAADIN/themes/liferay	Overwrite Vaadin themes and widgets

Of course, you can overwrite files in other folders such as errors, layouttpl, wap, and so on. The following table shows the folders with sample code:

Folder	sample	ext-web	portal-web	Description
errors	404.jsp	/docroot	/docroot	404 error page
custom	1_2_1_columns.tpl	/docroot/layouttpl	/docroot/layouttpl	Layout template custom file
standard	pop_up.tpl	/docroot/layouttpl	/docroot/layouttpl	Layout template standard files
common	init.jsp	/docroot/wap	/docroot/wap	WAP theme common JSP
portal	layout.jsp	/docroot/wap	/docroot/wap	WAP theme portal layout JSP
templates	portal_normal.vm	/docroot/wap/themes	/docroot/wap/themes	WAP default theme VM
jsp	_servlet_context_include.jsp	/docroot/WEB-INF	/docroot//WEB-INF	Include JSP servlet context

As you can see, the Ext plugin is the most powerful tool to extend the portal core. You can do almost anything in the Ext plugin, including generating services, models, and SQL scripts.

Note that support for Service-Builder in Ext plugins will be deprecated in future versions, thus it is not recommended to use Service-Builder in Ext plugins.

Ext plugins are designed to override the portal core code that cannot be done with hooks, layout templates, portlets, or themes. The Ext plugin is not meant to contain new custom services. Thus try to migrate `service.xml` of 5.x to a portlet plugin.

By the way, if you are using `ext-ejb` instead of `ext-impl`, you must first upgrade to Liferay 5.2 and then migrate your code to the Ext plugin.

Upgrading a legacy Ext environment

The Ext plugin is an evolution of the extension environment provided in 5.2 and previous versions. Thus, the extension environment needs to be migrated into the Ext plugin.

Ant target `upgrade-ext` within `ext/build.xml` provides capability to upgrade the old extension environment into the Ext plugin. Supposed that the old extension environment folder is `/workspace/ext`, and the Ext plugin name is `hello-world`, you can run the following Ant target.

```
ant upgrade-ext -Dext.dir=/workspace/ext -Dext.name=hello-world -Dext.
display.name="Hello World"
```

As you can see, `ext.dir` is a command line argument to the location of the old Extension environment, such as `/workspace/ext`, `ext.name` is the name of the Ext plugin that you want to create, like `hello-world`, and `ext.display.name` is the display name, saying "Hello World".

This task will build an Ext plugin from a legacy Ext environment. The files in the directory, denoted by `${ext.dir}`, will be copied into the Ext plugin directory named `${ext.name}-ext`. The property `${ext.dir}` must point to a legacy Ext environment and the Ext plugin directory named `${ext.name}-ext` must not already exist.

After executing the Ant target `upgrade-ext`, you would see the logs taking files from the Ext environment and copying them into the equivalent directory within the Ext plugin.

What's happening?

The Ant target `upgrade-ext` has been defined in `build.xml` as follows:

```
<target name="upgrade-ext">
<!-- see details in build.xml -->
<copy todir="${ext.name}-ext/docroot/WEB-INF/ext-impl/src"
failonerror="false">
  <fileset dir="${ext.dir}/ext-impl/src" />
</copy>
<copy todir="${ext.name}-ext/docroot/WEB-INF/ext-lib/global"
failonerror="false">
  <fileset dir="${ext.dir}/ext-lib/global" />
</copy>
<!-- see details in build.xml -->
</target>
```

As you can see in the preceding code, it takes files from the Ext environment and copies them into the equivalent directory within the Ext plugin.

In addition, you would find other Ant targets such as `create` specified in `build.xml`, and more Ant targets defined in `build-common-plugin.xml` such as `merge`, `deploy`, `direct-deploy`, `compile`, `build-wsdd`, `build-service`, `build-db`, `build-client`, and so on.

Deploy processes

In general, there are at least three deploying approaches: **sandbox deploy**, **auto deploy**, and **hot deploy**. The real deploy process could start from sandbox deploy or auto deploy first, then goes to the hot deploy. It could also start from hot deploy directly, like using the portlet `Plugins Installation` in the Control Panel.

In particular, there are two methods for deploying and redeploying Ext plugins in production: **redeploying plugin WAR file** and **generating an aggregated WAR file**.

The method **redeploying plugin WAR file** can be used in any application server that supports auto deploy such as **Tomcat**, **JBoss**, and so on. The only artifact that needs to be transferred to the production system is the `.war` file, produced using the Ant target `deploy`. To do so, you need to copy the Ext plugin `.war` into the auto deploy directory. Once the Ext plugin is detected and deployed, restart the portal server.

The method of **generating an aggregated WAR file** can be used for application servers that don't support auto deploy such as WebSphere, Weblogic, and so on. All Ext plugins are merged before deployment to production, so that a single .war file will contain the portal plus the changes from Ext plugins. To do so, you can deploy the Ext plugin first to the portal Tomcat bundle. Once it is deployed, you could create a .war file by zipping the folder $CATALINA_HOME/webapps/ROOT. In particular, you need to copy all the libraries from the directory $CATALINA_HOME/lib/ext, associated with all the Ext plugins, to the application server's global class-path.

> Note that we must be careful, because Weblogic randomly reads WEB-INF/lib libraries, so we have 50 percent of changes that our Ext plugin can deploy. If Weblogic read portal-impl.jar first, then we would not see the changes on the site.

What's happening?

After deployment, you would see the results of the Ext plugin in the application server. The following table shows the original files in the Ext plugin and targets files in the application server:

Ext plugin location	Application server location	Description
ext-service/ src	$CATALINA_HOME/lib/ext/ ext-${ext.name}-ext-service.jar	Overwrite portal service
ext-lib/ global/ ojdbc14.jar	$CATALINA_HOME/lib/ext/ ojdbc14.jar	Overwrite global lib
ext-lib/ portal/ commons-configuration. jar	$PORTAL_ROOT_HOME/ WEB-INF/lib/ commons-configuration.jar	Overwrite portal lib
ext-impl/src	$PORTAL_ROOT_HOME/WEB-INF/lib/ ext-${ext.name}-ext-impl.jar	Overwrite the portal implementation
ext-util-bridges/src	$PORTAL_ROOT_HOME/WEB-INF/lib/ ext-${ext.name}-ext-util-bridges.jar	Overwrite the portal bridges utilities
ext-util-java/ src	$PORTAL_ROOT_HOME/WEB-INF/lib/ ext-${ext.name}-ext-util-java.jar	Overwrite the portal Java utilities

Ext plugin location	Application server location	Description
`ext-util-taglib/src`	`$PORTAL_ROOT_HOME/WEB-INF/lib/ ext-${ext.name}-ext-util-taglib.jar`	Overwrite the portal taglib utilities
`ext-web/docroot/html/common/themes/bottom-ext.jsp`	`$PORTAL_ROOT_HOME/ html/common/themes/bottom-ext.jsp, bottom-ext.jsp.backup`	The original file `${file.name}` is renamed to `${file.name}.backup`.
`ext-web/docroot /WEB-INF/struts-config-ext.xml`	`$PORTAL_ROOT_HOME/WEB-INF/ struts-config-ext.xml, struts-config-ext.xml.backup`	If the same file doesn't exist, add this file directly as we did with `liferay-portlet-ext.xml`, `portlet-ext.xml`, and `tiles-defs-ext.xml`. Otherwise, the original file `${file.name}` is renamed to `${file.name}.backup`.

An XML file named `ext-${ext.name}-ext.xml` was generated in `$PORTAL_ROOT_HOME/WEB-INF`. The following is a snippet of the Ext plugin "hello-world":

```
<ext-info>
  <servlet-context-name>hello-world-ext</servlet-context-name>
  <files>
   <file>ext-impl/classes/com/liferay/portal/action/LoginAction.class
   </file>
    <!-- see details in ext-${ext.name}-ext.xml -->
  </files>
</ext-info>
```

Deployer

In fact, the portal provides a service interface `Deployer` as follows:

```
public void copyDependencyXml(String fileName, String targetDir)
throws Exception;
// see details in Deployer.java
public void updateWebXml(File webXml, File srcFile, String
displayName, PluginPackage pluginPackage)throws Exception;
```

As shown in the preceding code, the `Deployer` provides interfaces to copy dependency XML, JAR files, property files, TLD files, and XML files.

The interface `Deployer` was implemented by the abstract class `BaseDeployer`, and is furthermore extended by `ExtDeployer`, `HookDeployer`, `LayoutTemplateDeployer`, `PortletDeployer`, `ThemeDeployer`, and `WebDeployer`.

> Note that if you deploy your plugin, the `deployer` will unpack it, change `web.xml` and other XML files, and pack it again. If you directly copy the WAR file to the folder `webapps`, the plugin won't work.

Sandbox deploy

Sandbox deploy requires a directory, which is defined in the class `SandboxDeployDir`. The portal specified the following properties for sandbox deploy in `portal.properties`:

```
sandbox.deploy.listeners=\
// see details in portal.properties
sandbox.deploy.dir=${liferay.home}/sandbox
sandbox.deploy.interval=10000
```

As shown in the preceding code, sandbox-style plugins are limited to `portlet` and `theme`. In addition, you can enable/disable the sandbox-style plugin development as well. The portal also sets the directory `${liferay.home}/sandbox` to scan for sandbox style plugins, and it sets the interval in milliseconds on how often to scan the directory for changes.

Actually, the `SandboxDeployDir` class defined the methods to handle the preceding settings, and it has the following methods:

```
getDeployDir()
getInterval()
getListeners()
// see details in SandboxDeployDir.java
start()
stop()
```

The `SandboxHandler` interface defines the following interfaces: `deploy`, `undeploy`, and `getdisplayName`:

```
public static final String SANDBOX_MARKER = "-SANDBOX-";
// see details in SandboxHandler.java
public void undeploy(File dir) throws SandboxDeployException;
```

The interface SandboxHandler was implemented by the class BaseSandboxHandler and extended by PortletSandboxHandler and ThemeSandboxHandler. In particular, BaseSandboxHandler uses Deployer as its construction parameter.

The class SandboxDeployScanner uses the class SandboxDeployerDir to auto scan plugins in the folder ${liferay.home}/sandbox, while setting the interval in milliseconds.

In addition, the utility class SandboxDeployUtil defined a set of functions such as getDir, registerDir, and unregisterDir. Of course, you can leverage this utility in your plugins for the sandbox deploy.

```
public static SandboxDeployDir getDir(String name) {}
public static void registerDir(SandboxDeployDir sandboxDeployDir) {}
public static void unregisterDir(String name) {}
```

Sandbox deploy listener

The sandbox deploy listener, SandboxDeployListener, defines the following interfaces: deploy and undeploy.

```
public void deploy(File dir) throws SandboxDeployException;
public void undeploy(File dir) throws SandboxDeployException;
```

The SandboxDeployListener was implemented by the classes PortletSandboxDeployListener and ThemeSandboxDeployListener only. This is the reason that why the sandbox deploy currently only supports the plugins theme and portlet. If you need support on other plugin types such as Ext and hook, you can write your own custom classes such as ExtSandboxDeployListener and HookSandboxDeployListener, implementing the interface SandboxDeployListener.

Auto deploy

Similar to the sandbox deploy, auto deploy requires a directory, which is defined in the class autoDeployDir. The portal specified the following properties for auto deploy in portal.properties:

```
auto.deploy.listeners=\
  com.liferay.portal.deploy.auto.ExtAutoDeployListener,\
  com.liferay.portal.deploy.auto.HookAutoDeployListener,\
  // see details in portal.properties
auto.deploy.enabled=true
auto.deploy.deploy.dir=${liferay.home}/deploy
auto.deploy.dest.dir=
// see details in portal.properties
```

As shown in the preceding code, the property `auto.deploy.deploy.dir` sets the directory to scan for layout templates, hooks, Ext, portlets, webs, and themes to auto deploy. The property `auto.deploy.dest.dir` sets the directory where auto deployed WAR files are copied. The application server or servlet container must know how to listen on that directory. Different containers have different hot deploy paths. For example, Tomcat listens on `${catalina.base}/webapps` whereas JBoss listens on `${jboss.server.home.dir}/deploy`. The property `auto.deploy.dest.dir` sets a blank directory to automatically use the application's server-specific directory.

The property `auto.deploy.custom.portlet.xml` is set to `true` if you want the deployer to rename `portlet.xml` to `portlet-custom.xml`. This is only needed when deploying the portal on WebSphere `6.1.x` with a version before `6.1.0.7`, since WebSphere's portlet container will try to process a portlet at the same time that Liferay is trying to process a portlet.

The property, `auto.deploy.tomcat.conf.dir`, sets the path to Tomcat's configuration directory. This property is used to auto deploy exploded WAR files. Tomcat context XML fields found in the auto deploy directory will be copied to Tomcat's configuration directory. The context XML file must have the attribute `docBase` pointing to a valid WAR directory.

The property `auto.deploy.tomcat.lib.dir` sets the path to Tomcat's global class loader. Note that this property is only used by Tomcat in a standalone environment.

In fact, the class `AutoDeployDir` defined the methods to handle the preceding settings, and it has following methods:

```
getDeployDir()
getDestDir()
getInterval()
start()
stop()
```

The class `AutoDeployScanner` uses the class `AutoDeployerDir` to auto scan plugins in the folder `${liferay.home}/deploy`, with the interval set in milliseconds.

Similar to the class `SandboxDeployUtil`, the utility class `AutoDeployUtil` defined a set of functions such as `getDir`, `registerDir`, and `unregisterDir`. Obviously, you can leverage this utility in your plugins for the auto deploy feature.

```
public static autoDeployDir getDir(String name) {}
public static void registerDir(AutoDeployDir autoDeployDir) {}
public static void unregisterDir(String name) {}
```

Auto deploy listener

Similar to the hot deploy listener `HotDeployListener`, the interface `AutoDeployListener` defined an interface `deploy` to auto deploy plugins.

```
public void deploy(File file) throws AutoDeployException;
```

The interface `AutoDeployListener` was implemented in the abstract class `BaseAutoDeployListener`. This abstract class provides a set of functions, as shown in the following table:

Methods	Input	Conditions	Description
`isExtPlugin`	File	`file.getName().contains("-ext")`	Test if it is an Ext plugin
`isHookPlugin`	File	`isMatchingFile(file, "WEB-INF/liferay-plugin-package.properties") && (file.getName().contains("-hook")) && (!file.getName().contains("-portlet"))`	Test if it is a hook plugin and not a portlet plugin
`isThemePlugin`	File	`isMatchingFile(file, "WEB-INF/liferay-look-and-feel.xml") ||` `(isMatchingFile(file, "WEB-INF/liferay-plugin-package.properties") && file.getName().contains("-theme"))`	Test if it is a theme plugin
`isWebPlugin`	File	`isMatchingFile(file, "WEB-INF/liferay-plugin-package.properties") && file.getName().contains("-web")`	Test if it is a web plugin
`isMatchingFile`	File, String	`!isMatchingFileExtension(file)`	Test if a file is matched with the target file
`isMatchingFileExtension`	File	`fileName.endsWith(".war") || fileName.endsWith(".zip")`	Test if a filename has the extensions `.war` or `.zip`

The class `BaseAutoDeployListener` was extended in a set of classes such as `ExtAutoDeployListener`, `HookAutoDeployListener`, `layoutTemplateAutoDeployListener`, `PortletAutoDeployListener`, `ThemeAutoDeployListener`, and `WebAutoDeployListener`. This is the reason that auto deploy supports all plugins types such as `Ext`, hook, `layout-template`, `portlet`, and web.

Auto deployer

The interface `AutoDeployer` defines the interface `autoDeploy` as follows:

```
public void autoDeploy(String file) throws AutoDeployException;
```

This interface (`AutoDeployer`) was implemented by a set of classes, such as `ExtAutoDeployer`, `ExtAutoListener`, `HookAutoDeployer`, `HookAutoListener`, `PortletAutoDeployer`, `PortletAutoListener`, and so on. Moreover, the class `ExtAutoDeployer` extends the class `ExtDeploy` and implements the interface `AutoDeployer`.

The class `ExtDeployer` extends the abstract class `BaseDeployer`. More specifically, the method named `getExtraContent` defined the Ext context listener `ExtContextListener` as follows:

```
StringBundler sb = new StringBundler(6);
// see details in ExtContextListener.java
sb.append("<listener>");
sb.append("<listener-class>");
sb.append("com.liferay.portal.kernel.servlet.ExtContextListener");
sb.append("</listener-class>");
sb.append("</listener>");
return sb.toString();
```

In particular, the abstract class `BaseDeployer` consumes the class `ExtRegistry` and provides a set of methods, as shown in the following table. Note that the table does not provide a full list of methods. For example, a set of methods such as `deploy`, `deployDirectory`, `deployFile`, and so on, is not included.

Methods	References and Conditions	Description
addExtJar	`ExtRegister`, `DeployUtil`; `"ext-" + servletContextName + resource. substring(3);`	Add a prefix `ext-`
addRequiredJar	`DeployUtil`;	Add the required JAR files

Methods	References and Conditions	Description
`checkArguments`	`ServerDetector;`	Application server types:
	`baseDir, destDir, appServerType, jbossPerfix`	`ServerDetector.GERONIMO_ID, ServerDetector.GLASSFISH_ ID, ServerDetector.JBOSS_ID, ServerDetector.JONAS_ID, ServerDetector.JETTY_ID, ServerDetector.OC4J_ID, ServerDetector.RESIN_ID, ServerDetector.TOMCAT_ID, ServerDetector.WEBLOGIC_ID, ServerDetector.WEBSPHERE_ID`
`copyDependency Xml`	`DeployUtil;`	Copy dependency XML files
`copyJars`	`ServerDetector;`	Copy JARs
`copyPortal Dependencies`	`StringUtil, PortalUtil, DeployUtil;`	Copy portal dependencies: `jars, tdls, commons-logging*.jar, log4j*.jar`
`copyProperties`	`copyDependencyXml`	Copy properties: `log4j. properties, logging. properties`
`copyTlds`	`FileUtil;`	Copy TLD files:
	`auiTaglibDTD, portletTaglibDTD, portletExtTaglibDTD, securityTaglibDTD, themeTaglibDTD, uiTaglibDTD, utilTaglibDTD`	`liferay-aui.tld, liferay-portlet.tld, liferay-portlet-ext.tld, liferay-security.tld, liferay-theme.tld, liferay-ui.tld, liferay-util.tld`
`copyXmls`	`ServerDetector;`	Copy XML files: `geronimo-web. xml` or `weblogic.xml` or `ibm-web-ext.xmi;`
		and `web.xml`

Hot deploy

The portal specified the following property for hot deploy in `portal.properties`:

```
hot.deploy.listeners=\
    com.liferay.portal.deploy.hot.PluginPackageHotDeployListener,\
    com.liferay.portal.deploy.hot.ExtHotDeployListener,\
```

```
com.liferay.portal.deploy.hot.HookHotDeployListener,\
// see details in portal.properties
com.liferay.portal.deploy.hot.MessagingHotDeployListener
```

As shown in the preceding code, hot-deploy supports most plugins types, including `Ext`, `hook`, `layout-template`, `portlet`, plus plugin package, theme loader, and messaging.

The class `HotDeployEvent` defined a set of methods, specifying the context class loader, dependent servlet context names, plugin packages, and servlet content as follows.

```
public HotDeployEvent(ServletContext servletContext, ClassLoader
contextClassLoader) {}
public ClassLoader getContextClassLoader() { }
// see details in HotDeployEvent.java
protected void initDependentServletContextNames(){}
```

Based on the class `HotDeployEvent`, the utility class `HotDeployUtil` defined a set of functions such as `fireDeployEvent`, `fireUnDeployEvent`, `registerListener`, `reset`, `setCapturePrematureEvents`, and `unregisterListersener(s)`. Obviously, you can leverage this utility in your plugins for hot deploy.

```
public static void fireDeployEvent(HotDeployEvent event) {}
public static void fireUndeployEvent(HotDeployEvent event) {}
// see details in HotDeployUtil.java
public static void unregisterListeners() {}
```

Hot deploy listener

Based on the class `HotDeployEvent`, the interface `HotDeployListener` defined interfaces `invokeDeploy` and `invokeUndeploy` to invoke deploy or undeploy events, respectively.

```
public void invokeDeploy(HotDeployEvent event) throws
HotDeployException;
public void invokeUndeploy(HotDeployEvent event) throws
HotDeployException;
```

The interface was implemented in the abstract class `BaseHotDeployListener`, extended in a set of classes such as `ExtHotDeployListener`, `HookHotDeployListener`, `layoutTemplateHotDeployListener`, `MessagingHotDeployListener`, `PluginPackageHotDeployListener`, `PortletHotDeployListener`, `ThemeHotDeployListener`, and `ThemeLoaderHotDeployListener`. This is the reason that hot deploy supports most plugins types, such as `Ext`, `hook`, `layout-template`, and `portlet`, plus the plugin packages, theme loader and messaging. As you can see, the hot deploy does not support the plugin type `web`.

Let's have a deep look at the class `ExtHotDeployListener`. The class `HookHotDeployListener` will be addressed in detail in the coming section; while the rest of the classes will be addressed in the coming chapters.

The class `ExtHotDeployListener` extends the abstract class `BaseHotDeployListener` and implements the interface `HotDeployListener`. It uses the class `ExtRegistry` to register the plugin type Ext. The class `ExtRegistry` defined the following methods: `getFiles`, `unregisterExt`, `getConflicts`, `getServletContextNames`, `isRegistered`, `registerExt`, and `registerPortal`.

```
public static Set<String> getFiles(String servletContextName){}
public static void unregisterExt(String servletContextName){}
// see details in ExtRegistry.java
public static void registerPortal(ServletContext servletContext)
throws Exception {}
```

The class `ExtHotDeployListener` implements the methods `invokeDeploy` and `invokeUndeploy`, as shown in the following table:

Methods	Method references	Description
doInvokeDeploy (event)	invokeDeploy(HotDeployEvent event)	Deploy the Ext plugin
doInvokeUndeploy (event)	invokeUndeploy(HotDeployEvent event)	Undeploy the Ext plugin
copyJar	installExt(ServletContext servletContext, ClassLoader portletClassLoader)	Copy JAR files
copyWebFiles	installExt(ServletContext servletContext, ClassLoader portletClassLoader)	Copy web files
mergeWebXml	installExt(ServletContext servletContext, ClassLoader portletClassLoader)	Merge web XML files
removeJar	installExt(ServletContext servletContext, ClassLoader portletClassLoader)	Remove JAR files
resetPortal WebFiles	uninstallExt (String servletContextName)	Reset portal web files
resetWebXml	uninstallExt (String servletContextName)	Reset web XML files
installExt	doInvokeDeploy(HotDeployEvent event)	Install the Ext
uninstallExt	doInvokeUndeploy(Hot DeployEvent event)	Uninstall the Ext

Class loader proxy

Class loader proxy would be useful to share plugins services among different plugins. For example, let's say you have two plugins, `chat-portlet` and `knowledge-base-portlet`. Each one has its own WAR file. One of them, let's say `chat-portlet`, has a service named `StatusLocalService` and the service layer `StatusLocalServiceUtil`. Moreover, the second portlet, let's say `knowledge-base-portlet`, needs to use the service `StatusLocalServiceUtil.getStatuses` in order to find out who is online or offline. The class loader proxy class can achieve these requirements easily.

> Note that the portal core and built-in portlets services were deployed on an application server global lib, while the plugin services were deployed on the plugin's lib by default. It is also possible that you can deploy the plugin services on an application server global lib, thus these services will be shared among other plugins, even the portal core and built-in portlets.

The class `com.liferay.portal.kernel.util.ClassLoaderProxy` was defined in the `portal-service`. Thus this class is accessible in plugins. The class `ClassLoaderProxy` provides the following methods and attributes:

```
public ClassLoaderProxy(Object obj, ClassLoader classLoader){}
// see details in ClassLoaderProxy.java
private String _className;
```

As shown in the preceding code, the method `invoke` uses a class named `MethodHandler`, which implements the interface `Serializable`. These classes serialize model entities across web applications, so that they can be shared.

The class `MethodHandler` defines the following methods and attributes:

```
public Object[] getArguments() {}// see details in MethodHandler.java
private MethodKey _methodKey;
```

Generating the class loader proxy

In `service_clp.ftl`, Service-Builder specified the following code for the class `${entity.name}${sessionTypeName}ServiceClp`, where `${entity.name}` represents an entity name such as `Status` in `chat-portlet`, `${sessionTypeName}` represents the session type name such as `local`, and **Clp** is short for the class loader proxy.

```
public ${entity.name}${sessionTypeName}ServiceClp(ClassLoaderProxy
    classLoaderProxy) {
    _classLoaderProxy = classLoaderProxy;
```

```
        <#list methods as method>
          <#if !method.isConstructor() &&
              method.isPublic() && serviceBuilder.isCustomMethod(method)>
            <#assign parameters = method.parameters>
            _${method.name}MethodKey${method_index} =
              new MethodKey(_classLoaderProxy.getClassName(),
                "${method.name}"
            <#list parameters as parameter>
              , ${serviceBuilder.getLiteralClass(parameter.type)}
            </#list>
            );
          </#if>
        </#list>
}
```

The preceding code is the pattern for the ServiceClp class. For example, the class KBArticleLocalServiceClp has been generated as follows:

```
public class KBArticleLocalServiceClp implements KBArticleLocalService
{
public KBArticleLocalServiceClp(ClassLoaderProxy classLoaderProxy) {
_classLoaderProxy = classLoaderProxy;
_addKBArticleMethodKey0 = new MethodKey(_classLoaderProxy.
getClassName(), "addKBArticle", com.liferay.knowledgebase.model.
KBArticle.class);
// see details in the KBArticleLocalServiceClp.java
```

Once we run Ant target build-service, the class ${entity.
name}${sessionTypeName}ServiceClp will be generated for each entity such
as ArticleLocalServiceClp in knowledge-base-portlet, where the class
ClassLoaderProxy is the only parameter for the construction method.

In service_util.ftl, service builder defines the following ClassLoaderProxy for
the class ${entity.name}${sessionTypeName}ServiceUtil:

```
import com.liferay.portal.kernel.util.ClassLoaderProxy;
// see details in service_util.ftl
ClassLoader portletClassLoader = (ClassLoader)PortletBeanLocatorUtil.
locate(ClpSerializer.getServletContextName(), "portletClassLoader");
ClassLoaderProxy classLoaderProxy = new ClassLoaderProxy(object,
${entity.name}${sessionTypeName}Service.class.getName(),
portletClassLoader);
```

Therefore, in the utility class ${entity.name}${sessionTypeName}ServiceUtil
such as ArticleLocalServiceUtil from knowledge-base-portlet, the class
ClassLoaderProxy was imported and generated in the method getService.

Sharing plugin services

In general, there are two approaches to share plugins services across plugins. Let's say you have two plugins: `chat-portlet` and `knowledge-base-portlet`; the plugin `chat-portlet` has a service named `StatusLocalService` and its service layer is `StatusLocalServiceUtil`, while the plugin `knowledge-base-portlet` needs to use the service `StatusLocalServiceUtil.getStatuses`. Thus you would have the following approach to share these plugins services:

Put the service JAR `chat-portlet-service.jar` in the folder `$CATALINA_HOME/lib/ext` and remove the service JAR `chat-portlet-service.jar` in the folder `$PLUGINS_SDK_HOME/portlets/chat-portlet/docroot/WEB-INF/lib`.

Hooks

Hook is a plugin type and is the preferred way to customize the portal core features. **Hooks** are hot deployable and more forward compatible, filling a wide variety of the common needs for overriding the portal core functionality. Thus, whenever possible, hooks should be used in place of Ext plugins. Common scenarios which require the use of a hook are the need to perform custom actions on portal startup or user login, overwrite or extend portal JSPs, modify portal properties, replace a portal service with a custom implementation, modify search summaries, queries, and indexes, override struts actions, modify servlet filters and mappings, and so on.

In summary, there are several kinds of hooks: portal properties hooks, language properties hooks, custom JSP hooks, indexer post processor hooks, service wrapper hooks, servlet filters and servlets mapping hooks, and struts actions hooks.

Hook plugin project default template

Liferay plugins SDK provides a hook plugin project default template `hook_tmpl`. The hook plugin project folder name is represented as `@hook.name@-hook`. For example, the variable `@hook.name@` has a value named `mongodb` for the `Mongodb` hook. Under the folder `@hook.name@-hook`, there is a folder named `docroot` and the XML file `build.xml`. As you can see, `build.xml` has the following code:

```
<project name="@hook.name@-hook" basedir="." default="deploy">
  <import file="../build-common-hook.xml" />
</project>
```

As you must have noticed, the only special part of the hook plugin project is the XML file liferay-hook.xml under the folder docroot/WEB-INF. Moreover, the rest of the project structure is the same or similar to that of other plugin types such as portlet, web, and so on. Therefore, the hook plugin can be standalone or stay inside other plugin project such as portlet or web.

Of course, you can specify hooks as a standalone plugin or as part of web plugin. Here we are going to add the hooks capability in the portlet knowledge-base-portlet. We do this by adding liferay-hook.xml in the folder $PLUGINS_SDK_HOME/portlets/knowledge-base-portlet/docroot/WEB-INF with the following lines. Note that the following is a sample code, and we will add more features in the coming sections:

```
<hook>
  <portal-properties>portal.properties</portal-properties>
  <language-properties>content/Language_en.properties
  </language-properties>
  <struts-action>
    <struts-action-path>/portal/knowledge_base/find_article
    </struts-action-path>
    <struts-action-impl>
      com.liferay.knowledgebase.hook.action.FindArticleAction
    </struts-action-impl>
  </struts-action>
</hook>
```

As shown in the preceding code, it specified the portal properties hook portal-properties, language properties hook language-properties, and struts actions hook struts-action. You can find the **liferay-hook DTD** in svn://svn.liferay.com/repos/public/portal/trunk/definitions/liferay-hook_6_1_0.dtd.

Liferay hook DTD

In the DTD file, liferay-hook_6_1_0.dtd, the element hook is the root of the deployment descriptor for a **liferay-hook** descriptor that is used to define different kinds of hooks. The element hook is defined as follows:

```
<!ELEMENT hook (portal-properties?, language-properties*,
  custom-jsp-dir?, custom-jsp-global?,
  indexer-post-processor*, service*,
  servlet-filter*, servlet-filter-mapping*,
  struts-action*)
>
```

As shown in the preceding element type declarations, the element `hook` can have no more than one `portal-properties` child element, one or more `language-properties` child element, no more than one `custom-jsp-dir` and `custom-jsp-global` children element, and one or more `indexer-post-processor`, `service`, `servlet-filter`, `servlet-filter-mapping`, and `struts-action` children elements.

> Note that the order of these children elements is critical. When children elements are declared in a sequence separated by commas, these children elements must appear in the same sequence in the document.

The children elements `portal-properties`, `language-properties`, `custom-jsp-dir`, and `custom-jsp-global` were defined as follows. As you can see, there is no child element required:

```
<!ELEMENT portal-properties (#PCDATA)>
<!ELEMENT language-properties (#PCDATA)>
<!ELEMENT custom-jsp-dir (#PCDATA)>
<!ELEMENT custom-jsp-global (#PCDATA)>
```

The preceding elements with only parsed character data are declared with `#PCDATA` inside parentheses. The element `indexer-post-processor` has the following children element declarations:

```
<!ELEMENT indexer-post-processor (
  indexer-class-name, indexer-post-processor-impl)>
<!ELEMENT indexer-class-name (#PCDATA)>
<!ELEMENT indexer-post-processor-impl (#PCDATA)>
```

As shown in the preceding declarations, it declares only one occurrence of an element. For example, the element `indexer-post-processor` has two children elements, namely, `indexer-class-name` and `indexer-post-processor-impl`. The child elements `indexer-class-name` and `indexer-post-processor-impl` must occur once, and only once, inside the element `indexer-post-processor`.

Similarly, the element `service` has two children elements, namely, `service-type` and `service-name`. As shown in the following declarations, the children elements `service-type` and `service-name` must occur once, and only once, inside the element `service`:

```
<!ELEMENT service (
  service-type, service-impl)>
<!ELEMENT service-type (#PCDATA)>
<!ELEMENT service-impl (#PCDATA)>
```

The elements servlet-filter and servlet-filter-mapping were added in the DTD file liferay-hook_6_1_0.dtd. This allows adding new filters from hooks, as well as overriding existing filters. As shown in the following declarations, the element servlet-filter can have one, and only one, element servlet-filter-name and servlet-filter-impl. The child element init-param must occur never or once inside the element servlet-filter:

```
<!ELEMENT servlet-filter (servlet-filter-name,
  servlet-filter-impl, init-param*)>
<!ELEMENT servlet-filter-name (#PCDATA)>
<!ELEMENT servlet-filter-impl (#PCDATA)>
<!ELEMENT init-param (param-name, param-value)>
<!ELEMENT param-name (#PCDATA)>
<!ELEMENT param-value (#PCDATA)>
```

The preceding example declares that the children elements, param-name and param-value, must occur once, and only once, inside the element init-param.

In addition, new filter mappings can be added to new or existing filters as follows:

```
<!ELEMENT servlet-filter-mapping (servlet-filter-name,
  (after-filter | before-filter)?, url-pattern+, dispatcher*)>
<!ELEMENT after-filter (#PCDATA)>
<!ELEMENT before-filter (#PCDATA)>
<!ELEMENT url-pattern (#PCDATA)>
<!ELEMENT dispatcher (#PCDATA)>
```

The ? sign in the preceding example declares that the child element after-filter or before-filter can occur never or once inside the element servlet-filter-mapping. The * sign declares that the child element dispatcher can occur never or once inside the element servlet-filter-mapping. While the + sign declares that the child element url-pattern must occur once or more inside the element servlet-filter-mapping.

Similar to the element service, the element struts-action has two children elements, namely, struts-action-path and struts-action-impl. As shown in the following declarations, the children elements, service-type and service-name, must occur once, and only once, inside the element struts-action:

```
<!ELEMENT struts-action (
  struts-action-path, struts-action-impl)>
<!ELEMENT struts-action-path (#PCDATA)>
<!ELEMENT struts-action-impl (#PCDATA)>
```

Portal properties hooks

Through portal properties hooks, we can change certain configuration properties dynamically and inject behavior into the hooks defined in the `portal.properties` file. All of the hooks that we have discussed here will revert, and their targeted functionality will be disabled immediately as soon as they are undeployed from the portal. Moreover, each type of hook can easily be disabled through the `portal.properties` file. Note that a `portal.properties` file must exist in the plugin `WEB-INF/src` folder, such as `$PLUGINS_SDK_HOME/portlets/knowledge-base-portlet/docroot/WEB-INF/src`, if the portal properties hooks are enabled. As mentioned earlier, you can leverage Ext plugins to override portal properties through `portal-ext.properties`. However, the Ext plugins approach is not recommended; instead, you should leverage the `portal.properties` in a hook.

For example, let's say you have enabled the portal properties hooks in the XML `liferay-hook.xml` under the folder `$PLUGINS_SDK_HOME/portlets/knowledge-base-portlet/docroot/WEB-INF`. You can modify the `servlet.service.events.pre` portal property. In general, it is safe to modify these portal properties from multiple hooks, and they won't interfere with one another. You can determine which type a particular property will be by looking in `portal.properties`.

In addition to defining custom events, hooks can also override portal properties to define custom actions, model listeners, validators, generators, content sanitizers, upgrade processes, authentication public paths that don't require authentication, and so on. As shown in the following code, it will override properties `upgrade.processes`, `auth.public.paths`, `servlet.service.events.pre`, and `value.object.listener.com.liferay.portal.model.Group`:

```
upgrade.processes=\
// see details in plugin's portal.properties
auth.public.paths=\
  /portal/knowledge_base/find_article
servlet.service.events.pre=com.liferay.knowledgebase.hook.events.
ServicePreAction
value.object.listener.com.liferay.portal.model.Group=com.liferay.
knowledgebase.hook.listeners.GroupListener
```

Note that not all portal properties can be overridden through a hook. The supported properties are listed as follows. Of course, you can find these portal properties details in the `portal.properties`:

```
admin.default.group.names
admin.default.role.names
admin.default.user.group.names
// see details in liferay-hook_6_1_0.dtd
users.screen.name.validator
value.object.listener.*
```

You could find the same list through static `String Array SUPPORTED_PROPERTIES` in the class `HookHotDeployListener`. Note that the class `HookHotDeployListener` extends the class `BaseHotDeployListener`, implementing the interface `PropsKeys`.

Event handlers

Liferay portal has a few event handler connection points throughout its lifecycle. These event handlers are designed to conveniently hook-in the custom logic. The following table shows the available events:

Description	Properties
Application startup events	`application.startup.events`
Application shutdown events	`application.shutdown.events`
Global startup events	`global.startup.events`
Global shutdown events	`global.shutdown.events`
Login events	`login.events.pre, login.events.post`
Logout events	`logout.events.pre, logout.events.post`
Servlet service events	`servlet.service.events.pre, servlet.service.events.post`

The portal properties hooks could perform custom actions on these events. These event actions are defined in `portal.properties`, which could be overwritten by the portal properties hooks.

The servlet service events include pre-service events and post-service events. The pre-service events have an associated error page and will forward to that page if an exception is thrown during the execution of the events. The pre-service events are processed before Struts processes the request. The post-service events are processed after Struts processes the request.

For instance, a guest user that signs in will cause the original portlet authentication token to become stale. This could be fixed in the plugin by using a pre-service event hook before Struts processes the request.

First, add the portal properties hook in the `liferay-hook.xml` as follows:

```
<hook>
  <portal-properties>portal.properties</portal-properties>
</hook>
```

Then, add the following line in the `portal.properties`:

```
servlet.service.events.pre=com.liferay.knowledgebase.hook.events.
ServicePreAction
```

Finally, add the custom logic in `ServicePreAction.java` as follows:

```
public void run(HttpServletRequest request, HttpServletResponse
response) {
    try { doRun(request, response);
    } catch (Exception e) {_log.error(e, e); }
}
protected void doRun( HttpServletRequest request,
    HttpServletResponse response) throws Exception {
    ThemeDisplay themeDisplay = (ThemeDisplay)request.getAttribute(
        WebKeys.THEME_DISPLAY);
    //see details in ServicePreAction.java
    String redirect = HttpUtil.setParameter(
        themeDisplay.getURLCurrent(), "p_p_auth", actual_p_p_auth);
    response.sendRedirect(redirect);
}
```

As shown in the preceding code, the class `ServicePreAction` overwrites the method `run`. Generally speaking, servlet service events should extend the abstract class `com.liferay.portal.kernel.events.Action`. The `Action` class defined the following methods:

```
public abstract void run(HttpServletRequest request,
    HttpServletResponse response) throws ActionException;
// see details in Action.java
public void run(RenderRequest renderRequest,
    RenderResponse renderResponse) throws ActionException {
    // see details in Action.java
}
```

Similarly, you can define custom actions such as post-service events, login pre-events or post-events, and logout pre-events or post-events for using hooks. These custom actions must extend the abstract class `Action`. In the same way, you can override application startup or shutdown events and global startup or shutdown events while these custom actions must extend the abstract class `com.liferay.portal.kernel. events.SimpleAction`.

Model listeners

Model listeners have similar behaviors to the portal event handlers, except that they handle events with respect to models. As mentioned earlier, service builder will generate model listeners for each entity.

For example, knowledge-based articles contain group IDs. When a specific group is removed, associated knowledge-based articles should be removed accordingly. This can be implemented through portal properties hooks in the plugin in the following steps:

1. First, add the portal properties hook in the `liferay-hook.xml` as follows:

```
<hook>
  <portal-properties>portal.properties</portal-properties>
</hook>
```

2. Then, add the following line in `portal.properties`:

```
value.object.listener.com.liferay.portal.model.Group=com.liferay.
knowledgebase.hook.listeners.GroupListener
```

3. Finally, add the custom model listener class `com.liferay.knowledgebase.hook.listeners.GroupListener` with the following code:

```
public void onBeforeRemove(Group group) throws
ModelListenerException {
    try {
        doOnBeforeRemove(group);
    } catch (Exception e) { throw new ModelListenerException(e); }
}
// see details in GroupListener.java
protected void doOnBeforeRemove(Group group) throws Exception {
    ArticleLocalServiceUtil.deleteGroupArticles(group.
getGroupId());
    // add custom logic
    TemplateLocalServiceUtil.deleteGroupTemplates(group.
getGroupId());
}
```

The preceding code shows that before the action `Remove Group`, the portal will delete group-based articles and templates. Similarly, you can add custom logics such as `onAfterRemove`. Furthermore, you would trigger actions on other model listeners such as `ContactListener`, `LayoutListener`, `LayoutSetListener`, `PortletPreferencesListener`, `UserListener`, `UserGroupListener`, `JournalArticle`, `JournalTemplate`, and so on

These listeners implement the `com.liferay.portal.model.ModelListener` interface. You can add a listener for a specific class by setting the property `value.object.listener` with a list of comma-delimited class names that implement the interface `ModelListener`. These classes are pooled and reused and must be thread-safe.

In general, the interface `ModelListener` defined the following methods in the table:

Model listener function	Parameters	Description
`onAfterAdd Association`	Object `classPK`, String `associationClassName`,Object `associationClassPK`	Triggered after the action `Add Association`
`onAfterCreate`	T model	Triggered after the action `Create`
`onAfterRemove`	T model	Triggered after the action `Remove`
`onAfterRemove Association`	Object `classPK`, String `associationClassName`,Object `associationClassPK`	Triggered after the action `Remove Association`
`onAfterUpdate`	T model	Triggered after the action `Update`
`onBeforeAdd Association`	Object `classPK`, String `associationClassName`,Object `associationClassPK`	Triggered before the action `Add Association`
`onBeforeCreate`	T model	Triggered before the action `Create`
`onBeforeRemove`	T model	Triggered before the action `Remove`
`onBeforeRemove Association`	Object `classPK`, String `associationClassName`,Object `associationClassPK`	Triggered before the action `Remove Association`
`onBeforeUpdate`	T model	Triggered before the action `Update`

The following table shows event handlers hooks implementation, value object listener implementation, authentication token implementation, CAPTCHA engine implementation, sanitizer implementation, and so on:

Properties	Sample	Interface	Description

`application.startup.events`	`AppStartupAction`
	
	`ChannelHubAppStartupAction`
		`com.liferay.portal.kernel.events.SimpleAction`	Application startup event that runs once for every website instance of the portal that initializes.

`application.shutdown.events`	`AppShutdownAction`
	
	`ChannelHubAppShutdownAction`
		`com.liferay.portal.kernel.events.SimpleAction`	Application shutdown event that runs once for every website instance of the portal that shuts down.

`global.startup.events`	`GlobalStartupAction`	`com.liferay.portal.kernel.events.SimpleAction`	Global startup event that runs once when the portal initializes.
`global.shutdown.events`	`GlobalShutdownAction`	`com.liferay.portal.kernel.events.SimpleAction`	Global shutdown event that runs once when the portal shuts down.
`servlet.service.events.pre`	`ServicePreAction`	`com.liferay.portal.kernel.events.Action`	The pre-service events process before Struts processes the request.
`servlet.service.events.post`	`ServicePostAction`	`com.liferay.portal.kernel.events.Action`	The post-service events process after Struts processes the request.

Properties	Sample	Interface	Description
`login.events.pre`	`LoginPreAction`	`com.liferay.portal.kernel.events.Action`	The login pre-events process before processing a login request.
`login.events.post`	`ChannelLoginPostAction,` `DefaultLandingPage Action, LoginPostAction`	`com.liferay.portal.kernel.events.Action`	The login post-events process after processing a login request.
`logout.events.pre`	`LogoutPreAction`	`com.liferay.portal.kernel.events.Action`	The logout pre-events process before processing a logout request.
`logout.events.post`	`LogoutPostAction,` `DefaultLogoutPage Action,` `SiteMinderLogoutAction`	`com.liferay.portal.kernel.events.Action`	The logout post-events process after processing a logout request.
`value.object.listener.*`	`ContactListener,` `LayoutListener,` `LayoutSetListener,` `PortletPreferences Listener, UserListener,` `UserGroupListener,` `JournalArticle,` `JournalTemplate`	`com.liferay.portal.model.ModelListener`	Portal model listener, a listener for a specific class by setting the property `value.object.listener` with a list of comma-delimited class names.
`auth.token.impl`	`SessionAuthToken`	`com.liferay.portal.security.auth.AuthToken`	This class is used to prevent CSRF attacks.

Properties	Sample	Interface	Description
`captcha.engine.impl`	`ReCaptchaImpl, SimpleCaptchaImpl`	`com.liferay.portal.kernel.captcha.Captcha`	Generates captchas. reCAPTCHA uses an external service that must be configured independently but provides an audible alternative which makes the captcha accessible to the visually impaired.
`sanitizer.impl`	`DummySanitizerImpl`	`com.liferay.portal.kernel.sanitizer.Sanitizer`	This class is used to sanitize content.

The following table shows the document library hook implementation, document library repository implementation, mail hook implementation, upgrade processes, convert processes, and so on.

Properties	Sample	Interface	Description
`dl.hook.impl`	AdvancedFileSystemHook, CMISHook, FileSystemHook, JCRHook, S3Hook, DocumentumHook	`com.liferay.documentlibrary.util.Hook`	The document library server will use this to persist documents.
`dl.repository.impl`	CMISAtomPub Repository, CMISWebServices Repository	`com.liferay.portal.kernel.repository.BaseRepositoryImpl`	

Properties	Sample	Interface	Description
`mail.hook.impl`	CyrusHook, DummyHook, FuseMailHook, GoogleHook, SendmailHook, ShellHook	`com.liferay.mail.util.Hook`	The mail server will use this class to ensure that the mail and portal servers are synchronized on user information.
`upgrade.processes`	UpgradeProcess_6_1_0	`com.liferay.portal.upgrade.UpgradeProcess`	These classes will run on startup to upgrade older data to match with the latest version.
`convert.processes`	ConvertDocumentLibrary, ConvertDocumentLibrary ExtraSettings, ConvertPermissionAlgorithm, ConvertPermissionTuner, ConvertWikiCreole	`com.liferay.portal.convert.ConvertProcess`	Document library, database, permission algorithm, and tuner conversion

What's happening?

The method `doInvokeDeploy` of the class `HookHotDeployListener` initializes properties, auto logins, model listeners, and events in a specific order. Note that events have to be loaded last, as they may require model listeners to have been registered. The following sample code demonstrates this:

```
// see details in HookHotDeployListener.java
if (portalPropertiesConfiguration != null) {
  Properties portalProperties
    portalPropertiesConfiguration.getProperties();
  if (portalProperties.size() > 0) {
    _portalPropertiesMap.put(servletContextName, portalProperties);
    initPortalProperties(servletContextName, portletClassLoader,
        portalProperties);
    // see details in HookHotDeployListener.java
  }
 }
}
```

As shown in the preceding code, it initializes properties, auto logins, model listeners, and events in a specific order.

Language properties hooks

Language properties hooks allow us to install new translations or override messages in existing translations. Language properties hooks allow you to change any of the messages displayed by the portal to satisfy your needs. To do so, you can create a language file for the language whose messages you want to customize, and then refer to it in the `liferay-hook.xml` file. For example, to override the translations to English and German, the following two lines would be added to the file `$PLUGINS_SDK_HOME/portlets/knowledge-base-portlet/docroot/WEB-INF/liferay-hook.xml`:

```
<hook>
  <portal-properties>portal.properties</portal-properties>
  <language-properties>content/Language_en.properties
  </language-properties>
  <language-properties>content/Language_de.properties
  </language-properties>
  <!-- see details in liferay-hook.xml -->
</hook>
```

For example, you are going to rename `Custom Attributes` to `Custom Fields` in the user editing mode or the organization editing mode of the Control Panel. You can create the folder `content` under the plugin `WEB-INF/src`, and then you could create the properties files `Language_en.properties` and `Language_de.properties` under the plugin `WEB-INF/src/content`. Finally, add the following line at the end of `Language_en.properties`:

```
custom-attributes=Custom Fields
```

The preceding code shows that the message key `custom-attributes` will have the display text `Custom Fields`.

In the same way, add the following line at the end of `Language_de.properties`:

```
custom-attributes=Kundenspezifische Felder
```

The preceding code shows that the message key `custom-attributes` will have the display text `Kundenspezifische Felder`.

Multiple languages

The Liferay portal supports up to 44 languages, called locales. The portal has the following default settings for languages in the `portal.properties` file:

```
locales=ar_SA,eu_ES,bg_BG,ca_AD,ca_ES,zh_CN,zh_TW,hr_HR,cs_CZ,nl_
NL,nl_BE,en_US,en_GB,et_EE,fi_FI,fr_FR,gl_ES,de_DE,el_GR,iw_IL,hi_
IN,hu_HU,in_ID,it_IT,ja_JP,ko_KR,nb_NO,fa_IR,pl_PL,pt_BR,pt_PT,ro_
RO,ru_RU,sr_RS,sr_RS_latin,sl_SI,sk_SK,es_ES,sv_SE,tr_TR,uk_UA,vi_VN
```

As shown in the preceding settings, the portal specifies the available locales. Of course, this number is growing as supported languages are being added. How can we add a new language, for example, be_BY Belarusian for Belarus? In brief, you could add a new language in either the portal core or plugins. The following steps could be used to add a language through plugins:

1. Add a locale such as be_BY in the property `locales` of the `portal-ext.properties`.

2. Build a file named `Language_be.properties` through the Ant target `build-lang`.

3. Add a translation from English to Belarusian in the file `Language_be.properties`.

4. Hook the file `Language_be.properties` in the plugins.

Messages corresponding to a specific language are specified in the properties files with filenames matching that of `content/Language_${locale}.properties`. Of course, these values can also be overridden in the property files with filenames matching that of `content/Language-ext_${locale}.properties` at the folder `$PORTAL_ROOT_HOME/WEB-INF/classes`. Obviously, you can use a comma to separate each entry. Note that all locales must use UTF-8 encoding.

Actually, you would find all language property files in the folder `$PORTAL_SRC_HOME/portal-impl/src/content`. For each language, you would find one language property file matched.

What's happening?

The method `doInvokeDeploy` of the class `HookHotDeployListener` initializes language properties as follows:

```
LanguagesContainer languagesContainer = new LanguagesContainer();
_languagesContainerMap.put(servletContextName, languagesContainer);
List<Element> languagePropertiesElements = rootElement.elements(
    "language-properties");
```

```
for (Element languagePropertiesElement :
languagePropertiesElements) {
 String languagePropertiesLocation =
  languagePropertiesElement.getText();
 try {
  URL url = portletClassLoader.getResource(
   languagePropertiesLocation);
   // see details in HookHotDeployListener.java
}
```

In addition, the portal provides several language-related servlets such as `LanguageServlet` and `I18nServlet` both extending `HttpServlet`.

For example, in `LanguageServlet.java`, it specifies the following code:

```
response.setHeader(HttpHeaders.CONTENT_DISPOSITION,
  _CONTENT_DISPOSITION);
  // see details in LanguageServlet.java
  private static final String _CONTENT_DISPOSITION =
  "attachment; filename=language.txt";
```

The preceding code fixes a **cross-site scripting** (**XSS**) vulnerability with the `LanguageServlet` when using Internet Explorer (IE) because IE incorrectly identifies the **MIME** type of a file. Thus an attacker cannot potentially exploit this security vulnerability to insert malicious JavaScript into a page through the `LanguageServlet`.

The `I18nServlet` automatically qualifies as language paths for better **search engine optimization** (**SEO**). The following code snippet explains this:

```
String i18nLanguageId = request.getServletPath();
// see details in I18nServlet.java
String i18nPath = StringPool.SLASH + i18nLanguageId;
Locale locale = LocaleUtil.fromLanguageId(i18nLanguageId);
```

Note that each language requires an entry in the property `locales` and a servlet mapping in `web.xml` for the servlet `I18nServlet`. For example, the language German has the following servlet mapping in `web.xml`:

```
<servlet-mapping>
    <servlet-name>I18n Servlet</servlet-name>
    <url-pattern>/de/*</url-pattern>
</servlet-mapping>
```

Custom JSP hooks

The custom JSP hooks provide a way to easily modify JSP files of the portal core without having to alter the portal core. The folder /META-INF/custom_jsps must exist in the folder docroot of the plugin, if the tag custom-jsp-dir is set as /META-INF/custom_jsps.

Under the folder /META-INF/custom_jsps, the same folder structure, such as html, as that of $PORTAL_ROOT_HOME/html will be used to override portal-core JSP files with custom JSP files. In runtime, the original JSPs, such as ${name}.jsp or ${name}.jspf, will be renamed as ${name}.portal.jsp or ${name}.portal. jspf, respectively, under $PORTAL_ROOT_HOME/html. Similarly, the custom JSP files, ${name}.jsp or ${name}.jspf, will be copied to the $PORTAL_ROOT_HOME/html folder.

For example, let's say you are going to override the view of the login portlet. You can put the custom JSP file login.jsp of the plugin in the folder /META-INF/ custom_jsps/html/portlet/login. Moreover, add the following line in the liferay-hook.xml file:

```
<root>
    <custom-jsp-dir>/META-INF/custom_jsps</custom-jsp-dir>
    <custom-jsp-global>true</custom-jsp-global>
</root>
```

During deployment, the portal will rename the original JSP login.jsp to login. portal.jsp under the folder $PORTAL_ROOT_HOME/html/portlet/login first, and then the portal will copy the custom JSP file login.jsp of the plugin in the folder / META-INF/custom_jsps/html/portlet/login to the folder $PORTAL_ROOT_HOME/ html/portlet/login. More interestingly, you can include the renamed original JSP as follows in the custom JSP file login.jsp of the plugin at /META-INF/custom_ jsps/html/portlet/login again.

```
<liferay-util:include page="/html/portlet/login/login.portal.jsp" />
```

Therefore, after deploying the hook plugin, you would see both login.jsp and login.portal.jsp under the folder $PORTAL_ROOT_HOME/html/portlet/login.

The custom JSP hooks can globally set the tag custom-jsp-dir that will overwrite portal-core JSP files. Of course, you can add the tag <custom-jsp-global>false</ custom-jsp-global> in the liferay-hook.xml file, so that it will not be applied globally. Each group can choose to have that particular hook to be applied just for that group.

Custom JSP files and path mapping

The custom JSP directory /META-INF/custom_jsps must exist in the path of the JSP file. In particular, the JSP filename must be a 100 percent match to that of the portal web JSP filename, and the JSP file path must be a 100 percent match to that of the portal web JSP file path. This means, only the matched JSP filename and path will be activated. The following table shows the JSP file path mappings:

Hook JSP path	Portal web JSP path	Description
/META-INF/custom_jsps	$PORTAL_SRC_HOME/portal-web/docroot	Portal web doc root mapping
/html	/html	The folder HTML mapping
/html/common, /html/common/themes	/html/common, /html/common/themes	Common JSP files and JSP files under the folder/themes
/html/portal,	/html/portal,	Portal JSP files
/html/portal/layout/edit,	/html/portal/layout/edit,	Portal layout edit JSP files
/html/portal/layout/view,	/html/portal/layout/view,	Portal layout view JSP files
/html/portal/css/portal,	/html/portal/css/portal,	Portal CSS JSP files
/html/portal/css/taglib	/html/portal/css/taglib	Portal CSS taglib JSP files
/html/portlet/activities,	/html/portlet/activites,	Portal core portlets JSP files
/html/portlet/login,	/html/portlet/login,	
/html/portlet/workflow_tasks, and so on	/html/portlet/workflow_tasks, and so on	
/html/taglib/aui,	/html/taglib/aui,	taglib aui JSP files
/html/taglib/portlet,	/html/taglib/portlet,	taglib portlet JSP files
/html/taglib/theme,	/html/taglib/theme,	taglib theme JSP files
/html/taglib/ui	/html/taglib/ui	taglib ui JSP files

What's happening?

The custom JSP hooks that deploy and undeploy processes have been defined
in the class `HookHotDeployListener`. The method `doInvokeDeploy` of the class
`HookHotDeployListener` initializes custom JSP hooks as follows:

```
String customJspDir = rootElement.elementText("custom-jsp-dir");
if (Validator.isNotNull(customJspDir)) {
    boolean customJspGlobal = GetterUtil.getBoolean(
    rootElement.elementText("custom-jsp-global"), true);
    List<String> customJsps = new ArrayList<String>();
    String webDir = servletContext.getRealPath(StringPool.SLASH);
    getCustomJsps(servletContext, webDir, customJspDir, customJsps);
    if (customJsps.size() > 0) {
        // see details in HookHotDeployListener.java
    }
}
```

As shown in the preceding code, it first checks the tag `custom-jsp-dir`. If the value
of the tag is not NULL, it checks the tag `custom-jsp-global`, it gets custom JSP files,
adds these JSP files in the custom JSP bag, and initiates this JSP bag.

In particular, the method `initCustomJspBag` provides the following code. The
custom JSP files were handled in different ways, based on the value of the tag
`custom-jsp-global`.

```
String customJspDir = customJspBag.getCustomJspDir();
boolean customJspGlobal = customJspBag.isCustomJspGlobal();
List<String> customJsps = customJspBag.getCustomJsps();
String portalWebDir = PortalUtil.getPortalWebDir();
for (String customJsp : customJsps) {
    int pos = customJsp.indexOf(customJspDir);
    String portalJsp = customJsp.substring(
        pos + customJspDir.length(), customJsp.length());
    if (customJspGlobal) {
        File portalJspFile = new File(portalWebDir + portalJsp);
// see details in HookHotDeployListener.java    }
    FileUtil.copyFile(customJsp, portalWebDir + portalJsp);
}
if (!customJspGlobal) {
    CustomJspRegistryUtil.registerServletContextName(servletContextNa
me);
}
```

Indexer post processor hooks

The indexer post processor hooks implement a post processing system on top of the existing indexer to allow modifying the search summaries, indexes, and queries. For example, the class `UserIndexer` extends the abstract class `BaseIndexer`, implementing the interface `Indexer`. The class `UserIndexer` specified the search summaries, indexes, and queries. As you know, the class `UserIndexer` was defined in the `portal-impl`. Moreover, new requirement says that you need to modify the search summaries, indexes, and queries of portal users. This requirement can be satisfied through the indexer post processor hooks of the plugin in the following steps:

1. First, add indexer post processor hooks to `liferay-hook.xml` as follows:

```
<hook>
  <indexer-post-processor>
    <indexer-model-name>com.liferay.portal.model.User
    </indexer-model-name>
    <indexer-post-processor-impl>
      com.liferay.knowledgebase.hook.indexer.
      UserIndexerPostProcessor
    </indexer-post-processor-impl>
  </indexer-post-processor>
</hook>
```

2. In this case, the tag `indexer-model-name` is the name of the model whose indexer you wish to change and the tag `indexer-post-processor-impl` is the name of your post processor class that implements `com.liferay. portal.kernel.search.IndexerPostProcessor`.

3. Then, create the post processor class `com.liferay.knowledgebase.hook. indexer.UserIndexerPostProcessor` with the following lines:

```
// see details in UserIndexerPostProcessor.java
public void postProcessDocument(Document document, Object obj)
    throws Exception {
    // add your own logic
    User user = (User)obj;
    // see details in UserIndexerPostProcessor.java
    document.addKeyword("projectTitles", user.getFullName());
}
```

Similarly, you would be able to overwrite other portal core indexers such as `PluginPackageIndexer`, `AssetIndexer`, `BlogsIndexer`, `CalIndexer` (Calendar), `DLIndexer` (Document Library), `OrganizationIndexer`, `JournalIndexer`, `MBIndexer` (Message Boards), `SCIndexer` (Software Catalog), and `WikiIndexer` in the plugins using the indexer post processor hooks.

What's happening?

The interface `IndexerPostProcessor` defines the following functions:

```
public void postProcessContextQuery(
    BooleanQuery contextQuery, SearchContext searchContext)
    throws Exception;
public void postProcessDocument(Document document, Object obj)
    throws Exception;
// see details in IndexerPostProcessor.java
public void postProcessSummary(
    Summary summary, Document document, String snippet,
    PortletURL portletURL);
```

As you can see, the interface `IndexerPostProcessor` defined a set of function to post process context query, document, full query, search query, and summary.

In fact, the method `doInvokeDeploy` of the class `HookHotDeployListener` initializes indexer post processor hooks as follows:

```
List<Element> indexerPostProcessorElements = rootElement.elements(
"indexer-post-processor");
for (Element indexerPostProcessorElement :
    indexerPostProcessorElements) {
// see details in IndexerPostProcessor.java
Indexer indexer = IndexerRegistryUtil.getIndexer(indexerClassName);
IndexerPostProcessor indexerPostProcessor =
    // see details in IndexerPostProcessor.java
}
```

As shown in the preceding code, it first gets index post processors. Then, for each indexer post processor, it finds the indexer, constructs an instance of the interface `IndexerPostProcessor`, and then registers it in both the indexer and the indexer post processor container.

Service wrappers hooks

The service wrapper hooks allow us to customize portal core services and models, that is, service wrapper hooks can override portal core services and models. All functionality provided by service builder is encapsulated behind a service layer, accessed from the frontend layer. Thus, it is possible to change how a portal core portlet behaves without changing the portlet itself by customizing the backend services. The service wrapper hooks provide a way to customize these backend services.

In general, the service builder automatically generates dummy wrapper classes for all of its services, for example, UserLocalServiceWrapper is created as a wrapper of the UserLocalService, which is used to add, remove, and retrieve user accounts. In order to modify the functionality of UserLocalService from the service wrapper hook, you can create a class that extends from UserLocalServiceWrapper, overriding its methods, and then use that class instead of the original one.

For example, to override UserLocalService, you can add the following lines in the liferay-hook.xml file first:

```
<hook>
  <service>
    <service-type>com.liferay.portal.service.UserLocalService
    </service-type>
    <service-impl>
       com.liferay.knowledgebase.hook.service.impl.
       KBUserLocalServiceImpl
    </service-impl>
  </service>
</hook>
```

As shown in the preceding code, the service was specified by the tags service-type and service-impl. The tag service-type provides the original service or model in the portal core, and the tag service-impl provides customized portal service or models, which will override the original service or model in the portal core. More interestingly, you can specify many service tags, if needed.

Then, add custom implementations of the model KBUserImpl and the service KBUserLocalServiceImpl as follows:

```
// add custom logic
public String getFirstName() {
    // see details in KBUserImpl
    return super.getFirstName();
}
```

Note that the custom implementation class KBUserImpl extends the model wrapper class UserWrapper:

```
//add custom logic
public User getUserById(long userId)
    throws PortalException, SystemException {
    // see details in KBUserLocalServiceImpl.java
    return new KBUserImpl(user);
}
```

> Note that the custom implementation class
> KBUserLocalServiceImpl extends the service
> wrapper class UserLocalServiceWrapper.

Similarly, you would be able to change other portal portlet services such as
OrganizationLocalService, GroupLocalService, LayoutLocalService,
IGImageLocalService, DLLocalServic, CalEventLocalService, and so on.

What's happening?

The service wrapper hooks' deploy and undeploy processes have been defined in
the class HookHotDeployListener, too. The method doInvokeDeploy of the class
HookHotDeployListener initializes service wrapper hooks as follows:

```
List<Element> serviceElements = rootElement.elements("service");
// see details in HookHotDeployListener.java
for (Element serviceElement : serviceElements) {
    String serviceType = serviceElement.elementText("service-type");
    String serviceImpl = serviceElement.elementText("service-impl");
    Class<?> serviceTypeClass =
      portletClassLoader.loadClass(serviceType);
    Class<?> serviceImplClass =
      portletClassLoader.loadClass(serviceImpl);
    // see details in HookHotDeployListener.java
    }
}
```

As shown in the preceding code, it first gets elements for the tag service. Then, for
each tag service, it finds the values of the tags service-type and service-impl.
Finally, it registers custom service wrappers with service type, service impl, service
impl constructor, service proxy, and it adds custom service wrappers in the
service container.

In the undeploy process, it will remove the custom service wrapper from the service
container and it will remove the related servlet context from service constructors, too.

Servlet filter and servlet filter mappings hooks

The portal created a delegation filter to handle all servlet-filtering needs. This allows
dynamically adding new servlet filters and servlet filters mapping, or overriding
existing servlet filters and servlet filters mapping. Current filters and mappings
are moved to the XML file liferay-filter-web.xml, read by this filter. Basically,
this filter takes over the job of the servlet container and allows optimizing filters in
addition to adding new filters dynamically.

For instance, to add the new servlet filter Knowledge Base Filter, you can leverage servlet filters and servlet filters mapping hooks. Firstly, you can add servlet filters and servlet filters mappings in the liferay-hook.xml as follows:

```
<hook>
  <servlet-filter>
    <servlet-filter-name>Knowledge Base Filter</servlet-filter-name>
    <servlet-filter-impl>
      com.liferay.knowledgebase.hook.filter.KBFilter
    </servlet-filter-impl>
    <init-param>
      <param-name>knowledge</param-name>
      <param-value>base</param-value>
    </init-param>
  </servlet-filter>
  <servlet-filter-mapping>
    <servlet-filter-name>Knowledge Base Filter</servlet-filter-name>
    <before-filter>SSO Open SSO Filter</before-filter>
    // see details in liferay-hook.xml
  </servlet-filter-mapping>
</hook>
```

After that, you should provide the servlet filter implementation class com.liferay. knowledgebase.hook.filter.KBFilter. Note that the servlet filter class does implement the Filter interface as follows:

```
public void destroy() {
    // add custom logic
}
public void doFilter(
    ServletRequest servletRequest, ServletResponse servletResponse,
    FilterChain filterChain)
    throws IOException, ServletException {
    String uri = (String)servletRequest.getAttribute(
        WebKeys.INVOKER_FILTER_URI);
    // see details in KBFilter.java
    filterChain.doFilter(servletRequest, servletResponse);
}
public void init(FilterConfig filterConfig) {
    // add custom logic
}
```

As you can see, the class KBFilter must implement the methods of the Filter interface: destroy, init, and doFilter. Filters perform filtering in the doFilter method. Every filter, such as KBFilter, has access to a FilterConfig object from which it can obtain its initialization parameters such as knowledge — a reference to the ServletContext which it can use.

What's happening?

In fact, the method doInvokeDeploy of the class HookHotDeployListener initializes servlet filter hooks and servlet filter mapping hooks as follows:

```
ServletFiltersContainer servletFiltersContainer =
    _servletFiltersContainerMap.get(servletContextName);
// see details in HookHotDeployListener.java
List<Element> servletFilterElements = rootElement.elements(
    "servlet-filter");
for (Element servletFilterElement : servletFilterElements) {
    String servletFilterName = servletFilterElement.elementText(
        "servlet-filter-name");
    String servletFilterImpl = servletFilterElement.elementText(
        "servlet-filter-impl");
    List<Element> initParamElements = servletFilterElement.elements(
        "init-param");
    // see details in HookHotDeployListener.java
}
List<Element> servletFilterMappingElements = rootElement.elements(
"servlet-filter-mapping");
for (Element servletFilterMappingElement :
    servletFilterMappingElements) {
    String servletFilterName =
      servletFilterMappingElement.elementText(
        "servlet-filter-name");
    String afterFilter = servletFilterMappingElement.elementText(
        "after-filter");
    String beforeFilter = servletFilterMappingElement.elementText(
        "before-filter");
    // see details in HookHotDeployListener.java
}
```

As shown in the preceding code, it first handles the tag servlet-filter and its children elements servlet-filter-name, servlet-filter-impl, and init-param. Then, it handles the tag servlet-filter-mapping, and its child elements such as servlet-filter-name, after-filter, before-filter, and so on.

Struts actions hooks

The struts action hook provides capabilities to override existing struts actions and/
or add new struts actions from plugins. With the struts action hook, you can either
add new struts actions to the portal core from plugins or override any existing action
within the portal core from plugins.

We will create a new simple hook in the plugin `knowledge-base-portlet`. This
hook will create a new struts action path, such as `/portal/knowledge_base/find_article`, and wrap an existing struts action related to the struts action path such as
`/message_boards/view`.

1. First, edit `liferay-hook.xml` and add the following fragment:

```
<hook>
    <portal-properties>portal.properties</portal-properties>
    <struts-action>
        <struts-action-path>/portal/knowledge_base/find_article
        </struts-action-path>
        <struts-action-impl>
            com.liferay.knowledgebase.hook.action.FindArticleAction
        </struts-action-impl>
    </struts-action>
    <struts-action>
        <struts-action-path>/message_boards/view
        </struts-action-path>
        <struts-action-impl>
            com.liferay.knowledgebase.hook.action.KBStrutsPortletAction
        </struts-action-impl>
    </struts-action>
</hook>
```

2. As shown in the preceding code, it specified at least three kinds of hooks:
   portal properties hooks, custom JSP hooks, and struts action hooks.

3. Secondly, add the following line in `$PLUGINS_SDK_HOME/portlets/knowledge-base-portlet/docroot/WEB-INF/src/portal.properties`:

   `auth.public.paths=/portal/knowledge_base/find_article`

4. The property `auth.public.paths` specifies public paths that don't
   require authentication.

5. Thirdly, create the JSP in `$PLUGINS_SDK_HOME/portlets/knowledge-base-portlet/docroot/admin/view_article.jsp`.

6. Last but not least, create struts actions: `com.liferay.knowledgebase.` `hook.action.KBStrutsPortletAction` and `FindArticleAction`, as described in the `liferay-hook.xml` file. The `FindArticleAction` extending `BaseStrutsAction`, which implements `StrutsAction`, is used as an implementation of the struts action path `/portal/knowledge_base/find_article`.

```
public String execute(StrutsAction originalStrutsAction,
    HttpServletRequest request, HttpServletResponse response)
    throws Exception {
    // see details in KBStrutsPortletAction.java
    long resourcePrimKey = ParamUtil.getLong(request,
      "resourcePrimKey");
    boolean maximized = ParamUtil.getBoolean(request, "maximized");
    // add your own logic
    return null;
}
```

The preceding code overwrites the `execute` method. You should add your own logic for the `execute` method based on your own requirements. In `FindArticleAction`, you would find other functions such as `getAdminPortletURL`, `getArticle`, `getArticleURL`, `getDisplayPortletURL`, and so on.

The `KBStrutsPortletAction` extending `BaseStrutsPortletAction`, which implements `StrutsPortletAction`, will actually wrap `ViewAction` of the **Message Boards** portlet with the struts action path `/message_boards/view`.

```
// add your own implementation for processAction and serveResource
public String render(StrutsPortletAction originalStrutsPortletAction,
    PortletConfig portletConfig, RenderRequest renderRequest,
    RenderResponse renderResponse) throws Exception {
    // add your own logic here
    // see details in KBStrutsPortletAction.java
    return originalStrutsPortletAction.render(
        portletConfig, renderRequest, renderResponse);
}
```

The preceding code overwrites the method `render`. You should add your own logic for the method `render` based on your own requirements. Of course, you should overwrite the methods `processAction` and `serveResource` based on real use cases.

What's happening?

There are two interfaces related to struts actions, namely, `com.liferay.portal.kernel.struts.StrutsAction` and `StrutsPortletAction`. The `StrutsAction` is used for regular struts actions such as `/c/portal/update_password` and `/c/portal/update_terms_of_use`, and `StrutsPortletAction` is used for those that are used from portlets such as `/message_boards/view` for the portlet Message Boards.

The interface `StrutsAction` has specified the following methods:

```
public String execute( HttpServletRequest request,
    HttpServletResponse response) throws Exception;
// see details in strutsAction.java
public String execute(StrutsAction originalStrutsAction,
    HttpServletRequest request, HttpServletResponse response)
    throws Exception;
```

Similarly, the interface `StrutsPortletAction` has specified the following functions:

```
public void processAction(PortletConfig portletConfig,
    ActionRequest actionRequest,ActionResponse actionResponse)
    throws Exception;
    // see details in StrutsPortletAction.java
public void serveResource(
    StrutsPortletAction originalStrutsPortletAction,
    PortletConfig portletConfig, ResourceRequest resourceRequest,
    ResourceResponse resourceResponse)
    throws Exception;
```

In fact, the method `doInvokeDeploy` of the class `HookHotDeployListener` initializes struts actions as follows:

```
StrutsActionsContainer strutsActionContainer =
    _strutsActionsContainerMap.get(servletContextName);
// see details in HookHotDeployListener.java
List<Element> strutsActionElements =
    rootElement.elements("struts-action");
for (Element strutsActionElement : strutsActionElements) {
    String strutsActionPath = strutsActionElement.elementText(
        "struts-action-path");
    String strutsActionImpl = strutsActionElement.elementText(
        "struts-action-impl");
    // see details in HookHotDeployListener.java
}
```

In brief, there are several kinds of hooks like portal properties, language properties, custom JSP, indexer post processors, service wrappers, servlet filters and servlet mappings, and struts actions. The class `HookHotDeployListener` specified how hooks work, as shown in the following table:

Hook types	Deploy/un-deploy	Specific methods	Description
portal properties	invokeDeploy doInvokeDeploy	initPortalProperties, initAuthFailures, initAutoDeployListeners, initAutoLogins, initAuthenticators, initHotDeployListeners, initModelListeners, initEvents	add properties, reset portal properties, and register public paths, auth token, CAPTCHA engine impl, control panel default entry class, Document Library hook and repository impl, LDAP attributes transformer impl, mail hook impl, sanitizer impl, user e-mail address generator, user full name generator and validator, user screen name generator and validator, release info build number and upgrade processes; register auto deploy listener, register auto login, and so on
portal properties	invokeUndeploy doInvokeUndeploy	destroyPortalProperties	Destroy portal properties
language properties	invokeDeploy doInvokeDeploy	getLocale languagesContainer.add Language	Add languages into the languages container
language properties	invokeUndeploy doInvokeUndeploy	languagesContainer. unregisterLanguages	Remove languages into the languages container
custom JSP	invokeDeploy doInvokeDeploy	initCustomJspBag	Add JSP files

Hook types	Deploy/un-deploy	Specific methods	Description
custom JSP	invokeUndeploy doInvokeUndeploy	destroyCustomJspBag	Remove JSP files
indexer post processor	invokeDeploy doInvokeDeploy	indexer. registerIndexerPost Processor; indexerPostProcessor Container. registerIndexerPost Processor	Register the indexer post processor in both the indexer and the container
indexer post processor	invokeUndeploy doInvokeUndeploy	indexerPostProcessor Container. unregisterIndexerPost Processor	Unregister the indexer post processor in the container
service wrappers	invokeDeploy doInvokeDeploy	initServices	Initiate services
service wrappers	invokeUndeploy doInvokeUndeploy	destroyServices	Destroy service wrappers
servlet-filter and servlet-filter-mappings	invokeDeploy doInvokeDeploy	servletFiltersContainer. registerFilter servletFiltersContainer. registerFilterMapping	Register servlet filters and servlet filter mappings
servlet-filter and servlet-filter-mappings	invokeUndeploy doInvokeUndeploy	servletFiltersContainer. unregisterFilterMappings	Unregister servlet filter mappings
struts actions	invokeDeploy doInvokeDeploy	initStrutsAction; StrutsActionContainer. registerStrutsAction; Proxy.newProxyInstance	Elements: struts-action, struts-action path, struts-action-impl
struts actions	invokeUndeploy doInvokeUndeploy	StrutsActionContainer. unregisterStrutsActions unregisterClpMessage Listeners	Remove servlet content name from the struts action container map, unregister the struts action, and unregister the CLP message listeners.

Summary

This chapter first introduced Ext plugins. It then addressed hooks. You would have learned about Ext plugin and project default templates, upgrading a legacy Ext environment, deploying processes, class loader proxy, hooks and project default templates, portal properties hooks, language properties hooks and multiple languages support, custom JSP hooks, indexer post processors, service wrappers hooks, servlet filters and servlet mappings hooks, and struts action hooks.

In the next chapter, we will address the enterprise content management system ECM.

5
Enterprise Content Management

An **Enterprise Content Management System** (ECM) is a formalized means of organizing and storing content, documents, details, and records, related to the organizational processes of an enterprise. ECM manages the organization's unstructured information content—images, documents, records, and so on, with all its diversity of format, authoring, versioning, permissions, and location.

When building the **Knowledge Base**, articles, images, documents, videos, and records would be part of the content. The portal provides a tool called **Document and Media Library**, allowing individuals to upload and manage images, documents, and videos to websites.

This chapter will introduce image management first. Then it will address implementation of basic documents and videos management in the Document and Media Library. In particular, this chapter will show how to customize features of the Document and Media Library. It will then address multiple repositories, **CMIS** (**Content Management Interoperability Services**) consumers and producers. Finally, it will address web scanning and **OCR (Optical Character Recognition)**-based **Record Management (RM)**.

By the end of this chapter, you will have learned the following:

- Image management
- Basic document management
- Video management
- Multiple repository and WebDAV
- CMIS consumers and producers
- Web-scanning and OCR-based record management
- Content relationship, content authoring, and content archiving

Image management

Document imaging is a process to capture, store, scale, and reprint images. The **Document and Media Library** provides a centralized repository to store images used throughout the portal, and it assigns a unique URL to each image. Image is one of the default document types (Basic Document, Image, and Video) in the Document and Media Library (DL). This section will show the kernel of image management.

Models and services

The following diagram depicts an overview of image management conceptually. An image (special document) called **DL Image** has a set of folders (called `DLFolder`) associated with them. Each folder may have many sub folders associated with them. Thus the folders and their sub folders form a hierarchy structure. Each folder (or sub folder) may have a set of file entries called `DLFileEntry`. Each DL Image has a unique URL that is to be referred to. More interestingly, each DL Image can have a thumbnail and, optionally, two custom thumbnails. In a real world scenario, each DL Image can have at least two images or up to four images associated with it:

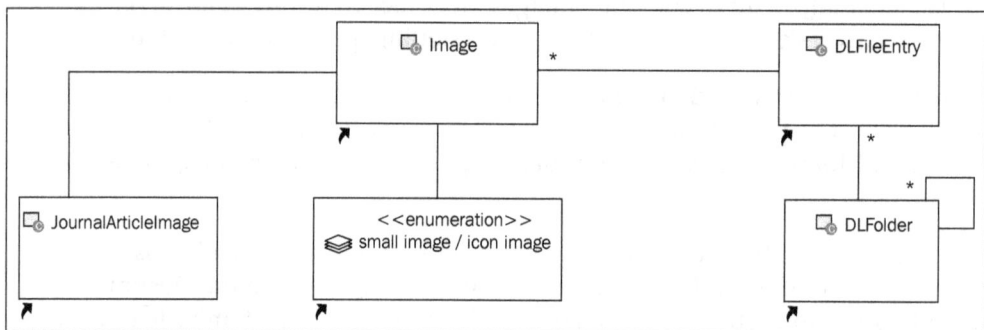

`DLFileEntry` table stores image metadata. The real image is stored in the table Image. The table Image not only stores images of the DL Image, but also images from other entities, for example, `JournalArticleImage`, `Journal Article` (web content), small image, page's icon image, and so on.

Models

The portal has defined the entity Image in the portal service, `service.xml svn://svn.liferay.com/repos/public/portal/trunk/portal-impl/src/com/liferay/portal/service.xml`, as follows:

```
<!-- PK fields -->
<column name="imageId" type="long" primary="true" />
<!-- Audit fields -->
```

```
<column name="modifiedDate" type="Date" />
<!-- Other fields -->
<column name="text" type="String" />
<column name="type" type="String" />
<column name="height" type="int" />
<column name="width" type="int" />
<column name="size" type="int" />
```

As shown in the previous code, an image is defined with the primary key column `imageId`, audit field `modifiedDate`, and other fields like `text`, `type`, `height`, `width`, and `size`. Each image would have a mime type, height, width, and size. Image binary would be stored in the field text if `DBStore` was in use. In versions prior to 6.1, `DatabaseHook`, `DLHook`, and `FileSystemHook` got supported. Since 6.1, only `DLStore` is supported.

The entity `DLFolder` has been defined in the DL `service.xml svn://svn.liferay.com/repos/public/portal/trunk/portal-impl/src/com/liferay/portlet/documentlibrary/service.xml` as follows:

```
<!-- PK fields -->
<column name="folderId" type="long" primary="true" />
<!-- Group instance -->
<column name="groupId" type="long" />
<!-- Audit fields -->
<!-- Other fields -->
<column name="repositoryId" type="long" />
<column name="mountPoint" type="boolean" />
<column name="parentFolderId" type="long" />
<column name="name" type="String" />
<column name="description" type="String" />
```

As you can see, the primary key of the entity is defined as `folderId`, the group instance is added as `groupId`, and the audit fields include `companyId`, `userId`, `createDate`, and `modifiedDate`. Each folder has its name and description. The folder hierarchy structure is defined as the column named `parentFolderId`. If the column `parentFolderId` has the value 0, it means that this is a root folder.

Similarly, the entity `DLFileEntry` has been defined in the DL `service.xml` as follows:

```
<!-- PK fields -->
<column name="fileEntryId" type="long" primary="true" />
<!-- see details in service.xml -->
<!-- Other fields -->
<column name="repositoryId" type="long" />
<column name="folderId" type="long" />
```

```
<column name="name" type="String" />
<column name="description" type="String" />
<column name="smallImageId" type="long" />
<column name="largeImageId" type="long" />
<column name="custom1ImageId" type="long" />
<column name="custom2ImageId" type="long" />
```

As shown in the previous code, the primary key of the entity is defined as `imageId`, and the group instance and audit fields have the same columns as that of the entity `DLFolder`. Each image has its name, description, and a folder — defined as the column `folderId`. If the column `folderId` has the value 0, it means that the image is stored in the root folder.

There are four columns for each **image**: `smallImageId` (pointing to the thumbnail image), `largeImageId` (pointing to the original image), `custom1ImageId`, and `custom2ImageId` (pointing to custom-defined images).

Thumbnails are reduced-size versions of pictures, which help in recognizing and organizing them. The DL automatically creates thumbnails for images, when they are uploaded (almost all image extensions got supported, such as BPM, PNG, GIF, JPG, TIF). And in addition, another two thumbnails with different custom sizes can be created, namely, `custom1` and `custom2`.

The following table shows models (`DLFolder`, `DLFileEntry`, and `Image`), interfaces, and their implementation:

Model	Interface	Implementation	Description
com.liferay. portlet. documentlibrary. model.DLFolder	DLFolderModel extends BaseModel<DLFolder>	DLFolderImpl, DLFolderModelImpl	Document and Media Library folder model and its metadata
com.liferay. portlet. documentlibrary. model. DLFileEntry	DLImageModel extends BaseModel<DLFileEntry>	DLFileEntryImpl, DLFileEntryModelImpl	Document and Media Library File Entry model and its metadata
com.liferay. portal.model. Image	ImageModel extends BaseModel<Image>	ImageImpl, ImageModelImpl	Global image model and its metadata like type, height, weight, size, and so on.

Base model

The base interface, `BaseModel`, is designed for all the model classes. This interface should never be used directly. The interface `BaseModel<T>` extends the interfaces `ClassedModel`, `Cloneable`, `Comparable<T>`, and `Serializable`.

The base interface `BaseModel` has defined following methods:

```
public void setNew(boolean n);
public void setCachedModel(boolean cachedModel);
public void setEscapedModel(boolean escapedModel);
// see details in BaseModel.java
public String toXmlString();
```

The previous code shows that it determines/sets if this model instance doesn't yet exist in the database, it determines/sets if this model instance was retrieved from the entity cache, and it determines/sets if this model instance is escaped, meaning that all strings returned from getter methods are HTML safe.

The interface `com.liferay.portal.model.ClassObject` defines a set of functions to get the model class, model class name, and primary key object as follows:

```
public interface ClassedModel
{
    public Class<?> getModelClass();
    public String getModelClassName();
    public Serializable getPrimaryKeyObj();
}
```

As shown in the previous code, `getModelClassName()` and `getModelClass()` got added into the interface `BaseModel`. Since all classes have this data anyways, the portal just exposes it as a friendly method. For example, `DLFileEntry.getModelClassName()` will return `com.liferay.portlet.documentlibrary.model.DLFileEntry`.

By the way, the interface `AuditedModel` got added too. Most of the base models have `companyId`, `createDate`, `modifiedDate`, `userId`, and `userName`. If a model like `DLFileEntry` has those fields, then it will also implement the `AuditedModel` interface as follows:

```
public interface AuditedModel
{
    public long getCompanyId();
    // see details in AuditedModel.java
    public void setUserUuid(String userUuid);
}
```

If a `BaseModel` is an `AuditedModel`, and if it has a group ID, then it is also a `GroupedModel` — it means that its data can be grouped into groups such as sites/communities or organizations.

```
public interface GroupedModel extends AuditedModel
{
    public long getGroupId();
}
```

The previous code shows that the interface `GroupedModel` extends the interface `AuditedModel`, and a group instance was added via group ID in the interface `GroupedModel`.

Services

The service builder generated a set of services for `Image`, `DLFileEntry`, and `DLFolder`. The following table shows the service interface, utilities, and service implementation:

Service	Utility	Implementation	Description
DLFileEntryLocal Service	DLFileEntryLocal ServiceUtil	DLFileEntryLocal ServiceImpl	DLFileEntry local service call. There is no permission check
DLFileEntryService	DLFileEntry ServiceUtil	DLFileEntryServiceImpl	DLFileEntry service call. Adds Permission check on the entity instance DLFileEntry
DLFolderLocal Service	DLFolderLocal ServiceUtil	DLFolderLocal ServiceImpl	DLFolder LocalService call. There is no permission check
DLFolderService	DLFolder ServiceUtil	DLFolderServiceImpl	DLFolder Service call. Adds Permission check on the entity instance DLFolder

Service	Utility	Implementation	Description
ImageLocalService	ImageLocal ServiceUtil	ImageLocalServiceImpl	Image LocalService call. There is no permission check
ImageService	ImageLocalService	ImageServiceImpl	Image Service call. Adds Permission check on the entity instance Image

As shown in the previous table, both LocalService and Service provide a similar function. The first one provides the LocalService call without permission checking; the second one provides the Service call with permission checking. Depending on your own requirements, you would be able to leverage one of them.

For example, both classes ImageLocalServiceImpl.java and ImageServiceImpl.java provide the function getImage(long imageId). The class ImageLocalServiceImpl.java provides method getImage, used for the LocalService call, which doesn't check for permission, as follows:

```
public Image getImage(long imageId)
{
    try
{
        if (imageId > 0)
{
            return imagePersistence.findByPrimaryKey(imageId);
}
}
    // see details in ImageLocalServiceImpl.java
}
```

The class ImageServiceImpl.java provides the same method. However, it is used for the Service call, which does check for permission, as follows:

```
public Image getImage(long imageId) throws PortalException,
SystemException
{
    DLFileEntryPermission.check( getPermissionChecker(),
    imageId, ActionKeys.VIEW);
    return imageLocalService.getImage(imageId);
}
```

Once an `Image` was uploaded in the Document and Media Library, you would be able to use it and its thumbnails in your JSP files. In order to use the thumbnails, you could do the following:

```
DLFileEntry fileEntry ; // getting the DLFileEntry
Image largeImage = ImageServiceUtil.getImage(fileEntry.
getLargeImageId());
Image smallImage = ImageServiceUtil.getImage(fileEntry.
getSmallImageId());
Image custom1Image = ImageServiceUtil.getImage(fileEntry.
getCustom1ImageId());
Image custom2Image = ImageServiceUtil.getImage(fileEntry.
getCustom2ImageId());
```

The previous code shows the methods for getting thumbnails—original image, `smallImage`, `custom1Image`, and `custom2Image`.

> Please note that you can use `ImageLocalServiceUtil`, other than `ImageServiceUtil`, if a permission check is not required.

Usage

There are at least two ways to use images from the Document and Media Library that are as follows:

- Call `DLFileEntryLocalServiceUtil`, `DLFolderLocalServiceUtil` or `DLFileEntryServiceUtil`, `DLFolderServiceUtil`
- Call `ImageLocalServiceUtil` or `ImageServiceUtil`

For example, for each Knowledge Base article, it was required to insert images into the content via the WYSIWYG editor. Thus, you can leverage the first approach by calling `DLFileEntryLocalServiceUtil`, `DLFolderLocalServiceUtil` or `DLFileEntryServiceUtil`, `DLFolderServiceUtil`. Once you have got a set of images, you could build your own presentation, like a slideshow, using Alloy UI or other JavaScript plus AJAX. Refer to the JSP at `svn://svn.liferay.com/repos/public/portal/trunk/portal-web/docroot/html/portlet/image_gallery_display/view_slide_show.jsp`.

Considering the Knowledge Base again, for each article, it was required to add small image as its thumbnail. Thus you can leverage the second approach by calling `ImageLocalServiceUtil` or `DLFileEntryServiceUtil`. How do we implement this?

First, add the `smallImage` columns in the DL `service.xml` as follows:

```
<column name="smallImage" type="boolean" />
<column name="smallImageId" type="long" />
<column name="smallImageURL" type="String" />
```

As shown in the previous code, the column `smallImage` shows a flag to indicate whether the `smallImage` is used for a Knowledge Base article or not. The column, `smallImageId`, stores the actual small image ID from the table Image. The column, `smallImageURL`, provides an option to use the image URL directly. This image URL could be images from the Document and Media Library Image or anywhere else.

Then, call `ImageLocalServiceUtil` or `DLFileEntryServiceUtil` in the `AdminPortlet` to save/get the `smallImage` via `smallImageId`.

Image processor

As you have noticed, the thumbnails (`smallImage`, `custom1`, and `custom2`) are configurable in the `portal.properties`. The property `dl.file.entry.thumbnail.max.*` sets the maximum thumbnail width in pixels as follows:

```
dl.file.entry.thumbnail.enabled=true
dl.file.entry.thumbnail.max.height=128
dl.file.entry.thumbnail.max.width=128
```

Another two thumbnail images with different custom sizes can be created: `custom1` and `custom2`. This means you would be able to specify different thumbnail images – you would be able to create a scaled image of that dimension. Of course, you can override the previous properties in `portal-ext.properties`.

In fact, the previous properties got checked and got saved as scaled images in the class `IGImageLocalServiceImpl.java` as follows:

```
// see functions deleteImage, updateImage, getImage
getImage(InputStream is,
   byte[] bytes, boolean cleanUpStream)
 {
    ImageBag imageBag = ImageToolUtil.read(bytes);
    RenderedImage renderedImage = imageBag.getRenderedImage();
    String type = imageBag.getType();
    Image image = new ImageImpl();
 }
```

The portal provides the interface `ImageTool` in order to scale the image and to generate scaled images with different dimensions. The class `ImageToolUtil` exposes the following functions for plugins:

```
public RenderedImage scale(RenderedImage renderedImage,
    int width);
public RenderedImage scale(RenderedImage renderedImage,
    int maxHeight, int maxWidth);
```

The first `scale` function scales the image, based on the given width along with the height, which is calculated to preserve aspect ratio. The second function scales the image, based on the maximum height and width given, while preserving the aspect ratio. If the image is already larger in both dimensions, the image will not be scaled.

The class `ImageToolImpl` (and `ImageToolUtil`) implements the interface `ImageTool`, by using `java.awt.Graphics` to draw images as follows:

```
// see details in ImageToolImpl (and ImageToolUtil).java
BufferedImage scaledBufferedImage = new BufferedImage(
    scaledWidth, scaledHeight, type);
Graphics graphics = scaledBufferedImage.getGraphics();
Image scaledImage = bufferedImage.getScaledInstance(
    scaledWidth, scaledHeight, Image.SCALE_SMOOTH);
graphics.drawImage(scaledImage, 0, 0, null);
```

The class `ImageProcessorImpl` (and `ImageProcessorUtil`) implements the interface `ImageProcessor`, by using `com.liferay.portal.kernel.image.`
`ImageToolUtil` to process images. Of course, you may leverage **ImageMagick** (referring to `http://www.imagemagick.org`) to implement the `scale` function and many more like format convert, transform, add transparency, draw, decorate, add special effects, add animation, add text and comments, and so on.

Image sprite processor

CSS sprite is the technique of combing images to lessen the number of calls that need to be made to the server. Therefore, you just shift the position of the background image to view the correct part of the image. The portal provides the **image sprite processor** for the same service.

First, the portal specifies the following properties for the image sprite processor in the `portal.properties`:

```
sprite.file.name=_sprite.png
sprite.properties.file.name=_sprite.properties
```

The previous code sets the filenames used for the auto-generated sprites. The default filename used to be `.sprite.png`, but now its name is `_sprite.png`, since **SiteMinder** doesn't allow filenames to start with a period. This property will not need to be changed unless your deployment has a conflict with filenames that start with an underscore.

Then, the portal provides the interface `SpriteProcessor` with the following code:

```
public Properties generate(
    // see details in SpriteProcessor.java
    int maxHeight, int maxWidth, int maxSize)
throws IOException;
```

As shown in the previous code, `properties.sprite.file.name` and `sprite.properties.file.name` are used to generate sprite properties. The following table shows the relationship among `SpriteProcessor`, `SpriteProcessorUtil`, and the implementation `SpriteProcessorImpl`:

Interface	Method	Implementation	Description
SpriteProcessor	generate	SpriteProcessorImpl	Provides functions to generate sprite properties
SpriteProcessorUtil	generate, getSpriteProcessor, setSpriteProcessor	_setSpriteImages at PortletLocalServiceImpl, ThemeLocalServiceImpl	Sprite processor utilities

When initiating the portlet or theme, it will set sprite images. For example, the implementation class `PortletLocalServiceImpl` (and `ThemeLocalServiceImpl`) has the following code to set sprite images:

```
// see details in PortletLocalServiceImpl.java
Properties spriteProperties = SpriteProcessorUtil.generate(
    images, spriteFileName, spritePropertiesFileName,
    spritePropertiesRootPath, 16, 16, 10240);
//for portlet application
portletApp.setSpriteImages(spriteFileName, spriteProperties);
// for theme, see details in ThemeLocalServiceImpl.java
theme.setSpriteImages(spriteFileName, spriteProperties);
```

As shown in the previous code, it first reads the properties settings `sprite.file.name` and `sprite.properties.file.name`, and the sprite properties root path. It then calls `SpriteProcessorUtil` to generate sprite properties. Finally, it sets sprite images for the portlet or the theme.

Permissions

Permissions in the DL are defined at three different levels, coinciding with the different sections of the XML file at the `svn://svn.liferay.com/repos/public/portal/trunk/portal-impl/src/resource-actions/documentlibrary.xml` file as follows:

```
<resource-action-mapping>
    <portlet-resource>
        <portlet-name>20</portlet-name>
        <permissions>
            <supports>
                <action-key>ACCESS_IN_CONTROL_PANEL</action-key>
                <!-- see details in documentlibrary.xml -->
            </supports>
            <!-- see details in documentlibrary.xml -->
        </permissions>
    </portlet-resource>
    <model-resource>
        <model-name>com.liferay.portlet.documentlibrary</model-name>
        <portlet-ref>
            <portlet-name>20</portlet-name>
        </portlet-ref>
        <permissions>
            <supports>
                <action-key>ADD_FOLDER</action-key>
                <action-key>ADD_DOCUMENT</action-key>
                <!-- see details in documentlibrary.xml -->
            </supports>
            <!--see details in documentlibrary.xml -->
        </permissions>
    </model-resource>
    <model-resource>
        <model-name>com.liferay.portlet.documentlibrary.model.DLFolder</model-name>
        <!-- see details in documentlibrary.xml -->
    </model-resource>
    <model-resource>
        <model-name>com.liferay.portlet.documentlibrary.model.DLFileEntry</model-name>
        <!-- see details in documentlibrary.xml -->
    </model-resource>
</resource-action-mapping>
```

First, in the `portlet-resource` section, actions and default permissions are defined on the portlet itself.

The second level of permissions is based on the scope of an individual instance of the portlet. These permissions are defined in the `model-resource` section. Notice that the `model-name` is not the name of an actual Java class, but simply of the Document and Media Library package.

The third level of permissions is based on the scope of models like `DLFileEntry` and `DLFolder`. The model resource is surrounded by the `model-resource` tag. The `model-name` is the name of an actual Java class of the model.

The `portlet-name`, which this model belongs to is defined under the `portlet-ref` tag. A model can belong to multiple portlets, which you may use multiple `portlet-name` tags to define.

Resource action mapping

The DTD for defining actions are specified at the `svn://svn.liferay.com/repos/public/portal/trunk/definitions/liferay-resource-action-mapping_6_1_0.dtd`. The `resource-action-mapping` is the root of the deployment descriptor for a resource action descriptor that is used to define actions that are supported on portal resources, such as portlets and models, as follows:

```
<!ELEMENT resource-action-mapping (portlet-resource*, model-
resource*,resource*) >
```

As shown in the previous code, the element `resource-action-mapping` can contain one or many sub-elements such as `portlet-resource`, `model-resource` and `resource`. The `portlet-resource` element defines the permissions of the portlet as follows:

```
<!ELEMENT portlet-resource (portlet-name, permissions?) >
```

The `portlet-name` element is the name of the portlet. The `permissions` element defines the default permissions granted and unsupported to community members, guest users, and layout managers.

```
<!ELEMENT permissions (supports, community-defaults?, guest-defaults?,
guest-unsupported?, layout-manager?, owner-defaults?) >
```

The `supports` element defines the actions supported by this resource as follows:

```
<!ELEMENT supports (action-key*) >
```

The `action-key` element defines the name of the action. The name will be translated as specified in the `Language.properties`. For example, if the name of the `action-key` is `VIEW`, then the key in `Language.properties` will be `action.VIEW`.

The `community-defaults` element specifies the actions that community members are permitted to perform by default. The `guest-defaults` element specifies the actions that the guest users are permitted to perform, by default. The `guest-unsupported` element specifies the actions that the guests are never permitted to perform. This disables the ability to assign permissions for these actions. You define actions here, only if you wish to prevent anyone from granting permissions to perform these actions.

The `layout-manager` element specifies the actions that layout (alternative name page instance) managers are permitted to perform. If omitted, then layout managers are granted permissions on all supported actions. If included, then the layout managers can only perform actions specified in this element. The `owner-defaults` element specifies the actions that the creator of the resource is permitted to perform. If omitted, then owners are granted permissions on all supported actions.

The `model-resource` element defines the `permissions` and `social-equity` rules of the model as follows:

```
<!ELEMENT model-resource (model-name, portlet-ref, permissions?,
social-equity?) >
```

The `model-name` element is the name of the model. The `portlet-ref` element is the name of the portlet that the model belongs to. The `social-equity` element specifies the social equity mappings for different actions that can be performed on the model as follows:

```
<!ELEMENT social-equity (social-equity-mapping*) >
```

The `social-equity-mapping` element specifies the social equity values that can be applied to a particular action on the model as follows:

```
<!ELEMENT social-equity-mapping (action-key, information-daily-limit?,
information-value?, information-lifespan?, participation-daily-limit?,
participation-value?, participation-lifespan?, social-activity-
mapping?, unique?) >
```

The `information-daily-limit` entity specifies the amount of added information (`information-value`) that can be applied to a user's social score for the action on an asset, and in turn, to its owner's contribution score on a daily basis. The `information-value` specifies the value of contributing information added to the asset, each time the action is performed. The `information-daily-limit` entity may affect this setting.

The `information-lifespan` entity specifies the length of time in days over which the corresponding `information-value` is linearly decreased to zero. The `participation-daily-limit` entity specifies the amount of participation (`participation-value`) that can be applied to a user's participation score for the action on an asset, on a daily basis. The `participation-value` entity specifies the value added to the user's participation score for performing the action. The `participation-lifespan` entity specifies the length of time in days, over which the corresponding `participation-value` is linearly decreased to zero.

The `social-activity-mapping` element specifies the `social-activity-mapping` class. The `unique` element specifies whether the action will provide value to the user's or asset's score, if it is performed more than once on the same asset by the user.

Last but not least, the `resource` element specifies an external file that contains `resource-action-mappings`. The attribute file specifies the external file that should be loaded to define resource actions.

Video management

As mentioned earlier, the DL provides the ability to define custom document types and metadata sets, based on **Dynamic Data Lists (DDL)** and **Dynamic Data Mappings (DDM)**. By default, the DL introduced the document types **Basic Document**, **Image**, and **Video** with the following metadata set:

Name	Fields	Description
Dublin Core metadata set	Contributor, coverage, creator, date, description, identifier, language, publisher, relation, right, source, and subject	Default document type Basic Document
Default Image's metadata set	Author, license, and location	Default document type Image
Default Video's metadata set	Author, license, location, running-time, and subtitles	Default document type Video

What's happening? In fact, the default metadata set got pre-loaded from the XML file `svn://svn.liferay.com/repos/public/portal/trunk/portal-impl/src/com/liferay/portal/events/dependencies/document-library-structures.xml`.

Adding default document types

The portal has specified the property to pre-load the default data—such as DL structure, page template, site template, and DDM structure, which is defined as follows:

```
application.startup.events=com.liferay.portal.events.
AddDefaultDataAction,
```

Application startup event runs once for every website instance of the portal that is initialized. The class `AddDefaultDataAction` loads/runs the classes `AddDefaultDocumentLibraryStructuresAction`, `AddDefaultLayoutPrototypesAction`, `AddDefaultLayoutSetPrototypesAction`, and `AddDefaultDDMStructuresAction` in sequence.

The class `AddDefaultDocumentLibraryStructuresAction` added the DDM structure's (defined at `document-library-structures.xml`) default document types, such as Image and Video, and DL raw metadata structures. This is the reason that the default metadata set and document types got pre-loaded.

Video and audio processors

The DL provides video/audio processors to handle video/audio preview and decoding/encoding using the **Xuggler**. The following table shows a summary of these processors:

Class	Extension	Interface	Description
VideoProcessor	DLPreviewable Processor	DLProcessor	VideoListener and VideoResizer extends com.xuggle.mediatool. MediaToolAdapter; preview type: flv; thumbnail type: jpg;
AudioProcessor	DLPreviewable Processor	DLProcessor	Preview type: mp3
RawMetadata Processor	none	DLProcessor	Generates the raw metadata associated with the file entry

Xuggler is the easy way to uncompress, modify, and re-compress any media file (or stream) from Java, allowing Java programs to decode, encode, and experience (almost) any video format. Refer to `http://www.xuggle.com/xuggler/`.

Antivirus scanner

The portal provides capability to integrate a third-party Antivirus Scanner — scanning for viruses in documents. By default, the portal has specified the following properties in `portal.properties`:

```
dl.store.antivirus.enabled=false
dl.store.antivirus.impl=com.liferay.portlet.documentlibrary.antivirus.
DummyAntivirusScannerImpl
```

The previous code sets the property `dl.store.antivirus.enabled` to `true` to enable the execution of an antivirus check, when files are submitted into a store. Setting this value to `true` will prevent any potential virus files from entering the store, but it won't allow for file quarantines.

The property `dl.store.antivirus.impl` sets the name of a class that implements `com.liferay.portlet.documentlibrary.antivirus.AntivirusScanner`. The Document Library server will use this to scan documents for viruses.

The following table shows the interface and its utility, wrapper, and implementation:

Class	Interface/ Extension	Utility/Wrapper	Description
BaseFileAntivirusScanner, BaseInputStreamAntivirus Scanner	AntivirusScanner	AntivirusScannerUtil, AntivirusScanner Wrapper	Basic file and input stream antivirus scanner
ClamAntivirusScanner Impl	BaseFileAntivirus Scanner	None	ClamAV: antivirus engine implementation, refer to http:// www.clamav. net/lang/en/
DummyAntivirus ScannerImpl	AntivirusScanner	None	Dummy antivirus scanner implementation

Document management

A **Document Management System (DMS)** is a computer system, used to track and store electronic documents and/or images of paper documents, while keeping track of the different versions created by different users. The Document Library provides one central place to aggregate and manage documents, images, videos, and any other document types. It provides document management that can be backed by different persistence systems, including capabilities like mounting existing CMIS repositories, check-in, check-out, metadata, versioning, document converting, and document imaging (live document preview) features.

Live document preview involves the following steps:

1. Upload documents (files with any extension) from a local box to the Document Library in the remote server, or mount pre-existing CMIS repositories.

2. Manage documents and its versions in the Document Library – move, revert, compare, update, and so on. Meanwhile, documents will be converted into different formats in the fly through **OpenOffice** (or **LibreOffice**) , PDF documents will be generated and managed in the Document Library, and moreover, PDF documents get imaged via **PDFBox** or **ImageMagic**.

3. Finally, the documents thumbnail preview and the documents page preview will be ready in the Document Library.

Models and services

The following diagram depicts an overview of the Document Library, conceptually. Document Library has a set of folders called `DLFolder`. Each folder may have many sub folders associated with them. Therefore, hierarchy structure is supported in folders. Each folder (or sub folder) may have a set of documents (called `DLFileEntry`). Each document has a unique URL to be referred to. Each document may have a list of versions (called `DLFileVersion`), ranks (called `DLFileRank`), and shortcuts (called `DLFileShortcut`). A repository, called `Repository`, is associated with the `DLFolder` folder, and it may contain many documents. It can also have many repository entries called `RepositoryEntry`:

Models

The portal has defined the entities, such as, `Repository`, `CMISRepository`, and `RepositoryEntry`, in the portal service `service.xml` as follows:

```
<!-- PK fields -->
<column name="repositoryId" type="long" primary="true" />
<!-- see details in service.xml -->
<!-- Other fields -->
<column name="classNameId" type="long" />
<column name="name" type="String" />
<column name="description" type="String" />
<column name="portletId" type="String" />
<column name="typeSettings" type="String" />
<column name="dlFolderId" type="long" />
```

As shown in the previous code, a repository is defined with the primary key columns `repositoryId`, group instance, audit fields, and other fields such as `classNameId`, `name`, `description`, `portletId`, `typeSettings`, and `dlFolderId`.

The entity `RepositoryEntry` has been defined as follows:

```
<!-- PK fields -->
<column name="repositoryEntryId" type="long" primary="true" />
<!-- Group instance -->
<column name="groupId" type="long" />
<!-- Other fields -->
<column name="repositoryId" type="long" />
<column name="mappedId" type="String" />
```

The entities, such as `DLApp`, `DLAppHelper`, `DLContent`, `DLFileEntryMetadata`, `DLFileEntryType`, `DLSync`, `DLFolder`, `DLFileEntry`, `DLFileVersion`, `DLFileShortcut`, and `DLFileRank`, have been defined in the DL `service.xml`.

The following table shows the models (`DLFileEntryType`, `DLFileEntry`, `DLFileVersion`, `DLFileShortcut`, `DLFileRank`, `Repository`, and `RepositoryEntry`), interfaces, and their implementation:

Model	Interface	Implementation	Description
com.liferay.portlet. documentlibrary. model. DLFileEntryType	DLFileEntryType Model extends BaseModel< DLFileEntryType >, GroupedModel	DLFileEntryType Impl, DLFileEntryType ModelImpl	Document and Media Library document type model and its metadata

Model	Interface	Implementation	Description
DLFileEntry Metadata	DLFileEntryMetadata Model extends BaseModel<DLFile EntryMetadata>, GroupedModel	DLFileEntryMetadataImpl, DLFileEntryMetadata ModelImpl	Document and Media Library file entry metadata model and its metadata
DLFileVersion	DLFileVersionModel extends BaseModel <DLFileVersion>	DLFileVersionImpl, DLFileVersionModelImpl	Document Library portlet file version model and its metadata
DLFileShortcut	DLFileShortcutModel extends BaseModel<DLFile Shortcut>, GroupedModel	DLFile Shortcut Impl, DL Shortcut ModelImpl	Document Library portlet file shortcut model and its metadata
DLFileRank	DLFileRankModel extends BaseModel <DLFileRank>	DLFileRankImpl, DLFileRankModelImpl	Document Library portlet file rank model and its metadata
com.liferay.portal. model.Repository	RepositoryModel extends BaseModel<Repository>	RepositoryImpl, RepositoryModelImpl	Global repository model and its metadata
com.liferay. portal.model. RepositoryEntry	RepositoryEntryModel extends BaseModel<Repository Entry>	RepositoryEntryImpl, RepositoryEntryModel Impl	Global repository entry model and its metadata

Services

There are at least three kinds of services generated for the Document Library: DLAppService, DLRepositoryService, and DLService. The following table shows these services, utilities, and service implementations:

Service	Utility	Implementation	Description
DLAppService	DLAppServiceUtil	DLAppServiceImpl extends DLAppServiceBaseImpl	DLAppService calls with permissions check
DLAppLocal Service	DLAppLocalService Util	DLAppLocalServiceImpl extends DLAppLocalService BaseImpl	DL App local service calls
DLRepository Service	DLRepositoryService Util	DLRepositoryLocalService Impl extends DLRepositoryLocal ServiceBaseImpl	DL Repository service calls with permission checking
DLRepository Local Service	DLRepositoryLocal ServiceUtil	DLRepositoryServiceImpl extends DLRepositoryService BaseImpl	DL Repository service calls with permission checking
DLService	DLServiceUtil	DLServiceImpl	DL local service calls with permission checking
DLLocalService	DLLocalServiceUtil	DLLocalServiceImpl	DL local service calls with permission checking

Attachments

Once documents exist in the Document Library, you could insert documents as links via the document-unique URL. When you build a Knowledge Base article, you may require a set of documents as attachments. Or when you build web content, you may upload documents as attachments in **Document Library document**. These attachments are stored as files in a repository. The interface of the method attachment is specified in the interface DLLocalService as follows:

```
dlLocalService.addFile(
    serviceContext.getCompanyId(),
    // see details in DLLocalService.java
    serviceContext, bytes);
```

The internal implementation is specified in the class DLLocalServiceImpl. Of course, you can leverage the global utility class DLServiceUtil or DLLocalServiceUtil in your plugins.

Document versioning

Document versioning is a process where by documents are checked in or out of a document management system. It allows users to retrieve previous versions and to continue work from a selected point. Document versioning is useful for documents that change over time and require updating, but it may be necessary to go back to or reference a previous copy.

The Document Library provides the ability to manage document versions. Once you have different versions of documents, you could convert documents from one format to another format, compare different versions, live document preview, and so on.

Converting document

The following table shows the possible formats for automatic conversion via OpenOffice (or LibreOffice). Obviously, the plain text of the previous document could be converted into **Portable Document Format (PDF)**, **OpenDocument Text (ODT)**, **OpenOffice.org 1.0 Text (SXW)**, **Rich Text Format (RTF)**, **Microsoft Word (DOC, DOCX)**, and so on. Refer to `http://www.openoffice.org/` for more information.

Category	From	To
Text Formats	OpenDocument Text (`*.odt`)	Portable Document Format (`*.pdf`)
	OpenOffice.org 1.0 Text (`*.sxw`)	OpenDocument Text (`*.odt`)
		OpenOffice.org 1.0 Text (`*.sxw`)
	Rich Text Format (`*.rtf`)	Rich Text Format (`*.rtf`)
	Microsoft Word (`*.doc, *.docx`)	Microsoft Word (`*.doc, *.docx`)
		Plain Text (`*.txt`)
	WordPerfect (`*.wpd`)	
	Plain Text (`*.txt`)	
Spreadsheet Formats	OpenDocument Spreadsheet (`*.ods`)	Portable Document Format (`*.pdf`)
		OpenDocument Spreadsheet (`*.ods`)
	OpenOffice.org 1.0 Spreadsheet (`*.sxc`)	OpenOffice.org 1.0 Spreadsheet (`*.sxc`)
	Microsoft Excel (`*.xls, *.xlsx`)	Microsoft Excel (`*.xls`)
		Comma-Separated Values (`*.csv`)
	Comma-Separated Values (`*.csv`)	Tab-Separated Values (`*.tsv`)
	Tab-Separated Values (`*.tsv`)	

Category	From	To
Presentation Formats	OpenDocument Presentation (`*.odp`)	Portable Document Format (`*.pdf`)
		Macromedia Flash (`*.swf`)
	OpenOffice.org 1.0 Presentation (`*.sxi`)	OpenDocument Presentation (`*.odp`)
		OpenOffice.org 1.0 Presentation (`*.sxi`)
	Microsoft PowerPoint (`*.ppt`, `*.pptx`)	Microsoft PowerPoint (`*.ppt`, `*.pptx`)
Drawing Formats	OpenDocument Drawing (`*.odg`)	Scalable Vector Graphics (`*.svg`)
		Macromedia Flash (`*.swf`)

The document conversion global service got defined in the `com.liferay.portal.kernel.util.DocumentConversionUtil`. It exposed two methods as follows:

```
public static File convert(
    String id, InputStream inputStream, String sourceExtension,
    String targetExtension)
    throws Exception
```

In fact, it uses the class `com.liferay.portal.kernel.util.PortalClassInvoker` to invoke the internal implementation class `com.liferay.portlet.documentlibrary.util.DocumentConversionUtil`. This implementation class `DocumentConversionUtil` provides functions to connect to OpenOffice, disconnect, convert, read the following properties, and so on:

```
openoffice.server.enabled=false
openoffice.server.host=127.0.0.1
openoffice.server.port=8100
## see details in portal.properties
openoffice.conversion.target.extensions[text]=doc,odt,pdf,rtf,sxw,txt
```

The previous code enables OpenOffice integration to allow the Document Library portlet and the Wiki portlet to provide conversion functionality. It then specifies the file extensions which allow conversions from source to target.

> Please note that entries must be limited by what is supported by OpenOffice, as shown in the previous table.

As you can see, the portal has provided an effective way to carry out method invoking (PortalClassInvoker), using the portal class loader PortalClassLoaderUtil. For example, the document conversion class com.liferay.portal.kernel. util.DocumentConversionUtil uses the invoker class PortalClassInvoker to invoke the implementation class com.liferay.portlet.documentlibrary. util.DocumentConversionUtil. Meanwhile, the portal also provides the PortletClassInvoker, which is very similar to PortalClassInvoker, except that it uses the portlet class loader.

Comparing versions

Diff is a file comparison utility that outputs the differences between two files, showing the changes between one version of a file and a former version of the same file. Diff displays the changes made on each line for text files.

The portal provides an interface called com.liferay.portal.kernel.util.Diff as a file (document, web content, or any other content types) comparison utility. For example, you would be able to compare two versions of a document and find changes.

The interface Diff defines the following methods, implemented by the class com. liferay.portal.util.DiffImpl:

```
public List<DiffResult>[] diff(Reader source, Reader target);
public List<DiffResult>[] diff(
    // see details in Diff.java
   String deletedMarkerEnd, int margin);
```

The class DiffImpl can compare two different versions of text by calling **Java-diff**. source refers to the earliest version of the text and target refers to a modified version of source. Changes are considered either as a removal from the source or as an addition to the target. This class detects changes to an entire line, and also detects changes within lines, such as, removal or addition of characters.

The class DiffResult represents a change between one or several lines. The changeType tells if the change happened in the source or target. The lineNumber holds the line number of the first modified line. This line number refers to a line in the source or target, depending on the changeType value. The changedLines is a list of strings; each string is a line that is already highlighted, indicating where the changes are.

The UI tag `liferay-ui:diff` uses Diff and `DiffResult` in the `$PORTAL_SRC_HOME/portal-web/docroot/html/taglib/ui/diff/page.jsp`. Of course, you can leverage the class utility `DiffUtil` in your plugin. By default, you can set which file extensions are comparable by the diff tool as follows:

```
dl.comparable.file.extensions=.css,.doc,.docx,.js,.htm,.html,.odt,.
rtf,.sxw,.txt,.xml
```

Any binary file listed here will only be comparable if either OpenOffice or LibreOffice is enabled and the file is convertible to text.

Java-diff is an implementation of the longest common sub sequences algorithm; its main method `Diff:diff()` returns a list of Difference objects, as two classes, its main method `Diff:diff()` returning a list of Difference objects, each of which describes an addition, deletion, or change between the two collections. Refer to `http://www.incava.org/` for more information.

Previewing a live document

As mentioned earlier, document imaging is the process of capturing, storing, scaling documents as images, and reprinting images. Live document preview is a nice feature that rescales documents as images for live preview. The portal provides a PDF processor utility called `com.liferay.portlet.documentlibrary.util.PDFProcessorUtil`. Which kind of image format is used for live document preview? The utility class `PDFProcessorUtil` provides a static string as follows:

```
public static final String PREVIEW_TYPE = ImageProcessor.TYPE_PNG;
public static final String THUMBNAIL_TYPE = ImageProcessor.TYPE_PNG;
```

Where are the thumbnail preview images and page preview images that are stored temporally? See the following snippet from `PDFProcessorUtil`:

```
private static final String _PREVIEW_PATH =
    SystemProperties.get(SystemProperties.TMP_DIR) +
        "/liferay/document_preview/";
private static final String _THUMBNAIL_PATH =
    SystemProperties.get(SystemProperties.TMP_DIR) +
        "/liferay/document_thumbnail/";
```

As you can see, the `PDFProcessorUtil` uses **Apache PDFBox** or **ImageMagic** (through **im4java**) to scale thumbnail preview images and page preview images. The following properties are involved in `PDFProcessorUtil`:

```
dl.file.entry.preview.enabled=true
## see details in portal.properties
imagemagick.enabled=false
imagemagick.global.search.path[windows]=C\:\\Program Files\\
ImageMagick
```

The previous code sets the values related to preview and thumbnail generation for Document Library files. Image generation will occur for all PDF files, if OpenOffice (or LibreOffice) is enabled for formats convertible to PDF. Image generation will use PDFBox by default, unless ImageMagick is enabled.

> Please note that PDFBox is less accurate in image generation and has trouble with certain fonts.

Apache PDFBox is an open source Java PDF library for working with PDF documents, allowing the creation of new PDF documents, manipulation of existing documents, and the ability to extract content from documents. Refer to http://pdfbox.apache.org/.

The im4java is a pure-java interface to the ImageMagick command line. Refer to http://im4java.sourceforge.net/.

The following is a sample to set up the preview UI via AUI. You may refer to the JSP file svn://svn.liferay.com/repos/public/portal/trunk/portal-web/docroot/html/portlet/document_library/view_file_entry.jsp for more details:

```
<aui:script use="aui-base,liferay-preview">
new Liferay.Preview( {
    actionContent: '#<portlet:namespace />previewFileActions',
    // see details in view_file_entry.jsp
    toolbar: '#<portlet:namespace />previewToolbar' }
).render();
</aui:script>
```

The JavaScript function of live document preview is specified at the svn://svn.liferay.com/repos/public/portal/trunk/portal-web/docroot/html/js/liferay/preview.js.

Document check-in and check-out

Document check-in and check-out functions are persisted by the entity Lock. Once a document is locked, nobody besides the owner can update that document. When the lock is expired, or it gets unlocked by the owner, everyone who has permissions can update that document.

The entity lock is specified in svn://svn.liferay.com/repos/public/portal/trunk/portal-impl/src/com/liferay/portal/service.xml as follows:

```
<!-- PK fields -->
<column name="lockId" type="long" primary="true" />
<!-- Audit fields, see details in service.xml -->
```

```
<!-- Other fields -->
<column name="className" type="String" />
<column name="key" type="String" />
<column name="owner" type="String" />
<column name="inheritable" type="boolean" />
<column name="expirationDate" type="Date" />
```

The previous code shows that the entity `lock` has a column `lockId` as its primary key, a set of audit fields, and other field columns such as `className`, `key`, `owner`, `inheritable`, and `expirationDate`. As you can see, a `lock` could be applied on any content type via the pair of class name and primary key, and document content type is one of them. For a given document, the `className` will have the value `com.liferay.portlet.documentlibrary.model.DLFileEntry` and the key will have that document primary key as its value.

Once a document is locked, one row of the `lock` table will be created; when that document gets unlocked, the same row will get deleted. If the owner locks a document for a while, but he/she forgets to unlock the same document in time, the document will get unlocked at a pre-defined expiration date/time. The default expiration time of `lock` is defined in `portal.properties` as follows:

```
lock.expiration.time.com.liferay.portlet.documentlibrary.model.
DLFolder=86400000
lock.expiration.time.com.liferay.portlet.documentlibrary.model.
DLFileEntry=86400000
lock.expiration.time.com.liferay.portlet.messageboards.model.
MBThread=0
```

The previous code sets the lock expiration time for each model. Locks for Document Library folders and files should expire after one day, but locks for message board threads should never expire. Obviously, the lock duration for both folder and file entry is measured in seconds.

The following table shows the lock model and services:

Name	Extension/Utility	Implementation	Description
Lock	LockModel extends BaseModel<Lock>	LockImpl extends LockModelImpl LockModelImpl extends BaseModelImpl<Lock>	Model, extension, and model implementation
LocalLocalService	LockLocalService Util	LockLocalServiceImpl	Local service, utility, and implementation

Name	Extension/Utility	Implementation	Description
LocalService	LockServiceUtil	LockServiceImpl	Service call with permission checking, utility, and implementation

Moving document

A document always has a folder associated to it. If the `folderId` has the value 0, it means that the folder is the root. This means documents are managed in a folder structure. In some use cases, you may be required to change the folder association of a given document. Thus the document moving from one folder to another is in the picture.

The signature `document moving` is specified in the utility class `DLAppServiceUtil`. The real implementation is specified in `DLAppLocalServiceImpl` as follows:

```
public FileEntry moveFileEntry(
    long userId, long fileEntryId, long newFolderId,
    ServiceContext serviceContext)
    throws PortalException, SystemException
{
    LocalRepository localRepository = getLocalRepository(0,
fileEntryId, 0);
    return localRepository.moveFileEntry(
        userId, fileEntryId, newFolderId, serviceContext);
}
```

More details of documents moving are specified in the class `DLRepositoryLocalServiceImpl`.

Document indexing

Document indexing functions are specified in the class `com.liferay.portlet.documentlibrary.util.DLIndexer`. The Document Library indexes metadata and text for readable documents as follows:

```
Document document = new DocumentImpl();
document.addUID(portletId, repositoryId, fileName);
document.addModifiedDate(modifiedDate);
// see details in DLIndexer.java
document.addKeyword("path", fileName);
document.addKeyword("extension", extension);
ExpandoBridgeIndexerUtil.addAttributes(document, expandoBridge);
```

As you can see, `repositoryId` and its modified date are added in the indexing document. Metadata path, extension, and many others are added as document keywords, while metadata name and description are added as document text. In addition, custom attributes of a given image are indexed as well. In particular, extracted text (from PDF, Excel, Word, PowerPoint, Publisher, and Visio) is indexed as a file. What's happening?

The `com.liferay.portal.kernel.util.File` interface specifies text extraction as follows. The utility class `FileUtil` exposes these methods as global ones:

```
public String extractText(InputStream is, String fileName);
```

The previous interface is implemented in the class `com.liferay.portal.util.FileImpl`. This is shown in the following code snippet:

```
Tika tika = new Tika();
boolean forkProcess = false;
if (PropsValues.TEXT_EXTRACTION_FORK_PROCESS_ENABLED)
{
    // see details in FileImpl.java
if (forkProcess)
{
    text = ProcessExecutor.execute(
    new ExtractTextProcessCallable(getBytes(is)),
    ClassPathUtil.getPortalClassPath());
}
else
{
    text = tika.parseToString(is);
}
```

Obviously, you would see many other file-related functions as well. The class `FileImpl` checks the following properties and uses file `Tika` to parse stream into text as follows:

```
text.extraction.fork.process.enabled=false
text.extraction.fork.process.mime.types=application/x-tika-ooxml
```

As you can see, you can set the property `text.extraction.fork.process.enabled` to `true`, if you want to carry out text extraction of certain MIME types to use separate Java processes. This will utilize extra resources from the operating system, while improving the portal's stability. The property `text.extraction.fork.process.mime.types` sets a list of comma-delimited MIME types that will trigger text extraction using a separate Java process.

Apache Tika is a toolkit for detecting and extracting metadata and structured text content from various documents using existing parser libraries (refer to `http://tika.apache.org/`). For example, it uses PDFBox to extract text from PDF files. Apache POI provides text extraction for all the supported file formats (such as Excel, Word, PowerPoint, Publisher, and Visio) that have access to the metadata associated with a given file such as title and author. In addition, POI works closely with the Apache Tika text extraction library (refer to `http://poi.apache.org`).

WebDAV

WebDAV (Web-based Distributed Authoring and Versioning) is defined as a set of methods, based on the HTTP that facilitates collaboration between users in editing and managing documents and files stored on WWW servers. WebDAV provides functionality to create, change, and move documents on a remote server and is supported by all major Operating Systems and Desktop Environments, including Windows, MacOS X, and Linux (KDE and GNOME).

The portal provides support for the WebDAV protocol, so users can upload and organize resources from both the web interface and the file explorer of their desktop operating system. It automatically generates WebDAV URL for the Document Library documents, images, and web content articles. How does the WebDAV URL get generated?

WebDAV storage

The portal generated the WebDAV URL for each Document Library document in `svn://svn.liferay.com/repos/public/portal/trunk/portal-web/docroot/html/portlet/document_library/view_file_entry.jsp` as follows:

```
String webDavUrl = themeDisplay.getPortalURL() + "/tunnel-web/
secure/webdav" + group.getFriendlyURL() + "/document_library" +
sb.toString();
```

You would find a similar expression for each Document and Media Library image and web content article.

This servlet can be protected by the secure filter `com.liferay.portal.servlet.filters.secure.SecureFilter`.

```
webdav.servlet.hosts.allowed=
webdav.servlet.https.required=false
```

The previous code shows that a list of comma-delimited IPs can access this servlet via the property `webdav.servlet.hosts.allowed`. Enter a blank list to allow any IP to access this servlet. You can set the property `webdav.servlet.https.required` to `true`, if this servlet can only be accessed via https.

It is the `WebDAVServlet` class that extends the `HttpServlet` class and also handles WebDAV URLs. To bring WebDAV into the Knowledge Base portlet, you can specify it with two tags as follows. You would find similar specification for Document Library, and web content in the portal core as follows:

```
<webdav-storage-token>knowledge_base</webdav-storage-token>
<webdav-storage-class> com.liferay.knowledgebase.admin.webdav.
KBWebDAVStorageImpl</webdav-storage-class>
```

The `webdav-storage-token` value is the WebDAV directory name for data managed by this portlet. The `webdav-storage-class` value must be a class that implements `com.liferay.portal.kernel.webdav.WebDAVStorage` and allows data to be exposed via the WebDAV protocol.

WebDAV models and services

The portal provides a set of models and services to support WebDAV, and to generate a WebDAV URL. The following table shows an overview of these models and services:

Model/Service	Utility	Implementation	Description
WebCacheItem, WebCachePool	WebCache PoolUtil	WebCachePoolImpl	Web cache management
Resource Status	WebDAVUtil	BaseResourceImpl DLFileEntryResourceImpl	WebDAV models: resource and status
WebDAVRequest	WebDAVUtil	WebDAVRequestImpl	WebDAV request interface
WebDAVStorage	WebDAVUtil	BaseWebDAVStorageImpl CompanyWebDAVStorageImpl GroupWebDAVStorageImpl DLWebDAVStorageImpl	WebDAV storage interface

Multiple repositories

On one hand, documents can be added into different repositories. On the other hand, an additional repository can be added into a specific folder—mounting existing CMIS repositories (per folder basis), that is, the portal supports multiple repositories.

Repository interface

The portal defines the repository access interface for access to third-party repositories, and it enables support for simultaneous access to the Liferay repository and third party repository at the folder level, that is, the interface `com.liferay.portal.kernel.repository.Repository` defines a set of signatures. The following code snippet demonstrates this:

```
public FileEntry addFileEntry(long folderId, String title,
String description, String changeLog,
InputStream is, long size, ServiceContext serviceContext)
throws PortalException, SystemException;
public Folder addFolder(
// see details in Repository.java
```

The interface `BaseRepository` extends the interface `Repository`. It brings the interface `LocalRepository` into the picture. This interface got implemented by the abstract class `BaseRepositoryImpl`. Third-party repository implementations should extend this class.

The interface `LocalRepository` got implemented by the class `BaseLocalRepositoryImpl`. This class is designed for third-party repository implementations. Since, the paradigm of remote and local services exist only within the portal, the assumption is that all permission-checking will be delegated to the specific repository.

There are also many calls within the class `BaseLocalRepositoryImpl` that are passed into a user ID as a parameter. These methods should only be called for administration of Liferay repositories and are hence not supported in all third-party repositories. This includes moving between Document Library hooks and LAR import/export.

Document hooks

The portal provides configurable hooks to bring document files into various persistence systems. The hooks include **File System Store, Advanced File System Store, CMIS Store, S3 Store**, and **JCR Store**. A new hook called **Documentum Hook** is available for allowing the Document Library to use **Documentum** as a repository. The default repository is set via the property `dl.store.impl` in `portal.properties` as follows:

```
#dl.store.impl=com.liferay.documentlibrary.util.AdvancedFileSystemStore
#dl.store.impl=com.liferay.portlet.documentlibrary.store.DBStore
#dl.store.impl=com.liferay.documentlibrary.util.CMISStore
dl.store.impl=com.liferay.documentlibrary.util.FileSystemStore
#dl.store.impl=com.liferay.documentlibrary.util.JCRStore
#dl.store.impl=com.liferay.documentlibrary.util.S3Store
```

The previous code sets the name of the class that implements the interface `com.liferay.documentlibrary.store.Store`. The Document Library server will use the interface `Store` to persist documents. `Store` defines a set of signatures to persist documents as follows:

```
public static final String DEFAULT_VERSION = "1.0";
public void addDirectory
// see details in Hook.java
```

The `Store` interface is implemented by the abstract class `BaseStore`. All specific hooks must extend this abstract class. The following table shows specific hooks and their implementation details:

Hook	Services	Interface	Description
CMISStore	CMISObject CMISUtil	Store BaseStore	Content Management Interoperability Services (CMIS) - a standard proposal consisting of a set of Web services for sharing information among disparate content repositories, which seeks to ensure interoperability for people, and applications using multiple content repositories.
DBStore	ava.sql.Blob	Store BaseStore	Saved directly to the server's database as Blob.

Hook	Services	Interface	Description
FileSystemStore	Java.io.File	Store BaseStore	Saved directly to the server's FileSystem and doesn't use any database or translation layer
AdvancedFileSystem Store	Java.io.File	extends FileSystemStore	Advanced File System Store extends File System Store by distributing the files in multiple directories, and thus avoiding filesystem limits on number of files per directory. It divides the data into smaller groups.
JCRStore	javax.jcr. Session, Node	Store BaseStore	Content Repository API for Java (JCR) - a specification for a Java platform API for accessing content repositories in a uniform manner; provides hooks to a for using Jackrabbit.
S3Store	S3Bucket S3Service	Store BaseStore	Amazon S3 (Simple Storage Service) is an online storage web service offered by Amazon Web Services. Amazon S3 provides unlimited storage through a simple web services interface.

Converting repositories

By default, the portal specifies File System Hook in `portal.properties` to persist documents. After a while, you may want to convert the repository from File System Store to **Database Store**. This conversion process can be done by the administration tool in the Control Panel.

As you can see, the conversion processes include database migration, Document Library hook migration, hook, and legacy permission algorithm migration. What's happening? The portal has specified the following properties for conversion processes:

```
convert.processes=\
  com.liferay.portal.convert.ConvertDatabase,\
  com.liferay.portal.convert.ConvertDocumentLibrary,\
  // see details in portal.properties
  com.liferay.portal.convert.ConvertWikiCreole
```

As shown previously, you could input a list of comma-delimited class names that implement `com.liferay.portal.convert.ConvertProcess`. These classes, such as, `ConvertDatabase`, `ConvertDocumentLibrary`, `ConvertDocumentLibraryExtraSettings`, `ConvertImageGallery`, `ConvertPermissionAlgorithm`, `ConvertPermissionTuner`, and `ConvertWikiCreole` provide capabilities to convert database, documents repositories, images repositories, and permission algorithms.

The abstract class `ConvertProcess` leverages the class `org.apache.commons.lang.time.StopWatch` and the utility class `com.liferay.portal.util.MaintenanceUtil` for the method `convert()`. This is the main reason that while converting, you will see a message about maintenance. By the way, the abstract methods `getDescription()`, `isEnabled()`, and `doConvert()` must get implemented by specific classes like `ConvertDocumentLibrary` and `ConvertDocumentLibraryExtraSettings`.

The class `ConvertDocumentLibrary` extends `ConvertProcess` and implements the methods `getDescription()`, `isEnabled()`, and `doConvert()`. This class is used to convert documents from one document repository to another document repository. Similarly, the class `ConvertDocumentLibraryExtraSettings` extends `ConvertProcess` and implements the methods `getDescription()`, `isEnabled()`, and `doConvert()` as well. This class is used to convert the Document Library's extra settings.

CMIS consumer and producer

The portal supports CMIS, acting as either a consumer or producer through **OpenCMIS**. CMIS Hook is built-in in the Document and Media Library, acting as a CMIS consumer. Furthermore, the portal allows the Document Library acting as a CMIS producer, much like that of WebDAV.

Apache Chemistry provides open source implementations of the Content Management Interoperability Services (CMIS) specification. OpenCMIS is the CMIS client and server library for Java. OpenCMIS provides two CMIS client APIs, which are called **Client API** and **Client Bindings API**. The OpenCMIS Server Framework handles both CMIS bindings on the server side and maps them to a common set of Java interfaces. The Apache Chemistry can be found at: `http://chemistry.apache.org/`.

The following table shows the main models for both CMIS and the Liferay local repository:

Model	Extends	Implementation	Description
RepositoryModel	GroupedModel, ClassedModel	None	Repository base model
CMISModel	None	CMISFileEntry CMISFileVersion CMISFolder	CMIS model
LiferayModel	LiferayBase	LiferayFileEntry, LiferayFileVersion, LiferayFolder	Liferay repository model
FileEntry	RepositoryModel <FileEntry>	CMISFileEntry, LiferayFileEntry	File entry for both CMIS and Liferay
FileVersion	RepositoryModel <FileVersion>	CMISFileVersion, LiferayFileVersion	File version for both CMIS and Liferay
Folder	RepositoryModel <Folder>	CMISFolder, LiferayFolder	Folder for both CMIS and Liferay

As a CMIS consumer, the portal is able to mount existing CMIS repositories into the Document Library through the **Atom Publishing Protocol (AtomPub)** or the web service. Similarly, as a CMIS producer, the portal has the capability to export the functionality of the Document Library through the AtomPub or web service.

The following table shows CMIS AtomPub and web services, along with their implementation:

Service	Extends	Implementation	Description
com.liferay. portal.kernel. repository.cmis. Session	none	com.liferay.portal.repository. cmis.SessionImpl	CMIS session and set Default Context
CMISRepository Handler	BaseRepository Impl	CMISAtomPubRepository CMISWebServicesRepository	CMIS Repository Handler
com.liferay. portal.kernel. repository.cmis. CMISRepository Util	none	com.liferay.portal.repository. cmis.CMISRepositoryUtil	CMIS repository utility; use PortalClassInvoke to invoke an internal implementation

SharePoint integration

The portal implements the **SharePoint** protocol, which allows us to save documents to the portal, as if it were a SharePoint server. In `portal.properties`, you will find the following configuration:

```
sharepoint.storage.tokens=document_library
sharepoint.storage.class[document_library]=com.liferay.portlet.
documentlibrary.sharepoint.DLSharepointStorageImpl
```

The previous code shows the integration of SharePoint in the portal. It sets the tokens for supported SharePoint storage paths first. It then sets the class names for supported SharePoint storage classes, for example, `com.liferay.portlet.documentlibrary.sharepoint.DLSharepointStorageImpl`. The class `DLSharepointStorageImpl` extends the abstract class `com.liferay.portal.sharepoint.BaseSharepointStorageImpl`, which implements the interface `com.liferay.portal.sharepoint.SharepointStorage`.

The following table shows SharePoint integration-related interfaces, abstract base implementation, and normal implementation:

Interface	Base Implementation	Implementation	Description
com.liferay. portal.sharepoint. SharepointStorage	BaseSharepoint StorageImpl	CompanySharepoint StorageImpl GroupSharepoint StorageImpl DLSharepoint StorageImpl	SharePoint storage: company-level, group-level, and Document Library implementation
com.liferay.portal. sharepoint,Response Element	none	Property Leaf Tree	SharePoint response element interface and its implementation
com.liferay.portal. sharepoint.dws. ResponseElement	none	RoleResponseElement MemberResponseElement	SharePoint Document Workspace Web service response element and its implementation

Interface	Base Implementation	Implementation	Description
com.liferay.portal. sharepoint.methods. Method	BaseMethodImpl	CreateURLDirectories MethodImpl	SharePoint integration methods
		GetDocsMetaInfoMethod Impl	
		GetDocumentMethodImpl	
		ListDocumentsMetaInfo MethodImpl	
		MoveDocumentMethod Impl	
		OpenServiceMethodImpl	
		PutDocumentMethodImpl	
		RemoveDocumentMethod Impl	
		UncheckoutDocument MethodImpl	
		UrlToWebUrlMethodImpl	

In addition to the previous interfaces, the portal provides the class `SharepointRequest` to set up **Sharepoint Storage**, **Http Servlet Request**, **Http Servlet Response**, and more. It also provides a set of filters and servlets to integrate SharePoint: `SharepointDocumentWorkspaceServlet`, `SharepointFilter` (extending `SecureFilter`), `SharepointServlet`, `SharepointWebServicesServlet`, and so on.

Documentum integration

Documentum, an **Enterprise Content Management** (ECM) platform, provides management capabilities for all types of content, including business documents, photos, videos, medical images, e-mails, web pages, fixed content, XML-tagged documents, and so on. The core of Documentum is a repository in which the content is stored securely under compliance rules. Refer to `http://www.emc.com/` for more information.

Besides the CMIS integration with the Documentum, the portal provides a `Hook` called `DocumentumHook`, so that you can integrate Documentum as a direct repository of the Document Library as follows:

```
dl.hook.impl=com.liferay.documentum.hook.DocumentumHook
```

The class `DocumentumHook` extends the abstract class `BaseHook`, implementing the interface `Hook`. Based on the web service calls, it provides implementation for a set of methods: `add directory`, `add file`, `delete directory`, `delete file`, `get file as stream` (downloading a file), `re-index`, `update file`, and so on.

In fact, the `Hook`, `DocumentumHook`, leverages a set of services provided by the Documentum web service client such as, `com.documentum.com.DfClientX`, `com.documentum.fc.client.IDfClient`, `IDfCollection`, `IDfDocument`, `IDfFolder`, `IDfSession`, `IDfSessionManager`, and so on.

The following properties could be used to configure the Documentum web service calls:

```
dfc.docbroker.host=localhost
dfc.docbroker.port=1489
dfc.globalregistry.repository=documentum
dfc.globalregistry.username=dm_bof_registry
dfc.globalregistry.password=test
```

The first two properties set the host and port to the Documentum server. The next three properties set the global repository and credentials for accessing Documentum.

Alfresco integration

Alfresco is an open source enterprise content management system for displaying documents, web, records, images, and collaborative content development. Refer to `http://www.alfresco.com` for more information.

In brief, Alfresco could be integrated in the portal, using the following approaches:

1. Web services: referring to the Alfresco Content portlet
2. RESTful services: OpenSearch, referring to the Alfresco Content portlet
3. RESTful services: web scripts, using Alfresco as the direct repository of the Document Library
4. CMIS: using CMIS Document Library Hook
5. Portlets: using the Alfresco web client as a set of portlets

Alfresco CMIS explores the benefits of introducing CMIS into the content applications. CMIS is an emerging standard for improving RESTful interoperability between ECM systems. For CMIS-based integration, Alfresco provides the following CMIS bindings:

1. CMIS AtomPub binding: This is used to see the AtomPub service document
2. CMIS web services binding: This is used to see WSDL documents

In fact, the class `CMISHook` extends the abstract class `BaseHook`, implementing the interface `Hook`. Based on the CMIS AtomPub binding or CMIS web service binding, it provides detailed implementation to add a directory and file, to delete a directory and file, get a file as stream (downloading a file), re-index, update a file, and so on. The class `CMISStore` could use the following properties to consume Alfresco CMIS:

```
dl.store.cmis.credentials.username=none
dl.store.cmis.credentials.password=none
cmis.repository.url= http://localhost:8080/alfresco/service/api/cmis
dl.store.cmis.system.root.dir=Liferay Home
```

Of course, you would be able to overwrite the previous properties in `portal-ext.properties`. As you can see, both CMIS version 1.0 and 0.61 got supported in the `CMISStore`. The following table shows details of the `CMISStore` implementation:

Name	Extends	Model	Description
CMISConstants_1_0_0	CMISConstants	None	CMIS 1.0 constants
CMISConstants_0_6_1	CMISConstants	none	CMIS 0.61 constants
CMISObject	org.apache.abdera.model. ExtensibleElementWrapper	org.apache. abdera. model. Element	CMIS Object
CMISRepositoryInfo	org.apache.abdera.model. ElementWrapper	org.apache. abdera. model. Element	CMIS repository information
CMISExtensionFactory	org.apache.abdera.util. AbstractExtensionFactory	none	CMIS extension factory

Apache Abdera provides a functionally-complete, high-performance implementation of the **IETF Atom Syndication Format** (RFC 4287) and **Atom Publishing Protocol (RFC 5023)** specifications, which are standards for creating, editing, and publishing web feeds and other web resources. Refer to `http://abdera.apache.org/` for more information.

Records management

Records management (RM) is the practice of maintaining the records of an organization from the time they are created up to their eventual disposal, including scanning, classifying, storing, securing, capturing, and tracking records, and automatic data extraction – using the **OCR** (**Optical Character Recognition**) component to convert **TIFF** and other unsearchable files to text. A record can be either a tangible object or digital information, for example, birth certificates, medical x-rays, office documents, databases, application data, fax, and e-mail.

The **United States Department of Defense standard DoD 5015.02-STD** defines records management as

> *The planning, controlling, directing, organizing, training, promoting, and other managerial activities involving the life cycle of information, including creation, maintenance (usage, storage, retrieval), and disposal, regardless of media.*

OCR is an electronic translation of scanned images of handwritten, typewritten, or printed text into machine-encoded text. OCR software enables us to extract text from an image and convert it into an editable text document. For example, you need the text from an image (such as, fax, e-mail, EDI, scanned document, scanned PDF, and so on). And you don't have to sit and type in the whole text. What can you do? Just scan the document and then use the OCR tool to convert it into editable text.

Records in Document Library

As you know, Document Library provides capabilities to manage documents with folders, file entries, searchable file content, and whether the file content is readable by `Tika`. **Apache Tika** is a toolkit for detecting and extracting metadata and structured text content from various documents, using existing parser libraries, that is, Document Library is able to manage documents and extract document content. Records management isn't in the picture, by default. This section will address how to build the records management system on top of Document Library, as well as that of documents management.

The records management system should have features: web-based, remote scanning, and remote site, capturing scanned document information using bar-code, regular expressions, and phrases.

Document scanning (or called image scanning) is the process of converting text and graphic paper documents, photographic film, photographic paper, or other files to digital images. Records are scanned documents, such as, insurance claims, mortgage files, patient records, tax reports, invoices, and sales orders coming via mail, fax, e-mail, and **EDI (Electronic Data Interchange)**. In general, a record can be either a tangible object or digital information—an un-editable and unsearchable document.

The regular data flow of records management should first include document tracking capability. Document tracking allows you to initiate document tracking right at the beginning of the process.

Then it covers document ingestion, such as, scanning, importing, and linking. Importable records would be fax, e-mail, EDI, or any scanned documents. And the scanners would be web scanner (using the local scanner device in web browsers and the store scanned document in the web application server) and other devices such as pen scanners, card scanners, or mobile scanners. All scanned documents are saved in the web application server. Generally speaking, it scans documents using web scanners or other devices like pen scanners, card scanners, and mobile scanners, and ingests documents using mailroom level scanners such as IBML, Opex, or NCR, or receives documents via fax from a fax server, e-mail from an e-mail server, or EDI (short for Electronic Data Interchange).

When uploading records, it will perform automatic data extraction via an OCR engine, that is, it captures appurtenant data from the records, and meanwhile, it extracts the full text from the records too. Most importantly, the OCR engine should show capability to recognize English text, other languages, and Unicode characters like Chinese.

Metadata information should cover dates, patient card ID, load numbers, policy numbers, claim numbers, invoice numbers, bar-coded values, and even a table, a line item, and so on. This metadata information can be retrieved through learning processes based on different content types—training the OCR engine to recognize special metadata by learning processes.

OCR-supported bar code formats should cover the following:

1. CODE 128 (128b, 128C, 128raw)
2. EAN (International Article Number) 8 and 13
3. UPC (Universal Product Code)
4. Code 3 of 9
5. Code interleaved 2 of 5

OCR-supported image formats should cover the following:

Format	Extension	Description
Adobe Photoshop	.psd	Photoshop's native format stores an image with support for most imaging options available in Photoshop.
Bitmap, Windows/OS2	.bmp, .dib	A raster graphics image file format used to store bitmap digital images
Cursor	.cur	The cursor file format is an almost identical image file format for non-animated cursors
Graphics Interchange Format	.gif	A bitmap image format
Icon	.ico	An image file format for icons; contains one or more small images at multiple sizes and color depths.
JPEG	.jpeg, .jpg	A commonly used method of lossy compression for digital images
Macintosh PICT Format	.pict, .pct	A graphics file format as standard metafile format
PCX Format	.pcx	A device-independent raster image format
Portable Network Graphics	.png	A bitmapped image format and video codec that employs lossless data compression
Sun Raster Format	.ras	A raster graphics file format
Tag Image File Format	.tif, .tiff	A file format for mainly storing raster images
Targa	.tga	A raster graphics file format; an acronym for Truevision Advanced Raster Graphics Adapter.
X Bitmap	.xbm	A plain text monochrome image format for storing cursor and icon bitmaps used in the X GUI.
X PixMap	.xpm	Primarily used for creating icon pixmaps, and supporting transparent color

In addition, Portable Document Format (PDF) is a file format widely used for all kinds of documents. PDF could be used to extract text, and then index the text extracted for search. Thus, OCR engine should be able to extract text from images stored in PDF files.

By the way, OCR engines should have a high-level of accuracy and page layout analysis, and should be able to recognize text in multiple languages such as, Arabic, English, Bulgarian, Catalan, Czech, Chinese (both simplified and traditional), Danish (standard and Fraktur script), German, Greek, Finnish, French, Hebrew, Croatian, Hungarian, Indonesian, Italian, Japanese, Korean, Latvian, Lithuanian, Dutch, Norwegian, Polish, Portuguese, Romanian, Russian, Slovak (standard and Fraktur script), Slovenian, Spanish, Serbian, Swedish, Tagalog, Thai, Turkish, Ukrainian, Vietnamese, and so on. Moreover, OCR engines should be flexibly trained to work in other languages too.

After OCR data extraction, it saves the original scanned document as a file entry — that is, a scanned document. It also saves metadata as part of the record metadata. And it saves the full text extracted by OCR engine as an extra string.

Once having scanned documents, metadata, and full text saved, it manages records in the Liferay Portal. And a record could be previewed as scanned document and searchable via its metadata and full text. Of course, the records management system would be able to allow the admin to update the full text of records — manually correcting OCR text extraction results, if needed.

Record model

The Document Library does have a model currently to support document management. For records management, we're not going to create a new wheel. Instead, reuse the current model, and make it support both document management and records management.

First, let's extend the model to support records management in the Document Library. To do so, add the following columns for the entity, `DLFileEntry`, in the DL, `service.xml`:

```
<column name="type" type="String" />
<column name="text" type="String" />
```

As shown in the previous code, it adds two columns: type and text. The column type should be a short string, such as, 75 characters; while the column text should be a long text.

The column type will be used to identify whether it is a document or a record. If it is a document, use Document Library's default processes. Otherwise, use the previous OCR-based data flow processes.

The column text will be used for the type record only, storing the full text extracted by an OCR engine. Keep this column blank, when the type is document.

Once the updated `service.xml` is ready, you can use the service-builder to re-generate models and services. From now on, the Document Library is going to support both documents management and records management.

Records validation and classification

During the OCR recognition phase, you would be able to review records, validate metadata extraction, train the OCR engine to recognize metadata from different record types, and classify records via record types in the records management systems (RMS).

Record classification includes determining document or file naming conventions and identifying metadata. The best way to ensure that the record can be retrieved is to group the records within a category. This process is called **classifying the record**, as they are grouped into record types. For example, the record type Patient Record must have metadata such as card ID, date of birth, and so on, while the record type Invoice Record should have metadata such as invoice date, part number, invoice total, state, and city. Obviously, RMS should have the capability to allow end users to define custom record types in runtime.

Records, where certain data fields are missing from OCR extraction, need to be validated by the user. This can be done by entering the correct data in the empty textboxes. And different data fields will be seen, depending on the type of record.

The previous tasks (records review, validation, and classification) can be done through a pre-defined workflow, and different workflows can be applied for the same purpose in runtime. Users can train the engine to recognize the documents by giving samples, and the RMS will learn them by utilizing several technologies like OCR.

Records indexing

Once a record is saved in the Document Library, the metadata and the full text of that record should be indexed as well. One simple option to present record metadata is by using custom attributes. The following is the sample code from the method `doGetDocument` of the class `com.liferay.portlet.documentlibrary.DLIndexer.java`:

```
String type = fileEntry.getType();
String text = fileEntry.getText();
document.addKeyword("type", type);
// see details in DLIndexer.java
ExpandoBridgeIndexerUtil.addAttributes(document, expandoBridge);
```

As shown in the previous code, it indexes the type as `addKeyword`, the text as `addText`, and record metadata is indexed as custom attributes.

OCR engines

The following OCR engines may meet your requirements for converting images into text:

1. **Tesseract**: This is an optical character recognition engine for various operating systems, and one of the most accurate open source OCR engines available. The source code will read a binary, gray, or color image and output text. A TIFF reader is built in and it reads uncompressed TIFF images. It also supports multiple language recognition. Refer to `http://code.google.com/p/tesseract-ocr` for more information.

2. **Readiris**: This converts your paper documents into editable text or PDF files that you can edit, share, and store. Refer to the **I.R.I.S.** at `http://www.irislink.com/` for more information.

3. **Asprise OCR**: This is an OCR engine used to transform images (for example, images scanned from paper documents) into editable text-based computer files. Its features include high-level of accuracy, format retention, and barcode recognition. Refer to `http://asprise.com/` for more information.

4. **ABBYY FineReader**: This is an OCR software for text recognition and for creating editable and searchable electronic files from scanned paper documents, PDFs, and digital photographs. Refer to `http://finereader.abbyy.com/` for more information.

5. **RecoStar**: This extracts text from bitmap documents, scans, or faxes, making the information accessible for file search, indexing, or data warehousing tools. The supported input formats include: TIFF, JPEG, BMP, PNG, GIF, and PDF. Output can be stored as Searchable PDF (PDF/A), plain text, or XML. Refer to OpenText at `http://www.captaris-dt.com/product/recostar/` for more information.

6. **OCRopus**: This is a state-of-the-art document analysis and OCR system, featuring pluggable layout analysis, pluggable character recognition, statistical natural language modeling, and multi-lingual capabilities. Refer to `http://code.google.com/p/ocropus/` for more information.

7. **GOCR**: This is an OCR program, converting scanned images of text back to text files. Refer to `http://jocr.sourceforge.net/` for more information.

8. **SimpleOCR**: This is the popular freeware OCR software, a royalty-free **OCR SDK** for custom applications. Refer to `http://www.simpleocr.com/` for more information.

9. **OmniPage**: This is an optical character recognition application, converting images, such as, scanned paper documents and PDF files into document file formats. Refer to `http://www.nuance.com/for-individuals/by-product/omnipage/` for more information.

10. **Microsoft OneNote**: This is simplicity personified. But it's not too great for handwritten characters or even fuzzy ones. **Microsoft Office Document Imaging** handles printed text ably.

11. **TopOCR** (called **SnapReader**): This is designed more for digital cameras and mobile phones along with scanners. Refer to `http://www.topocr.com/` for more information.

The following online OCR services may meet your needs to convert images into text.

1. **Google Docs**: These allow us to upload images or PDF files, scan the file, and use computer algorithms to convert the file into a Google document. Refer to `https://docs.google.com` for more information.

2. **FineReader Online**: This is an online OCR service to provide accurate and swift conversion of scanned and photographed images, and PDFs into editable Word, Excel, RTF, TXT, and searchable PDF documents. Refer to `http://finereader.abbyyonline.com` for more information.

3. **Free OCR**: This is a graphical frontend for Google's Tesseract OCR engine that is often considered as one of the most accurate text recognition engines around. Refer to `http://www.free-ocr.com/` for more information.

4. **OCR Terminal**: This is an online OCR service that converts image formats (TIFF, JPEG, PNG, PDF, and so on) to editable (RTF, DOC, TXT) and searchable PDF formats. Refer to `https://www.ocrterminal.com/` for more information.

5. **OCR Online**: This extracts text from image formats (JPG, JPEG, BMP, TIFF, and GIF) and converts it into editable Word, Text, Excel, PDF, and HTML output formats. Converted documents look exactly like the original — tables, columns, and graphics. Refer to `http://www.free-ocr.com/` for more information.

Building relationship

A relationship is a general term, covering the specific types of logical connections found on **class diagrams** and **object diagrams** of **UML**. Instance-level relationships of UML cover external link, association, aggregation, composition, dependency, and so on.

Relationships exist in the records management system. For example, record A and record B may have different relationships, such as external link (called reference), association, aggregation (like whole-part), and composition (like parent-child).

Relationships can exist among records and documents inside the Document Library. For example, record A is associated with document A and record B refers to document B.

Relationships can exist among different content types like Document Library, web content, and so on. For example, record A and document B are associated with image A.

This relationship could be a **one-one**, presented as **1:1**, or a **one-many**, presented as **1:n**, or a **many-one**, presented as **m:1**, or a **many-many**, presented as **m:n**. Moreover, relationships could exist among any entities. How to implement the same in the portal? The following section will propose a solution for this.

Model

First of all, define an entity called Relationship in the service XML file portal service.xml as follows:

```
<entity name="Relationship" uuid="true" local-service="true" remote-
service="true">
   <!-- PK fields -->
   <column name="relationshipId" type="long" primary="true" />
   <!-- Audit fields -->
   <!-- Other fields -->
   <column name="fromGroupId" type="long" />
   <column name="fromClassNameId" type="long" />
   <column name="fromClassPK" type="long" />
   <column name="toGroupId" type="long" />
   <column name="toClassNameId" type="long" />
   <column name="toClassPK" type="long" />
   <column name="type" type="String" />
   <!-- Finder methods -->
   <!-- see details in service.xml -->
</entity>
```

As shown in the previous code, the entity Relationship is defined with the primary key relationshipId, audit fields such as, companyId, userId, userName, and createDate, and other fields such as fromGroupId, fromClassNameId, fromClassPK, toGroupId, toClassNameId, toClassPK, type, and description.

As you can see, relationships are scoped into the portal instance level, that is, `from-entity` and `to-entity`, and must share the same `companyId`. For example, record A and document B are associated with image A, and record A, document B, and image A can be scoped into different groups, but they should be scoped into the same portal instance. Moreover, the `from-entity`, `fromClassPK` and the `to-entity`, `toClassPK` can be scoped into the same group, when the `from-group`, `fromGroupId` and the `to-group`, `toGroupId` have the same values. Alternatively, the `from-entity` and the `to-entity` can be scoped into different groups, when `from-group` and `to-group` have different values.

More specifically, the `from-entity`, `fromClassPK`, and the `to-entity`, `toClassPK` can belong to a same content type, when the `from-class-name`, `fromClassNameId` and the `to-class-name`, `toClassNameId` have the same values. Alternatively, the `from-entity` and the `to-entity` can belong to different content types, when the `from-class-name` and `to-class-name` are different.

The column type can have configurable values like external link, association, aggregation, composition, dependency, and so on. Of course, you will be able to predefine relationship types through the property `entity.relationship.types` in the `portal.properties` and be able to override the same in `portal-ext.properties` later.

Services

Once `service.xml` is ready, you could use the service builder to generate models and services in the portal core. Afterwards, you would see a set of models and services generated. Of course, it would be nice if you could add your own implementation in the source code `RelationshipLocalServiceImpl.java` and `RelationshipServiceImpl.java`.

Next, insert functions of updating relationships in the UI part, when updating an entity like image, document, record, web content, and so on. This can be done by calling relationship service utility `RelationshipLocalServiceUtil` or `RelationshipServiceUtil`.

As you can see, the previous model can present different relationships among different content types and/or entities, including a one-one, like 1:1; a one-many, like 1:n; a many-one, like m:1; or a many-many, like m:n.

Portal-instance level relationship

The portal has specified a few relationships in the portal-instance level. For example, the entity `Role` and `Group` have a many-many relationship, same as that of `Role` and `Permission`, and `Role` and `User`:

```
<!-- Relationships -->
<column name="groups" type="Collection" entity="Group" mapping-
table="Groups_Roles" />
<column name="users" type="Collection" entity="User" mapping-
table="Users_Roles" />
```

As shown in the previous code, the `entity Group` and `mapping-table`, `Groups_Roles` attributes are specified, but attribute `mapping-key` is not specified. The service builder will assume that you are specifying a many-many relationship.

Similarly, the portal has specified a many-many relationship between the entity `Team` and `User`, and `Team` and `User Group` as follows:

```
<!-- Relationships -->
<column name="users" type="Collection" entity="User" mapping-
table="Users_Teams" />
<column name="userGroups" type="Collection" entity="UserGroup"
mapping-table="UserGroups_Teams" />
```

You will find similar many-many relationships among the entities **User Group**, **Group**, **User**, **Team**, **Organization**, **Role**, and **Permission**. More details can be found in the portal service XML `service.xml`.

In particular, if the entity and `mapping-key` attributes are specified, but the `mapping-table` is not specified, then the service builder will assume that you are specifying a one-many relationship. For example:

```
<column name="shoppingItemPrices" type="Collection"
    entity="ShoppingItemPrice" mapping-key="itemId"
/>
```

The previous column specifies that there will be a getter called `pojo.getShoppingItemPrices()` that will return a collection. It will map to a column called `itemId` in the table that maps to the entity `ShoppingItemPrice`.

Content authoring

Authoring is the process of composing a course-ware, web page, or a multimedia application (presentation) with text, sound, still and video pictures, and animation. Authoring also includes creating and navigating other tools that allow interaction between the user and the application.

In the portal core, it would be nice to have the capability to add authoring information in any content database schema. For example, when adding a record into the Document Library, you would be able to add author information, and when auditing information, you would be able to see who updated the record and when the record got updated.

For content types, such as image, DL document/record, and web content article, the following fields are added for content creation or modification:

```
<column name="userId" type="long" />
<column name="userName" type="String" />
<column name="createDate" type="Date" />
<column name="modifiedDate" type="Date" />
```

As you can see, the model is able to store created date and modified date, that is, for a given entity like a record, you would know when it got created and when it got updated. However, there is one and only one username existing in the model. When an entity instance gets created, the username will be marked as the **content creator** (or called **content author**). When the entity instance gets updated, the username will be marked as the **content modifier**, where the original content creator information will get lost.

Document Library has added version-related user information as follows:

```
<column name="versionUserId" type="long" />
<column name="versionUserName" type="String" />
```

This is a good thing that will keep version-related content-creator information. As you know, Document Library will maintain different versions of documents or records. Content versioning is the process of assigning either unique version names or unique version numbers to unique states of content (such as documents, records, images, web content, and so on). Within a given version number category (either major or minor), these numbers are generally assigned in increasing order and correspond to new updates of content.

Obviously, content authoring is missing by default. But the content authoring is widely used in many real use cases. Therefore, it would be nice to add content authoring capabilities for different content types.

How to implement content authoring? You can simply add authoring fields for any content models. For example, add the following two fields in the Document Library (referring to the service XML documentlibrary DL service.xml):

```
<column name="authorId" type="long" />
<column name="authorName" type="String" />
```

As shown in the previous code, at least two use cases are covered as well. When adding a new content like a record, you would have a chance to input author information. This author could be a regular user inside the portal. Thus, the system will save selected user's ID and name as the author's user ID and author's name, respectively. This is one use case. Another use case is that the author is not a regular user of the portal yet. Thus the system should ask the end user to input the author's name manually.

Once author information becomes part of metadata of the content, the portal will be able to index the author's name as well. In any use case, the portal would have capabilities to associate author information with any content. Furthermore, all content will be searchable by author name.

Content archiving

An archive is defined as a collection of historical records, as well as the physical place where they are located. Archives contain primary source documents that are kept to show the function of an organization.

For many reasons, either known or unknown, the portal should have capabilities to archive historical documents and records in the Document Library and to manage all archives properly. How to implement this feature?

First, add a column called `archive` as the `Boolean` type in the entity `DLFileEntry` specification as follows:

```
<column name="archive" type="boolean" />
```

The previous code adds the `archive` flag on a document or a record. By default, it is `false`, meaning that the document or record is not archived yet. Once it is `true`, the document or record becomes part of the archives.

Then, use the service builder to update models and services in order to support archiving capabilities. Of course, you would be able to implement the same on other content types such as web content, and so on.

Last, but not least, don't forget the indexing of the archive flag. The following sample code should be added to the `doGetDocument` method of the class `com.liferay.documentlibrary.util.DLIndexer.java`:

```
boolean archive = fileEntry.isArchive();
document.addKeyword("archive", archive);
```

Expected features of content archiving are listed as follows. Of course, you may have your own specific requirements. What you can do is that you can use the same framework and add new functions on top of the framework. These functions are as follows:

1. The ability to auto-archive documents, based on a specific date
2. The ability to manage archives
3. The ability to make all archives searchable or classifiable
4. The ability to navigate archives in a very intuitive way, by using a calendar view

Summary

In this chapter, you learnt about video and image management, document management, WebDAV implementation, multiple repositories integration, CMIS consumers and producers, web scanning, OCR and record management, content relationships, content authoring, and content archiving.

In *Chapter 6, DDL and WCM*, we're going to introduce DDL and WCM.

6
DDL and WCM

A **Web Content Management (WCM)** system is designed to simplify the publication of web content to both regular websites and mobile devices. In particular, it allows content creators to submit the content without requiring technical knowledge of HTML or the uploading of files.

A WCM is a software system used to control a dynamic collection of web material, such as, HTML documents, images, and other forms of media. While a CMS facilitates document control, auditing, editing, and timeline management, a WCM typically facilitates automated templates, access control, scalable expansion, easily editable content, scalable feature sets, content virtualization, content syndication, multiple languages, versioning, and so on.

This chapter will introduce web content first. Then, it will address what custom attributes are and how they work. Afterwards, it will introduce **CKEditor**, **Dynamic Data Lists (DDL)**, and **Dynamic Data Mapping (DDM)**. Finally, assets, asset links, tagging, and categorization will be addressed in detail.

By the end of this chapter, you will have learned how to:

- Customize web content models and services
- Build web content structure
- Build a web content template
- Publish web content—asset publisher
- Integrate CKEditor and its plugins
- Use Expando—custom attributes
- Leverage DDL—dynamisc data lists
- Employ DDM—dynamic data mapping
- Manage assets, asset links, tags, and categories
- Publish assets with asset query

Web content management

Web content is the textual, visual, or aural content, as part of user experience, on websites. It may include, among other things, text, images, sounds, videos, and animations. The portal provides a Web Content Management (WCM) portlet, which manages the structured and unstructured content to be published in a website. The features cover tagging, categorization, versioning, multilanguage support, workflow, scheduled publishing, defining the fields of the web content by creating structures, editing the XML file with a desktop application through WebDAV, defining the look of the custom structures by using Velocity or XSL templates, dynamic publishing, and so on.

Models and services

The following figure depicts an overview of web content management, conceptually. Web content has a set of resources, called JournalArticleResource, associated with it. Each resource may have many versions of journal articles, called JournalArticle, associated with them. As you can see, web content supports versioning at the model level.

And each article called JournalArticle has a unique URL and a WebDAV URL to be referred. Each article like the JournalArticle can have a structure called JournalStructure and a template called JournalTemplate associated with it. The structure is a logical structure of the article — it only states what the article contains, while the template is the real article layout. Therefore, you can first define the fields of the web content by creating structures and then define your own look of the custom structures by defining custom velocity or XSL or FreeMarker template. The structure of the models and services is given as follows:

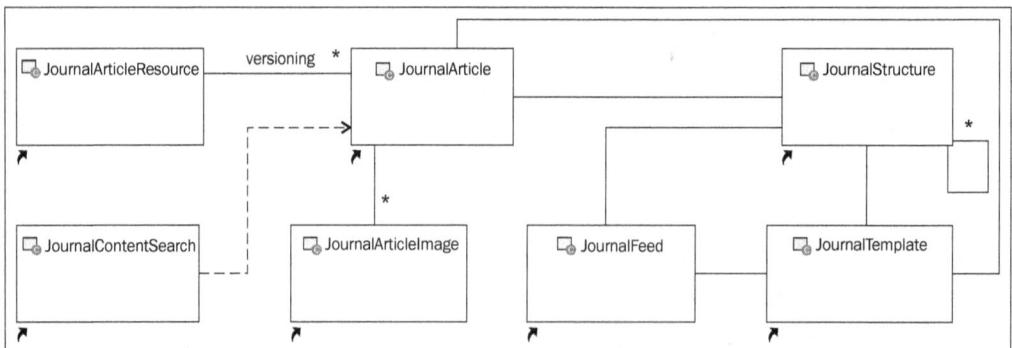

As you can see, based on `JournalStructure` and `JournalTemplate`, RSS feeds of journal articles can be built dynamically, by using `JournalFeed`. In addition, a `JournalArticle` article can have many images associated with it, called `JournalArticleImage`. For search purposes, a model called `JournalContentSearch` is defined, referring to the `JournalArticle` model as dependencies. That is, it provides the ability to search web content associated with journal articles.

Models

The portal has defined the entity `JournalArticleResourse`, in the journal service XML `svn://svn.liferay.com/repos/public/portal/trunk/portal-impl/src/com/liferay/portal/service.xml`, as follows:

```
<!-- PK fields -->
<column name="resourcePrimKey" type="long" primary="true" />
<!-- Other fields -->
<column name="groupId" type="long" />
<column name="articleId" type="String" />
<!-- Finder methods -->
```

As shown in the preceding code, a `JournalArticleResource` entity is defined with the primary key column `resourcePrimKey` and other fields, such as, `groupId` and `articleId`. That is, the `JournalArticleResource` entity mainly specifies association among `JournalArticleResource` and `JournalArticle`, with the help of `resourcePrimKey` and `articleId`, respectively.

In the same service XML, you will find the entity `JournalArticle`, specified as follows:

```
<!-- PK fields -->
<column name="id" type="long" primary="true" />
<!-- Resource -->
<column name="resourcePrimKey" type="long" />
<!-- Group instance -->
<!-- Audit fields -->
<!-- Other fields -->
<column name="smallImageId" type="long" />
<!-- see details in service.xml -->
```

The preceding code shows that the entity `JournalArticle` has a primary key field ID, a resource `resourcePrimKey`, a group instance, audit fields, and other fields; such as, `articleId`, version, title, `urlTitle`, description, content, type, `smallImage`, `smallImageId`, `smallImageURL`, and more.

In the same service XML, you will find other entities and their definitions, such as, `JournalArticleImage`, `JournalStructure`, `JournalTemplate`, `JournalFeed`, and `JournalContentSearch`. The following table shows a summary of these models, their extension, and implementation:

Name	Extension	Implementation	Description
`JournalArticle`	`JournalArticle Model extends BaseModel <JournalArticle>, GroupedModel, ResourcedModel`	`JournalArticleImpl extends JournalArticleModelImpl`	Journal article model
`JournalArticle Display`	`Serializable`	`JournalArticle DisplayImpl`	Journal article display model
`JournalArticle Image`	`JournalArticle ImageModel extends BaseModel <JournalArticle Image>`	`JournalArticleImageImpl extends JournalArticle ImageModelImpl`	Journal article image model
`JournalArticle Resource`	`JournalArticle ResourceModel extends BaseModel <JournalArticleRe source>`	`JournalArticle ResourceImpl extends JournalArticle ResourceModelImpl`	Journal article resource model, for versioning
`JournalContent Search`	`JournalContent SearchModel`	`JournalContentSearchImpl extends JournalContent SearchModelImpl`	Journal content search model, for web content search capabilities
`JournalFeed`	`JournalFeedModel`	`JournalFeedImpl extends JournalFeedModelImpl`	Journal article RSS feed model
`Journal Structure`	`JournalStructure Model`	`JournalStructureImpl extends JournalStructure ModelImpl`	Journal article structure model
`Journal Template`	`JournalTemplate Model`	`JournalTemplateImpl extends JournalTemplateModelImpl`	Journal article template model

In fact, each journal article has a different workflow status; such as approved, pending, inactive, denied, and so on. This kind of status is predefined in the class workflow constant `com.liferay.portal.kernel.workflow.WorkflowConstants`.

Services

`JournalArticle` is also called web content. Based on the previous `service.xml` file, the service builder generates a set of services, such as, `JournalArticleResource`, `JournalArticle`, `JournalStructure`, `JournalTemplate`, `JournalFeed`, and `JournalContentSearch`. The following table shows service interface, utilities, wrappers, and service implementation:

Name	Utility/Wrapper	Implementation	Description
JournalArticle(Local)Service	JournalArticle(local) ServiceUtil JournalArticle(local) ServiceWrapper	JournalArticle(Local) ServiceImpl extends JournalArticle(Local) ServiceBaseImpl	Journal article service with permission checking and local service
JournalArticle Resource (Local)Service	JournalArticleResource (Local)ServiceUtil JournalArticleResource (Local)ServiceWrapper	JournalArticleResource (Local) ServiceImpl extends JournalArticleResource (Local)ServiceBaseImpl	Journal article resource service and local service
JournalStructu re(Local) Service	JournalStructure (Local)ServiceUtil	JournalStructure (Local) ServiceImpl extends JournalStructure (Local)ServiceBaseImpl	Journal structure service and local service
JournalTemplate (Local)Service	JournalTemplate(Local) ServiceUtil	JournalTemplate(Local) ServiceImpl extends JournalTemplate(Local) ServiceBaseImpl	Journal template service and local service
JournalFeed (Local)Service	JournalFeedServiceUtil JournalFeedLocal Service	JournalFeed(Local) ServiceImpl extends JournalFeed(Local) ServiceBaseImpl	Journal feed service and local service
JournalArticle Image(Local) Service	JournalArticleImage ServiceUtil JournalArticleImage LocalServiceUtil	JournalArticleImage (Local) ServiceImpl extends JournalArticleImage (Local)ServiceBaseImpl	Journal article image service and local service
JournalContent Search(Local) Service	JournalContent Search(Local) ServiceUtil	JournalContentSearch (Local) ServiceImpl extends JournalContentSearch (Local)ServiceBaseImpl	Journal content search service and local service

By the way, the class `JournalArticleConstants` defines the following journal article constants:

```
public static final String CANONICAL_URL_SEPARATOR = "/-/";
// see details in JournalArticleConstants.java
public static final String[] TYPES =
    PropsUtil.getArray(PropsKeys.JOURNAL_ARTICLE_TYPES);
```

As shown in the preceding code, the default version will start with 1.0, and the canonical URL separator will be /-/.

Comparator services

Journal articles can be displayed with columns, such as, ID, title, version, created date, display date, modified date, review date, structure primary key, and so on. And these columns can be sorted in ascending or descending order. Eventually, these sortable features are specified in a set of comparators. The following table shows these comparator services:

Name	Extension	Package	Description
ArticleCreateDate Comparator	com.liferay. portal. kernel.util. OrderByComparator	com.liferay. portlet.journal. util.comparator	Compare to object Date create date
ArticleDisplay DateComparator	OrderByComparator implements Comparator, Serializable	com.liferay. portlet.journal. util.comparator	Compare to object Date display date
ArticleID Comparator	OrderByComparator implements Comparator, Serializable	com.liferay. portlet.journal. util.comparator	Compare to object Long ID
ArticleModified DateComparator	OrderByComparator implements Comparator, Serializable	com.liferay. portlet.journal. util.comparator	Compare to object Date modified date
ArticleReview DateComparator	OrderByComparator implements Comparator, Serializable	com.liferay. portlet.journal. util.comparator	Compare to object Date review date
ArticleTitle Comparator	OrderByComparator implements Comparator, Serializable	com.liferay. portlet.journal. util.comparator	Compare to object String Title

Name	Extension	Package	Description
ArticleVersion Comparator	OrderByComparator implements Comparator, Serializable	com.liferay. portlet.journal. util.comparator	Compare to object Double version
StructurePK Comparator	OrderByComparator implements Comparator, Serializable	com.liferay. portlet.journal. util.comparator	Compare to object Long Structure Primary Key

In the same way, you will find comparator services for the **Document Library (DL)**, for instance, FileRankCreateDateComparator, FileVersionComparator, RepositoryModelCreateDateComparator, RepositoryModelModifiedDateComparator, RepositoryModelNameComparator, RepositoryModelReadCountComparator, and RepositoryModelSizeComparator, in the package com.liferay.portlet.documentlibrary.util.comparator.

Journal content services

The portal defines a set of journal content services in the interface JournalContent. The JournalContent constants, static variables, and their values are abstracted from the interface JournalContent:

```
public static final String CACHE_NAME = JournalContent.class.
getName();
// see details in JournalContent.java
public static final String VIEW_MODE_SEPARATOR = "_VIEW_MODE_";
```

Content that is displayed needs to be cached, depending on the protocol. Journal templates have a token called @protocol@, which returns either HTTP or HTTPS, depending on the protocol used by the user to access the page. In fact, the cached function interface is specified in the interface JournalContent.java, as follows:

```
public void clearCache();
public void clearCache(long groupId, String articleId, String
templateId);
```

The other two function interfaces are specified in the interface JournalContent. java. They are getContent, which returns a string, and getDisplay, which returns the interface JournalArticleDisplay.

The interface JournalContent is implemented by JournalContentImpl, and all the methods are exposed to the end user in the utility class JournalContentUtil. That means, in your plugins, you can leverage these methods via the class JournalContentUtil.

Journal tokens

At runtime, several tokens (called journal tokens) included in the journal elements, such as `JournalArticle`, `JournalStructure`, and `JournalTemplate`, will be translated to their applicable runtime value at processing time. Tokens have this form: `@token_name@`.

For example, you can add a view counter through the `JournalArticle` token. You can just add a token `@view_counter@` to either the content of `JournalArticle` or the output of the `JournalArticle` template used. This token is automatically translated to the logic of view counter increment. In fact, the logic (replacing the counter token with the increment call) has been defined in the class `ViewCounterTransformerListener.java`, in the package `com.liferay.portlet.journal.util`, as follows:

```
protected String replace(String s)
{
    Map<String, String> tokens = getTokens();
    // see details in ViewCounterTransformerListener.java
    s = StringUtil.replace(s, counterToken, sb.toString());
    return s;
}
```

The preceding code shows same logic as that of the `JournalArticle` JSP file. Since it is AJAX-based, even if the page is cached somewhere in a proxy, you will get the correct number of views counted. The following table shows a few transformer listeners:

Listener	Extension	Interface	Description
ViewCounterTrans formerListener	BaseTransformer Listener	Transformer Listener	View counter transformer listener, for the token @view_ counter@
TokensTrans formerListener	BaseTransformer Listener	Transformer Listener	Tokens transformer listener
RegexTrans formerListener	BaseTransformer Listener	Transformer Listener	Regex transformer listener
PropertiesTrans formerListener	BaseTransformer Listener	Transformer Listener	Properties transformer listener
LocaleTrans formerListener	BaseTransformer Listener	Transformer Listener	Locale transformer listener, for the token @language_id@
ContentTrans formerListener	BaseTransformer Listener	Transformer Listener	Content transformer listener

Besides the token `@view_counter@`, there are a set of tokens that you can use at runtime, translating to their applicable runtime value at processing time. The following is a subset of the list of tokens and their runtime values:

```
@cdn_host@: themeDisplay.getCDNHost()
// ignore details
@language_id@: the language id of the current request
```

Of course, you are able to add custom journal tokens in the `portal-ext.properties`, as follows:

```
journal.article.token.page.break=@page_break@
journal.article.custom.tokens=custom_token_1,custom_token_2
journal.article.custom.token.value[custom_token_1]=token1
journal.article.custom.token.value[custom_token_2]=token2
```

As shown in the preceding code, you can set the token `@page_break@`, which is used when inserting simple page breaks in articles, and set a list of custom tokens that will be replaced, when article content is rendered. For example, if `custom_token_1` is set, `@custom_token_1@` will be replaced with its token value before an article is displayed.

You can also find the same details in the utility class `com.liferay.portlet.journal.util.JournalUtil`. The following is the code snippet to populate custom tokens:

```
// see details in JournalUtil.java
for (String customToken :
PropsValues.JOURNAL_ARTICLE_CUSTOM_TOKENS)
{
    _customTokens.put(customToken, value);
}
```

In addition, there are several meta-elements, called **reserved elements**, which are added to an article's XML before they are processed by the template. The following is an abstracted list of reserved elements. Of course, you can find the same list in the class `com.liferay.portlet.journal.model.JournalStructureConstants`.

```
reserved-article-asset-tag-names
// ignore details
reserved-article-version
```

Retrieving structures, templates, and articles

There are a few backend journal services calls allowing us to retrieve structures, templates, and articles, for use in various ways. The following table shows details about these backend call services:

URL	Service action	Parameters	Parameters' values

`/journal/get_article`	`com.liferay.portlet.journal.action.GetArticleAction`	`groupId=${groupId}`
		
		 `articleId=${articleId}`
			Group Id, and article Id; article Id is different from resource primary key; output `ContentTypes.TEXT_XML_UTF8`

`/journal/get_article_content`	`GetArticleContentAction`	`xml=${xml}`	Input xml, Output `ContentTypes.TEXT_XML_UTF8` and file name `article.xml`
`/journal/get_articles`	`GetArticlesAction`		

`/journal/get_latest_article_content`	`GetLatestArticleContentAction`	`groupId=${groupId}`
		
		 `articleId=${articleId}`
			Group Id, and article Id; output `ContentTypes.TEXT_XML_UTF8`

`/journal/get_structure`	`GetStructureAction`	`groupId=${groupId}`
		
		 `structureId=${structureId}`
			Group Id, and structure Id; output `ContentTypes.TEXT_XML_UTF8`

`/journal/get_structure_content`	`GetStructureContentAction`	`xml=${xml}`	Input XML, Output `ContentTypes.TEXT_XML_UTF8` and file name `structure.xml`

`/journal/get_template`	`GetTemplateAction`	`groupId=${groupId}`
		
		 `templateId=${templateId}`
		
		 `transform=${transform}`
			Group Id, template Id and transform; output `ContentTypes.TEXT_XML_UTF8`

URL	Service action	Parameters	Parameters' values
`/journal/ get_template_ content`	`GetTemplate ContentAction`	`xslContent=${ xslContent}` `formatXsl=${ formatXsl }` `langType=${ langType}`	XSL content, format XSL and language type; output `ContentTypes`. `TEXT_XML_UTF8` UTF8 and file name `template.$ {langType}`

Content type constants have been defined in the interface `com.liferay.portal. kernel.util.ContentTypes`.

Structure

Structure is an XML (Extensible Markup Language) definition of the dynamic parts of journal articles. These parts may be a text, a textbox, a text area (HTML), an image, a Document Library image, a Document Library document, a Boolean flag (true or false), a selection list, a multiple selection list, a link to a page, selection break, and so on. Actually, the structure is a specific XML schema.

The main columns of journal structure have been defined in the journal service XML `service.xml` file, as follows:

```
<column name="structureId" type="String" />
<column name="parentStructureId" type="String" />
<column name="xsd" type="String" />
```

As shown in the preceding code, each journal structure has an ID column called `structureId` and a parent ID column called `parentStructureId`—value 0 means that there is no parent structure. Thus, `structureId` and `parentStructureId` form journal structure hierarchy.

Besides ID columns, there are other columns, called name, description, and xsd. The value of the journal structure is stored as XML in the field xsd.

Types

The field xsd of journal structure is made up of a set of rows. Each row can have subrows as its children. Rows are placed in order, FIFO first in (the place) first out (to be displayed).

Each row has a set of attributes, such as, name, type, index type, and repeatable. The attribute name and type are required. The following table shows the predefined types and their default values:

Type	Value	Description
text	`<aui:option label="text-field" value="text" />`	Input text
text_box	`<aui:option label="text-box" value="text_box" />`	Input textbox
text_area	`<aui:option label="text-area" value="text_area" />`	Text area HTML, using WYSIWYG
boolean	`<aui:option label="checkbox" value="boolean" />`	Checkbox
list	`<aui:option label="select-box" value="list" />`	Select box
multi-list	`<aui:option label="multi-selection-list" value="multi-list" />`	Multiple selection list
image	`<aui:option label="image-uploader" value="image" />`	Upload image into Image table
image_gallery	`<aui:option label="image-gallery" value="image_gallery" />`	Display image using image URL from the Document Library /journal/select_image_gallery
document_library	`<aui:option label="document-library" value="document_library" />`	Display document link using image URL from the Document Library /journal/select_document_library
link_to_layout	`<aui:option label="link-to-page" value="link_to_layout" />`	Display page link using page friendly URL
selection_break	`<aui:option label="selection-break" value="selection_break" />`	Display selection break

Each row can have optional attributes, such as, index type, predefined value, repeatable, required, and localized. The following table shows these optional attributes:

Column	Value	Description
Index-type: Not searchable,	none keyword	Attribute Index type could have values: not searchable
searchable keyword,	text	Searchable keyword,
searchable text		Searchable text
predefinedValue	text	Predefined values
Repeatable	checkbox	Repeatable structure fields
Required	checkbox	Required structure fields
Localized	checkbox	Localized field; this property is active only in journal article render processes

For more details, you can refer to `svn://svn.liferay.com/repos/public/portal/trunk/portal-web/docroot/html/portlet/journal/edit_article_structure_extra.jspf`. Of course, you can add custom types; such as date, polls, and Knowledge Base articles, by modifying this JSP file using JSP hooks in plugins.

Value format

The value of the field xsd has the root element `<root></root>`, which contains many rows. Each row is presented as the element `<dynamic-element>`. Each row has many attributes, such as, name, type, index-type, and repeatable. Each row may have many subrows. Subrows are presented as the element `<dynamic-element>`, too. The following is an example of the value of the field xsd:

```
<root>
    <dynamic-element name='link-to-page' type='link_to_layout'
        index-type='' repeatable='false'></dynamic-element>
    </dynamic-element>
</root>
```

Template

Template (or **web template**) is a pattern to rapidly generate and mass-produce web pages that are associated with a structure. A template defines the layout of journal articles, and determines how the content items will be arranged.

The main columns of journal template have been defined in the journal service XML `service.xml` file, as follows:

```
<column name="templateId" type="String" />
<column name="structureId" type="String" />
<column name="smallImageURL" type="String" />
```

As shown in the preceding code, each journal template has an ID column called `templateId` and an associated journal structure called `structureId`. Besides ID columns, there are other columns called name, description, and xsd. The value of journal structure is stored as XML, in the field xsd.

Each journal template can have an image as its thumbnail, stored in the table image as the file `samllImageId`, or the image can be an external image URL or an image URL from the Document Library.

In addition, each journal template can be cacheable, set by the column `cacheable`. Most importantly, each journal template can have a different language type, presented as the column `langType`.

Language types

Each journal template can be presented as different template languages, such as, **CSS**, **FreeMarker**, **VM (Velocity template)**, or **XSL**. The following table shows these template language types:

Type	Property	Value
css	journal.template.language.content	com/liferay/portlet/journal/dependencies/template.css
	journal.template.language.parser	
ftl	journal.template.language.content	com/liferay/portlet/journal/dependencies/template.ftl
	journal.template.language.parser	com.liferay.portlet.journal.util.FreeMarkerTemplateParser
vm	journal.template.language.content	template.vm
		VelocityTemplateParser
	journal.template.language.parser	
xsl	journal.template.language.content	template.xsl
		XSLTemplateParser
	journal.template.language.parser	

Variables and values

Considering the previous example, the dynamic element `main-text` can be accessed in the following ways (velocity template variables are defined in the interface `VelocityVariables.java` and its implementation class `VelocityVariablesImpl.java`):

- `$main-text.getName()`: This is the name in the article for the field `main-text`.

- `$main-text.getData()`: This is the data in the article for the field `main-text`.

- `$main-text.getType()`: This is the type in the article for the field `text-area`.

- `$main-text.getChildren()`: This is a collection of two nodes, for example, subimage and subtext.

- `$main-text.getSiblings()`: This is a collection of elements with the name `main-text`. This will only return more than one element, if this element is repeatable.

- Element of type `multi-list`: `$ms-list.getOptions()` is a collection with up to three string entries that can be used in the `#foreach` clause.

- Element of type `link_to_layout`: `$linkToPage.getUrl()` is the URL that links to the selected page in the current site, organization, and so on.

The variable `$journalTemplatesPath` can be used to include another journal template, for example, `#parse("$journalTemplatesPath/LAYOUT-PARENT")`. By the way, the variable `$viewMode`, specifies the mode in which the article is being viewed. For example, if `$viewMode` is set to print, it means that the user clicked the print icon to view this article.

Custom CSS

You may have your own CSS to display articles. Fortunately, you can add this CSS inside the journal template, in the following format. This CSS should stay at the beginning of the template text:

```
<style type="text/css">
/*add your own CSS*/
</style>
```

Custom JavaScript

Similarly, you may have your own JavaScript to display articles. Obviously, you can add this JavaScript inside the Journal template, in following format. The JavaScript could stay either at the beginning of the template text or at the end of the template text.

```
<aui:script>
// add your own JavaScript
</aui:script>
```

The preceding code uses the AUI script tag. You can also use normal a JavaScript tag, shown as follows:

```
<script type="text/javascript">
// add your own JavaScript
</script>
```

Localization

Internationalization (i18n) and **localization (L10n)** are the means of adapting computer software to different languages, regional differences, and the technical requirements of different target markets. Localization is defined as the process of adapting internationalized software for a specific region or language by adding locale-specific components and translating text.

Liferay portal supports up to 42 languages or locales. The portal framework is flexible enough to include any new locales. The following section will discuss how to add localization for the title, description, and content of many content types; web content is one of these content types.

Localized column

As mentioned earlier, the localized value specifies whether or not the value of the column can have different values for different locales. For example, the columns title and description have been specified as `localized="true"`. The service builder will use `model.ftl` and `model_impl.ftl` to generate model interface and implementation, respectively. The following is an example code snippet, abstracted from `model_impl.ftl`:

```
<#if column.localized>
    public String get${column.methodName}(Locale locale)
{
    String languageId = LocaleUtil.toLanguageId(locale);
```

```
      return get${column.methodName}(languageId);
   }
   // see details in model_impl.ftl
   </#if>
```

The following code snippet is abstracted from `model.ftl`. `${column.type}` here presents `String`, and `${column.methodName}` presents column method name, say, title, description, and so on:

```
   public ${column.type} get${column.methodName}(Locale locale);
   public Map<Locale, String> get${column.methodName}Map();
```

Value format

The value of the field title, description, and content, is persisted in the database in the following XML format. The keyword **Title** is used as an example only:

```
   <?xml version='1.0' encoding='UTF-8'?>
   <root available-locales="en_US" default-locale="en_US">
   <Title language-id="en_US">Test</Title>
   </root>
```

The preceding code shows that the first line is XML version, that is, **1.0**, and XML encoding, that is, **UTF-8**. The second line defines available locales, such as en_US, and a default locale, say en_US, with element root.

What's happening? The model `JournalArticleModel`, implemented by `JournalArticleModelImpl`, has defined getters/setters. That is, the localized title of this journal article, optionally using the default language if no localization exists for the requested language, . The following code snippet illustrates this:

```
   // see details in JournalArticleModelImpl.java
   public void setTitle(String title, Locale locale, Locale
   defaultLocale)
   {
      String languageId = LocaleUtil.toLanguageId(locale);
      String defaultLanguageId =
         LocaleUtil.toLanguageId(defaultLocale);
   }
```

In the same way, the model `JournalArticleModel` has defined the getters/setters, that is, the localized description (and content) of this journal article.

Localization interface

The interface `com.liferay.portal.kernel.util.Localization` stores and retrieves localized strings from XML, and provides utility methods for updating localizations from JSON, portlet requests, and maps, used for adding localization to strings, most often for model properties.

Caching of the localized values is done in this class rather than in the value object, since value objects get flushed from cache quickly. Although lookups performed on a key based on an XML file are slower than lookups done at the value object level in general, the value object will get flushed at a rate that works against the performance. The cache is a soft hash map that prevents memory leaks within the system while enabling the cache to live longer than in a weak hash map.

The following table shows the localization interface, utility, and implementation:

Interface	Implementation	Utility	Description
Localization	LocalizationImpl	Localization Util	Stores and retrieves localized strings from XML and JSON
Cloneable, Serializable	java.util.Locale	LocaleThread Local LocaleUtil	Represents a specific geographical, political, or cultural region.

A `java.util.Locale` object represents a specific geographical, political, or cultural region. An operation that requires a locale to perform its task is called locale-sensitive and uses the locale to tailor information for the user. For example, displaying a number is a locale-sensitive operation; the number should be formatted according to the customs/conventions of the user's native country, region, or culture.

You can create a `Locale` object using the constructors in the following class:

```
Locale(String language)
Locale(String language, String country, String variant)
```

Indexer

In order to find web content fast and easily, all web content gets indexed with a search engine, such as, **Lucene** (a high-performance, full-featured text search engine library, written entirely in Java) and/or **Solr** (enterprise search platform). This search engine indexing is used to collect, parse, and store data, to facilitate fast and accurate information retrieval.

The web content indexer is specified in the class `JournalIndexer.java`, which extends `BaseIndexer`, as follows:

```
// see details in JournalIndexer.java
public static final String[] CLASS_NAMES =
   {JournalArticle.class.getName()};
// UID
document.addUID(PORTLET_ID, groupId, articleId);
// title and localized title
document.addKeyword(Field.TITLE,
   article.getTitle(defaultLocale), true);
document.addLocalizedText("titleMap", titleMap);
// see details in JournalIndexer.java
// related custom attributes
ExpandoBridgeIndexerUtil.addAttributes(document,
   expandoBridge);
```

The preceding code first shows an indexer class name. It is called `JournalArticle.class.getName()`, in this indexer, which is used in the indexer registration process. Then it adds a **UID (Unique Identification Number)**, generated by three elements, `PORTLET_ID`, `groupId`, and `articleId`. As you can see, there is one and only one version that gets indexed, since the entity `articleId` is a unique ID for all the versions of that article. If you want to index all versions, you can use the `articleId` plus the version number, such as, 1.0, 1.2, 2.0, and so on, instead of using the `articleId` only.

As mentioned earlier, the title, description, and content get localized. The portal improves the search by indexing localized content as separate fields, and it adds the `Locale` parameter to search methods, such as, `addLocalizedKeyword` and `addLocalizedText`, from the interface `Document`. The portal adds support, so that when a field is localized from the service builder level, you just need to pass the map to the document. The following is an example code snippet, abstracted from the class `DocumentImpl`, which implements the interface `Document`:

```
// see details in DocumentImpl.java
public void addLocalizedText(String name,
   Map<Locale, String> values)
{
   _fields.put(name, field);
}
```

The structure content fields get indexed as well. Besides these, the category names list, the category IDs list, and the tag names list get indexed as keywords. All related custom attributes get indexed as well, for example, `ExpandoBridgeIndexerUtil.addAttributes(document, expandoBridge)`. We will address the details of custom attributes in the coming section.

XML security

As you have noticed, structure, template, and localized content are specified by XML values, which are stored in the database. Similarly, the XSL Content portlet provides the ability to publish XML-based content. A security vulnerability exists within the XSL Content portlet that can potentially allow execution of code on the server. Specifically, the XML/XSL specification allows for potentially dangerous code to be executed. Therefore, the question about XML security arises.

XML security should adhere to security best practices and minimize the opportunities for threats based on XML security mechanisms. Refer to `http://www.w3.org/TR/2010/WD-xmlsec-reqs-20100204/`.

However, this can be a feature that is useful for portals. The portal is now able to set permission in roles to determine who can add the XSL Content portlet to a page. By default, users with a personal site will no longer be able to add the XSL Content portlet to their personal pages. If users were given permission to add an XSL Content portlet to their personal pages, additional permissions must be granted to the users.

Programmatically, the class `com.liferay.portlet.xslcontent.util.XSLContentUtil` transforms XSL content XML to stream. The following code snippet demonstrates this:

```
// see details in XSLContentUtil.java
String xsl = HttpUtil.URLtoString(xslUrl);
StreamSource xslSource = new StreamSource(new
UnsyncStringReader(xsl));
```

The class `XSLTemplateParser` extends `VelocityTemplateParser` and `BaseTemplateParser`, which implements `TemplateParser`. The class `XSLTemplateParser` provides the ability to parse XML content with XSL structure and values, as shown in the following table:

Interface	Implementation	Extension	Description
Template Context	XSLContext	None	Template context
FreeMarker Context	FreeMarker ContextImpl	TemplateContext	FreeMarker template context

Interface	Implementation	Extension	Description
Velocity Context	Velocity ContextImpl	TemplateContext	Velocity template context
Template Parser	BaseTemplate Parser	VelocityTemplate Parser	Template parser
		FreeMarkerTemplate Parser	
		XSLTemplate Parser	

Sanitizer

What are sanitizers? **Sanitizers** are filtering elements that sanitize web content, usually HTML or JavaScript code, so that it doesn't contain inappropriate content, for example, JavaScript malicious code or swearwords.

The portal provides the interface com.liferay.portal.kernel.sanitizer. Sanitizer, a filtering element that sanitizes web content usually HTML or JavaScript code. The following is the code snippet for sanitizer constants, abstracted from the interface Sanitizer:

```
public static final String MODE_ALL = "ALL";
public static final String MODE_XSS = "XSS";
```

The following table shows Sanitizer interface, implementation, wrapper, and utility:

Interface	Wrapper	Implementation	Utility
Sanitizer	SanitizerWrapper	BaseSanitizer SanitizerImpl	SanitizerUtil
	none	DummySanitizerImpl	none

The following property has been provided in the portal.properties element, allowing the use of a custom sanitizer:

```
sanitizer.impl=com.liferay.portal.sanitizer.DummySanitizerImpl
```

The preceding code sets the name of a class that implements the interface Sanitizer. This class is used to sanitize content. As you can see, you can use custom sanitizers by setting the property sanitizer.impl.

Before entering the contents into the database, the sanitizer can be applied to any entity, either portal core entities, such as, wiki pages, blog entries, message board threads, journal articles, and so on, or custom entities such as Knowledge Base articles in plugins. For example, you can use the utility class `SanitizerUtil` in the model service wrapper hook `WikiPageLocalServiceWrapper` for wiki pages, or the model service wrapper hook `BlogsEntryLocalServiceWrapper` for blogs entries, or the model service wrapper hook `JournalArticleLocalServiceWrapper` for journal articles. For custom entities such as Knowledge Base articles, you can apply the utility class `SanitizerUtil` in the local service class implementation `KBArticleLocalServiceImpl`; more specifically, inside the method `addKBArticle`, use the utility class `SanitizerUtil`, to sanitize the content. The following is an example code snippet, abstracted from the class `KBArticleLocalServiceImpl`:

```
String sanitizedContent = SanitizerUtil.sanitize(
    // see details in KBArticleLocalServiceImpl.java
    ContentTypes.TEXT_HTML, content);
```

Antisamy

OWASP AntiSamy is an API that helps you make sure that clients don't supply malicious cargo code in the HTML that they supply for their profile, comments, and so on, that get persisted on the server. Refer to `https://www.owasp.org/index.php/Category:OWASP_AntiSamy_Project`.

AntiSamy can be used as a starting point that may be interested in implementing your custom sanitizers. How does it work? The following are the main steps that you can follow to bring AntiSamy into the portal. Of course, in the same process, you will be able to bring other sanitizers into the portal as well:

1. Create a hook plugin project, for example, `antisamy-hook`, and add the following line to `portal.properties`:

   ```
   sanitizer.impl=com.liferay.antisamy.hook.sanitizer.
   AntiSamySanitizerImpl
   ```

2. The preceding code sets the name of the class `AntiSamySanitizerImpl` that implements the interface `Sanitizer`. This class is used to sanitize content.

3. Add the portal properties hook by adding the following line in `liferay-hook.xml`:

   ```
   <portal-properties>portal.properties</portal-properties>
   ```

4. Bring the AntiSamy API (downloadable at `https://www.owasp.org/index.php/Category:OWASP_Download`) into the plugin. For example, copy the JAR file `antisamy.jar` and its dependent JAR files, such as, `batik-css.jar`, `batik-util.jar`, and `xml-apis-ext.jar` into the folder `/docroot/WEB-INF/lib`.

5. Finally, provide an implementation of `com.liferay.antisamy.hook.sanitizer.AntiSamySanitizerImpl` in the folder `/docroot/WEB-INF/src`, as follows:

```
public class AntiSamySanitizerImpl implements Sanitizer
{
    public byte[] sanitize(
    // see details in AntiSamySanitizerImpl.java
    byte[] bytes, Map<String, Object> options)
{
        // add custom logic here
        return bytes;
}
 // see details in AntiSamySanitizerImpl.java
}
```

As shown in the preceding code, the class `AntiSamySanitizerImpl` implements the interface `Sanitizer`.

ClassName-classPK pattern

The journal portlet provides the interesting functionality of storing structured content and then applying templates to it. This functionality is also useful outside the world of web content, since a common pattern can use its backend to build third-party applications on top of it. Therefore, the data stored in `JournalArticle` by those applications also appears as web content.

One possible solution is to apply the `className-classPK` pattern to separate the `JournalArticle` entries for web content (for example, `classNameId=0`) from those that have other purposes. To implement the same, you can add the following lines inside the entry `JournalArticle`, from the service XML `/journal/service.xml`:

```
<column name="classNameId" type="long" />
<column name="classPK" type="long" />
```

The preceding code uses the column `classNameId` to present different content type. It shows web content if the value of `classNameId` is 0. The column `classPK` presents a different content table primary key.

WYSIWYG editor

The WYSIWYG editor will be helpful in building content on top of the portal, for example, blog entries, forum topics, articles, journal articles, and so on. The portal is integrated with the WYSIWYG editors. Thus, content creation and publishing in the portal is simple and straightforward.

The WYSIWYG editor of the portal is highly configurable. In general, you can configure individual JSP pages to use a specific implementation of the available WYSIWYG editors: **liferay**, **CKEditor**, **FCKeditor**, **simple**, **tinymce**, or **tinymcesimple**. Moreover, you can include the WYSIWYG editor in the edit page of blog entries, web content, wiki pages, mail configuration, and custom assets such as Knowledge Base articles.

The following table shows WYSIWYG editor system files, runtime files and folders, and integration connections. You will be able to find the system files in the folder `$PORTAL_SRC_HOME/portal-web/third-party` and the runtime files in the folder `$PORTAL_SRC_HOME/portal-web/docroot/html/js/editor`:

Name	System file	Runtime folder	Integration Connection
CKEditor	`ckeditor_3 .x.x.zip`	CKEditor	`ckeditor_diffs,` `ckeditor.jsp`
FCKeditor	`FCKeditor_2 .x.x.zip`	FCKeditor	`fckeditor_diffs,` `fckeditor.jsp`
tinymce	`tinymce_3_ x_x.zip`	`tiny_mce`	`tiny_mce, tinymce.jsp`
tinymcesimple			`Tinymcesimple.jsp`
codepress	`codepress-v .x.x.x.zip`	codepress	`codepress_diffs`
simple	none	none	`simple.jsp`
liferay	none	`liferay`	none

CKEditor integration

CKEditor (previously called FCKeditor) is a web-based HTML text editor with powerful formatting capabilities. It brings to the web much of the power of desktop editors such as MS Word. Moreover, it is the most-used rich HTML editor on the Web. It's also lightweight and doesn't require any kind of installation on the client's computer. Refer to `http://ckeditor.com` for more details.

The **CKEditor File Browser Connector** offers a unique interface that can be used by all server-side languages that are developed completely on JavaScript DHTML; integration is available by XML.

The portal sets CKEditor as the default WYSIWYG editor included in the edit page of blog entries, web content, wiki pages, mail configuration, and so on. The following section will show more integration details.

CKEditor structure

The following table shows the CKEditor folder structure:

Folder name	Subfolders	Files
_sample	adobeair, api_dialog, asp, assets, php	sample.css, sample.js, *.html
_source	adapters, core, lang, plugins, skins, themes/ default	theme.js and more
adapters	none	jquery.js
images	none	spacer.gif
lang	none	c_languages.js, af.js, ar.js, en.js, en-au.js, en-ca.js, en-gb.js, zh.js, zh-cn.js, and so on
plugins	a11yhelp, about, scaty, xml, and so on	For example, option.js, toolbar.css under the folder scayt/dialogs
skins	kama, office2003, v2	For example, dialog.css, editor.css, skin.js, template.css under the folder kama
themes	default	theme.js

In addition, you will find a set of configuration files in the root, such as, ckeditor.js, ckeditor_basic.js, ckeditor_source.js, ckeditor_basic_source.js, config.js, and so on.

CKEditor diffs

The portal uses two folders, `ckeditor_diffs` and `fckeditor_diffs`, to integrate CKEditor/FCKeditor. The following table shows the integration details:

Name	Folder	Overwrite file	Description
`ckeditor.jsp`	root	none	ckeditor integration specification
`fckeditor.jsp`	root	none	fckeditor integration specification
`ckeditor.js`	`ckeditor_diffs`	`ckeditor.js`	Overwrite CKEditor core JavaScript
`ckconfig.jsp`	`ckeditor_diffs`	`config.js`	Overwrite CKEditor configuration JavaScript - `CKEDITOR.config.toolbar` definition
editor	`fckeditor_diffs`	none	`/filemanager/browser/liferay`
			images
			js and files

The main entry point of CKEditor integration is the file `ckconfig.jsp`. The following code snippet shows this:

```
CKEDITOR.replace( '<%= name %>',
{// see details in ckconfig.jsp
toolbar: '<%= TextFormatter.format(HtmlUtil.escape(toolbarSet),
TextFormatter.M) %>'
}
);
```

The preceding code shows how to load `ckconfig.jsp` and `/ckeditor/editor/filemanager/browser/liferay/browser.html`. You can find details in the file `/editor/ckeditor.jsp`.

To upgrade CKEditor, download the latest version and unzip it to CKEditor. Then, add custom configuration to `fckeditor/fckconfig.jsp`, and copy `fckeditor/editor/filemanager/browser/default` to `ckeditor/editor/filemanager/browser/liferay`. Modify `browser.html`, `frmresourceslist.html`, `frmresourcetype.html`, and `frmupload.html`.

CKEditor plugins

By default, CKEditor has a lot of built-in plugins, specified in the folder `$PORTAL_SRC_HOME/portal-web/docroot/html/js/editor/ckeditor/plugins`. The following table shows some of the built-in plugins:

Name	Folders	Files	Description
a11yhelp	dialogs, lang	a11yhelp.js, en.js, he.js	Help
about	dialogs	about.js, logo_ckeditor.png	about
adobeair	none	plugin.js	Adobe air
ajax	none	plugin.js	AJAX
autogrow	none	plugin.js	Auto grow
clipboard	dialogs	paste.js	Clipboard
colordialog	dialogs	colordialog.js	Colour dialog
dialog	none	dialogDefinition.js	Dialog

Besides the previous built-in plugins, you will see more plugins under the same folder, such as, `div`, `find`, `flash`, `forms`, `iframe`, `inframedialog`, `image`, `link`, `liststyle`, `pagebreak`, `pastefromword`, `pastetext`, `placeholder`, `scayt`, `showblocks`, `smiley`, `specialchar`, `styles`, `table`, `tablesize`, `tabletools`, `templates`, `uicolor`, `wsc`, and `xml`.

Custom plugins

By default, the portal provides three custom plugins, as shown in the following table, in the folder `$PORTAL_SRC_HOME/portal-web/docroot/html/js/editor/ckeditor_diffs/plugins`. In the portal building process, these plugins will get copied into the folder `/ckeditor/plugins`:

Name	Folder	Files	Description
BBcode	none	bbcode_data_processor.js, bbcode_parser.js, plugin.js, ckconfig_bbcode.js	Bulletin Board Code or BBCode is a lightweight markup language used to format posts in many message boards.
Creole	none	creole_data_processor.js, creole_parser.js, plugin.js, ckconfig_creole.js	Creole is a lightweight markup language for formatting wiki text.

Name	Folder	Files	Description
Wiki link	`dialogs`	`link.js, plugin.js`	Wiki link is created simply by smashing together capitalized words, at least two of them.

As you can see, JavaScript `CKEditor.plugins.add` gets specified in the file `plugin.js`. Let's see one more custom example, adding a plugin to implement pull quote function in the CKEditor.

A **pull quote** is a quotation or excerpt from an article that is typically placed in a larger or more distinctive typeface, on the same page, serving to entice readers into an article, or to highlight a key topic. Authors would need to duplicate the text excerpt. This feature could be implemented as a plugin called `pullquote` in the CKEditor, automating and simplifying the use of pull quotes with the following main functions:

1. Remove the need to duplicate excerpts.
2. Automatically add opening and closing quotation marks to the pull quote.
3. Leave the excerpt unchanged in the body text.
4. Format the pull quote to match your site's design by using CSS.

You can implement `pullquote` by performing the following steps:

1. First create a folder named `pullquote`.
2. Then create a folder `dialogs`, and add a JavaScript file `pullquote.js`, and a CSS file `pullquote.css`. Of course, workable code is required here.
3. Finally, add a JavaScript file `plugin.js` in the folder `pullquote`.

Expando—custom attribute

The portal provides a feature called **custom attribute** (or called **custom field**), which allows extending the profile of users and organizations, with fields, to store custom information. In fact, it allows extending any core entities, such as, Document Library folders and documents, web content, wiki pages, blogs entries, bookmarks entries, calendar events, users, and organizations, and custom entities such as Knowledge Base articles. The Custom attribute is safely stored within the database and is fully indexed.

Models and services

As shown in the following figure, a custom attribute is defined by four entities: ExpandoTable, ExpandoColumn, ExpandoRow, and ExpandoValue. As you can see, the entity ExpandoTable can have many entities, such as, ExpandoColumn, ExpandoRow, and ExpandoValue. In other words, each ExpandoColumn, ExpandoRow, and ExpandoValue will have an ExpandoTable associated with it. And especially, each ExpandoValue will have ExpandoColumn, ExpandoRow, and ExpandoTable associated with it. That is, an ExpandoValue is always unique and is identified by ExpandoColumn, ExpandoRow, and ExpandoTable. This is shown as follows:

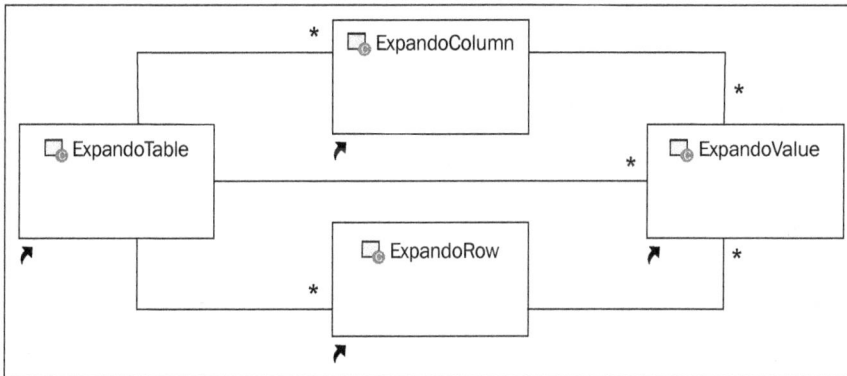

Models

The entity ExpandoTable has been specified as follows, in the service XML / expando/service.xml:

```
<!-- PK fields -->
<column name="tableId" type="long" primary="true" />
<!-- Audit fields -->
<column name="companyId" type="long" />
<!-- Other fields -->
<column name="classNameId" type="long" />
<column name="name" type="String" />
```

The preceding code shows that the entity ExpandoTable is defined as a set of columns, for example, tableId, companyId, classNameId, and name. Custom fields are scoped on company-level objects, such as, users, organizations, and so on. In order to support group-level objects, you can add the audit field groupId, in the table ExpandoTable. When the value of groupId is 0, it means custom fields are scoped on company-level objects. Otherwise, custom fields are scoped on group-level objects.

Of course, you could find other entities and their column specifications in the same service XML, such as, ExpandoColumn, ExpandoRow, and ExpandoValue. The following table shows these models plus the models CustomAttributesDisplay and ExpandoBridge, their extension, and implementation:

Name	Extension	Implementation	Description
ExpandoTable	ExpandoTableModel extends BaseModel <ExpandoTable>	ExpandoTableImpl extends ExpandoTable ModelImpl	Expando table model
ExpandoColumn	ExpandoColumnModel extends BaseModel <ExpandoColumn>	ExpandoColumnImpl extends ExpandoColumn ModelImpl	Expando column model
ExpandoRow	ExpandoRowModel extends BaseModel <ExpandoRow>	ExpandoRowImpl extends ExpandoRow ModelImpl	Expando row model
ExpandoValue	ExpandoValueModel extends BaseModel <ExpandoValue>	ExpandoValueImpl extends ExpandoValue ModelImpl	Expando value model
ExpandoBridge	none	ExpandoBridgeImpl	Expando bridge
CustomAttributes Display	none	BaseCustom AttributesDisplay	Custom attribute display model

Services

The service builder has generated a set of services based on the service XML. The following table shows service interface, implementation, and utility classes:

Interface	Utility	Implementation	Description
ExpandoTable LocalService	ExpandoTableLocal ServiceUtil	ExpandoTableLocal ServiceImpl extends ExpandoTableLocal ServiceBaseImpl	Expando Table service
ExpandoColumn LocalService	ExpandoColumnLocal ServiceUtil	ExpandoColumnLocal ServiceImpl extends ExpandoColumnLocal ServiceBaseImpl	Expando Column service

Interface	Utility	Implementation	Description
ExpandoRow LocalService	ExpandoRowLocal ServiceUtil	ExpandoRowLocal ServiceImpl extends ExpandoRowLocal ServiceBaseImpl	Expando Row service
ExpandoValue LocalService	ExpandoValueLocal ServiceUtil	ExpandoValueLocal ServiceImpl extends ExpandoValueLocal ServiceBaseImpl	Expando Value service
ExpandoBridge	none	ExpandoBridgeImpl	getExpandoBridge at ExpandoBridge Factory(Impl)

Taglib

There are three tags related to custom attributes: `liferay-ui:custom-attribute-list`, `liferay-ui:custom-attributes-available`, and `liferay-ui:custom-attribute`.

The tag `liferay-ui:custom-attribute-list` generates a list of all non-hidden and viewable tags for a given entity type and portal instance; the tags `liferay-ui:custom-attributes-available` and `iferay-ui:custom-attribute` generate a view of a specific attribute for a given entity type and portal instance.

Data types

Custom attributes support data types, both primitive (such as, Boolean, Integer, String, Short, and so on) and preset (such as, textbox, selection, and so on). The following table shows these types:

Name	Value	Label	Description
BOOLEAN, BOOLEAN_ARRAY	1 2	custom.field.boolean custom. field.boolean.array	Primitive data type, Boolean, and Boolean list
DATE, DATE_ ARRAY	3 4	custom.field.java.util.Date custom.field.java.util.Date. array	Data type: Date and Date list
DOUBLE, DOUBLE_ARRAY	5 6	custom.field.double custom. field.double.array	Primitive data type: double and double list
FLOAT, FLOAT_ ARRAY	7 8	custom.field.float custom. field.float.array	Primitive data type: float and float list

Name	Value	Label	Description
INTEGER, INTEGER_ARRAY	9 10	custom.field.int custom. field.int.array	Primitive data type: int and int list
LONG, LONG_ ARRAY	11 12	custom.field.long custom. field.long.array	Primitive data type: long and long list
SHORT, SHORT_ ARRAY	13 14	custom.field.short custom. field.short.array	Primitive data type: short and short list
STRING, STRING_ARRAY	15 16	custom.field.java.lang.String custom.field.java.lang. String.array	Data type: String and String list

You can look up the details in the class ExpandoColumnConstants.java.

Default Expando table constants get defined in the class ExpandoTableConstants. java, as follows:

```
public static final String DEFAULT_TABLE_NAME = "CUSTOM_FIELDS";
```

Indexer

The custom fields can be indexed as none (not indexed), Keyword (exact matching only plus faceted support and sorting), Text (prose plus stop words, language analysis, and no sorting) In the summary, all custom field types can be indexed.

The following table shows custom field indexer interface, implementation, utility, and factory:

Interface	Utility	Implementation
ExpandoBridgeIndexer	ExpandoBridgeIndexerUtil	ExpandoBridge IndexerImpl
ExpandoBridgeFactory	ExpandoBridgeFactoryUtil	none
ExpandoBridge	ExpandoConverterUtil	ExpandoBridgeImpl

You can find different data types and indexing details in the class ExpandoBridgeIndexerImpl.java. And, moreover, you may leverage converting functions (from string to attribute, and from attribute to string) from the utility class ExpandoConverterUtil.java. Date functions, such as, date compareTo, date equals, ISO date format, UTC date format, locale, and time zone, are specified in the utility class DateUtil.java.

NoSQL adapter

NoSQL is a broad class of database management systems that differ from classic relational database management systems. Data stores may not require fixed table schemas, usually avoid join operations, and typically scale horizontally. Loosely speaking, NoSQL is schema-free and has easy replication support, a simple API, and a huge amount of data.

MongoDB (a kind of NoSQL) is a scalable, high-performance, open source, document-oriented database. Refer to http://www.mongodb.org/. The portal can be a prime candidate as a viable platform for scaling dynamically via a NoSQL-like MongoDB backend. The most obvious way to leverage a NoSQL solution is with the most dynamic aspect of the portal — Expandos and their custom fields.

An adapter using a hook pattern can be used to build a backend for Expando on MongoDB. You can find implementation details in the plugin mongodb-hook.

Dynamic data lists and dynamic data mapping

The portal provides capabilities to build Dynamic Data Lists (DDL) and Dynamic Data Mapping (DDM). Through DDL and DDM, users can define web form, document types, metadata set, and columns of various input styles, such as, free form, drop-down list, combo-box, date, number, text, and predefined list values (such as list of users, list of order types, and list of inventory types). Some columns can be drop-downs with predefined values that only allow you to choose one of the options defined. Other columns can be drop-downs with predefined values that are a collection of all previously entered values in that column and that allow you to enter a new value. The other columns may allow selecting more than one value. The DDL and DDM can be tied to a service to retrieve values.

Models and services

The following figure depicts DDL models, DDM models, and their relationships. The entity DDLRecordSet is associated with the entity DDMStructure. It may contain many entities, such as, DDLRecord and DDLRecordVersion. The entity DDLRecord is associated with the entity DDMStructureLink. The entity DDMStructure may have many entities such as DDMStructureLink. Each DDMStructure can have many DDMStorageLink entities, and each DDMTemplate may be associated with a DDMStructure.

Each `DDMContent` may refer to `DDMStructure`, `DDMStorageLink`, and `DDMTemplate`, as follows:

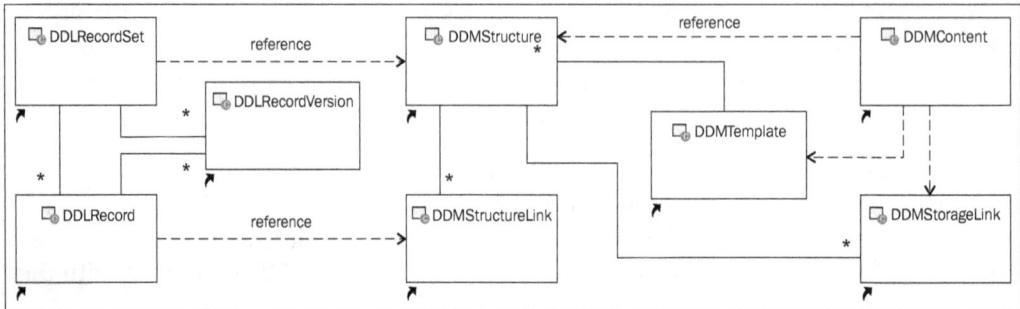

Models

DDL and DDM functions are defined as a set of models: `DDLRecordSet`, `DDLRecord`, `DDLRecordVersion`, `DDMStructure`, `DDMStructureLink`, `DDMTemplate`, `DDMStorageLink`, and `DDMContent`. The following table shows DDL and DDM models, their extensions and implementation:

Model	Extension	Implementation	Description
DDLRecord	DDLRecordModel extends BaseModel <DDLRecord>	DDLRecordImpl extends DDLRecordModelImpl	DDL record model
DDLRecord Version	DDLRecordVersion Model extends BaseModel <DDLRecordVersion>	DDLRecordVersionImpl extends DDLRecordVersion ModelImpl	DDL record version model
DDLRecordSet	DDLRecordSetModel extends BaseModel <DDLRecord>	DDLRecordSetImpl extends DDLRecordModelImpl	DDL record set model
DDMContent	DDMContentModel extends BaseModel<DDM Content>, Grouped Model	DDMContentImpl extends DDMContentModelImpl	DDM content model
DDMStorage Link	DDMStorageLinkModel extends BaseModel <DDMStorageLink>	DDMStorageLinkImpl extends DDMStorageLink ModelImpl	DDM storage link model
DDMStructure	DDMStructureModel extends BaseModel <DDMStructure>, GroupedModel	DDMStructureImpl extends DDMStructure ModelImpl	DDM structure model

Model	Extension	Implementation	Description
DDMStructure Link	DDMStructureLink Model extends BaseModel <DDMStructureLink>	DDMStructureLinkImpl extends DDMStructureLink ModelImpl	DDM structure link model
DDMTemplate	DDMTemplateModel extends BaseModel <DDMTemplate>, GroupedModel	DDMTemplateImpl extends DDMTemplateModelImpl	DDM template model

These models have been defined well in the service XML /dynamicdatamapping/ service.xml and /dynamicdatalists/service.xml.

Services

Based on the previous service XML files, the service builder generated a set of services. The following table shows DDL service interface, utility, wrapper, and implementation:

Interface	Utility	Implementation	Wrapper	Description
DDLRecord (Local) Service	DDLRecord (Local) ServiceUtil	DDLRecord(Local) ServiceImpl extends DDLRecord(Loca) ServiceBaseImpl	DDLRecord (Local) Service Wrapper	DDL record local service and service
DDLRecord Set(Local) Service	DDLRecordSet (Local) ServiceUtil	DDLRecordSet(Local) ServiceImpl extends DDLRecordSet(Local) ServiceBaseImpl	DDLRecord Set(Local) Service Wrapper	DDL record set local service and service
DDLRecord Version (Local) Service	DDLRecord Version(Local) ServiceUtil	DDLRecordVersion (Local)ServiceImpl extends DDLRecord Version(Local) ServiceBaseImpl	DDLRecord Version (Local) Service Wrapper	DDL record version service and local service

Similarly you can find the DDM service interface, utility, wrapper, and implementation in the package com.liferay.portlet.dynamicdatamapping.service.

Storage adapter

The portal provides a set of service interface, implementation, and utility class for DDM storage, storage query, and XML/XSD. The following table shows details of these services:

Interface	Utility/ Implementation	Model/Constant	Description
`DDMXML`	`DDMXMLUtil`	`DDMFieldConstants`	DDM XML interface
`DDMSXD`	`DDXSDUtil`	`DDMFieldConstants`	DDM SXD interface
`StorageEngine extends StorageAdapter`	`StorageEngine Util,` `BaseStorage Adapter,` `StorageEngine Impl,`	`Field, Fields` `StorageType`	DDM storage, engine, and type
`FieldCondition extends Condition`	`FieldCondition Impl`	`ComparisonOperator,` `LogicalOperator`	DDM storage query field condition
`Junction extends Condition`	`JunctionImpl`	`ComparisonOperator,` `LogicalOperator`	DDM storage query junction
`ConditionFactory`	`ConditionFactory Util`	`ComparisonOperator,` `LogicalOperator`	DDM storage condition factory

Asset, tagging, and categorization

An **asset** can be defined formally as a resource, controlled by the entity as a result of past events, and from which future economic benefits are expected to flow to the entity. The portal uses assets to present any kind of entities, either core entities, such as, `DLFileEntry`, `JournalArticle`, `BookmarkEntry`, `MBMessage`, `BlogsEntry`, and so on, or custom entities, such as, `KBArticle`, `MicroblogsEntry`, `PMUserThread`, and so on.

Folksonomies are a user-driven approach to organizing content through tags, co-operative classification, and communication through shared metadata. The portal implements folksonomies through tags. A tag may be associated with content. With tags, you can tag almost anything: bookmarks entries, blog entries, wiki articles, Document Library documents and images, journal articles, message board threads, custom entities such as Knowledge Base articles, and so on.

Taxonomies are a hierarchical structure used in scientific classification schemes. Although taxonomies are common, it can be difficult to implement them. The portal implements taxonomies as vocabulary, category, and category hierarchy, in order to tag contents and classify them.

Models and services

The following figure depicts an overview of asset tags, asset categories, and asset entries. An asset called `AssetEntry` may be associated with many tags such as `AssetLink`.

A tag called `AssetTag` may be associated with many assets, whereas an asset may have many tags associated with it. This is called **tagging content**. Also, a tag may have many properties associated with it. Each property, called `AssetTagProperty`, is made up of a name-value pair.

You can have more than one vocabulary, which forms a top-level item of the hierarchy. Each vocabulary, called `AssetVocabulary`, may have many categories. That is, a category called `AssetCategory` can't be a top-level item of the hierarchy. However, a category can have other categories as its child or siblings. Therefore, vocabulary and categories form a hierarchical tree structure.

In the same way, a category may have many properties. Each property, called `AssetCategoryproperty`, is made up of a name and a value. In addition, a predefined category will be applied to any asset. In a word, assets can be managed and grouped by categories:

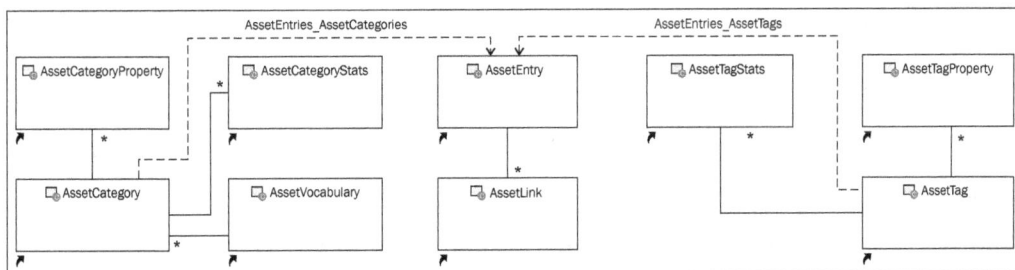

Models

The portal extends asset model to store the `layoutUuid` value of the default display page. Asset tags, asset categories, and asset entries are defined in the service XML `/asset/service.xml`, as follows:

```
<!-- PK fields -->
<column name="entryId" type="long" primary="true" />
<!-- Group instance -->
<!-- Audit fields -->
<!-- Other fields -->
<column name="classNameId" type="long" />
<column name="classPK" type="long" />
<!-- see details in service.xml -->
<column name="viewCount" type="int" />
<!-- Relationships -->
<column name="categories" type="Collection" entity="AssetCategory"
mapping-table="AssetEntries_AssetCategories" />
<column name="tags" type="Collection" entity="AssetTag" mapping-
table="AssetEntries_AssetTags" />
```

The preceding code gives detailed column specification for the entity `AssetEntry`. Based on these columns, we should be able to summarize the following items:

1. Each asset can be scoped into both company-level and group-level categories.
2. Associated content is presented in a `classNameId-classPK` pattern. As you can see, the class `Name` can be any entity. Thus, the `classNameId-classPK` pattern can be used to present any content type and, furthermore, any content instance.
3. The **UUID** `layoutUuid` is stored for the default display page.
4. Relationships, categories, and tags get recorded in different database tables — `AssetEntries_AssetCategories` and `AssetEntries_AssetTags`.
5. View count number is recorded based on individual assets.

Similarly, you will find more entities in the same service XML, such as, `AssetLink`, `AssetTag`, `AssetTagProperty`, `AssetTagStat`, `AssetCategory`, `AssetCategoryProperty`, `AssetVocabulary`, and so on. The following table shows these models:

Entity	Extension	Implementation	Wrapper	Description
Asset Entry	AssetEntryModel extends BaseModel <AssetEntry>, GroupedModel	AssetEntryImpl extends AssetEntryModel Impl	AssetEntry Wrapper	Asset entry model
Asset Link	AssetLinkModel extends BaseModel <AssetLink>	AssetLinkImpl extends AssetLinkModelImpl	AssetLink Wrapper	Asset link model – a link among entries
AssetTag	AssetTagModel extends BaseModel<AssetTag>, GroupedModel	AssetTagImpl extends AssetTagModelImpl	AssetTag Warpper	Asset tag model
AssetTag Property	AssetTagProperty Model extends AuditedModel, BaseModel <AssetTagProperty>	AssetTagProperty Impl extends AssetTagProperty ModelImpl	AssetTag Property Wrapper	Asset tag property model
Asset TagStats	AssetTagStatsModel extends BaseModel <AssetTagStats>	AssetTagStatsImpl extends AssetTagStats ModelImpl	Asset TagStats Wrapper	Asset tag stats model
Asset Category	AssetCategory Model extends BaseModel <AssetCategory>, GroupedModel	AssetCategoryImpl extends AssetCategory ModelImpl	Asset Category Warpper	Asset category model
Asset Category Property	AssetCategory PropertyModel extends AuditedModel, BaseMo del<AssetCategoryPr operty>	AssetCategory PropertyImpl extends AssetCategory PropertyModelImpl	Asset Category Property Wrapper	Asset category property model
Asset Category Stats	AssetCategory StatsModel extends BaseModel<Asset CategoryStats>	AssetCategory StatsImpl extends AssetCategory StatsModelImpl	Asset Category Stats Wrapper	Asset category stats model
AssetVoca bulary	AssetVocabulary Model extends BaseM odel<AssetVocabular y>,GroupedModel	AssetVocabulary Impl extends AssetVocabulary ModelImpl	Asset Vocabulary Wrapper	Asset vocabulary model

As you can see, the entity `AssetLink` provides the ability to link one `AssetEntry` entity called `entryId1` with another `AssetEntry` entity called `entryId2`. This kind of link can present any association, specified by column type and weight, as follows:

```
<column name="entryId1" type="long" />
<column name="entryId2" type="long" />
<column name="type" type="int" />
<column name="weight" type="int" />
```

The portal provides the ability for an asset to link different assets via the model `AssetLink`. This feature gets implemented as the taglibs `<liferay-ui:input-asset-links>` and `<liferay-ui:asset-links>`. The first taglib will be applied to all assets, to link one asset to another; the second taglib will show the list of related assets linked to the current asset.

Services

As shown in the following table, a set of services have been generated for the entities `AssetEntry` and `AssetLink`, via the service builder:

Service	Utility	Wrapper	Implementation	Description
AssetEntry (Local) Service	AssetEntry (Local) ServiceUtil	AssetEntry (Lolcal) ServiceWrapper	AssetEntry(Local) ServiceImpl extends AssetEntryLocal ServiceBaseImpl	Asset entry service and local service
AssetLink (Local) Service	AssetLink (Local) ServiceUtil	AssetLink (Local) ServiceWrapper	AssetLink(Local) ServiceImpl extends AssetLink(Local) ServiceBaseImpl	Asset link service and local service

View count

As mentioned earlier, view count number gets recorded, based on individual asset, using the `className-classPK` pattern. Anyway, you can increase the view count using any portal core entities or custom entities in the following code:

```
AssetEntry(Local)ServiceUtil.incrementViewCounter(
    String className, long classPK)
```

The following table shows how to record view count for any content types, no matter whether they are portal core entities or custom entities, with a few examples. As you can see, the entity `AssetEntry` can be used to present any kind of content types:

Asset Type	Class Name	Class PK	Description
Web content article	`JournalArticle.class.getName()`	`JournalArticle.getResourcePrimKey()`	Journal article @view_counter@ does have the same function
Wiki page	`WikiPage.class.getName()`	`WikiPage.getResourcePrimKey()`	Wiki pages
Blogs entry	`BlogsEntry.class.getName()`	`entry.getEntryId()`	Blogs entries
Message Board thread	`MBThread.class.getName()`	`thread.getThreadId()`	Forums threads
Bookmark entry	`BookmarkEntry.class.getName()`	`entry.getEntryId()`	Bookmarks
Document Library documents	`DLFileEntry.class.getName()`	`fileEntry.getFileEntryId()`	Document Library documents
Knowledge Base article	`KBArticle.class.getName()`	`KBArticle.getResourcePrimKey()`	Knowledge Base articles

Based on view count, you can easily find out which assets are being viewed the most (called most popular assets) at either group level (by the key `groupId`) or asset-type level (by the key `className`). Obviously, the least viewed assets will be available at both group level and content-type level, too. Whenever an asset is viewed, the portal will increase the view count number.

Tag

Tags are scoped into the group instance. That is, a different group (either a site or organization) will have its own non-shared tags set, since the entity `AssetTag` gets defined with `companyId` and `groupId`. Thus the tag name must be unique for a given group. The following code snippet explains this:

```
<column name="tagId" type="long" primary="true" />
<!-- Group instance -->
<!-- Audit fields -->
<!-- Other fields -->
<column name="name" type="String" />
<column name="assetCount" type="int" />
```

Services

The following table shows services related to the entities `AssetTag`, `AssetTagProperty`, and `AssetTagStats`:

Interface	Utility	Implementation	Wrapper	Description

`AssetTag(Local)`
`Service`
	`AssetTag`
	`(Local)`
	`ServiceUtil`
		`AssetTag(Local)`
		`ServiceImpl`
		`extends`
		`AssetTag(Local)`
		`ServiceBaseImpl`
			`AssetTag`
			`(Local)`
			`Service`
			`Wrapper`
				Asset tag (local) service, group-wise

`AssetTagProperty`
`(Local)Service`
	`AssetTag`
	`Property`
	`(Local)`
	`ServiceUtil`
		`AssetTagProperty`
		`(Local)`
		`ServiceImpl`
		`extends`
		`AssetTagProperty`
		`(Local)`
		`ServiceBaseImpl`
			`AssetTag`
			`Property`
			`(Local)`
			`Service`
			`Wrapper`
				Asset tag property (local) service

`AssetTagStats`
`(Local)Service`
	`AssetTagStats`
	`(Local)`
	`ServiceUtil`
		`AssetTagStats`
		`(Local)`
		`ServiceImpl`
		`extends`
		`AssetTagStats(`
		`Local)`
		`ServiceBaseImpl`
			`Asset`
			`TagStats`
			`(Local)`
			`Service`
			`Wrapper`
				Asset tag stats (local) service, content-type wise.

Tags cloud

The tag group-wise popularity (presented as **tags cloud**) is recorded in the column `AssetCount`. The following is the code snippet showing how to calculate the tag popularity based on the group-wise asset count:

```
int count = tag.getAssetCount();
int popularity = (int)(1 + ((maxCount - (maxCount - (count -
minCount))) * multiplier));
```

The preceding code shows group-wise tag popularity. You can check details in the JSP file `$PORTAL_SRC_HOME/portal-web/docroot/html/taglib/ui/asset_tags_navigation/page.jsp`. Of course, you leverage a tag cloud through the entity `AssetTagStats`. As you can see, columns `tagId`, `classNameId`, and `assetCount` get specified in the entity `AssetTagStats`, as follows:

```
<column name="tagStatsId" type="long" primary="true" />
<!-- Other fields -->
<column name="tagId" type="long" />
<column name="classNameId" type="long" />
<column name="assetCount" type="int" />
```

Category

Categories are scoped into a group instance. Furthermore, a category must have a container associated, called `AssetVocabulory`. Again, `AssetVocabulory` is scoped into a group instance. Therefore, category name must be unique for a given vocabulary. In addition, a category can have a parent category, identified by `parentCategoryId`, which forms a category hierarchy. A category can have a left category and right category associated with it, which can be used to improve category retrieval capability. This is shown in the following code snippet:

```
<column name="categoryId" type="long" primary="true" />
<!-- Group instance -->
<!-- Audit fields -->
<!-- Other fields -->
<column name="parentCategoryId" type="long" />
<column name="leftCategoryId" type="long" />
<column name="rightCategoryId" type="long" />
<column name="name" type="String" />
<column name="vocabularyId" type="long" />
```

Services

The following table shows services related to the entities `AssetCategory`, `AssetCategoryProperty`, and `AssetVocabulary`:

Interface	Utility	Implementation	Wrapper	Description
Asset Category (Local) Service	AssetCate gory(Local) ServiceUtil	AssetCategory (Local) ServiceImpl extends AssetCategory (Local) ServiceBaseImpl	AssetCategory (Local) ServiceWrapper	Asset Category (local) service, group-wise
Asset Category Property (Local) Service	AssetCate goryProp erty(Local) ServiceUtil	AssetCategory Property (Local)ServiceImpl extends AssetCategory Property (Local) ServiceBaseImpl	AssetCategory Property(Local) ServiceWrapper	Asset Category property (local) service
AssetVoca bulary (Local) Service	AssetVoca bulary (Local) ServiceUtil	AssetVocabulory (Local)ServiceImpl extends AssetVocabulory (Local) ServiceBaseImpl	AssetVocabulory (Local) ServiceWrapper	Asset Vocabulory (local) service, group-wise

Categories cloud

Categories cloud capability isn't supported at the time of writing. One method of adding categories cloud capability is shown in the following steps:

1. Add column `AssetCount` inside the specification of the entity `AssetCategory`. The column `AssetCount` will be used to present group-level asset count for a given category, as follows:

   ```
   <column name="assetCount" type="int" />
   ```

2. Add an entity called `AssetCategoryStats` to present the asset-type-level asset count for a given category. When the model is ready, use the service builder to generate required models and services, shown as follows:

   ```
   <!-- PK fields -->
   <column name="categoryStatsId" type="long" primary="true" />
   <!-- Other fields -->
   <column name="categoryId" type="long" />
   <column name="classNameId" type="long" />
   <column name="assetCount" type="int" />
   ```

3. Update UI taglib `liferay-ui:asset-categories-navigation` to support category cloud.

4. Add category cloud capability in the configuration of the portlet `asset-category-navigation`.

Category tree

As mentioned earlier, any category must have a vocabulary associated with it, and it may have a `parentCategoryId` entity associated, too. Meanwhile each category has `leftCategoryId` and `rightCategoryId` associated. The entities; such as `parentCategoryId`, `categoryId`, `leftCategoryId`, and `rightCategoryId`, form a tree called **category tree**. The following code shows how the category tree gets built:

```
protected void expandTree(AssetCategory assetCategory)
   throws SystemException
{
   // see details in AssetCategoryPersistenceImpl.java
   assetCategory.setLeftCategoryId(leftCategoryId);
   assetCategory.setRightCategoryId(rightCategoryId);
}
```

Asset query

As shown in the following table, the portal provides asset-query capability to find out asset entries by category, tag, group, asset type, date, and so on:

Group	Parameters	Description
All	`_allcategoryIds,_allTagIds`	All category ids, all tag ids
Any	`_anyCategoryIds, _anyTagIds,_classNameIds,_groupIds`	Any category ids, any tag ids, any class name ids, any group ids
not	`_notAllCategoryIds,`	Not all category ids,
	`_notAllTagIds,_notAnyCategoryIds, _notAnyTagIds`	not all tag ids, not any category ids, not any tag ids
Order	`_orderByCol1, _orderByCol2, _orderByType1,_orderByType2`	Order by column 1, Order by column 2, Order by type 1, Order by type 2
Date	`_publishDate,_expirationDate`	Publish date, expiration date
Integer	`_end,_start`	Pagination end number, Pagination start number
boolean	`_excludeZeroViewCount, _visible`	Whether exclude zero view count or not, where it is visible or not

For more details, you can refer to the class `AssetEntryQuery.java`.

The following table shows two methods `countEntries` and `findEntries`, the interface `AssetEntryFinder`, implementation, utility, and involved database tables:

Method	Interface	Utility	Implementation	Database tables
count Entries	AssetEntry Finder	AssetEntry FinderUtil	AssetEntry FinderImpl	AssetEntry,
				AssetEntries_ AssetTags,
				AssetTag,
				AssetEntries_ AssetCategories
				AssetCategory
find Entries	AssetEntry Finder	AssetEntry FinderUtil	AssetEntry FinderImpl	AssetEntry,
				AssetEntries_ AssetTags,
				AssetTag,
				AssetEntries_ AssetCategories
				AssetCategory

Related content

Related content is the kind of content related to the main topic featured on the page. These links may be populated by the content management system, based on same or partially same tags and/or categories. The idea is that if you are interested in the article on this page, you may want to read additional articles on similar subjects, presented as either tags or categories. This is in contrast to **Read More**, reading more of the article that you are currently reading.

Based on number of tags and/or categories (such as, `_anyTagIds` and/or `_anyCategoryIds`) existing in original content, related content can be further divided into the groups most-related content and regular-related content. Most-related content is a set of content that has at least the same set of tags and/or categories as that of the original content. Regular-related content is a set of content that has at least one tag and/or category as that of the original content.

Range query

Range queries allow one to match documents the fields' values of which are between the lower and upper bound specified by the range query. Range queries can be inclusive or exclusive of the upper and lower bounds. Sorting is done **lexicographically**.

In some use cases, you may want to get most viewed content and/or related content in any time period, no matter how long it is. Some use cases may require a time period based on most viewed and/or related content. For example, you may require related content and most viewed content on a weekly, monthly, or yearly basis. These can be implemented by a date query with conditions `displayDateLT` and `displayDateGT`, as follows:

```
displayDate before displayDateLT
displayDate after displayDateGT
```

Similar scenarios can occur with the most shared content.

> Please note that the entity `RatingEntry` gets involved in the methods `countEntries` and `findEntries`, of the class `AssetEntryFinderImpl`. The rating will be addressed in *Chapter 7, Collaborative and Social API*.

Asset publishing

Asset publisher is a flexible tool for publishing many types of assets with tags and categories. It allows for the showing of lists of web content, blog entries, images, documents, bookmark entries, wiki pages, and so on. Each element on the list can be displayed as a title, a summary (that is, an abstract), in full detail, and many other ways. And most importantly, all of them are configurable.

The following code shows the utility class of the Asset publisher:

```
public static void addAndStoreSelection
// see details in AssetPublisherUtil.Java
public static void removeRecentFolderId(PortletRequest
portletRequest, String className, long classPK) {}
```

For more details about the class `AssetPublisherUtil`, refer to the source code `AssetPublisherUtil.java`.

Asset renderer framework

The portal provides a framework called **asset renderer** framework with the tag `AssetRendererFactory`, in the file `liferay-portlet-app_6_1_0.dtd`. This framework will allow registering custom asset types, so that generic portlets such as `Asset Publisher` can be used to publish them.

> ![icon] Please note that the `AssetRendererFactory` value in the core
> or custom asset types must be a class that implements `com.`
> `liferay.portlet.asset.model.AssetRendererFactory`
> and is called by `AssetPublisher`.

The following table shows `AssetRendererFactory` and `AssetRenderer`, and their
implementation:

Interface	Abstract implementation	Implementation examples	Description
Asset Renderer Factory	BaseAsset Renderer Factory	LayoutRevisionAssetRendererFactory, BlogsEntryAssetRendererFactory, BookmarksEntryAssetRendererFactory, CalEventAssetRendererFactory, UserAssetRendererFactory, DLFileEntryAssetRendererFactory, JournalArticleAssetRendererFactory, MBMessageAssetRendererFactory, WikiPageAssetRendererFactory, KBArticleAssetRendererFactory	Asset render factory
Asset Renderer	BaseAsset Renderer	LayoutRevisionAssetRenderer, BlogsEntryAssetRenderer, BookmarksEntryAssetRenderer, CalEventAssetRenderer, UserAssetRenderer, DLFileEntryAssetRenderer, JournalArticleAssetRenderer, MBMessageAssetRenderer, WikiPageAssetRenderer, KBArticleAssetRenderer	Asset render

Summary

In this chapter, you learnt how to customize web content models and services,
build web content structure and templates, publish web content via asset publisher,
integrate CKEditor and its plugins, use `Expando`—custom attributes, leverage DDL
(dynamic data lists) and DDM (dynamic data mapping), manage assets, asset links,
tags, and categories, and publish assets with asset query.

In *Chapter 7, Collaborative and Social API*, we're going to introduce the collaborative
API and the social API.

7
Collaborative and Social API

The portal is the best ECM for team collaboration, supporting industry standards such as **Web Experience Management Interoperability (WEMI)**, **CMIS**, **WebDAV**, and **JCR**. Event data can be specific to a group within a company. In any organization, some data will be relevant at a team level and some other data will be relevant across the whole business. The portal supports such things very well. The portal's collaboration and social networking features take advantage of the benefits of today's virtualized work environment.

Social office gives us a social collaboration on top of the portal—a full virtual workspace that streamlines communication and builds up group cohesion. All components in social Office are tied together seamlessly, getting everyone on the same page by sharing the same look and feel. More importantly, dynamic activity tracking gives us a bird's eye view of who has been doing what and when within each individual site. **Social equity** can be used to measure the contribution and participation of a user, and the information value of an asset. The activities that award equities include adding contributions, rating, commenting, viewing content, searching and tagging, and more.

This chapter will introduce collaboration tools first. Then it will address collaborative assets management and assets collaborations. Afterwards, it will introduce social networking, social coding, social office, social activity, social equity, open social API, and many other features.

By the end of this chapter, you will have learned about the following:

- Collaboration tools—wiki, blogs, calendar events, message boards, bookmarks, and polls
- Collaborative assets management—both core assets and custom assets
- Assets collaboration building—both core assets and custom assets
- Social networking, social coding, and social office
- Social activity and social equity
- OpenSocial

Collaboration

The portal provides a collaboration suite, which takes advantage of the benefits of the virtualized work environment for collaboration. These collaboration tools include blogs, calendar event, web mail, message boards, polls, RSS feeds, Wiki, AJAX chat client, dynamic friend list, activity wall, activity tracker, alerts and announcements, and more.

Wiki

The Wiki portlet provides a straightforward wiki solution. The following figure shows Wiki from viewpoint of models. Wiki articles are presented by the entity `WikiPage`. Each `WikiPage` has a unique resource-primary-key associated. These resource-primary-keys are defined in the entity `WikiPageResource`. All wiki pages are grouped as Wiki nodes and presented as the entity `WikiNode`. Each `WikiNode` may have many wiki page resources and wiki pages associated. In particular, `WikiPageResource` connects between `WikiNode` and `WikiPage`. So, there is a many-to-many relationship between `WikiPage` and `WikiNode`, shown as follows:

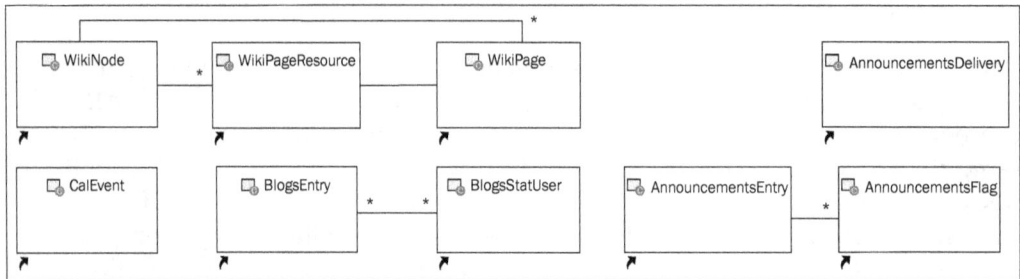

Wiki models

The following table shows the wiki models `WikiPage`, `WikiPageResource`, `WikiNode`, and their implementation:

Interface	Extension	Implementation	Description
WikiNode	WikiNodeModel extends BaseModel<WikiNode>, GroupedModel	WikiNodeImpl extends WikiNode ModelImpl	Wiki node model, extension, and implementation
WikiPage Display	none	WikiPage DisplayImpl	Wiki page display

Interface	Extension	Implementation	Description
`WikiPage`	`WikiPageModel extends BaseModel<WikiPage>, GroupedModel, ResourcedModel`	`WikiPageImpl extends WikiPageModelImpl`	Wiki page model, extension, and implantation
`WikiPage Resource`	`WikiPageResource Model extends BaseModel<Wiki PageResource>`	`WikiPageResource Impl extends WikiPageResource ModelImpl`	Wiki page resource model, extension, and implementation

Wiki services

Based on the service XML model `svn://svn.liferay.com/repos/public/portal/trunk/portal-impl/src/com/liferay/portlet/wiki/service.xml`, the service builder generated a set of services for Wiki pages and nodes. The following table shows a summary of these services:

Interface	Utility	Wrapper	Main methods
`WikiNode(Local)Service`	`WikiNode(Local)ServiceUtil`	`WikiNode(Local)ServiceWrapper`	`addNode, deleteNode, getNode, importPages, subscribeNode, unsubscribeNode, updateNode`
`WikiPage(Local)Service`	`WikiPage(Local)ServiceUtil`	`WikiPage(Local)ServiceWrapper`	`add*, changeParent, delete*, get*, movePage, revertPage, subscribePage, unsubscribePage, update*`
`WikiPage Resource LocalService`	`WikiPageResource LocalServiceUtil`	`WikiPageResource LocalService Wrapper`	`add*, create*, delete*, dynamicQuery, get*, set*, update*`

Wiki engines

The portal provides the interface `com.liferay.portlet.wiki.engines.WikiEngine` with functions like `convert`, `getOutGoingLinks`, `setInterWikiConfiguration`, `setMainConfiguration`, and `validate`. The function `convert` converts the content of the given page to HTML using the view and edit URLs to build links. The function `getOutGoingLinks` gets a map with the links included in the given page. The key of each map entry is the title of the linked page. The value is a Boolean object that indicates if the linked page exists or not.

The function `setInterWikiConfiguration` sets the configuration to support quick links to other wikis. The format of the configuration is specific to the `WikiEngine`. While the function `setMainConfiguration` sets the main wiki configuration as a `String`. And the function `validate` validates the content of a wiki page for this engine.

A specific wiki engine must implement the interface `WikiEngine`. The following table shows several integrated Wiki engines: Text wiki, HTML wiki, JSP wiki, and JAM wiki:

Name	Interface	Engine	Description
HtmlEngine	`WikiEngine`	Built-in	HTML wiki engine
TextEngine	`WikiEngine`	Built-in	Text wiki engine
JSPWikiEngine	`WikiEngine`	JSPWiki	JSP wiki is a wiki software built around the standard J2EE components of Java, servlets, and JSP. Refer to `http://www.jspwiki.org/`
MediaWikiEngine	`WikiEngine`	JAMWiki	JAM wiki is a wiki software built around the standard components of Java, servlets, and JSP. It is very similar to MediaWiki. Refer to `http://jamwiki.org/wiki/en/JAMWiki`

In addition, you may want to order wiki pages by created date, title, and version. You can leverage the comparator utilities, such as `PageCreateDateComparator`, `PageTitleComparator`, and `PageVersionComparator`, respectively. The Wiki portlet supports versioning, RSS feeds, and different languages, such as Creole, text, and HTML. Of course, it leverages WYSIWYG editors to edit the wiki page. By default, it supports workflow on the wiki pages.

Blogs

The Blogs portlets provide a straightforward Blogs solution, including full WYSIWYG editing capability and publication date, RSS support, workflow support, threaded user and guest comments, tags and labels, social bookmarking links, e-mail notifications of blog replies, and an entry rating system.

As shown in the previous diagram, blogs got defined in two entities, namely, `BlogsEntry` and `BlogsStatsUser`. The entity `BlogsEntry` covers the following special columns in the service XML `/blogs/service.xml`:

```
<column name="trackbacks" type="String" />
<column name="smallImageId" type="long" />
<column name="smallImageURL" type="String" />
```

As shown in the previous code, each blog entry could have a column `displayDate` or be called `publishDate` to show whether the blogs entry would be visible to the guest users or not by that date. And each blog entry will have trackbacks — either allowing ping backs or allowing track backs. In particular, each blog entry can have an image as its thumbnail. This image can be stored in the table image referred by the filed `samllImageId`, or this image can be an external image URL or an image URL from the Image Gallery.

Similarly, the entity `BlogsStatsUser` shows detailed information about the recent bloggers, covering the following special columns in the service XML `/blogs/service.xml`:

```
<column name="ratingsTotalScore" type="double" />
<column name="ratingsAverageScore" type="double" />
```

The previous code shows detailed blogger information, like blog entry counts, last post date ratings, total entries ratings, total score ratings, and average score ratings. These messages would get displayed in the **Recently Blogs** portlet.

Based on the service XML `/blogs/service.xml`, the service builder generates Blogs models: `BlogsEntry`, `BlogsStatsUser`, wrappers, and their implementation.

The following table shows the blog entries services, their services' utilities, wrappers, and implementation:

Service	Utility	Wrapper	Main methods
BlogsEntry(Local)Service	BlogsEntry(Local)ServiceUtil	BlogsEntryServiceWrapper	add*, delete*, get*, subscribe, unsubscribe, update*
BlogsStatsUserLocalService	BlogsStatsUserLocalServiceUtil	BlogsStatsUserLocalServiceWrapper	add*, create*, delete*, dynamicQuery, get*, set*, update*

Shared calendar

The calendar portlet provides calendar information and shares the calendar among users from different departments. Based on the **iCal**, we can import/export calendar events from/to other calendars like **iGoogle**. It also supports connections of **AIM**, **ICQC**, **MSN**, and **YM**. The calendar events got defined via an entity called CalEvent in the service XML /calendar/service.xml. The following code shows the other fields of the entity CalEvent:

```
<column name="firstReminder" type="int" />
<column name="secondReminder" type="int" />
```

The previous code shows the title, description, and type of the calendar events. Each event can have location information, start-date, and end-date. Each event can have a duration of time in hours and minutes, whether it should be all day or not. Each event can be time zone sensitive, for example, repeating with recurrence text. Or it has reminder interval, such as, first reminder and second reminder time interval.

Similarly, the shared calendar has simple services, as shown in the following table:

Interface	Utility	Wrapper	Implementation	Main methods
CalEvent(Local)Service	CalEvent(Local)ServiceUtil	CalEvent(Local)ServiceWrapper	CalEvent(Local)ServiceImpl extends CalEvent(Local)ServiceBaseImpl	add*, delete*, get*, has*, export*, importICal4j, update*

Announcements

Announcements and **Alerts** are two separate portlets, which are responsible for broadcasting messages to a list of users within a scope. Essentially, these portlets provide a mass messaging engine and one-way messaging. All Announcement and/or Alert entries are tracked, so that they can be *read* by each individual user, and each user can individually hide an entry.

The portal defines a set of entities like `AnnouncementsDelivery`, `AnnouncementsEntry`, and `AnnouncementsFlag` in the service XML/announcements/service.xml.

Based on the previous service XML, `Service-Builder` generates a set of services, utilities, wrappers, and main method implementation, as shown in the following table:

Interface	Utility	Wrapper	Main methods
Announcements Entry(Local) Service	Announcements Entry(Local) ServiceUtil	Announcements Entry(Local) ServiceWrapper	addEntry, deleteEntry, updateEntry
Announcements Delivery(Local) Service	Announcements Delivery(Local) ServiceUtil	Announcements Delivery(Local) ServiceWrapper	updateDelivery
Announcements Flag(Local) Service	Announcements Flag(Local) ServiceUtil	Announcements Flag(Local) ServiceWrapper	addFlag, deleteFlag, updateFlag

Message Boards

Message Boards is a full-featured forum solution with threaded views, categories, RSS capability, avatars, file attachments, previews, dynamic list of recent posts, and forum statistics. Message Boards work with the fine-grained permissions and role-based access control model to give detailed levels of control to administrators and users.

The following diagram depicts a forum structure overview of Message Boards. A forum is made up of a set of categories. Each category, called `MBCategory`, may have many subcategories and threads. In addition each category can have many mailing lists called `MBMailingList`. Furthermore, each thread called `MBThread` may have many posts (in the form of replies).

The thread refers to the collection of messages called `MBMessage`. A thread itself is a post, too. The posts may be displayed in flat chronological order by date of posting, or in a question-answer order. Actually, threads can be regarded as the root-level posts. Sub-posts are also supported, which enable comments in one of the replies to start another thread that remains linked to the original. Moreover, you can enable flags, called `MBMessageFlag`, thereby allowing users to flag content as inappropriate.

In addition, banned users are specified in the entity `MBBan`, and users' message boards stats are defined in the entity `MBStatsUser`. The entity `MBDiscussion` defined assets' comments, which were associated with the entity `MBThread`. This is shown as follows:

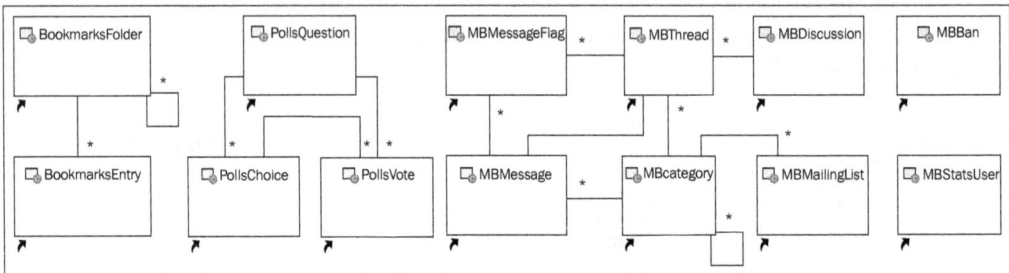

Models

Message Boards models got specified in the service XML `/messageboards/service.xml`. The following table gives an overview of these models, their wrapper, extension and implementation:

Model Interface	Extension	Wrapper	Implementation	Model Constants
MBBan	MBBanModel extends BaseModel<MBBan>, GroupedModel	MBBan Wrapper	MBBanImpl extends MBBanModel Impl	none
MBCategory	MBCategoryModel extends BaseModel <MBCategory>, GroupedModel	MBCategory Wrapper	MBCategory Impl extends MBCategory ModelImpl	MBCategory Constants
MBCategory Display	none	none	MBCategory DisplayImpl	none
MBThread	MBThreadModel extends BaseModel <MBThread>	MBThread Wrapper	MBThreadImpl extends MBThread ModelImpl	MBThread Constants

Model Interface	Extension	Wrapper	Implementation	Model Constants
MBTree Walker	Serializable	none	MBTreeWalker Impl	none
MBMessage	MBMessageModel extends BaseModel <MBMessage>, GroupedModel	MBMessage Wrapper	MBMessageImpl extends MBMessage ModelImpl	MBMessage Constants
MBDiscu ssion	MBDiscussionModel extends BaseModel <MBDiscussion>	none	MBDiscussion Impl extends MBDiscussion ModelImpl	none
MBMailing List	MBMailingListModel extends BaseModel <MBMailingList>, GroupedModel	MBMailing List Wrapper	MBMailingList ModelImpl extends BaseModelImpl <MBMailing List>	none
MBMessage Flag	MBMessageFlagModel extends BaseModel <MBMessageFlag>	MBMessage Flag Wrapper	MBMessage FlagImpl extends MBMessage FlagModelImpl	MBMessage Flag Constants
MBStats User	MBStatsUserModel extends BaseModel <MBStatsUser>	MBStatsUser Wrapper	MBStatsUser ModelImpl extends BaseModelImpl <MBStatsUser>	none

Services

Based on the previous service XML, the service builder generates a set of services, as shown in the following table:

Interface	Utility	Wrapper	Main Methods
MBBan(Local) Service	MBBan(Local) ServiceUtil	MBBan(Local) ServiceWrapper	addBan, deleteBan
MBCategory (Local)Service	MBCategory (Local)Service	MBCategory(Local) ServiceWrapper	add*, delete*, get*, subscribe*, unsubscribe*, update*
MBDiscussion LocalService	MBDiscussion LocalService Util	MBDiscussionLocal ServiceWrapper	add*, create*, dynamicQuery, get*, set*, update*

Interface	Utility	Wrapper	Main Methods
MBMailingList LocalService	MBMailingList LocalService Util	MBMailingList LocalService Wrapper	add*, create*, dynamicQuery, get*, set*, update*
MBThreadFlag LocalServiceI	MBThreadFlag LocalServiceI Util	MBThreadFlag LocalServiceI Wrapper	add*, create*, dynamicQuery, get*, set*, update*
MBMessage (Local)Service	MBMessage (Local) ServiceUtil	MBMessage(Local) ServiceWrapper	add*, delete*, get*, subscribe*, unsubscribe*, update*
MBStatsUser LocalService	MBStatsUser LocalService Util	MBStatsUser LocalService Wrapper	add*, create*, dynamicQuery, get*, set*, update*
MBThread (Local)Service	MBThread (Local) ServiceUtil	MBThread(Local) ServiceWrapper	Delete*, get*, lock*, move*, split*, unlock*

Bookmarks

Bookmarks are retrievable names and URLs (that is, web page locations). Their primary purpose is to catalog and access web pages that users have visited easily either by name or by URL. The Bookmarks portlet provides the ability for users to keep track of URLs in the portal. An administrator can use bookmarks to publish relevant links to a group of users. In addition, bookmarks can be imported or exported via LAR files.

The portlet Bookmarks defines a set of folders to hold entries. Each folder called BookmarksFolder can have many sub folders. Thus the folders form a hierarchy. Each folder can have many entries. Each entry, called BookmarksEntry, can have one URL, name, description, and priority. More interestingly, entries can be classified by categories, and entries can have many tags associated — thus end-users can group entries in their own way. Of course, each bookmark entry can have multiple custom attributes.

The portal has specified bookmark models in the service XML /bookmarks/service.xml.

The portal has generated a set of services for polls via the service builder. The following table shows an overview of these services, their wrappers, and their main method implementations:

Service interface	Utility	Wrapper	Main methods
BookmarksEntry (Local)Service	BookmarksEntry (Local)ServiceUtil	BookmarksEntry (Local)Service Wrapper	add*, delete*, get*,open*, update*
BookmarksFolder (Local)Service	BookmarksFolder (Local)ServiceUtil	BookmarksFolder (Local)Service Wrapper	add*, delete*, get*, update*

As you can see in the previous table, the local service `BookmarksEntryLocalService` is the interface for the local service, containing the signature of every method in `BookmarksEntryLocalServiceBaseImpl` and `BookmarksEntryLocalServiceImpl`. The regular service `BookmarksEntryService` is the interface for the permission-checking service, containing the signature of every method in the `BookmarksEntryServiceBaseImpl` and `BookmarksEntryServiceImpl`.

Polls

The **Polls** portlet allows us to create multiple choice polls that keep track of votes and display results on a page where a lot of separate polls could be managed, and it is configurable to display a specific poll's results; while the Polls Display portlet allows us to vote for a specific poll's question and view the results.

As shown in the previous diagram, polls are made up of questions called `PollsQuestion`, that is, polls will have many questions associated with them. Each question must have two or more choices, called `PollsChoice`. In turn, each choice may have many votes called `PollsVote` associated with it. Note that a given user on a specific question can have, at the most, one vote.

The polls models got defined in the service XML `/polls/service.xml`.

The portal has generated a set of services for polls via the service builder. You can leverage these services in your custom plugins. The following table shows an overview of these services:

Service Interface	Utility	Wrapper	Main methods
PollsQuestion (Local)Service	PollsQuestion (Local)ServiceUtil	PollsQuestion (Local) ServiceWrapper	add*, delete*, get*, update*
PollsChoice LocalService	PollsChoiceLocal ServiceUtil	PollsChoiceLocal ServiceWrapper	add*, create*, dynamicQuery, get*, set*, update*
PollsVote (Local)Service	PollsVote(Local) ServiceUtil	PollsVote(Local) ServiceWrapper	addVote

Asset management

The portal has a set of built-in assets, called portal core assets. And the portal also provides a framework in which custom assets can be plugged through plugins easily. We have introduced a set of core assets like polls, bookmarks, message boards, announcements, shared calendar, blogs, wiki, in the previous section. In this section, we are going to introduce more portal core assets and typical custom assets.

Software Catalog

The **Software Catalog** portlet allows building a catalog of software products and making them available to the visitors of the site. The software catalog covers a set of features like license management, framework management, ratings, tagging, screenshots, ability to specify a direct download link or a download page, allowing users to register their products, tracking of product versions, export of liferay-plugin-repository.xml for the whole repository, integration with permission system, and so on.

As shown in the following diagram, the software catalog defines a few entities, namely, SCFrameworkVersion, SCProductVersion, SCLicense, SCProductEntry, and SCProductScreenshot. Each product version may have many framework versions associated, and each product entry may have many product versions, licenses, and screenshots associated with it:

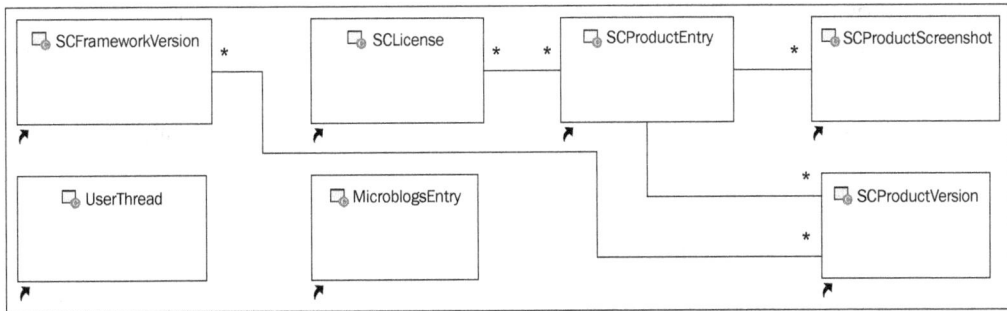

These entities get defined in the service XML `/softwarecatalog/service.xml`.

Similarly, the portal generates a set of services — utilities, wrappers, and implementation: `SCProductEntry(Local)Service`, `SCProductScreenshotLocalService`, `SCProductVersion(Local)Service`, `SCLicense(Local)Service`, and `SCFrameworkVersion(Local)Service`. The common methods include `add*`, `delete*`, `get*`, `update*`, `where*`, and the present model's name, such as, **FrameworkVersion**, **License**, **ProductEntry**, **ProductVersion**, and **ProductScreenshot**.

Private messaging

A private message, often shortened to PM, is like an e-mail sent from one user to another user on Message Boards. Private messages are forums and the like, where users don't personally know the other users and might not be comfortable with giving out their personal e-mail address.

The private message got defined via the entity `UserThread` as follows:

```
<!-- see details in /privatemessage/service.xml-->
<column name="read" type="boolean" />
<column name="deleted" type="boolean" />
```

As shown in the previous code, the private message has columns, such as `mbThreadId` and `topMBMessageId` associated with the Message Boards, using Message Boards backend, and the columns read and deleted to indicate its status.

Microblogs

Microblogging is a broadcast medium in the form of blogging. Microblog content is typically smaller in both actual and aggregate file size. The fact is the differences between microblog entries and normal blog entries are insignificant. Microblogs are, well, micro. They are shorter, real-time, and addressable.

The microblogs portlet allows users to broadcast short messages to other users of the service, and microposts can be made public and/or distributed to a private group of subscribers, called followers.

The microblogs got specified through the entity `MicroblogsEntry` as follows:

```
<!-- see details in /microblogs/service.xml -->
<column name="receiverMicroblogsEntryId" type="long" />
<column name="socialRelationType" type="int" />
```

As shown in the previous code, each `MicroblogsEntry` has defined columns, content, and type to present blog's content and types, and columns such as `receiverUserId`, `receiverMicroblogsEntryId`, and `socialRelationType` for the present receiver user, receiver microblogs entry, and social relation type, respectively. Of course, you can use this service XML as a basis and add your own custom fields. Once your service XML is ready, you can go further and generate models and services, using the service builder in the plugins.

Shopping cart

Shopping portlet provides all you need to have an online store with a shopping cart. As shown in the following diagram, the shopping cart got defined within a set of entities like `ShoppingCart`, `ShoppingCategory`, `ShoppingCoupon`, `ShoppingItem`, `ShoppingItemField`, `ShoppingItemPrice`, `ShoppingOrder`, and `ShoppingOrderItem`, shown as follows:

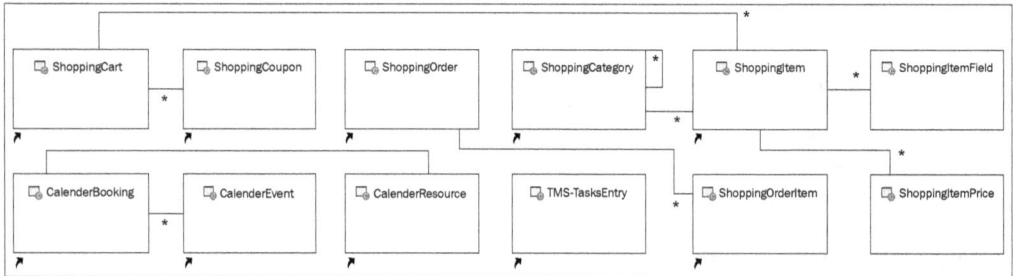

Shopping cart entities get specified in the service XML /shopping/service.xml.
The following table shows a summary of these entities:

Entity name	Extension	Wrapper	Implementation
ShoppingCart	ShoppingCartModel extends BaseModel<Shopping Cart>, GroupedModel	ShoppingCart Wrapper	ShoppingCart Impl extends ShoppingCart ModelImpl
Shopping CartItem	Comparable<Shopping CartItem>, Serializable	none	ShoppingCart ItemImpl
Shopping Category	ShoppingCategory Model extends BaseModel<Shopping Category>, GroupedModel	Shopping Category Wrapper	ShoppingCategory Impl extends ShoppingCategory ModelImpl
Shopping Coupon	ShoppingCoupon Model extends BaseModel<Shopping Coupon>, GroupedModel	Shopping CouponWrapper	ShoppingCoupon Impl extends ShoppingCoupon ModelImpl
ShoppingItem	ShoppingItemModel extends BaseModel<Shopping Item>, GroupedModel	Shopping ItemWrapper	ShoppingItem Impl extends ShoppingItem ModelImpl
Shopping ItemField	ShoppingItemField Model extends BaseModel<Shopping ItemField>	ShoppingItem FieldWrapper	ShoppingItem FieldImpl extends ShoppingItem FieldModelImpl
Shopping ItemPrice	ShoppingItemPrice Model extends BaseModel<Shopping ItemPrice>	ShoppingItem PriceWrapper	ShoppingItem PriceImpl extends ShoppingItem PriceModelImpl
ShoppingOrder	ShoppingOrder Model extends BaseModel<Shopping Order>, GroupedModel	Shopping OrderWrapper	ShoppingOrder Impl extends ShoppingOrder ModelImpl
Shopping OrderItem	ShoppingOrderItem Model extends BaseModel<Shopping OrderItem>	ShoppingOrder ItemWrapper	ShoppingOrder ItemImpl extends ShoppingOrder ItemModelImpl

Based on this service XML, the portal generates a set of services — utilities,
wrappers, and implementation for the shopping cart. You can leverage the
same in your plugins.

Advanced calendar

As mentioned earlier, the portal has provided a shared calendar within the entity called `CalEvent`. Obviously, you can define an advanced calendar in the plugin. Let's see a sample of an advanced calendar. Of course, you can use this advanced calendar as reference and thereby develop your own customized advanced calendar.

The advanced calendar is made of three entities: `Calendar Booking`, `Calendar Event`, and `Calendar Resource`. Each calendar booking can have one, and only one, calendar event and calendar resource associated, as shown in the following code:

```
<!--see details in /advanced-calendar/service.xml -->
<column name="classNameId" type="long" />
<column name="classPK" type="long" />
<column name="location" type="String" />
```

The previous code shows that each calendar booking can have one, and only one, calendar event via the name `calendarEventId` and calendar resource via the name `calendarResourceId` associated. Each calendar booking can have columns such as title, description, location, and so on. Most importantly, each calendar booking has included the pattern `classNameId-classPK`. Therefore, each calendar booking can be associated with any content type and content.

Tasks management

Task management is the process of managing a task or a task portfolio through its life cycle. It can either help individuals achieve goals, or help groups of individuals collaborate and share knowledge for the accomplishment of collective goals. An effective task management supposes being able to manage all aspects of a task, including its status, priority, time, human and financial resources assignments, recurrences, notifications, and so on. The portal framework can reach the same and the tasks could be defined in the plugins via the entity `TasksEntry`:

```
<!-- Audit fields see details in /tasks/service.xml --><column
name="dueDate" type="Date" />
<column name="finishDate" type="Date" />
<column name="status" type="int" />
```

The previous code shows that each task entry will have columns such as title and priority—high, lower, and normal—to identify tasks or task portfolios. The columns `assigneeUserId` and `resolverUserId` indicate the assignee and resolver; while the columns `dueDate`, `finishDate`, and `status` indicate the task due-date, finish-date, and current status—all, open, *%-percent-complete, reopen, and resolved.

Online chat and mail

The Chat portlet is an **AJAX Enterprise Instant Messaging** client that allows users to automatically chat with other logged-in portal users. Chat sessions are persisted across portal pages and are as secure as other portal functionalities. It allows you to enter chat rooms and converse with other online users. In addition, chat portlet integrates Jabber servers (like OpenFire, http://www.igniterealtime.org/projects/openfire/) in nature. As shown in the following diagram, chat is defined by the entities Chat-Entry and Chat-Status. Both of them are associated with the portal core asset User, which is shown as follows:

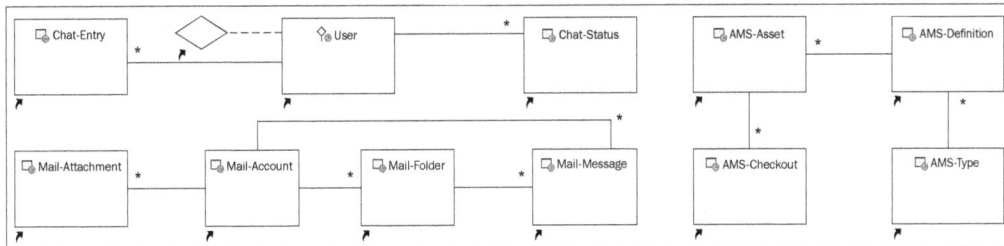

The Mail portlet is a full AJAX-based webmail client that can be configured to interface with many popular IMAP e-mail servers. It allows users to send and check their e-mail directly through the portal, and it also allows them to visualize all e-mails of a given account from several e-mail accounts. As shown in the previous diagram, the mail got specified within the entities Mail-Attachment, Mail-Account, Mail-Folder, and Mail-Message.

Chat

Chat entities get specified in the service XML. The following table shows the chat models, its extension, wrapper, and implementation:

Model interface	Extension	Wrapper and Clp	Implementation
Entry	EntryModel extends BaseModel<Entry>	EntryWrapper EntryClp	EntryImpl extends EntryModelImpl
Status	StatusModel extends BaseModel<Status>	StatusWrapper StatusClp	StatusImpl extends StatusModelImpl

There are a set of chat services generated by the service builder (service XML /chat/ service.xml). The following table shows these services, their wrappers, utilities, and implementations:

Interface	Utility	Wrapper	Clp	Main methods
EntryLocal Service	EntryLocal ServiceUtil	EntryLocal ServiceWrapper	EntryLocal ServiceClp	add*, create*, delete*, dynamicQuery, get*, set*, update*
StatusLocal Service	StatusLocal ServiceUtil	StatusLocal ServiceWrapper	StatusLocal ServiceClp	add*, create*, delete*, dynamicQuery, get*, set*, update*

Mail

Mail-related entities got specified in the service XML. As shown in the following table, the mail models, its extension, wrapper, **clp** (**Class Loader Proxy**), and implementation get generated by the service builder:

Model Interface	Extension	Wrapper and Clp	Implementation
Account	AccountModel extends AuditedModel, BaseModel<Account>	AccountWrapper AccountClp	AccountImpl extends AccountModelImpl
Attachment	AttachmentModel extends BaseModel <Attachment>	AttachmentWrapper AttachmentClp	AttachmentImpl extends Attachment ModelImpl
Folder	FolderModel extends AuditedModel, BaseModel<Folder>	FolderWrapper FolderClp	FolderImpl extends FolderModelImpl
MailFile	none	none	none
Message	MessageModel extends AuditedModel, BaseModel<Message>	MessageWrapper MessageClp	MessageImpl extends MessageModelImpl
Message Display	none	none	none
Messages Display			

The mail services could be summarized as shown in the following table (service XML /mail/service.xml):

Interface	Utility	Wrapper and Clp	Main methods
AccountLocal Service	AccountLocal ServiceUtil	AccountLocal ServiceWrapper AccountLocal ServiceClp	add*, create*, delete*, dynamicQuery, get*, set*, update*
Attachment LocalService	Attachment LocalServiceUtil	AttachmentLocal ServiceWrapper AttachmentLocal ServiceClp	add*, create*, delete*, dynamicQuery, get*, set*, update*
FolderLocal Service	FolderLocal ServiceUtil	FolderLocal ServiceWrapper FolderLocal ServiceClp	add*, create*, delete*, dynamicQuery, fetch*, get*, set*, update*
MessageLocal Service	MessageLocal ServiceUtil	MessageLocal ServiceWrapper MessageLocal ServiceClp	add*, create*, delete*, dynamicQuery, get*, set*, update*, populate*

In addition, the mail portlet has defined a set of service utilities for mailbox and IMAP connection. The following table shows a summary of these services:

Service	Interface	Extension/Utility	Description
Connection Listener	javax.mail. event. Connection Listener	none	Mail connection listener
IMAPAccessor	none	none	IMAP accessor
IMAPAttachment Handler	Attachment Handler	DefaultAttach mentHandler HtmlContentUtil	IMAP attachment handler
IMAPConnection	none	none	IMAP connection
IMAPMailbox	Mailbox	BaseMailbox	IMAP mail box

Service	Interface	Extension/Utility	Description
PasswordRetriever	none	PasswordUtil	Mail password retriever
AccountLock	none	none	Mail account lock

Asset management system

Assets would be expensive to purchase and maintain. **Asset management system (AMS)** features include online asset inventory, helping you track your items in real-time; organization of data based on asset type, asset definition, and checkout; automatic contract expiration notifications; utilization tracking and auditing, so that you know what is being used, and more.

How can you model the asset management system? As shown in the previous diagram, AMS can be modeled via the entities Asset, Definition, Type, and Checkout. Each type could have many definitions, and each definition could have many assets. Each asset will have many checkouts.

These entities are summarized in the following table (service XML /ams/service. xml):

Model	Extension	Wrapper/Clp	Implementation	Description
Asset	AssetModel extends AuditedModel, BaseModel<Asset>	AssetWrapper AssetClp	AssetImpl extends AssetModelImpl	AMS Asset model
Checkout	CheckoutModel extends AuditedModel, BaseModel <Checkout>	Checkout Wrapper CheckoutClp	CheckoutImpl extends CheckoutModel Impl	AMS Checkout model
Definition	DefinitionModel extends AuditedModel, BaseModel <Definition>	Definition Wrapper DefinitionClp	DefinitionImpl extends Definition ModelImpl	AMS Definition model
Type	TypeModel extends AuditedModel, BaseModel<Type>	TypeWrapper TypeClp	TypeImpl extends TypeModelImpl	AMS Type model

Human resource management

Human resource management (**HR**) is the management of an organization's employees, including employment and arbitration in accord with the law, and with a company's directives. Its features include organizational management, personnel administration, manpower management, and industrial management.

Based on the portal framework, HR can be built within management organization chart, asset, billing, expense, and timesheet (in the service XML `/hr/service.xml`).

Marketplace

Marketplace is a hub for sharing, browsing, and downloading Liferay-compatible applications. The marketplace is defined as a plugin called `marketplace-portlet` by the entities (in the service XML `/marketplace/service.xml`) App and Module, while the entity App is specified with the main columns, `remoteAppId` and version; the entity Module is specified with main columns, `appId` and `contextName`.

Assets collaboration

We have discussed collaboration capabilities with the portal core assets and custom assets to enable productive discussion around all your collective knowledge. This section will address assets collaboration.

In the previous chapter, we had introduced custom attributes, DDL and DDM—to add custom document types and custom fields easily into any entities. It has also applied asset views, tags, and categories on any entities. Thus, most viewed and most related content could be identified in nature in the portal framework. In this section, we're going to introduce more asset collaborative capabilities, like rating, comment, flagging, subscribing, and so on. The following diagram depicts an overview on the viewpoint of modeling:

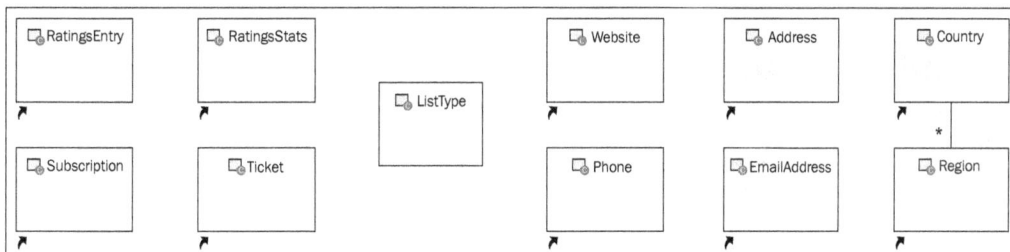

For example, the entities `RatingsEntry` and `RattingsStats` present asset ratings; the entity `Subscription` presents subscription capability. Other entities like `Ticket`, `Website`, `Phone`, `Address`, and `EmailAddress` can be applied on as many assets as you want. The entity `ListType` provides dynamic selection list type, while the entities `Country` and `Region` provide the ability to present all countries and their regions around the world.

Asset ratings

Ranking a page or portlet or asset would be very useful in order to find its popularity. The portal provides rating capability, so that a user can add a ranking on any asset, like a page, portlet, asset, and so on. For a specific user, he/she would have only one chance to rank a specific page, or portlet, or asset. Of course, he/she should have a chance to update his/her rankings at any time.

Asset ratings entities are defined in the service XML, `/ratings/service.xml`.

The following table shows the services of the entities `RatingsEntry` and `RatingsStats` for asset ratings:

Service Interface	Utility	Wrapper	Main methods
RatingsEntry (Local)Service	RatingsEntry(Local) ServiceUtil	RatingsEntry(Local) ServiceWrapper	
RatingsStats LocalService	RatingsStatsLocal ServiceUtil	RatingsStatsLocal ServiceWrapper	

In order to use the ratings entities and services in plugins, you should add the ratings reference in the service XML `service.xml` as follows:

```
<reference package-path="com.liferay.portlet.ratings"
    entity="RatingsStats" />
```

UI taglib liferay-ui:ratings

Ranking a page or a portlet or an asset could be used to measure popularity. Adding ranking to any assets can be done within the tag `liferay-ui:ratings`, since the portal provides a way to extend a page or a portlet or asset's capabilities via UI tags simply:

```
<liferay-ui:ratings-score score="<%= score %>" />
<liferay-ui:ratings
    className="<%= KBArticle.class.getName() %>"
    classPK="<%= kbArticle.getResourcePrimKey() %>"
/>
```

The tag `liferay-ui:ratings-score` can have only one required attribute, `score`, while the tag `liferay-ui:ratings` can have required attributes, such as `className` and `classPK`, which are used to present any asset, like a Knowledge Base article, and optional attributes like `numberOfStars`, `ratingsEntry`, `ratingsStars`, `type`, and `url`. The value of `type` can be `thumbs` or `stars`. For the type `stars`, you can specify the number of stars, such as `5` or `10`.

Asset comments

Adding comments on a page or a portlet or an asset could be useful, too. The portal provides asset comments capability, so that a user can add many comments on any asset, such as, page, portlet, assets, and so on. A user can have a chance to update one or many comments on a specific page, or portlet, or asset. Obviously, the user should have a chance to update his/her comments at any time.

Model

The entity `MBDiscussion` has been defined within the following columns: `discussionId`, `classNameId`, `classPK`, and `threadId`. The pattern `classNameId`-`classPK` can be used to represent any asset:

```
<column name="classNameId" type="long" />
<column name="classPK" type="long" />
<column name="threadId" type="long" />
```

The model `MBDiscussion` extends the model `MBDiscussionModel` and `MBDiscussionModel` extends `AttachedModel` and `BaseModel<MBDiscussion>`.

Service

Asset comments services are defined in the message boards such as `MBMessageLocalService` and `MBMessageLocalServiceUtil`. For example, in the UI taglib JSP `/taglib/ui/discussion/page.jsp`, you can find the following code consuming service `MBMessageLocalService`:

```
MBMessageDisplay messageDisplay = MBMessageLocalServiceUtil.getDi
scussionMessageDisplay(userId, scopeGroupId, className, classPK,
WorkflowConstants.STATUS_ANY, threadView);
```

UI taglib liferay-ui:discussion

Actually, adding comments to a portlet or any asset can be done with the tag
liferay-ui:discussion by extending portlet capabilities via UI tags. The
attributes className and classPK are used to represent these assets, as shown
in the following snippet:

```
<liferay-ui:discussion
    className="<%= BlogsEntry.class.getName() %>"
    classPK="<%= entry.getEntryId() %>"
    // see details in UI taglibs
    userId="<%= entry.getUserId() %>"
/>
```

The tag liferay-ui:discussion should have the required attributes, such as
className, classPK, formAction, subject, and userId, and optional attributes
such as formName, permissionClassName, permissionClassPK, ratingsEnabled,
and redirect. Here the attributes className and classPK are used to represent any
asset generated by service builder in the portal core or custom plugins. Refer to the
book *Liferay User Interface Development* for details about UI taglibs.

Asset flags

Asset flags allow the end user to flag the contents available on that page, as a way
to allow end users to flag the user as inappropriate. They are a form of AJAX-based
flagging that avoids a full page reload. They send an e-mail to the administrators, so
that they can take the appropriate action.

The entity FlagsEntry got defined in the service XML /flags/service.xml. The
following table shows asset flags' model and service:

Name	Wrapper	Utility	Description
FlagsRequest	None	none	Flags request
FlagsEntry Service	FlagsEntry ServiceWrapper	FlagsEntry ServiceUtil	Use MessageBusUtil. sendMessage (DestinationNames. FLAGS, flagsRequest);

For example, in the UI taglib JSP page, /html/taglib/ui/flags/page.jsp, it
consumes the previous service as follows:

```
popup.plug(
    A.Plugin.IO,
    {
```

```
        data:
{

        className: '<%= className %>',
        classPK: '<%= classPK %>',
        //see details in UI taglibs
} );
```

UI taglib liferay-ui:flags

You may flag the content from either portal core portlet or custom plugins portlet as inappropriate via the tag `liferay-ui:flags` as follows:

```
<liferay-ui:flags
className="<%= assetEntry.getClassName() %>"
classPK="<%= assetEntry.getClassPK() %>"
// see details in UI taglibs
/>
```

As shown in the previous code, the tag `liferay-ui:flags` required attributes such as `className`, `classPK`, and `contentTitle`, and optional attributes such as `message` and `reportedUserId`.

Assets subscription

The portal has defined an entity called `Subscription` (a service that can be paid periodically rather than all at once) in the service XML `service.xml`. As shown in the following code, the table `Subscription` has defined the following columns `classNameId`, `classPK`, and `frequency`:

```
<column name="classNameId" type="long" />
<column name="classPK" type="long" />
<column name="frequency" type="String" />
```

As shown in the previous code, the model `Subscription` can be applied on any asset, since the pattern `classNameId-classPK` represents any asset type via `classNameId` and the asset primary key via `classPK`.

The interface `Subscription` extends `SubscriptionModel`, and the interface `SubscriptionModel` extends `AttachedModel`, `AuditedModel`, and `BaseModel<Subscription>`. The wrapper class `SubscriptionLocalServiceWrapper` implements the service `SubscriptionLocalService`.

The utility `SubscriptionLocalServiceUtil` specifies the following methods for the `Subscription` local service:

```
public Subscription addSubscription(long userId,
    long groupId, String className, long classPK);
public Subscription getSubscription(long companyId,
    long userId, String className, long classPK);
```

In order to use the `Subscription` entity and services in plugins, you should add the `Subscription` reference in the portal service XML `service.xml` as follows:

```
<reference package-path="com.liferay.portal" entity="Subscription" />
```

E-mail notification

Once an event happens, the portal may be required to send an e-mail notification. The e-mail notification in the settings of the Control Panel covers the tabs `Sender`, `Account Created Notifications`, and `Password Changed Notifications`. The following table shows the e-mail account models interface, mail message, and mail service:

Model/Service	Extension/Util	Example	Description
IMAPAccount	Account implements Serializable	IMAPAccount(protocol, secure, port);	IMAP account
POPAccount	Account implements Serializable	POPAccount(protocol, secure, port);	POP account
SMTPAccount	Account implements Serializable	SMTPAccount(protocol, secure, port);	SMTP account
MailMessage	implements Serializable	MailMessage(from, to, processedSubject, processedBody, htmlFormat);	Mail message model
MailService	MailService Util	MailServiceUtil. sendEmail(mailMessage);	Mail service to send e-mail

For example, in the method `sendEmail(InternetAddress to, Locale locale)` of the class `com.liferay.portal.util.SubscriptionSender`, it specifies the following code:

```
// see details in SubscriptionSender.java
MailServiceUtil.sendEmail(mailMessage);
```

The previous code first initiates the object `MailMessage`. Then it processes the object `MailMessage`. Finally, it calls the method `MailServiceUtil.sendEmail` to send subscription e-mail notification.

RSS feeds

RSS (Really Simple Syndication) is a family of web feed formats used to publish frequently updated works—such as blog entries, news headlines, audio, and video—in a standardized format. A web feed (or news feed) is a data format used for providing users with frequently-updated content. Content distributors syndicate a web feed, thereby allowing users to subscribe to it.

The portal first provides secure RSS feeds. All secure RSS feeds transparently support BASIC Authentication. Liferay portlet supports RSS feed type, that is, **ATOM 1.0, RSS 1.0**, and **RSS 2.0**.

The portal includes the **Rome API** by default. In addition to being fluent in the many flavors of RSS, the Rome API is easy to use and intuitive to understand. Rome is an open source Java API for reading and publishing RSS feeds in a relatively format-neutral way. The following table shows the usage of Rome API:

Interface	Implementation	Sample code	Description
SyndEnclosure	SyndEnclosure Impl	`enclosure.setLength(image. getSize());`	Syndication enclosure
		`enclosure.setUrl(portalURL + url);`	
SyndLink	SyndLinkImpl	`link.setHref(portalURL + url);`	Syndication link
		`link.setLength(image. getSize());`	
SyndFeed	SyndFeedImpl	`syndFeed.setTitle(feed. getName());`	Syndication feed
		`syndFeed.setLink(feedURL. toString());`	
SyndEntry	SyndEntryImpl	`syndEntry. setAuthor(author);`	Syndication entry
		`syndEntry.setLink(link);`	
SyndContent	SyndContent Impl	`syndContent. setType(RSSUtil.DEFAULT_ ENTRY_TYPE);`	Syndication content
		`syndContent. setValue(value);`	

By the way, you can check for more details in the utilities `com.liferay.portlet.`
`journal.util.JournalRSSUtil.java` and `com.liferay.portlet.journal.`
`action.RSSAction.java`.

Attached model

The portal has added `getModelClassName()` and `getModelClass()` to the
`BaseModel`, through the model interface `AttachedModel`; since all the classes
have that data anyway, just expose it as a friendly method. The model interface
`AttachedModel` defines the following methods:

```
public String getClassName();
public long getClassNameId();
public long getClassPK();
```

For example, `MBMessage.getModelClassName()` will return the model `com.`
`liferay.portlet.messageboards.model.MBMessage`. The following table
shows a set of portal core models, which extend the attached model:

Model Name	Extension	Wrapper	Implementation	Description
Ticket	TicketModel extends AttachedModel, BaseModel<Ticket>	Ticket Wrapper	TicketImpl extends TicketModel Impl	Ticket Model
Address	AddressModel extends AttachedModel, AuditedModel, BaseModel<Address>	Address Wrapper	AddressImpl extends AddressModel Impl	Address model
Email Address	EmailAddressModel extends AttachedModel, AuditedModel, BaseModel<Email Address>	EmailAddress Wrapper	EmailAddress Impl extends EmailAddress ModelImpl	E-mail address model
Phone	PhoneModel extends AttachedModel, AuditedModel, BaseModel<Phone>	PhoneWrapper	PhoneImpl extends PhoneModel Impl	Phone model
Website	WebsiteModel extends AttachedModel, AuditedModel, BaseModel<Website>	Website Wrapper	WebsiteImpl extends WebsiteModel Impl	Website model

The portal also provides the `AuditedModel` interface. Most of the base models have `companyId`, `createDate/modifiedDate`, and `userId/userName`. If a model has those fields, then it will also implement the `AuditedModel` interface. Similarly, if a base model is an `AuditedModel`, and also has a `groupId`, then it is also a `GroupedModel` – meaning that its data can be grouped into `sites/communities`.

Social identity repository

The portal supports **social networking** – you can easily manage your Facebook, MySpace, Twitter, and other social network accounts. In addition, you can manage your instant messenger accounts, such as AIM, ICQ, Jabber, MSN, Skype, and YM, smoothly.

Social office gives us a social collaboration suite on top of the portal – a full virtual workspace that streamlines communication and builds up group cohesion. All components in social office are tied together seamlessly, getting everyone on the same page by sharing the same look and feel. Social office isn't another separate portal, but a specific instance of the portal.

Social networking

The following figure depicts entities and their relationships among social networking, social coding, and social office. As you can see, the social networking plugin defines the entities `MeetupsEntry` for meet-ups entries, `MeetupsRegistration` for meet-ups registration, and `WallEntry` for wall entries. The social coding plugin defines entities such as `SVNRevison`, `SVNRepository`, `JIRAAction`, `JIRAChangeGroup`, `JIRAChangeItem`, and `JIRAIssue`:

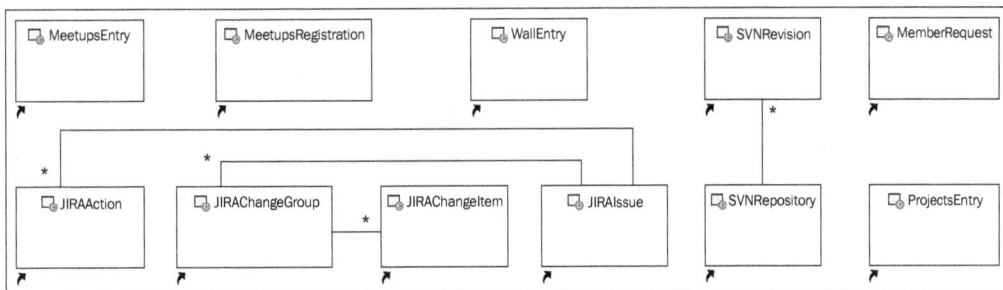

Models

As mentioned earlier, social networking plugin defines three entities, such as, `MeetupsEntry`, `MeetupsRegistration`, and `WallEntry`. The following table shows these entities, model extension, wrapper, clp (class loader proxy), and gives a description:

Model Interface	Extension	Wrapper/Clp	Implementation	Description
Meetups Entry	MeetupsEntryModel extends AuditedModel, BaseModel<Meetups Entry>	MeetupsEntry Wrapper MeetupsEntry Clp	MeetupsEntry Impl extends MeetupsEntry ModelImpl	Meet-ups entry model
Meetups Registr ation	MeetupsRegistration Model extends AuditedModel, BaseModel<Meetups Registration>	MeetupsRegi stration Wrapper MeetupsRegi strationClp	MeetupsRegist rationImpl extends MeetupsRegi strationModel Impl	Meet-ups registration model
WallEntry	WallEntryModel extends BaseModel<Wall Entry>, GroupedModel	WallEntry Wrapper WallEntryClp	WallEntryImpl extends WallEntry ModelImpl	Wall entry model

Services

The social networking plugin showcases how to build a social network by leveraging social networking services. The following table shows a list of the portlets (service XML `/socialnetworking/service.xml`):

Portlet	Related services	Service Utility	Related UI Taglib example
Friends	UserLocalService	UserLocal ServiceUtil	`<liferay-ui:user-display userId="<%=friend.getUserId() %>" userName="<%= friend.getFullName() %>" />`
Friends activities	SocialActivity LocalService	SocialActivity LocalService Util	`<liferay-ui:social-activities activities="<%= activities %>" feedEnabled="<%= true %>" />`

Portlet	Related services	Service Utility	Related UI Taglib example

map	Google maps	`MessageBusUtil`
		
		`IPGeocoderUtil`
			`<aui:script> google.`
			`load("maps", "2.x",`
			`{"language" : "ja_`
			`JP"}); google.setOnLo`
			`adCallback(<portlet:n`
			`amespace />initMap);`
			`</aui:script>`

meetups	`MeetupsRegistration`
	`LocalService`
	
	`MeetupsEntry`
	`LocalService`
		`MeetupsRegi`
		`stration`
		`LocalService`
		`Util`
		
		`MeetupsEntry`
		`LocalService`
		`Util`
			none

members	`UserLocalService`	`UserLocal`
		`ServiceUtil`
			`<liferay-ui:user-`
			`display userId="<%=`
			`member.getUserId()`
			`%>" userName="<%=`
			`member.getFullName()`
			`%>" />`

Members activities	`SocialActivity`
	`LocalService`
		`SocialActivity`
		`LocalService`
		`Util`
			`<liferay-ui:social-`
			`activities`
			`activities="<%=`
			`activities %>"`
			`feedEnabled="<%= true`
			`%>" />`

Summary	`SocialRequest`
	`LocalService`
	
	`UserLocalService`
		`SocialRequest`
		`LocalService`
		`Util`
		
		`UserLocal`
		`ServiceUtil`
			`<liferay-ui:icon />`

Wall	`WallEntryLocal`
	`Service`
	
	`UserLocalService`
		`WallEntryLocal`
		`ServiceUtil`
		
		`UserLocal`
		`ServiceUtil`
			`<liferay-ui:input-`
			`field model="<%=`
			`WallEntry.class %>"`
			`bean="<%= null %>"`
			`field="comments" />`

Social coding

Social coding is a plugin containing two collaborative applications: integration with **SVN** (Apache Subversion) and **JIRA** (a proprietary issue tracking system).When these applications get displayed in a user's personal page, they will display all the information about the development activity of that user in different projects.

The following table shows these applications' models, their extensions, wrappers, clp (Class Loader Proxy), and implementation (service XML /socialcoding/ service.xml):

Interface	Extension	Wrapper/Clp	Implementation	Description
JIRAAction	JIRAActionModel extends BaseModel<JIRA Action>	JIRAAction Wrapper JIRAActionClp	JIRAActionImpl extends JIRAAction ModelImpl	JIRA Action model
JIRAChange Group	JIRAChangeGroup Model extends BaseModel<JIRA ChangeGroup>	JIRAChange GroupWrapper JIRAChange GroupClp	JIRAChange GroupImpl extends JIRAChange GroupModel Impl	JIRA Change Group model
JIRAChange Item	JIRAChangeItem Model extends BaseModel <JIRAChangeItem>	JIRAChange ItemWrapper JIRAChange ItemClp	JIRAChange ItemImpl extends JIRAChange ItemModel Impl	JIRA Change Item model
JIRAIssue	JIRAIssueModel extends BaseModel<JIRA Issue>	JIRAIssue Wrapper JIRAIssueClp	JIRAIssue Impl extends JIRAIssue ModelImpl	JIRA Issue model
SVNRepo sitory	SVNRepository Model extends BaseModel <SVNRepository>	SVNRepository Wrapper SVNRepository Clp	SVNRepository ModelImpl extends BaseModelImpl <SVNReposi tory>	SVN Repository model
SVNRevision	SVNRevisionModel extends BaseModel <SVNRevision>	SVNRevision Wrapper SVNRevision Clp	SVNRevision ModelImpl extends BaseModelImpl <SVNRevision>	SVN Revision model

Social office

Social office is a social collaboration solution for the enterprise. It allows people to collaborate effectively and efficiently. One of the handy features of social office is its usage of Microsoft Office integration. In general, all of the features of social office are available in the portal as well. In fact, the portal is the framework and social office is a customization of this framework.

Models

The social office plugin (so-portlet) defines a few entities in the service XML: `MemberRequest` and `ProjectsEntry`. The following table shows these entities, their extension, wrapper, clp (class loader proxy), and implementation:

Model	Extension	Wrapper/Clp	Implementation	Description
Member Request	MemberRequest Model extends BaseModel<Member Request>, GroupedModel	MemberRequest Wrapper MemberRequest Clp	MemberRequest Impl extends MemberRequest ModelImpl	Member request model
Projects Entry	ProjectsEntry Model extends AuditedModel, BaseModel <ProjectsEntry>	ProjectsEntry Wrapper ProjectsEntry Clp	ProjectsEntry Impl extends ProjectsEntry ModelImpl	Project entry model

Services

The social office plugin (`so-portlet`) defines a set of portlets: activities, contacts, expertise, invite-members, notifications, and sites. The following table depicts these portlets, their related services, utilities, and the involved models (service XML `/socialoffice/service.xml`):

Portlet	Related services	Related service utility	Involved model
Activities	SocialActivity InterpreterLocal Service	SocialActivity InterpreterLocal ServiceUtil	SocialActivity
Contacts	ProjectsEntry LocalService	ProjectsEntry LocalServiceUtil	ProjectsEntry
Expertise	ProjectsEntry LocalService	ProjectsEntry LocalServiceUtil	ProjectsEntry
Invite_ members	UserLocalService GroupLocalService RoleLocalService	UserLocalService Util GroupLocalService Util RoleLocalService Util	User Group Role

Portlet	Related services	Related service utility	Involved model
Notifications	SocialRequest LocalService	SocialRequest LocalServiceUtil	SocialRequest User
	SocialRequest Interpreter LocalService	SocialRequest Interpreter LocalServiceUtil	MemberRequest Group
	UserLocal Service	UserLocalServiceUtil MemberRequestLocal ServiceUtil	
	MemberRequest LocalService		
	GroupLocal Service	GroupLocalService Util	
Sites	GroupLocal Service	GroupLocalService Util	Group LayoutSet Prototype Layout
	LayoutSet PrototypeService	LayoutSetPrototype ServiceUtil	
	LayoutLocalServic	LayoutLocalService Util	

As you can see, the contacts information of social office is accessible via the contacts portlet.

Hooks

The plugin `so-portlet` specifies portal properties hooks. First, the portal properties hook got defined in `liferay-hook.xml` as follows:

```
<portal-properties>portal.properties</portal-properties>
```

In the `portal.properties`, it specifies the following properties and their values:

```
users.form.my.account.identification=expertise
users.form.update.identification=expertise
```

As you can see, the default values of these properties are addresses, phone numbers, additional e-mail addresses, websites, instant messenger, social network, SMS, OpenID. Now, they are overwritten as expertise.

The plugin `so-portlet` indeed specifies JSP hooks. The following table shows a summary of these JSP hooks:

Name	Type	Relative path	Root path	Description
social_office.png	icons	html/icons	/META-INF/custom_jsps	Overwrites icons
expertise.jsp	portlet	html/portlet/enterprise_admin/user	/META-INF/custom_jsps	Overwrites the JSP file
login.jsp	portlet	html/portlet/login	/META-INF/custom_jsps	Overwrites the JSP file
page_site_name.jsp	taglib	html/taglib/ui/my_places	/META-INF/custom_jsps	Overwrites ui taglib

The plugin `so-portlet` leveraged indexer-post-processor hook — allowing hooks to add an `IndexerPostProcessor` to modify user's search summaries, queries, and indexes. It implements a post processing system on top of the existing indexer to allow the plugin hook to modify the search summaries, indexes, and queries. In `liferay-hook.xml`, the plugin `so-portlet` adds the following hook definition:

```
<indexer-post-processor>
    <indexer-class-name>com.liferay.portal.model.User</indexer-class-name>
    <indexer-post-processor-impl>com.liferay.so.hook.indexer.UserIndexerPostProcessor</indexer-post-processor-impl>
</indexer-post-processor>
```

`indexer-model-name` is the name of the model whose indexer you wish to change and `indexer-post-processor-impl` is the name of your `post processor` class that implements `com.liferay.portal.kernel.search.IndexerPostProcessor`.

The plugin `so-portlet` also leverages the `struts-action` hook — allowing the overriding of struts actions from hook plugins. The `struts-action` hook added a new action element `struts-action` into `liferay-hook.xml`, defining `com.liferay.portal.kernel.struts.StrutsAction` and `com.liferay.portal.kernel.struts.StrutsPortletAction` interfaces.

The following table shows these `struts-action` hooks defined in the `so-portlet` plugin:

Name	Model	Path	Implementation	Service Utility
Enterprise admin	User Projects Entry	/enterprise_ admin/edit_ user	com.liferay. so.hook.action. EditUserAction	ProjectsEntry LocalService Util
Enterprise admin users	User Projects Entry	/enterprise_ admin_users/ edit_user	com.liferay. so.hook.action. EditUserAction	ProjectsEntry LocalService Util
My account	User Projects Entry	/my_account/ edit_user	com.liferay. so.hook.action. EditUserAction	ProjectsEntry LocalService Util

Contacts

The Contacts plugin (`contacts-portlet`) enables users to manage customers and friends, including phone numbers, addresses, birthdays, companies, e-mails, and so on. The contact list shows all the people on various sites, as well as friends, and provides a quick way to message them and to find their information. Contacts Centre helps in following a user to receive updates about their activity; managing friends and friend requests and improving the way a user can locate people within the system.

As shown in the following table, the Contacts plugin defines a set of portlets: Chat, Contacts Centre, Profile, My Contacts, and Members:

Portlet	Related service	Related service utility	Related models
Chat	Liferay.Chat.Manager. registerBuddyService PortletLocalService	PortletLocal ServiceUtil	User Portlet
Contacts Center	UserLocalService SocialRequestLocalService PhoneService EmailAddressService	UserLocal ServiceUtil SocialRequest LocalService Util PhoneService Util EmailAddress ServiceUtil	User SocialRequest Phone EmailAddress

Portlet	Related service	Related service utility	Related models
Members	UserLocalService	UserLocal ServiceUtil	User
My Contacts	UserLocalService	UserLocal ServiceUtil	User
Profile	UserLocalService	UserLocal ServiceUtil	User

Most interestingly, user's **Contact Center Profiles** are accessible via the **Chat** portlet. To do so, deploy both the Chat portlet and Contacts portlet. As you can see, your buddies should have a contact index, when hovering over them in the buddy list. How does it work? The following would be the simple answer:

1. First, the Chat portlet defines the utility class ChatExtensionsUtil — an extension system for the Chat portlet that allows us to add in buttons to the buddy list to extend interaction with the buddy with their own portlet. The extension system allows other plugins to register changes to the Chat portlet.

2. Second, register the Chat extension when deploying the plugin. The following code sample shows how to do this:

```
protected void registerChatExtension() throws Exception {
    PortletClassInvoker.invoke(
    false, "1_WAR_chatportlet", _registerMethodKey,
    "contacts-portlet", "/chat/view.jsp"); }
// see details in HotDeployMessageListener.java
private MethodKey _registerMethodKey = new MethodKey(
    "com.liferay.chat.util.ChatExtensionsUtil", "register",
    String.class, String.class);
```

Similarly, the contact's information of social office is accessible via the contacts-portlet. An extension system for the contacts-portlet allows us to add contacts information of social office (or any plugin) to contacts-portlet. In fact, the contacts-portlet defines a utility class ContactsExtensionsUtil.

Social activity

The portal provides the capability to track social activity. Recorded social activities will appear in the Activities portlet. Entities of SocialActivity include SocialActivity, SocialRelation, and SocialRequest. Social equity gets specified via the entities SocialActivityAchievement, SocialActivityCounter, SocialActivityLimit, and SocialActivitySetting.

In addition, in the `OpenSocial` plugin, it defines the entities `Gadget`, `OAuthConsumer`, and `OAuthToken`. In this section, we're going to introduce the `SocialActivity` first. Social equity and `OpenSocial` will get addressed in the coming sections. The following diagram shows the structure of social activity:

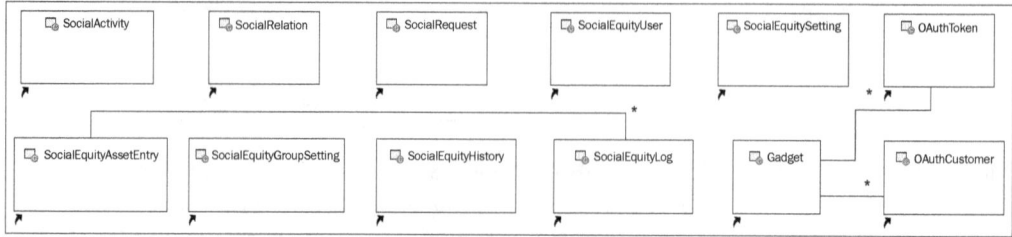

Models

The following table shows the `SocialActivity` models, their extension, wrapper, and implementation:

Model Interface	Extension	Wrapper	Implementation
SocialActivity	SocialActivity Model extends AttachedModel, BaseModel<Social Activity>	SocialActivi tyWrapper	SocialActivity Impl extends SocialActivity ModelImpl
SocialActivity Interpreter	SocialActivity FeedEntry	none	BaseSocialActivity Interpreter
SocialRequest Interpreter	SocialActivity FeedEntry	none	BaseSocialRequest Interpreter
SocialRelation	SocialRelation Model extends BaseModel<Social Relation>	SocialRelat ionWrapper	SocialRelationImpl extends SocialRelation ModelImpl
SocialRequest	SocialRequest Model extends AttachedModel, BaseModel<Social Request>	SocialRequest Wrapper	SocialRequestImpl extends SocialRequest ModelImpl

Services

The following table shows the `SocialActivity` services, their utilities, wrapper, and main methods implementation:

Service Interface	Utility	Wrapper	Main methods
SocialActivity InterpreterLocal Service	SocialActivity InterpreterLocal ServiceUtil	SocialActivity InterpreterLocal ServiceWrapper	add*, delete*, get*, interpret, set*
SocialActivity LocalService	SocialActivity LocalServiceUtil	SocialActivity LocalService Wrapper	add*, create*, delete*, dynamicQuery, get*, set*, update*
SocialRelation LocalService	SocialRelation LocalServiceUtil	SocialRelation LocalService Wrapper	add*, create*, delete*, dynamicQuery, get*, has*, is*, set*, update*
SocialRequest InterpreterLocal Service	SocialRequest InterpreterLocal ServiceUtil	SocialRequest InterpreterLocal ServiceWrapper	add*, delete*, get*, interpret, process*, set*
SocialRequest LocalService	SocialRequest LocalServiceUtil	SocialRequest LocalService Wrapper	add*, create*, delete*, dynamicQuery, get*, set*, update*

UI taglib liferay-ui:social-activities

Social activities could be displayed through the tag `liferay-ui:social-activities` as follows. Refer to the book, *Liferay User Interface Development*, for more details on UI taglibs:

```
<liferay-ui:social-activities
    activities="<%= activities %>"
    // see details in UI taglibs
/>
```

As shown in the previous code, the tag `liferay-ui:social-activities` can have optional attributes such as `activities`, `className`, `classPK`, `feedEnabled`, `feedLink`, `feelLinkMessage`, and `feedTitle`.

Adding social activity tracking

How do we add social activity tracking on a portlet? Let's use a Knowledge Base article as an example to show the steps to add social activity tracking to any portlets:

1. First, add the social activity reference in the plugin service XML `service.xml` as follows:

   ```
   <reference package-path="com.liferay.portlet.social"
   entity="SocialActivity" />
   ```

2. Second, create the activity interpreter `com.liferay.knowledgebase.admin.social.AdminActivityInterpreter` that extends `BaseSocialActivityInterpreter`. The activity interpreter class needs a `getClassNames()` method that returns an array of class names. It includes a `doInterpret(SocialActivity, ThemeDisplay)` method that returns a `SocialActivityFeedEntry`. It also parses the `SocialActivity` argument to create the `SocialActivityFeedEntry`. In particular, it covers a link, a title, and a body as follows:

   ```
   // see details in AdminActivityInterpreter.java
   return new SocialActivityFeedEntry(link, title, body);
   ```

3. Third, add the following lines in `liferay-portlet.xml` to register social activity in a portlet:

   ```
   <social-activity-interpreter-class>
   com.liferay.knowledgebase.admin.social.AdminActivityInterpreter
   </social-activity-interpreter-class>
   ```

As you have noticed, the portal provides the tag `social-activity-interpreter-class` value (it must be a class that implements `com.liferay.portlet.social.model.SocialActivityInterpreter`), and it is called to interpret activities into friendly messages that are easily understandable by a human being. The tag `social-activity-interpreter-class` adds social activity tracking to a portlet.

Requests and activities

The portlet Requests allows us to register social friendship requests for either confirmation or rejection, referring to the JSP file `/html/portlet/requests/view.jsp`, while the portlet Activities exposes social activities, referring to the JSP file `/html/portlet/activities/view.jsp`. The following table shows a summary of these portlets:

Portlet	Related service	Related service utility	Related model	UI taglib
Activities	`GroupLocal Service` `SocialActivity LocalService`	`GroupLocal Service Util` `SocialActivity LocalService Util`	`Group` `Social Activity`	`<liferay- ui:social- activities />`
Requests	`SocialRequest InterpreterLocal Service` `SocialRequest InterpreterLocal Service`	`SocialRequest Interpreter Local ServiceUtil` `SocialRequest Interpreter LocalService Util`	`Social Request` `Social Request FeedEntry`	`<liferay- ui:user- display />` `<liferay- ui:icon-list />` `<liferay- ui:icon />` `<liferay- ui:message />`

Social bookmarks

Social bookmarking links (such as Twitter, Facebook, and Google + 1) can be added in any page via the tags `liferay-ui:social-bookmarks` and `liferay-ui:social-bookmark`. The details are specified in the JSP files `twitter.jsp`, `facebook.jsp`, and `plusone.jsp`, respectively, at the folder `/html/taglib/ui/social_bookmark`. The following is the sample code to add the social bookmarks into any pages:

```
<liferay-ui:social-bookmarks
    displayStyle="<%= socialBookmarksDisplayStyle %>"
    target="_blank"
    title="<%= entry.getTitle() %>"
    url="<%= bookmarkURL.toString() %>"
/>
```

The previous code shows that the tag `liferay-ui:social-bookmarks` requires the attributes, `title`, and `url`, and optional attributes such as `target` and `types`. By the way, you can use the tag `liferay-ui:social-bookmarks` to add social bookmarks in your pages, too. The tag `liferay-ui:social-bookmark` can have the required attributes, such as `title`, `type`, and `url`, and the optional attribute `target`.

Social equity

The portal provides a social equity framework to build a dynamic social capital system by measuring the contribution and participation of a user, and the information value of an asset. Social equity can be used to measure the contribution and participation of a user and the information value of an asset. The activities that award equities include adding contributions, rating, commenting, viewing content, searching, and tagging. The social equity will cover the following aspects:

- Logically, the social equity framework is assets-agnostic.

- It operates on assets directly and uses action keys defined in the `resource-actions` XML.

- Thus liferay-social activity service calls need to be configured for the respective services such as Web Content, Knowledge Base, and so on.

Models

As mentioned earlier, social equity got specified via the entities `SocialActivityAchievement`, `SocialActivityCounter`, `SocialActivityLimit`, and `SocialActivitySetting`. The following table displays these entities, their extension, wrapper, and implementation:

Model Interface	Extension	Wrapper	Implementation
`SocialActivity Achievement`	`SocialActivity AchievementModel extends BaseModel<Social Activity Achievement>`	`SocialActivity Achievement Wrapper`	`SocialActivity AchievementImpl extends SocialActivity AchievementModel Impl`
`SocialActivity Counter`	`SocialActivity CounterModel extends BaseModel <SocialActivityCo unter>`	`SocialActivity CounterWrapper`	`SocialActivity CounterImpl extends SocialActivity CounterModelImpl`
`SocialActivity Limit`	`SocialActivity LimitModel extends BaseModel<Social ActivityLimit>`	`SocialActivity LimitWrapper`	`SocialActivity LimitImpl extends SocialActivity LimitModelImpl`
`SocialActivity Setting`	`SocialActivity SettingModel extends BaseModel <SocialActivitySe tting>`	`SocialActivity SettingWrapper`	`SocialActivity SettingImpl extends SocialActivity SettingModelImpl`

Services

The following table displays social equity services, their utility, wrapper, and main methods implementation:

Service interface	Utility	Wrapper	Main methods
SocialActivity CounterLocal Service	SocialActivity CounterLocal ServiceUtil	SocialActivity CounterLocal ServiceWrapper	add*, create*, delete*, dynamicQuery, get*, is*, update*
SocialActivity LimitLocal Service	SocialActivity LimitLocal ServiceUtil	SocialActivity LimitLocal ServiceWrapper	add*, create*, delete*, dynamicQuery, get*, is*, update*
SocialActivity SettingLocal Service	SocialActivity SettingLocal ServiceUtil	SocialActivity SettingLocal ServiceWrapper	add*, create*, delete*, dynamicQuery, get*, set*, update*
SocialActivity Achievement LocalService	SocialActivity AchievementLocal ServiceUtil	SocialActivity Achievement LocalService Wrapper	add*, clear*, create*, delete*, dynamicQuery, get*, set*, update*

Adding social equity services on custom assets

The portal specifies the social equity definition in a `liferay-social` DTD file, referring to `svn://svn.liferay.com/repos/public/portal/trunk/definitions/liferay-social_6_1_0.dtd` as follows:

```
<!ELEMENT liferay-social (activity*)>
<!ELEMENT activity (model-name, activity-type, language-key?, log-
activity?, processor-class?, contribution-value?, contribution-limit?,
contribution-limit-period?, participation-value?, participation-
limit?, participation-limit-period?, counter*, achievement*)>
```

As shown in the previous element type declarations, the element `liferay-social` can have one or more `activity`. The element `activity` can have only one `model-name` and `activity-type`, no more than one `language-key`, `log-activity`, `processor-class`, `contribution-value`, `contribution-limit`, `contribution-limit-period`, `participation-value`, `participation-limit`, and `participation-limit-period`, and one or many `counter` and `achievement`.

The social equity of the portal core assets was specified in a `liferay-social.xml` file, referring to `svn://svn.liferay.com/repos/public/portal/trunk/portal-web/docroot/WEB-INF/liferay-social.xml`. The social activity model names include Blogs entry, Message Boards message, and Wiki page.

In general, you can apply social equity via `liferay-social.xml` on custom assets like a Knowledge Base article in plugins. For example, the activity type `TYPE_VIEW` for the model named Knowledge Base article can be specified in the XML file `/docroot/WEB-INF/liferay-social.xml` as follows:

```
<liferay-social>
  <!-- see details in the liferay-social.xml -->
  <activity>
    <model-name>com.liferay.knowledgebase.model.KBArticle</model-name>
    <activity-type>${com.liferay.portlet.social.model.
SocialActivityConstants.TYPE_VIEW}</activity-type>
    <language-key>VIEW</language-key>
    <log-activity>false</log-activity>
    <participation-value>1</participation-value>
  </activity>
</liferay-social>
```

Social activity statistics and top users

There are a few portlets related to social equity: `SocialActivity`, user statistics, and group statistics. The following table shows a summary of these portlets, related services, utilities, models, and UI taglib:

Portlet	Related service	Related service utility	Related model	UI taglib
Social activity	`SocialActivity CounterLocal Service,` `SocialActivity`	`SocialConfi gurationUtil`	`SocialActivity Definition`	`<aui:script use="liferay-social-activity-admin">`
User statistics	`SocialActivity CounterLocal Service`	`SocialActivity CounterLocal ServiceUtil`	`SocialActivity Counter`	`<liferay-ui:user-display />`
Group statistics	`SocialActivity CounterLocal Service`	`SocialActivity CounterLocal ServiceUtil,` `AssetTagLocal ServiceUtil`	`SocialActivity Counter`	`<liferay-ui:panel>`

OpenSocial

OpenSocial is a set of common APIs for web-based social networking applications. Based on HTML and JavaScript, OpenSocial includes four APIs for social software applications to access data and core functions on participating social networks. Each API addresses a different aspect; there is one for the general JavaScript API, one for people and friends, one for activities, and one for persistence.

The portal features an OpenSocial container based on **Shindig**. OpenSocial Gadgets present as first-class citizens, just like portlets. Apache Shindig is an OpenSocial container and helps you to start hosting OpenSocial apps quickly by providing the code to render gadgets, proxy requests, and handle **REST** and **RPC** requests. For more information, refer to http://shindig.apache.org/.

Gadget models

As mentioned earlier, in the OpenSocial plugins, it defines entities such as Gadget, OAuthConsumer, and OAuthToken. As you can see, **OAuth (Open Authorization)** is supported by default in the portal. The following table shows these entities, their extension, wrapper, and implementation:

Model Interface	Extension	Wrapper/Clp	Implementation
Gadget	GadgetModel extends BaseModel<Gadget>	GadgetWrapper GadgetClp	GadgetImpl extends GadgetModelImpl
OAuthConsumer	OAuthConsumerModel extends BaseModel<OAuthConsumer>	OAuthConsumerWrapper OAuthConsumerClp	OAuthConsumerModelImpl extends BaseModelImpl <OAuthConsumer>
OAuthToken	OAuthTokenModel extends AuditedModel, BaseModel<OAuthToken>	OAuthTokenWrapper OAuthTokenWrapper	OAuthTokenModelImpl extends BaseModelImpl <OAuthToken>

Gadget services

As shown in the following table, gadgets services got displayed with the service interface, its utilities, wrappers, and main methods implementation:

Service interface	Utility	Wrapper	Main methods
`Gadget(Local)` `Service`	`Gadget(Local)` `ServiceUtil`	`Gadget(Local)` `ServiceWrapper`	`addGadget,` `deleteGadget`
`OAuthConsumer` `LocalService`	`OAuthConsumer` `LocalServiceUtil`	`OAuthConsumer` `LocalService` `Wrapper`	`add*, create*,` `dynamicQuery,` `fetch*, get*, set*,` `update*`
`OAuthToken` `Local`	`OAuthTokenLocal` `Util`	`OAuthToken` `LocalWrapper`	`add*, create*,` `dynamicQuery,` `fetch*, get*, set*,` `update*`

Shindig services extension

Based on the Shindig, the plugin OpenSocial features an OpenSocial container. The following table shows Shindig services extensions:

Name	Type	Shindig Extension	Main methods
`SerializerUtil;` `ShindigUtil`	Utility	none	`copy*,` `get*, is*,` `has*,` `update*`
`ShindigFilter`	Servlet	`InjectedFilter`	`Destroy,` `doFilter`
`LiferayJsonContainer` `Config`	Configuration	`JsonContainerConfig`	`get*`
`LiferayModule`	Module	`AbstractModule`	`configure`
`LiferayOAuthModule;` `LiferayOAuthStore;` `LiferayOAuthStore` `Provider`	OAuth	`AbstractModule;` `OAuthStore;` `Provider<OAuthStore>`	`configure,` `set*, get*,` `remove*`
`LiferayActivityService;` `LiferayAlbumService;` `LiferayAppDataService;` `LiferayMediaItemService;` `LiferayPersonService`	Service	`ActivityService;` `AlbumService;` `AppDataService;` `MediaItemService;` `PersonService`	`create*,` `delete*,` `get*, do*,` `update*`

Gadget portlets

The plugin OpenSocial defines a set of portlets, namely, `adhoc_gadget`, `admin`, `editor`, and `gadget`. The following table shows a summary of these portlets:

Portlet	Related service	Related service utility	Related model	UI taglib
adhoc_gadget	none	none	Gadget	`<liferay-ui:icon />`

admin	`GadgetLocalService; OAuthConsumerLocal Service`	`GadgetLocalService Util`
		
		`OAuthConsumerLocal ServiceUtil`
			Gadget
			
			OAuth Consumer
				`<liferay-ui:header />`
				`<liferay-ui:search-container>`

editor	`Liferay.OpenSocial. Editor; Liferay. Util.getOpener(). Liferay.fire`	`ShindigUtil`	Gadget	none
gadget	`Liferay. OpenSocial.Gadget; ExpandoValueService`	`ShindigUtil; ExpandoValueService Util`	Gadget JSONObject	none

Summary

In this chapter, we first introduced how to use collaborative tools — wiki, blogs, calendar event, message boards, polls, bookmarks. Then we addressed how to manage more collaborative assets — both core assets and custom assets, and how to collaborate assets — both core assets and custom assets. Afterwards, we introduced how to use social networking, social coding, and social office. Finally, we addressed social activity, social equity capabilities, and the OpenSocial API.

In *Chapter 8, Staging, Scheduling, Publishing, and Cache Clustering*, we're going to introduce staging, scheduling, publishing, caching, and clustering.

8
Staging, Scheduling, Publishing, and Cache Clustering

Websites or WAP sites often need the capability to assemble, review, and approve new versions before going into production. **Scheduling** is the process of deciding how to commit resources between various possible tasks. Ehcache can scale from an in-process cache on one or more nodes through to a mixed in-process capable of terabyte-sized caches. Hibernate offers both a first-level cache and a second-level cache. In general, the portal provides the capabilities for staging, scheduling, publishing locally or remotely, caching, and clustering.

This chapter will first introduce the pattern Portal-Group-Page-Content. Then we will introduce LAR export and import mechanisms. Based on this, we will address the local staging and publishing processes. Then, we will discuss remote staging and publishing, either by scheduling or non-scheduling event. Finally, we will address caching and clustering mechanisms.

By the end of this chapter. you will have learned:

- The pattern: Portal-Group-Page-Content (PGPC)
- LAR exporting and importing
- Local staging and publishing
- Remote staging and publishing
- Scheduling and messaging
- Caching and clustering

The pattern: Portal-Group-Page-Content

According to the pattern **Portal-Group-Page-Content**, we have addressed a lot about the content in the previous chapters. This section will focus on the other concepts that is, portal, group, and page. As you can see, the portal is implemented by portal instances. A portal can manage multiple portal instances in one installation. Of course, you can install multiple portal instances in multiple installations, separately.

As shown in the following diagram, each portal instance, represented as an entity called Company, can have many groups. Each group, represented as an entity called Group, is implemented as an organization, a site, a user group, a page, or a user.

More specifically, organizations are presented as an entity called **Organization**. Each organization can have one and only one parent organization associated, and vice versa. It may have many associated child organizations. An organization which doesn't have a child organization is called **Location**; otherwise, it is called a **Regular Organization**. Similarly, each user group, represented as an entity **UserGroup**, can have one and only one parent user group associated. That is, a user group can have many child user groups associated with it, since it has a column called `parentUserGroupId`.

Moreover, each user presented as an entity called **User**, has a group associated with it—that is, there is one and only one user in that group. In a group, a set of users can be grouped into a team, presented as an entity **Team**. The notion of a team is somewhat similar to a role, but a role is a portal-wide entry while a team is restricted to a particular group-like site or organization.

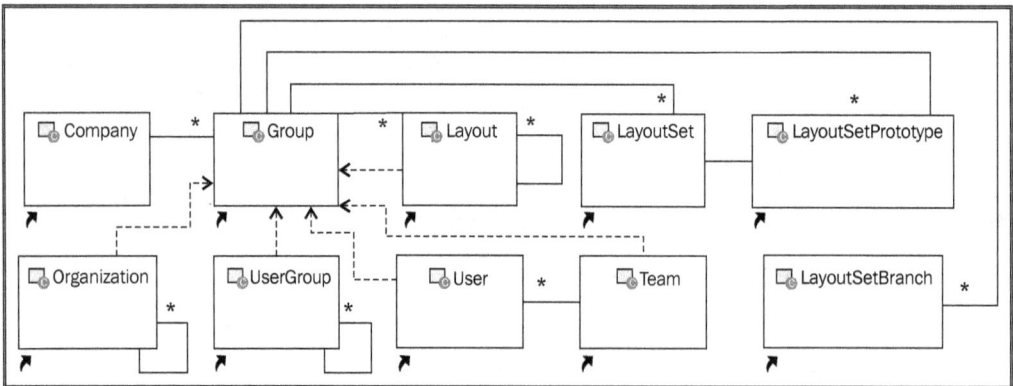

You may be interested in the entire portal service's specification. Eventually, you could find service definition details in the portal core XML file `/portal/service.xml`.

Portal

The interface `Portal` defines the portal with constants and a set of functions (such as `getCDHost`, `getBaseModel`, `getCompany`, `getPortalURL`, `getCurrentURL`, `getUser`, and so on), implemented by the class `PortalImpl`. The constants cover a friendly URL separator, path image, path main, path portal layout, and portal realm.

The default standard portlet XML filename is defined as `portlet.xml`, while the default custom XML filename is defined as `portlet-custom.xml`. This is the reason why you will find `portlet-custom.xml` only at the folder `$PORTAL_SRC_HOME/portal-web/docroot/WEB-INF`, while `portlet.xml` gets in use as the default portlet definitions when being used as plugins.

Base models

The portal defines the base model interface, such as `BaseModel<T>`, `AuditedModel`, `AttachedModel`, `ClassedModel`, `ResourcedModel`, `WorkflowedModel`, `PersistedModel`, and `GroupedModel`. This interface `BaseModel` should never be used directly. By the way, the base model implementation `BaseModelImpl<T>` is used for all model classes as shown in the following diagram, using the entity `KBArticle` as an example. According to the same rule, this class should never be used directly. Instead, you can modify the implementation class `KBArticleImpl`.

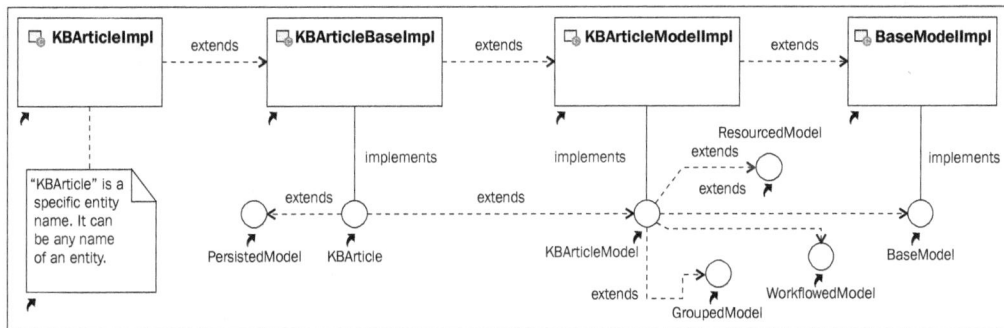

The following table shows an overview of these base models:

Interface	Extension	Listener/ Implementation	Main functions
BaseModel<T>	ClassedModel, Cloneable, Comparable<T>, Serializable	BaseModel Listener<T extends BaseModel<T>> BaseModel Impl<T>	isNew, isCacheModel,is EscapedModel, getPrimaryKeyObj, getExpandoBridge
AttachedModel	none	none	getClassName, getClassNameId, getClassPK
AuditedModel	none	none	getCompanyId, getCreeteDate, getModifiedDate, getUserName, getUserUuid
ClassedModel	none	none	getExpandoBridge, getModelClass, getModelClassName, getPrimaryKeyObj
GroupedModel	none	none	getGroupId
ResourcedModel	none	none	getResourcePrimKey, isResourceMain
WorkflowedModel	none	none	getStatus, getStatusByUserId, getStatusByUserName, getStatusDate, isApproved, isDraft, isExpired, isPending
PersistedModel	none	none	persist

As you can see, the portal adds getModelClassName and getModelClass to BaseModel by extending ClassedModel. Since all the classes have that data, just expose it as a friendly method. The portal also adds the AuditedModel interface. Most of the portal base models have companyId, createDate/modifiedDate, userId/userName. If a model has those fields, then it will also implement the AuditedModel interface. Furthermore, if a base model is an AuditedModel, and also has a groupId, then it also extends a GroupedModel. This means that its data can be grouped into sites/organizations.

In brief, the portal abstracts out the portal core services to the interfaces, so that they can be called from other web applications; while implementation is still in the portal there aren't any additional library dependencies.

Model listener

A **model listener** is a special call-back class, including core portal model or any model defined in the plugins. It is similar to the term **hibernate listener**, allowing writing reaction on any action with the object. In fact, the portal defines the model listener interface named `com.liferay.portal.model.ModelListener` with the following methods:

```
public void onAfterAddAssociation();
// see details in ModelListener.java
public void onBeforeUpdate(T model);
```

As you can see, these methods cover the **On-After** and **On-Before** methods, such as adding association, creating a model, removing a model, removing association, and updating a model.

The interface `ModelListener` is implemented by the abstract class `BaseModelListener<T extends BaseModel<T>>`. Any model listener, either from portal core or from plugins, must extend the class `BaseModelListener<T extends BaseModel<T>>` directly, as shown in the following diagram, using entities named `User` and `JournalArticle` as examples:

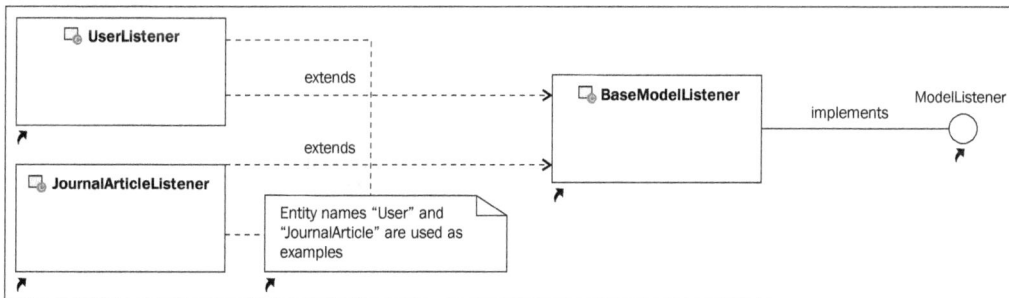

The following table shows these model-listener implementations.

Model listener	Extension	Model	Overridden methods
ContactListener	BaseModel Listener <Contact>	Contact	onAfterCreate(Contact obj)
LayoutListener	BaseModel Listener <Layout>	Layout	onAfterCreate(Layout obj), onAfterRemove(Layout obj), onBeforeRemove(Layout obj), onAfterUpdate(Layout obj)
LayoutSetListener	BaseModel Listener <LayoutSet>	LayoutSet	onAfterRemove(LayoutSet obj), onAfterUpdate(LayoutSet obj)
PortletPreferences Listener	BaseModel Listener <Portlet Preferences>	Portlet Preferences	onAfterRemove(PortletPref erences obj), onAfterUpdat e(PortletPreferences obj)
UserGroupListener	BaseModel Listener <UserGroup>	UserGroup	onAfterAddAssociation (Object o1, String o2, Object o3)
UserListener	BaseModel Listener <User>	User	onAfterAddAssociation (Object o1, String o2, Object o3), onAfterCreate(User obj)
JournalArticle Listener	BaseModel Listener <Journal Article>	Journal Article	onAfterRemove (JournalArticle obj), onAfterUpdate (JournalArticle obj)
JournalTemplate Listener	BaseModel Listener <Journal Template>	Journal Template	onAfterRemove (JournalTemplate obj), onAfterUpdate (JournalTemplate obj)

By the way, ModelListener does have the power to stop the current transaction, since the service class's transaction has been configured to rollback whenever the SystemException and PortalException exceptions occur. The portal implemented the same as well. It added an exception thrown from the ModelListener, configured in the Spring configuration to signal a rollback.

Portal instance

The portal instances allow the administrators to run more than one portal instance on a single server or a single installation, called **multitenancy**. The data for each portal instance is kept separately from every other portal instance, either in the same database or in a different database called **sharding**. Refer to the book *Liferay Portal 6 Enterprise Intranets* for the sharding configuration.

The portal instances are defined in the class `PortalInstances`. The class defines a set of company IDs, web IDs, and virtual hosts.

Each portal instance is persisted within the following entities: `Company`, `Account`, `VirtualHost`, and `Shard`.

The following table shows the service interfaces of the entities: `Company`, `Account`, `VirtualHost`, and `Shard`, their utility classes, wrapper classes, and implementation.

Interface	Utility	Wrapper	Main methods	JSP
Company (Local) Service	CompanyLocal ServiceUtil	Company (Local) ServiceWrapper	add*, deleteLogo, get*, remove*, update*	/portlet/ admin/ Instances. jspf
Account (Local) ServiceI	Account (Local) ServiceIUtil	Account (Local) ServiceIWrapper	add*, create*, delete*, dynamicQuery, get*, set*, update*	none
Virtual HostLocal Service	VirtualHost LocalService Util	VirtualHost LocalService Wrapper	add*, create*, delete*, dynamicQuery, fetch*, get*, set*, update*	none
Shard Local Service	ShardLocal ServiceUtil	ShardLocal ServiceWrapper	add*, create*, delete*, dynamicQuery, get*, set*, update*	none

Group

As mentioned earlier, a portal can have many portal instances based on one installation. And each portal instance can have many groups: sites, organizations, user groups, teams, and users. In fact, the entity Group is specified with a set of columns in the portal core service XML. The following code block shows the main columns, and the pattern classNameId-classPK is included, obviously.

```
<column name="classNameId" type="long" />
<column name="classPK" type="long" />
<column name="parentGroupId" type="long" />
<column name="liveGroupId" type="long" />
<column name="name" type="String" />
<column name="type" type="int" />
```

The column classNameId points to any class name like Group, Organization, User Group, Team, Layout, Layout Prototype, Layout Set Prototype, and User.

A site can have a type called site type, such as Open, Restricted, Private, or System. They are explained as follows. The default type value is Open.

- **Open**: Allows the users to join and leave a site whenever they want to.

- **Restricted**: Requires a site administrator or owner to add users to the site or to remove users from the site. Users cannot join the site themselves, instead they can request membership. Of course, users can leave the site whenever they want to.

- **Private**: The process of adding users doesn't show up at all. Neither do users have the ability to join the site, nor do they have the ability to request membership.

- **System**: For system usage only, for example, Global group, Control Panel group, User Personal Site group, User group, Scoped Page group (defined by the tag <scopeable>), Layout Prototype group, and Layout Set Prototype group.

Eventually, site type information is defined in the class GroupConstants. The following code snippet illustrates this:

```
// see details in GroupConstants.java
public static final int TYPE_SITE_OPEN = 1;
public static final String USER_PERSONAL_SITE_FRIENDLY_URL =
    "/personal_site";
```

As you can see, this class defines four site types—Open, Private, Restricted, and System. Besides, it also defines a name for user personal site, Control Panel, and guest. Obviously, the default live group ID and default parent group ID get defined as well.

Similarly, an organization could be defined as different types, such as **Location** or **Regular Organization**. This type of information gets defined in the class OrganizationConstants.

Services

Once you have a list of models handy, you could leverage these entity's services and apply these services on your plugins. The following table shows the services' interface, utilities, wrappers, and implementation.

Interface	Utility	Wrapper	Main methods
Group(Local) Service	Group(Local) ServiceUtil	Group(Local) ServiceWrapper	add*, delete*, get*, has*, search*, set*, unset*, update*
Organization (Local) Service	Organization (Local) ServiceUtil	Organization(Local) ServiceWrapper	add*, delete*, get*, set*, unset*, update*
UserGroup (Local) Service	UserGroup (Local) ServiceUtil	UserGroup(Local) ServiceWrapper	add*, delete*, get*, unset*, update*
User(Local) Service	User(Local) ServiceUtil	User(Local) ServiceWrapper	add*, delete*, get*, has*, set*, unset*, update*
Team(Local) Service	Team(Local) ServiceUtil	Team(Local) ServiceWrapper	add*, delete*, get*, has*, update*

System groups

There are a few system groups such as a company group called Global group, Control Panel group, Guest Site group, Scoped Page group, and User Personal Site group. When the server starts, the portal checks to ensure if all the system groups exist. Any missing system group will be created by the portal. The following code snippet illustrates this:

```
// see details in CompanyLocalServiceImpl.java
roleLocalService.checkSystemRoles(companyId);
groupLocalService.checkSystemGroups(companyId);
groupLocalService.checkCompanyGroup(companyId);
passwordPolicyLocalService.checkDefaultPasswordPolicy(companyId);
```

The **Global** group (called **Global Scope**) is a place for the data that is common to all organizations, sites, user groups, and users of the portal instance, that is, same company ID. The Global group doesn't have associated pages and can only be accessed from the Control Panel. The content in the Global group can be shared across organizations and sites. Also, the scope of the portlet (called **Scoped group**) can be the default group of the current page or the Global group or the Scoped selected-page group. The following code snippet shows how to create the Global group:

```
// see details in GroupLocalServiceImpl.java
public void checkCompanyGroup(long companyId) {
    groupLocalService.addGroup(defaultUserId,
        Company.class.getName(), companyId, null,
    null, 0, null, false, true, null);
}
```

The following table shows a summary of information of these groups (0 - system, 1 - open, and 3 - private).

Group name	Type	Class name	Class PK	Name	Site	Parent Group ID	Friendly URL
Company group—Global	0	Company	companyId	company Id	No	0	/null
Control Panel	3	Group	groupId	Control Panel	Yes	0	/control_panel
Guest	1	Group	groupId	Guest	Yes	0	/guest
User Personal Site	3	User Personal Site	default UserId	User Personal Site	No	0	/personal_site
User	0	User	User Id	User Id	No	0	/${user.id}
Scoped page	0	Layout	Layout Id	Layout Id	No	${layout.group.id}	/${layout.group.id}
Layout Prototype	0	Layout Prototype	Layout Prototype Id	Layout Prototype Id	No	0	/template-${Layout Prototype.Id}
LayoutSet Prototype	0	LayoutSet Prototype	LayoutSet Prototype Id	LayoutSet Prototype Id	No	0	/template-${Layout SetProto type.Id}

As you can see, content can be shared by the shared group and the Global group. That is, content in the Global group would be visible to the other groups from the same portal instance. Besides this Global group, content could be shared based on **shared-by-permission**, **shared-by-organization-hierarchy**, **shared-by-membership**, and **shared-by-subscription**. These shared mechanisms could be implemented in the group level of the same portal instance.

User

Loosely speaking, a user is a person, organization, or other entity that employs the services provided by a telecommunication system, or by an information-processing system, for the transfer of information. Or, a user is a person who uses a product. The portal defines a user as a person who can take any action limited by role-permissions.

When adding a new user or updating an existing user, the portal would take the following steps:

- Create a user ID by calling `counterLocalService.increment()`
- Update the user by calling `userPersistence.update`
- Add the user resource by calling `resourceLocalService.addResources()`
- Create the user contact ID by calling `contactPersistence.create(user.getContactId())`
- Update the user contact by calling `contactPersistence.update()`
- Add the user's group information by calling `groupLocalService.addGroup()`
- Add the user's user group by calling `groupLocalService.addUserGroups()`
- Add default groups by calling `groupLocalService.addUserGroups(userId, groupIds)`
- Update the asset by calling `user.setExpandoBridgeAttributes(serviceContext)`
- Set the custom fields by calling `user.setExpandoBridgeAttributes(serviceContext)`
- Index the user object by calling `indexer.reindex(user)`
- Set up the workflow by calling `WorkflowHandlerRegistryUtil.startWorkflowInstance`

Of course, you can check all the methods and details in the class `UserLocalServiceImpl`. The entities include `Contact`, `UserIdMapper`, `UserPersonalSite`, and `UserNotificationEvent`.

The interface `UserPersonalSite`, as a place holder, defines fine-grained control of a user's permission in the user's personal site. Based on the preceding entity's models, the portal generates a set of services, which you can refer to in your plugins development as well.

Layout set

Similar to a site, each group will have two different page layout sets: public pages and private pages. These page layout sets are presented by the entity `LayoutSet`, including the logo, theme, CSS, page count, settings — for example, site public pages or private pages, explained as follows — virtual host settings, JavaScript, and so on.

- **Private page**: A private page is a page on a site that can only be accessed by users who've logged in and are part of the site. If a user isn't logged in (that is, the user is a guest) or if a user doesn't belong to your site, then the user can't access the private pages.

- **Public page**: A public page is a page on a site that can be accessed by guests. As long as the guest has the appropriate URL, he/she can access any public page.

A layout set represents a group of layout pages, and thus, a layout set can be thought of as a website. Since each user has a group associated with them, this allows each individual user to maintain his/her own custom sites — either public or private sites. The entity `LayoutSet` presents the group's public pages and private pages.

The entity `LayoutSetPrototype` presents layout set templates, that is, site template. Here, a site template is a hierarchical set of pages and content, used as a template for creating new sites. For example, you can use site templates to create users, organizations, and sites, as long as they don't have any existing public page or private page. The creation form would shows the selected boxes for using a site template for public pages, private pages, or both. When a site template is applied, a copy of its pages and its contents is created. In fact, there is a non-existing link to the original template, so that any change to the site template will not have any side effect on pages that originated from it.

The entity `LayoutSetBranch` presents the layout set brand (versioning) information. In general, a brand can be defined as an identity of a specific product, service, or business. The entities include `LayoutSet`, `LayoutSetPrototype`, and `LayoutSetBranch`.

Layout

A **layout** (also called single web page) is an instance of a single page, composed of one or many portlets arranged inside various columns. Layouts are stored in the `Layout` table. As shown in the following diagram, each group can have two sites: public site and private site. Each site is made up of many page layouts, presented by the entity `Layout`. Each layout is a member of the layout set. The theme and color scheme assigned to a layout can either be set individually for the layout or inherited from its layout set.

The portal adds the ability to create pages for users based on a page template. A **page template** is a page created to be included in other pages. Templates usually contain repetitive material that might need to show up on any number of pages. The entity `LayoutPrototype` presents layout templates, that is, the page template.

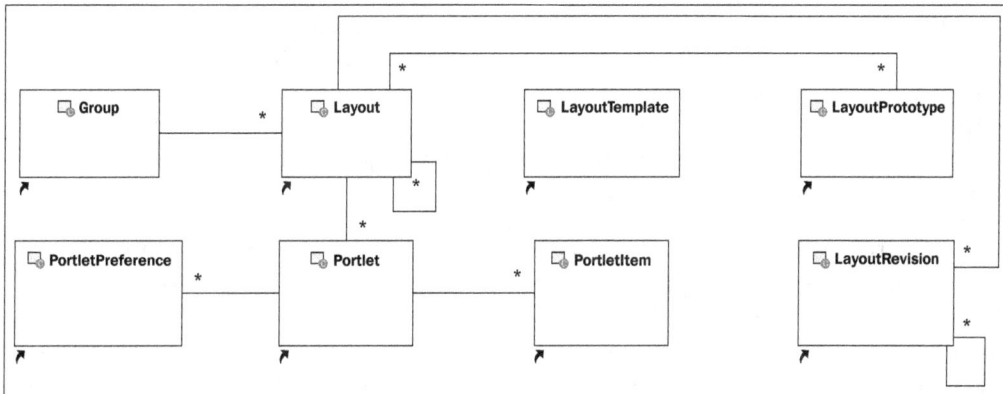

The entity `LayoutRevision` presents the layout reversion information. Reversion or reverting is the abandonment of one or more recent changes in favor of a return to a previous version of the material at hand. The portal adds revision control capability to the layouts — to manage the changes of the page layouts. The entities include `Layout`, `LayoutRevision`, and `LayoutPrototype`.

Layout template

Layout template is the way of choosing how the portlets will be arranged on a page. The portal defines a layout template interface called `LayoutTemplate`, extending `Comparable<LayoutTemplate>`, `Plugin`, and `Serializable`.

The layout templates can either be standard (for example, `exclusive`, `max`) or custom (for example, `freeform`, `1_column`), defined in the class `LayoutTemplateConstants`.

Portlet

In the previous chapters, we have discussed the terms plugin and portlet. In this section, we're going to provide an overview of the plugin- and portlet-related entities. The interfaces or classes cover `PluginSettings`, `Plugin`, `Portlet`, `PortletItem`, `PortletPreferences`, `PortletCategory`, `PortletApp`, `PortletFilter`, `PortletInfo`, and `PortletURLListener`.

Especially, the content of the portlet is scopeable, that is, you are able to change the scope from the current group to the Global group, or a Page group. Logically, the content of a portlet can be scoped into any group of current portal instance. To enable the scope, you can add the following line to the plugin's `liferay-portlet.xml` file.

```
<scopeable>true</scopeable>
```

The DTD file `liferay-portlet-app_6_1_0.dtd` has specified the tag `scopeable`. If `scopeable` is set to `true`, an administrator will be able to configure the scope of the data of the portlet to the current site (default), global group, the current layout, or the scope of any other layout of the site that already exists. Portlets that want to support this, must be programmed to obtain the proper scope group ID according to the configuration, and scope their data accordingly. The default value is `false`.

To summarize, groups are the most used in the portal as a resource container for permission and content scoping purposes. For instance, a site is a group, meaning that it can contain layouts, web content, wiki entries, and so on. However, a single layout can also be a group containing its own unique set of resources. An example of this would be a site that has several distinct wiki on different layouts. Each of these layouts will have its own group, and all of the nodes in the wiki for a certain layout would be associated with that layout's group. This allows the users to be given different permissions on each of the wiki entries, even though they are all within the same site. In addition to sites and layouts, users and organizations are also groups.

Groups also have a second, partially conflicting purpose in the portal. For legacy reasons, groups are also the model used to represent sites (known as communities before v6.1). Confusion may arise from the fact that a site group is both the resource container and the site itself, whereas a layout or organization would have both a primary model and an associated group.

LAR export and import

Data export and import generally revolve around the concept of storing data outside the portal, either permanently or temporarily. The portal does this by handling the creation and interpretation of the LAR files.

LAR is short for Liferay Archive. A LAR is mainly used to export the existing page data in a portal group for backup and to import data into another portal group. The following diagram shows the processes of LAR export and import. More specifically, the portal could export both portal core assets and custom assets associated with an existing page or all pages of a given site as a LAR file. The portal could also import from a LAR file, which contains both portal core assets and custom assets associated with an existing page or all pages of a given site — into a page or site — respectively.

Note that LAR export and import should be used for backup only, and not for upgrading, since the source (portal instance) and the target (portal instance) must have exactly the same version.

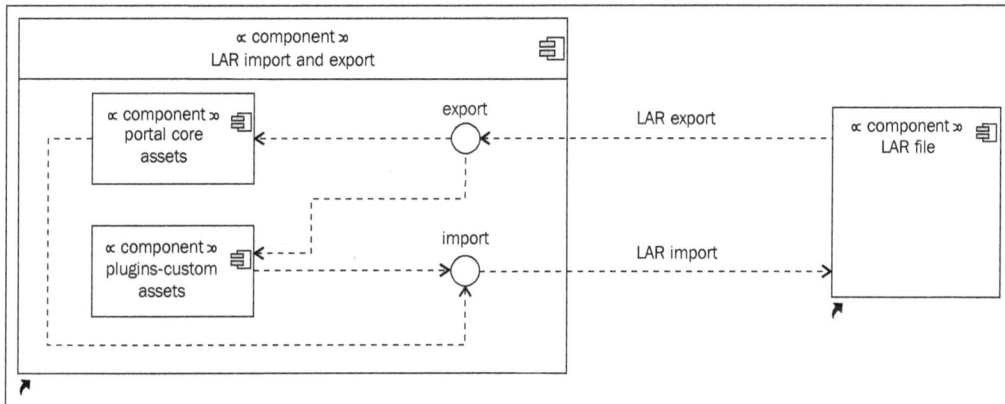

Portlet data handler

An interface called `PortletDataHandler` is a special class capable of exporting and importing portlet-specific data to a Liferay Archive file (LAR) when a site's layouts are exported or imported. The implementations of the `PortletDataHandler` class are defined by placing a `portlet-data-handler-class` element in the portlet section of the `liferay-portlet.xml` file.

Interface

The interface `PortletDataHandler` defines a set of methods as follows:

```
public String exportData(
    PortletPreferences obj3);
public PortletPreferences importData(PortletDataContext obj1,
    String obj2, PortletPreferences obj3, String obj4);
// see details in PortletDataHandler.java
```

The method `deleteData` deletes the data created by the portlet. It can optionally return a modified version of preferences, if it contains reference to data that doesn't exist anymore. The method `exportData` returns a string of data to be placed in the `portlet-data` section of the LAR file. This data will be passed as the data parameter of the method `importData` in String XML format.

The method `getExportControls` returns an array of the controls defined for this data handler. These controls enable us to create fine-grained control over the export behavior. The controls are rendered in the export UI. The method `getImportControls` returns an array of the controls defined for this data handler. These controls enable the developer to create fine-grained control over the import behavior. The controls are rendered in the import UI.

The method `importData` handles any special processing of the data when the portlet is imported into a new layout. It can optionally return a modified version of preferences to be saved in the new portlet.

The method `isAlwaysExportable` returns `true` to allow the user to export data for this portlet even though it may not belong to any pages. The method `isPublishToLiveByDefault` returns whether the data exported by this handler should be included by default when publishing to live. This should only be `true` for data that is meant to be managed in a staging environment, such as CMS content, but not for data meant to be input by users, such as wiki pages or message board posts.

Portlet data context

The interface `PortletDataContext` extends the interface `Serializable`. In addition, it holds the context information that is used during exporting and importing portlets. The interface `PortletDataContext` defines the constants root path groups, layouts, and portlets.

It also defines a set of methods to add the following items: asset categories, asset tags, class model, comments, locks, permissions, primary key, ratings entries, and zip entry.

In addition, the interface `PortletDataContext` defines the methods `createServiceContext`, `formXML`, getters, `import*`, setters, `has*`, and `is*`. This interface is implemented by the class `PortletDataContextImpl`.

Portlet data context listener

The interface `PortletDataContextListener` defines the following methods:

```
public void onAddZipEntry(String path);
public void onGetZipEntry(String path);
```

As shown in the preceding code, the listener has added the methods `onAddZipEntry` and `onGetZipEntry`. That is, when adding the zip entry or getting the zip entry, the portal will take some actions. By the way, this listener is implemented by the class `PortletDataContextListenerImpl`. If required, you can override this implementation.

Services

The portal provides a set of services for the portlet data handler, context, listener, and strategies. The following table contains an overview of these services:

Service Interface	Extension	Implementation	Description
PortletData Handler	none	BasePortletData Handler	Portlet data handler interface
PortletData Context	Serializable	PortletData ContextImpl	Portlet data context
PortletData ContextListener	none	PortletData ContextListener Impl	Portlet data content listener
PortletData HandlerBoolean	PortletData HandlerControl	none	Portlet data handler Boolean
PortletData HandlerChoice	PortletData HandlerControl	none	Portlet data handler Choice
PortletData HandlerKeys	none	none	Portlet data handler keys
UserIdStrategy	none	AlwaysCurrent UserIdStrategy	User ID strategy
		CurrentUser IdStrategy	

The portlet data handler is implemented in three aspects: layout, permission, and portlet. For layout, the portlet provides the implementation classes `LayoutExporter` and `LayoutImporter`. Similarly, the implementation classes `PermissionExporter` and `PermissionImporter` are available for the permission import and export, and the implementation classes `PortletExporter` and `PortletImporter` for the portlet import and export, as well.

You can find a summary of these implementations in the following table:

Class name	Associated services	Main functions	Description
LayoutCache	GroupLocalServiceUtil, OrganizationLocalServiceUtil, ResourceLocalServiceUtil, RoleLocalServiceUtil, TeamLocalServiceUtil, UserGroupLocalServiceUtil	getEntity GroupId, getEntityMap, getGroupRoles, getGroupUsers, getResource, getRole, getUser, getUserRole	Layout cache
Layout Exporter Layout Importer	GroupLocalServiceUtil, ImageLocalServiceUtil, LayoutLocalServiceUtil, LayoutSetLocalServiceUtil, LayoutSetPrototypeLocal ServiceUtil	export* import*	Layout exporter and importer
Permission Exporter Permission Importer	GroupLocalServiceUtil, PermissionLocalServiceUtil, ResourcePermissionLocal ServiceUtil, RoleLocalServiceUtil	export* import*	Permission exporter and importer
Portlet Exporter Portlet Importer	PortletItemLocalServiceUtil, PortletLocalServiceUtil, PortletPreferencesLocal ServiceUtil	export* import*	Portlet exporter and importer

Portal core assets

The portal provides the ability to export and import LAR file for most of the portal core assets, such as document library, DDM, web content, and so on. As shown in the following table, export/import controls mainly cover assets, categories, tags, comments, ratings, and so on.

Implementation	Interface/ Abstract class	Portlet	Export controls	Import controls
DLDisplayPortlet DataHandlerImpl DLPortletData HandlerImpl	BasePortlet DataHandler PortletData Handler	DL Display DL	_foldersAnd Documents, _ shortcuts, _ranks, _ comments, _ratings, _tags	_foldersAnd Documents, _shortcuts, _ranks, _comments, _ ratings, _tags
DDMPortletData HandlerImpl	BasePortlet DataHandler PortletData Handler	DDM	_structures, _ templates	_structures, _templates
JournalContent PortletData HandlerImpl JournalPortlet DataHandlerImpl	BasePortlet DataHandler PortletData Handler Journal Creation Strategy	Journal Content Journal	_articles, _ structures TemplatesAndFeeds, _embeddedAssets, _images, _comments, _ratings, _tags	_articles, _structures Templates AndFeeds, _images, _comments, _ ratings, _tags

Portlet exporter and importer

As mentioned earlier, export/import controls mainly the cover assets, links, categories, tags, comments, ratings, custom fields, and so on. As shown in the following table, we're going to address the details of the portlet exporter and portlet importer:

Items	Model interface	Zip entry path	Root	Description
ROOT	none	/manifest.xml	"root"	ROOT
Layouts	LayoutExorter, LayoutImporter, Portlet, Permission	/layout.xml	"layout"	Layout page exporter and importer
Portlets	Portlet Preferences, PortletItems, Permission	/portlet-data.xml /portlet.xml	"portlet"	Portlet import and export
Permissions	Permission Importer, Permission Exporter	/portlet-data-permissions.xml	"portlet-data-permissions"	Import/ export Users, roles, and permissions

Items	Model interface	Zip entry path	Root	Description
Asset Categories	AssetEntry, AssetCategory, AssetVocabulary	/categories-hierarchy.xml	"categories-hierarchy"	Asset categories, vocabulary import and export
AssetLinks	AssetEntry, AssetLink	/links.xml	"links"	Asset links import and export
AssetTags	AssetEntry, AssetTag	/tags.xml	"tags"	Asset tags import and export
Comments	MBMessage	/comments.xml	"comments"	Comments import and export
Expando Table	ExpandoTable, ExpandoColumn	/expando-tables.xml	"expando-tables"	Custom attributes import and export
Locks	Lock	/looks.xml	"lock"	Locks the importer and exporter
Ratings Entries	RatingsEntry	/ratings.xml	"ratings"	Ratings of the importer and exporter

By the way, the portal uses **XStream** (http://xstream.codehaus.org/) to serialize the objects to XML and back again in the LAR export and import processes.

Setup archive

In general, the portlets can have an associated configuration page, configuring parameters of the portlet to set up how it will be shown to all the other users. It is generally used to allow each user to configure their own preferences and not affect the other users.

Any portlet which has setup capability will be able to customize setup and archive the setup. For these portlets, you can save these settings, and moreover, revert these changes later. This feature can be achieved through archive setup.

Configuration action

How can we implement a configuration page for a new plugin portlet? Let's use knowledge base portlet as an example.

1. First, specify the configuration action class, and define it as the value of the tag `configuration-action-class` in the `liferay-portlet.xml`. The `configuration-action-class` value is a class that extends `com.liferay. portal.kernel.portlet.DefaultConfigurationAction`, implementing `ConfigurationAction`. This class is called to allow the users to configure the portlet at runtime.

2. Then implement the `processAction` and `render` methods as defined in the interface `ConfigurationAction`.

3. Create the file `configuration.jsp` containing the form that the page administrator will edit to set up the portlet. The file `configuration.jsp` is defined in the abstract class `DefaultConfigurationAction`.

As you can see, in a few steps you can add the configuration action to the portlet.

Portlet preferences and portlet item

The portlet configuration is saved in the table `PortletPreferences` and the setup archive is saved in the table `PortletItem`. The following table shows the service utilities, interfaces, their related models, and the main methods:

Utility	Interface	Related models	Main methods
Portlet Preferences FactoryUtil	Portlet Preferences Factory	Layout, Portlet, PortletPre ferencesIds	fromXML, getLayoutPortletSetup, getPortalPreferences, getPortletPreferences, getPortletSetup, getPreferences, toXML
Portlet Preferences ServiceUtil	Portlet Preferences Service	PortletItem, Portlet Preferences	deleteArchivePreferences, restoreArhcivePreferences, updateArchivePreferences

Note that this feature is available for the portlets for which the `Setup` tab is visible because the portal specifies this function in the portlet configuration file `archived_ setup_action.jsp` and `edit_archived_setups.jsp` under the folder `/html/ portlet/portlet_configuration`. More details and archives are stored in the portlet preferences of the portal instance. Therefore, you shouldn't use this feature for backing up the data from one portal instance to another portal instance.

Local staging and publishing

The portal provides local staging and publishing capabilities. Users can stage their work—the ability to work on a working copy of the website. For example, as a content creator, you can manipulate this working copy and preview it as if it were the website. You should be able to preview a working copy at any time without disrupting the live pages. The purpose of the staging feature is to deploy a new version of the website in a fully-functional form, which can be tested and reviewed by the content producers or the content editors. The content producers or content editors, who are evaluating the web content changes, are able to navigate to the site without having to choose which version to see.

Similarly, it would be nice if the users can publish web content smoothly—to push one or more assets from a staging to a live (or called local production) environment. Generally speaking, publishing should include the capability to publish to both the local portal instances and the remote portal instances. From the functional point of view, publishing should be as simple as a push of a button or it should be included as a step in a workflow. Most importantly, publishing shouldn't disrupt the production environment except the published change. The portal provides the ability to stage and publish web content either locally or remotely.

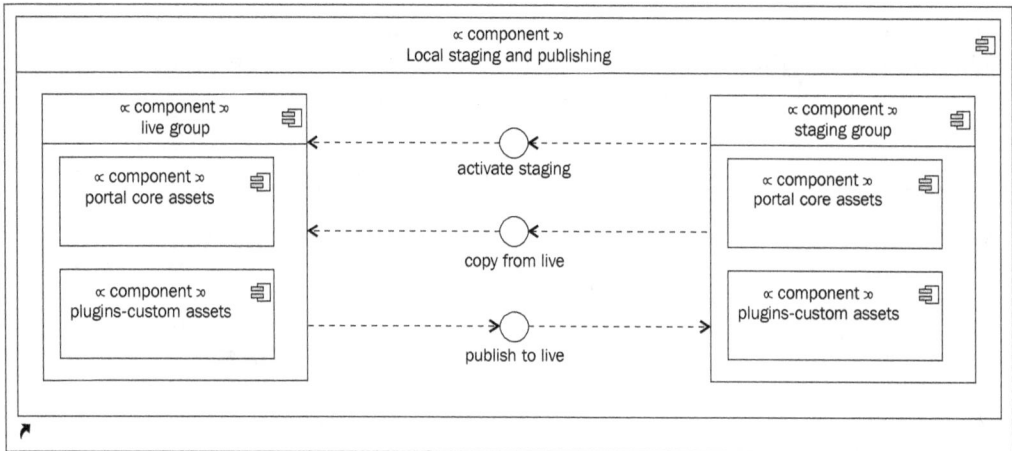

Activating staging

The portal provides local or remote staging and publishing capabilities through which the users can select subsets of pages and data (both portal core assets and custom assets), and transfer them to the live site—that is, local group instance or remote portal instance. There are two types of staging: local live and remote live.

- **Local live**: Within the current portal environment, a clone of the current site will be created. This clone contains the copies of all existing pages and the data of portlets. This clone becomes the local staging while the original becomes the local live.

- **Remote live**: A connection is built between this site and the target existing in a remote instance. The connection settings cover the persistent network configuration, which defines how to locate the remote instance when the publishing event occurs. This site becomes the remote staging while the remote site becomes the remote live.

In the next section, we will discuss local live staging. Remote live staging will be addressed in a later section.

Local staging interface

As shown in the preceding diagram, local staging and publishing contain the following main functions:

- Activate staging: Create a new group (called **staging group**) for a given group (called **live group**) and copy the pages (either public pages or private pages or both) from the live group to the staging group. When disabling staging, the portal will remove the staging group from the current portal instance.

- Copy from live: Copy the pages from the live group to the staging group.

- Publish to live: Publish the selected pages or an entire website from the staging group to the live group.

Once activating local live staging, you would see the following data or similar data stored in the field typeSettings of the table Group_.

```
stagedRemotely=false
branchingPrivate=true
staged=true
```

As you can see, there is a set of properties for the staging mode Local Live, such as staged-portlet_*, branchingPublic, and branchingPrivate. Of course, the property stagedRemotely has false value while the property staged has true value.

The portal defines an interface called Staging, implemented by the class StagingImpl. The class ServiceContext is widely used in the class StagingImpl. Most importantly, the staging and publish functions work well on page-level only, since the portal defines an interface called LayoutStaging, implemented by the class LayoutStagingImpl.

The following table shows main methods and attributes of these classes:

Class name	Implements	Main methods or attributes	Description
StagingImpl	Staging	copyFromLive, copyPortlet, copyRemoteLayouts, publishLayout, publishLayouts, publishToLive	The interface Staging and its implementation
Layout StagingImpl	Layout Staging	getLayoutRevision, getLayoutStagingHandler, isBranchingLayout, isBranchingLayoutSet	The interface LayoutStaging and its implementation
ServiceContext	Cloneable, Serializable	_addGroupPermissions, _addGuestPermissions, _assetCategoryIds	Service context

Local staging services

As mentioned earlier, the portal provides the capabilities of local staging and publishing , and to copy pages from the live and to publish pages to the live. As shown in the following table, these functions are implemented in the class StagingImpl:

Function	Service utilities	Main methods	Description
enableLocal Staging	GroupLocal ServiceUtil	addGroup, updateGroup,	Create a local staging group, copy pages from the live group to the staging group, and update the live group (export and import)
	LayoutLocal ServiceUtil	exportLayoutsAsFile, importLayouts	
disable Staging	GroupLocal ServiceUtil, LayoutLocal ServiceUtil	deleteGroup, updateGroup, deleteLayout SetBranches	Delete the staging group and update the live group (typeSettings)
copyFrom Live	GroupLocal ServiceUtil, LayoutLocal ServiceUtil	getGroup, exportLayoutsAsFile, importLayouts	Copy pages from the live group to the staging group (export and import)
publish ToLive	GroupLocal ServiceUtil, LayoutLocal ServiceUtil	getGroup, exportLayoutsAsFile, importLayouts	Publish pages from the staging group to the live group (export and import)

By the way, the staging Spring beans are defined in the XML file /META-INF/
staging-spring.xml. You may use it as references.

Remote staging and publishing

The portal provides remote staging and publishing capabilities through which the
users can select subsets of pages and data, and transfer them to the live site of the
remote portal instance. By this feature, we can export the selected data to the group
of a remote portal instance or to another group in the same portal instance. The
LAR export and import features are used for remote staging and publishing. These
features are implemented in the PortletDataHandler API. As mentioned earlier,
the intent of this API is to import and export application content to and from the
portal in a database-agnostic fashion for the portal core assets and custom assets.

The following diagram depicts an overview of remote staging and remote
publishing. The staging has a set of portal core assets, custom assets, and groups of
users. First, the portal will export related portal core assets and custom assets based
on the current user's permission as a LAR ZIP file. Then, the portal transfers this LAR
ZIP file to the live site through the tunnel-web HTTP or HTTPS call. The live site will
import the related portal core assets and custom assets, as a LAR ZIP file, based on
the same user's permission.

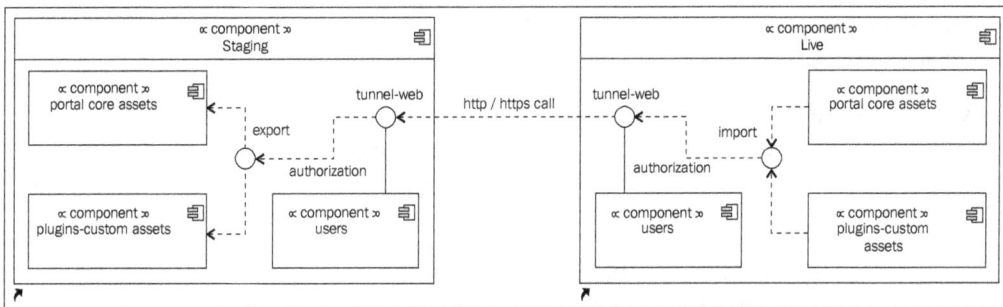

Local staging and publishing means that we have only one box and only one Liferay
portal instance. For a given group, for example, Book Street, the portal will create
a staging group Book Street (Staging) —a working copy of the Book Street
group— when activating Local Live. Now, users can work only on the staging
group. When they are ready, they can publish the pages of the Book Street
(Staging) staging group to the pages of the Book Street live group. As the staging
and publishing happen in one box, and the Book Street (Staging) staging group
and the Book Street live group belong to the same portal instance, it is called **local
staging and publishing**. This will be useful when the website is small with less
traffic and a small group of end users.

However, when the website is huge — high traffic, big groups of end users — we have to consider the **remote staging and publishing** feature. As shown in the preceding figure, there are one or many staging boxes and many production boxes. All of the boxes have only live groups. For instance, the `Book Street` live group in the staging box will be mapped into the `Book Street` live group in the production boxes. Thus, the `Book Street` live group in the staging box could be called as a staging group of the `Book Street` live group in the production boxes.

All of the internal content management users are working only in the staging box. They can use the CMS and WCM tools to manage the portal core assets and custom assets, for example, building a live website. They can also apply the workflow to approve or reject the portal core assets and custom assets. That is, the staging box is used only for the internal content management team. Once the pages are approved, the content management team can publish these pages to the production boxes.

Activating remote live

Once you activate remote live, you would see the following data or similar data stored in the field `typeSettings` of the table `Group_`:

```
stagedRemotely=true
remoteAddress=localhost
remoteGroupId=10457
remotePort=8080
staged=true
```

As you can see, a few additional properties are added for the staging mode `Remote Live` only, such as `secureConnection`, `remoteAddress`, `remoteGroupId`, `remoteHost`, and `remotePort`. Of course, the property `stagedRemotely` has a value of `true`.

When the staging is disabled, either local live or remote live, the portal will remove all the properties from the field `typeSettings` of the table `Group_`. How come? The following code is a snippet from the method `disableStaging` of the class `StagingImpl`:

```
GroupLocalServiceUtil.updateGroup(
    liveGroup.getGroupId(), typeSettingsProperties.toString());
```

Remote staging services

As mentioned earlier, the portal provides the capabilities of remote staging and publishing that you can either enable or disable in staging, and publish pages to the live site. As shown in the following table, these functions are implemented in the class `StagingImpl`:

Function	Service utilities	Main methods	Description
enableRemote Staging	GroupLocalServiceUtil UnicodeProperties	getGroup, hasStaging Group, updateGroup,	Enable/disable remote live and update the live group
disable Staging	GroupLocalServiceUtil LayoutLocalServiceUtil	updateGroup	update the live group (typeSettings)
publishTo Remote	GroupLocalServiceUtil, LayoutLocalServiceUtil	getGroup, copyRemote Layouts	Publish pages from the local live group to the remote live group (export and import)
copyRemote Layouts	UserLocalServiceUtil, GroupServiceHttp, LayoutLocalServiceUtil, LayoutServiceHttp	getGroup	Export pages from the local live group, and import pages to the remote live group

Tunnel-web services

Tunneling is a technology that enables one network to send its data via another network's connections. It works by encapsulating a network protocol within packets carried by the second network. **HTTP Tunneling** is a technique by which communications performed using various network protocols are encapsulated using the HTTP protocol, belonging to the TCP/IP family of protocols. The HTTP protocol, therefore, acts as a wrapper for a covert channel that the network protocol being tunneled uses to communicate.

The portal implements HTTP tunneling via the tunnel-web like remote HTTP services and web services. This section is going to address remote HTTP services, while the web services will be addressed in the next chapter.

The following table shows a summary of tunnel servlet, tunnel utility, and method handler used in the tunnel web:

Class name	Interface/method	Related services/interfaces	Description
TunnelServlet	HttpServlet – doPost	HttpServletRequest, HttpServletResponse, HttpPrincipal, PrincipalThreadLocal	Servlet mappings /liferay/* /secure/ liferay/*
TunnelUtil	invoke, _ getConnection	HttpServletRequest, HttpURLConnection, HttpPrincipal, HostnameVerifier, HttpsURLConnection, SSLSession	URL – /tunnel-web/ liferay/do /tunnel- web/secure/ liferay/do
MethodHandler	Serializable – invoke	java.lang.reflect. Method, java.lang. reflect.Modifier	Method handler for the Tunnel servlet and utility

Copying remote layouts

As mentioned earlier, the method copyRemoteLayouts is one of the main signatures of the interface Staging, implemented by the class StagingImpl. This implementation takes the following main steps:

1. Get the current user information through the class PermissionChecker. The following is the code snippet:

   ```
   User user = UserLocalServiceUtil.getUser(
       permissionChecker.getUserId());
   ```

2. Build HTTP principal as shown in the following code:

   ```
   HttpPrincipal httpPrincipal = new HttpPrincipal(
       url, user.getEmailAddress(), user.getPassword(),
       user.getPasswordEncrypted());
   ```

3. Ping the remote host and verify that the group exists. As you can see, it leverages the class GroupServiceHttp:

   ```
   GroupServiceHttp.getGroup(httpPrincipal, remoteGroupId);
   ```

4. Export the layouts from the local staging group. The following is the sample code:

```
LayoutLocalServiceUtil.exportLayouts(
    sourceGroupId, privateLayout, layoutIds, parameterMap,
    startDate, endDate);
```

5. Import layouts of the local staging group into the remote live group. As you can see, it leverages the class `LayoutServiceHttp`.

HTTP services

As stated previously, two HTTP services `GroupServiceHttp` and `LayoutServiceHttp` are involved in the `copyRemoteLayouts` process. These classes provide an HTTP utility for the `${packagePath}.service.${entity.name}ServiceUtil}` service utility. The static methods of these classes call the same methods of the service utility. However, the signatures are different, since it requires an additional `{com.liferay.portal.security.auth.HttpPrincipal}` parameter.

The benefit of using the HTTP utility is that it is fast and allows for tunneling without the cost of serializing the text. However, the drawback is that it only works with Java.

The following table shows a summary of the classes `GroupServiceHttp` and `LayoutServiceHttp`:

HTTP service	Main methods	Related services	Description
GroupService Http	addGroup, addRoleGroups, deleteGroup, getGroup	MethodKey, MethodHandler, TunnelUtil	Group HTTP service
LayoutService Http	addLayout, deleteLayout, exportLayout, importLayout, updateLayout	MethodKey, MethodHandler, TunnelUtil	Layout HTTP service

As you can see, many portal core assets have HTTP services, such as `AccountServiceHttp`, `AddressServiceHttp`, and so on. What's happening? The service builder is able to generate HTTP services in the following steps:

1. The portal provides a template file called `service_http.ftl` for HTTP services in the service-builder; the `service_http.ftl` has defined the following code:

```
public class ${entity.name}ServiceHttp {
    <#assign hasMethods = false>
    <#list methods as method>
/* see details in service_http.ftl */
}
```

2. The service builder generates HTTP services in the `ServiceBuilder` class.

As you can see, if an entity has remote service settings set to `true`, the service builder will generate service, implementation, base implementation, factory, utility, clp, JSON, and SOAP service. In depth, if the remote filename is not null, the service builder will generate the HTTP service.

Protecting tunnel-web In order to communicate with the remote server, and moreover, to protect the HTTP connection, we need to set up a tunnel-web in the `portal-ext.properties`. This means that we need to add the following lines at the end of the `portal-ext.properties`:

```
tunnel.servlet.hosts.allowed=127.0.0.1,69.198.171.104
tunnel.servlet.https.required=false
```

The preceding code shows a `tunnel.servlet.hosts.allowed` property with a list of allowed hosts, for example, `69.198.171.104`. As stated earlier, we used these hosts as examples only. You can have your own real hosts. Meanwhile, it specifies the `tunnel.servlet.https.required` property. By default, it is set to `false`. You can set it to `true`, if you want to use HTTPS.

Securing users' information

Let's take a look at a scenario. There are clustered staging servers and clustered product servers. By default, there is a dummy user in both staging and product servers. All editorial users exist in the staging server only. Their daily work is to create/update press release, and schedule to publish the product. Thus, the use case is that we need to secure the users' information in the staging server when using the remote publishing function.

How can we implement this? Here, we provide a simple implementation as follows:

1. First, in the staging server, predefine a dummy user-screen name in `portal.properties`. This dummy user will impersonate all the users who have the permission to handle staging and remote publishing.

```
tunnel.dummy.user.enabled=false
tunnel.dummy.user.screenname=test
```

2. Then, before calling the remote group, impersonate the current user using the dummy user. The following is the code snippet:

```
User user = UserLocalServiceUtil.getUserByScreenName(
        permissionChecker.getCompanyId(),
        _TUNNEL_DUMMY_USER_SCREENNAME);
// see details in StagingImpl.java
```

Scheduling and messaging

Scheduling refers to the way processes are assigned to run on the available CPUs. The portal uses the **Quartz scheduler** as the scheduling service, where you would see a set of tables in the database, such as QUARTZ_JOB_DETAILS, QUARTZ_JOB_ LISTENERS, QUARTZ_TRIGGERS, and so on. Definitely, you can refer the entire quartz tables in the the SQL file $PORTAL_SRC_HOME/sql/quartz-tables.sql.

Quartz is a full-featured, open source job-scheduling service that can be integrated with the smallest standalone application to the largest e-commerce system. The Quartz scheduler includes many enterprise-class features, such as JTA transactions, clustering, and so on. Refer to http://www.quartz-scheduler.org/ for more details.

The portal uses **JMS** — **Java Message Service** API — a **Java Message Oriented Middleware (MOM)** API for sending messages between two or more clients. In general, the JMS API supports two models: **point-to-point** and **publish and subscribe**. In the point-to-point model, a sender — who knows the destination of the message and posts the message directly to the receiver's queue — posts messages to a specific queue and a receiver reads the messages from the queue. In the publish/subscribe model, neither the publisher nor the subscriber know each other, subscribers may register their interest in receiving the messages on a particular message topic.

Scheduler

The portal has specified the scheduler in portal.properties as follows.

```
scheduler.enabled=true
scheduler.job.name.max.length=80
```

You can set the property `scheduler.enabled` to `false` in `portal-ext.properties` to disable all the scheduler classes defined in `liferay-portlet.xml`. The class `QuartzSchedulerEngine` checks whether this property is `true` or `false`. In addition, you can set the maximum length of the description, group name, and job name fields. The interface `SchedulerEngine` will read these properties for the fields — maximum length of description, group name, and job name.

Interfaces

The portal provides a set of interfaces for the scheduler. The following table shows a summary of these interfaces:

Interface	Utility	Associated classes	Implementation
Trigger	Trigger FactoryUtil	TriggerState, TriggerType	BaseTrigger, CronTrigger, IntervalTrigger
Scheduler Engine	Scheduler EngineUtil	JobState, StorageType	ClusterSchedulerEngine, SchedulerEngineProxyBean, QuartzSchedulerEngine
Scheduler Entry	none	TimeUnit	SchedulerEntryImpl

Services

The portal provides a set of service interface implementations. The following table shows the scheduler services implementation:

Service	Interface	Related models	Description
ClusterScheduler Engine	IdentifiableBean, SchedulerEngine, SchedulerEngine ClusterManager	SchedulerEngine, StorageType, Trigger, TriggerState, SchedulerResponse	Cluster scheduler engine
SchedulerEngine ProxyBean	BaseProxyBean implements SchedulerEngine	SchedulerEngine, Trigger, SchedulerResponse	Scheduler engine proxy bean
MessageSender	org.quartz.Job	org.quartz. JobDataMap, JobDetail, JobExecutionContext, Scheduler, Trigger	Message sender
ScriptingMessage Listener	BaseMessage Listener	Message, SchedulerEngine, ScriptingUtil	Scripting message listener

Service	Interface	Related models	Description
PortalJobStore	JobStoreTX	org.quartz.impl.jdbcjobstore.DB2v8Delegate, DriverDelegate	Portal job store
QuartzConnectionProvider	ConnectionProvider	Connection, DataSource	Quartz connection provider
QuartzSchedulerEngine	SchedulerEngine	CronTrigger, JobDataMap, JobDetail, Scheduler, SimpleTrigger, Trigger, StdSchedulerFactory	Quartz scheduler engine
SybaseDelegate	MSSQLDelegate	PreparedStatement	Particular Sybase delegate

The scheduler Spring beans is defined in the XML file /META-INF/scheduler-spring.xml. The following table shows the details of scheduler Spring beans:

Name	Class	Method	Interface
messagingProxyAdvice	SchedulerEngineProxyBean	Invoker	extends BaseProxyBean implements SchedulerEngine
com.liferay.portal.scheduler.ClusterSchedulerEngineService	ClusterSchedulerEngine	schedulerEngine/createClusterSchedulerEngine	implements IdentifiableBean, SchedulerEngine, SchedulerEngineClusterManager
SchedulerEngineUtil	ClusterSchedulerEngineService	schedulerEngine	none

Clustering scheduler

The portal has added cluster support for the scheduler. It adds memory scheduler to handle the non-permanent jobs, including singleton jobs that schedule once in the whole cluster and non-singleton jobs that schedule in each instance. It also adds cluster support for the memory scheduler. Also, it migrates the non-permanent jobs to the memory scheduler, modifies the interfaces to support both memory scheduler and permanent scheduler.

Especially, the portal added a property to cluster the schedulers in `portal.properties` as follows:

```
memory.cluster.scheduler.lock.cache.enabled=false
```

In addition, you would see other properties starting with `memory.scheduler.org.quartz.*` and `persisted.scheduler.org.quartz.*` for scheduler memory settings and scheduler persistence, respectively.

The interfaces `SchedulerEngineClusterManager` and `SchedulingConfigurator` are addressed in the following table:

Interface	Implementation	Signature	Main methods
SchedulerEngine ClusterManager	Cluster Scheduler Engine	Lock updateMemory SchedulerCluster Master()	createCluster SchedulerEngine, delete, getScheduledJob, getScheduledJobs, pause, resume, schedule, start
Scheduling Configurator	Abstract Scheduling Configurator, Default Scheduling Configurator, Plugin Scheduling Configurator	destroy, init, setMessageBus, setScheduler Engine, setScheduler Entries	ClassLoader getOperating Classloader()

Messaging

The portal has defined messaging Spring beans in the XML files `/META-INF/messaging-core-spring.xml` and `messaging-misc-spring.xml`.

The portal defined different packages for messaging, such as `basis`, `async`, `config`, `jmx`, `proxy`, and `sender`. The following table shows the details of these packages:

Type	Listener	Extension	Interface	Related models
basis	Global Destination EventListener, Bridging Message Listener, DummyMessage Listener, Invoker Message Listener	BaseDestination EventListener, BaseMessage Listener, BaseMessage StatusMessage Listener	Destination EventListener, Message Listener	Destination, Message, MessageBatch, MessageBus, MessageStatus
async	Async Message Listener	BaseMessage Listener	Message Listener	Async
config	Default Messaging Configurator, Plugin Messaging Configurator	Abstract Messaging Configurator	Messaging Configurator	Destination
jmx	JMXMessage Listener	BaseDestination EventListener	Destination EventListener	Destination Manager, MessageBus Manager, Destination Statistics Manager
proxy	ProxyMessage Listener	none	Message Listener	ProxyMode, ProxyRequet, ProxyResponse
sender	Synchronous Message Listener	none	Message Listener	MessageSender, Synchronous MessageSender

Note that the class `MessagingHotDeployListener` extends the abstract class `BaseHotDeployListener`, which implements the interface `HotDeployListener`. It provides the capabilities to invoke, deploy, and undeploy the processes by using the classes `Message` and `MessageUtil`.

Scheduling layouts publishing

The portal provides the scheduling capability to publish pages. In order to publish pages either locally or remotely, we should select the scope of publishing — all of the pages, or the selected pages of a given site (for example, Book Street) — in the **Pages** tab first, and then use the **Scheduler** tab to add an event (that is, a job for publishing). You can provide Description, Start Date, End Date, and a repeatable feature. In the class StagingImp, a set of methods are defined.

As you can see, the feature scheduling layouts publishing takes place at the layout level, either for a page or for a set of pages. In fact, the service interface LayoutService defines the following scheduling functions:

```
public void schedulePublishToLive;
public void schedulePublishToRemote;
public void unschedulePublishToLive;
public void unschedulePublishToRemote;
```

The service interface LayoutService is implemented by the abstract class LayoutServiceBaseImpl, extended by the class LayoutServiceImpl. Of course, the service utility class LayoutServiceUtil is available for the preceding functions.

Scheduling portal core assets and custom assets

The portal provides scheduling framework for both portal core assets and plugins' custom assets. The following table shows the samples of a scheduler in the portal core assets:

Listener class	Extension	Interface	Description
CheckEquityLog MessageListener	BaseMessage Listener	MessageListener	Checks equity log message listener
ExpireBanMessage Listener, MailingListMessage Listener	BaseMessage Listener	MessageListener	Expire ban message listener, Mailing list message listener
CheckArticle MessageListener	BaseMessage Listener	MessageListener	Checks article's message listener
AudioProcessor MessageListener, VideoProcessor MessageListener	BaseMessage Listener	MessageListener	Audio processor and video processor message listeners

How to leverage the scheduling framework for the plugin's custom assets? Here, we will use the daily-check-attachments of the knowledge base plugin as an example. The following steps would help on how to add the scheduler on the custom asset, for example, `KBArticle`:

1. First, prepare a method called `checkAttachments()` in the class `KBArticleLocalServiceImpl`.

2. Then prepare the class `CheckAttachmentsMessageListener`, extending the abstract class `BaseMessageListener`, implementing the interface `MessageListener`:

    ```
    protected void doReceive(Message message) throws Exception {
        KBArticleLocalServiceUtil.checkAttachments();
    }
    ```

3. Finally, configure the scheduler entry in the XML file `liferay-portlet.xml` as follows:

    ```
    <scheduler-entry>
        <scheduler-event-listener-class>    com.liferay.knowledgebase.
    admin.messaging.CheckAttachmentsMessageListener</scheduler-event-
    listener-class>
        <trigger>
            <simple>            <simple-trigger-value>1</simple-trigger-
    value>
                <time-unit>day</time-unit>
            </simple>
        </trigger>
    </scheduler-entry>
    ```

As shown in the preceding code, the `scheduler-entry` element contains the declarative data of a scheduler. The `scheduler-event-listener-class` value must be a class that implements `com.liferay.portal.kernel.messaging.MessageListener`. This class will receive a message at a regular interval specified by the trigger element. The `trigger` element contains the configuration data to indicate when to trigger the class specified in `scheduler-event-listener-class`.

Cache clustering

The portal can be deployed in clusters of multiple instances for availability and scalability. It leverages Ehcache-distributed or replicated cache. Without a distributed or replicated cache, the application clusters exhibit a number of undesirable behaviors.

Portal cache interfaces

The portal has defined a set of cache interfaces, such as portal cache, single VM pool, multi-VM pool, thread local cache, and so on. The following table shows an overview of these cache interfaces:

Interface	Utility/Implementation	Main functions/ Related models	Description
PortalCache	BasePortalCache, Blocking PortalCache	Destroy, get, put, registerCache Listener, remove, unregister CacheListener	Portal cache
PortalCache Manager	none	clearAll, getCache, reconfigureCaches, removeCache	Portal cache manager
SingleVMPool	SingleVMPoolUtil	Clear, get, put, remove	Simple VM pool
MultiVMPool	MultiVMPoolUtil	Clear, get, put, remove	Multiple VM pool
ThreadLocal Cache<T>	ThreadLocal CacheAdvice extends Annotation ChainableMethodAdvice	Lifecycle, ThreadLocal Cachable, ThreadLocal	Thread local cache
ThreadLocal CacheManager	ThreadLocal CacheAdvice extends Annotation ChainableMethodAdvice	Lifecycle, ThreadLocalCache, ThreadLocal	Thread local cahce manager

Ehcache

Ehcache is an open source, widely used, java-distributed cache for general purpose caching, such as Java EE and light-weight containers. It features memory and disk stores, replicates listeners, cache loaders, cache extensions, cache exception handlers, a GZIP caching servlet filter, RESTful and SOAP APIs, referring to `http://ehcache.org/`.

> Using **Terracotta** for Ehcache-distributed caching is the recommended method of operating Ehcache in a distributed or scaled-out application environment. It provides the highest level of performance, availability, and scalability.

Replicated cache

In addition to the built-in distributed caching, Ehcache has a pluggable cache replication scheme, which enables the addition of cache replication mechanisms. The following additional replicated caching mechanisms are available: RMI, JGroups, JMS, and cache server. Cache discovery is implemented via multicast or manual configuration. Updates are delivered either asynchronously or synchronously via custom RMI connections.

RMI is a point-to-point protocol, which can generate a lot of network traffic. Ehcache manages this through batching of communications for the asynchronous replicator. To set up RMI replicated caching, you need to configure the `CacheManager` with `PeerProvider` and `CacheManagerPeerListener`. Keep in mind that only `Serializable` elements are suitable for replication.

Ehcache provides two mechanisms for peer discovery of RMI: manual and automatic. **Automatic peer discovery** uses TCP multicast to establish and maintain a multicast group with minimal configuration and automatic addition to and deletion of members from the group, while **manual peer discovery** requires the IP address and port of each listener to be known. Peers can't be added or removed at runtime.

In order to achieve shared data, all JVMs read to and write from a **cache server**, which runs it in its own JVM. To achieve redundancy, the Ehcache inside the cache server can be set up in its own cluster.

JMS (Java Message Service) provides replication between cache nodes using a replication topic, pushing of data directly to cache nodes from external topic publishers, and a `JMSCacheLoader`, sending cache load requests to a queue. Each cache node subscribes to a predefined topic, configured as `topicBindingName` in the XML file `ehcache.xml`. Each replicated cache publishes cache elements to that topic. Replication is configured per cache.

The portal allows the plugins to configure and deploy the Ehcache configuration files to reconfigure the following types of caches: Single VM (`SingleVMPool`), Clustered portal caches (`MultiVMPool`), and Hibernate caches.

In fact, the portal updates `Cluster Link`-based replication allows the plugins to reconfigure the `PortalCacheManager` caches and the Hibernate caches. The Hibernate Spring beans are specified in the XML file `/META-INF/hibernate-spring.xml`.

The portal integrates Ehcache. The following table shows a summary of this integration:

Class	Interface	Involved models	Description
EhcachePortal Cache	BasePortal Cache implements PortalCache	net.sf.ehcache. Ehcache, Element, event.CacheEvent Listener, event. NotificationScope	Ehcache portal cache
EhcachePortal CacheManager	PortalCache Manager	net.sf.ehcache. Cache, CacheManager, Ehcache, config. CacheConfiguration, config.Configuration	Ehcache portal cache manager
Ehcache Configuration Util	none	CacheConfiguration, Configuration, Configuration Factory	Ehcache configuration utility
JGroupsManager	CacheManager PeerProvider CachePeer	org.jgroups.Address, JChannel, Message	Custom JGroups manager
JGroupsBootstrap CacheLoader	net.sf.ehcache. distribution. jgroups. JGroupsBootstrap CacheLoader	Ehcache	Custom JGroups Bootstrap cache loader
Modifiable EhcacheWrapper	net.sf.ehcache. Ehcache	net.sf.ehcache. CacheManager, Element, Statistics, Status	Modifiable Ehcache wrapper
PortalCache CacheEvent Listener	net.sf.ehcache. Ehcache	net.sf.ehcache. CacheManager, Element, Statistics, Status	Portal cache event listener
LiferayCache EventListener Factory	CacheEvent ListenerFactory	net.sf.ehcache.event. CacheEvent Listener	Custom cache event listener factory
LiferayBootstrap CacheLoader Factory	BootstrapCache LoaderFactory	net.sf.ehcache. bootstrap.Bootstrap CacheLoader	Custom bootstrap cache loader factory

The portal provides capacities to turn the cache on/off for all velocity ResourceLoaders. The portal specifies Journal content cache, Layout cache, Velocity cache, and FreeMarker cache.

Of course, you can apply portal cache on the plugin's custom assets, such as `PortalCache` and `MultiVMPoolUtil`. For example, the Knowledge base plugins defines a class called `KBArticleContentCacheUtil`, specifying multi-VM pool for articles and templates.

Replicated caching with JGroups

There are two different ways to configure the Ehcache cache replication using JGroups: **UDP Multicast** and **TCP Unicast**. JGroups can be used as the underlying mechanism for the replication operations in Ehcache. It offers a very flexible protocol stack and a reliable unicast and multicast message transmission. For more details refer to `http://www.jgroups.org/`.

In addition, the portal defines the following properties for UDP multicast:

```
cluster.link.channel.properties.control=UDP(*)
cluster.link.channel.properties.transport.0=UDP(*)
cluster.link.autodetect.address=www.google.com:80
```

The preceding code sets JGroups properties for each channel. It supports upto 10 transport channels and one single required control channel. Use as few transport channels as possible for best performance. By default, only one UDP control channel and one UDP transport channel are enabled. Channels can be configured by XML files that are located in the class path or by inline properties.

The portal also sets the property `cluster.link.autodetect.address` to autodetect the default outgoing IP address so that JGroups can bind to it. The property must point to an address that is accessible to the portal server, `www.google.com` or your local gateway.

By the way, these properties are consumed in the class `ClusterExecutorImpl`, which extends the abstract class `ClusterBase`, implementing the interfaces `ClusterExecutor` and `PortalPortEventListener`.

Clustered caching via Terracotta

In general, Ehcache distributed with **TSA (Terracotta Server Array)** is different to the other distribution mechanisms. Of course, you can set up clustered caching via Terracotta. Cache discovery is automatic and many options exist for tuning the cache behavior and performance for your use cases.

Loosely speaking, you can set up clustered caching via Terracotta as follows:

1. Copy all jars in `$TERRACOTTA_HOME/ehcache/lib` to `$TOMCAT_HOME/webapps/ROOT/WEB-INF/lib`, including jars `/common/terracotta-toolkit-1.0-runtime-<version>.jar`, `/quartz/quartz-terracotta-<version>.jar`, and `/quartz/quartz-all-<version>.jar`.

2. Create `terracotta-ehcache` folder (of course, you can have a different name) to `$TOMCAT_HOME/webapps/ROOT/WEB-INF/classes`, and create the XML files `hibernate-terracotta.xml` and `liferay-multi-vm-terracotta.xml`, adjusting `terracottaConfig` to point to Terracotta servers, such as `<terracottaConfig url="localhost:9510"/>`.

3. Configure EhCache, Hibernate second level cache, and Quartz scheduler as follows.

   ```
   ehcache.multi.vm.config.location=/terracotta-ehcache/liferay-
   multi-vm-terracotta.xml
   net.sf.ehcache.configurationResourceName=/terracotta-ehcache/
   hibernate-terracotta.xml
   org.quartz.jobStore.tcConfigUrl = localhost:9510
   ```

In addition, you should set up session replication in the application server, for example, Tomcat or JBoss.

Memcached

Memcached is a general purpose, distributed memory caching system used to speed up dynamic database-driven websites by caching data and objects in RAM to reduce the number of times an external data source (such as a database or API) must be read. Refer to `http://www.memcached.org/` for more details.

The portal adds Memcached support via the Spring beans specification in the XML file `/META-INF/memcached-spring.xml`. The following table depicts a summary of the Memcached integration:

Class	Interface	Factory	Description
`MemcachePortal Cache, PooledMemcache PortalCache`	`BasePortal Cache implements PortalCache`	`PooledMemcached ClientFactory implements MemcachedClient Factory,` `DefaultMemcached ClientFactory`	(Pooled) Memcache portal cache

Class	Interface	Factory	Description
`MemcachePortal CacheManager,` `PooledMemcache PortalCacheManager`	`PortalCache Manager`	`MemcachedClient PoolableObjectFactory` `implements` `PoolableObjectFactory`	(Pooled) Memcache cache manager

Cache clustering

Clustering allows us to run portal instances on several parallel servers (called **cluster nodes**). The load is distributed across different servers, and even if any of the servers fail, the portal is still accessible via the other cluster nodes. Clustering is crucial for scalable portal enterprise, as you can improve the performance by simply adding more nodes to the cluster.

The following diagram depicts an overview of the clustering of portal instances. A cluster allows us to distribute the traffic coming into website to several machines, so that the cluster can allow websites to handle more web traffic at a faster pace than it would be possible with a single machine. Definitely, the portal works well in a clustered environment.

In general, the clustering of portal instances involves a few main items: clustered document repository, clustered database, synced Lucene indexing, clustered Hibernate, and clustered multi-VM.

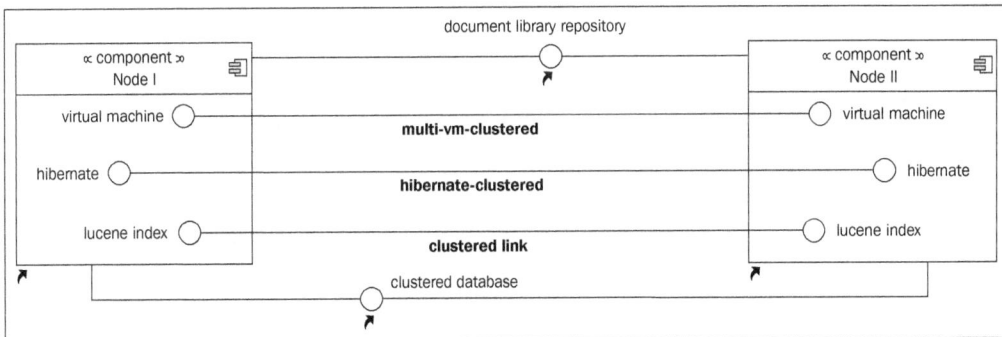

Clustering models and interfaces

The portal provides an entity called `ClusterGroup` in the service XML `/portal/service.xml`.

Class	Interface	Extension/Utility	Description
`AddressImpl`	`com.liferay.portal.kernel.cluster.Address`	none	Cluster address
`ClusterLinkImpl`	`ClusterLink`	`ClusterBase, ClusterLink Util`	Cluster link implementation
`ClusterNode, ClusterEvent, ClusterRequest, ClusterNodeResponse`	`Serializable`	none	Cluster nodes, events, request, and node response
`ClusterExecutorImpl`	`ClusterExecutor, PortalPort EventListener`	`ClusterBase`	Cluster executor implementation
`ClusterGroupImpl`	`ClusterGroup`	`ClusterGroup ModelImpl`	ClusterGroup Model extends BaseModel `<ClusterGroup>`

Clustering settings

The default clustering settings is UDP multicast. Of course, beside the UDP multicast, you can leverage either TCP unicast or Terracotta. For UDP multicast, you can add the following lines in `portal-ext.properties`. By the way, the cluster Spring beans are specified in the XML file `/META-INF/cluster-spring.xml`. You may use the same XML file as references:

```
net.sf.ehcache.configurationResourceName=/ehcache/hibernate-clustered.
xml
ehcache.multi.vm.config.location=/ehcache/liferay-multi-vm-clustered.
xml
dl.store.file.system.root.dir=/data/document_library
cluster.link.enabled=true
lucene.replicate.write=true
```

The property `cluster.link.enabled` is required, if you want to cluster indexing and other features that depend on the cluster link. Set `lucene.replicate.write` to `true`, if you want the portal to replicate an index write across all the members of the cluster. This is useful in some clustered environments, where you wish each server instance to have its own copy of the Lucene search index. This is only relevant when using the default Lucene indexing engine.

Summary

In this chapter, you have learned the Portal-Group-Page-Content (PGPC) pattern, LAR exporting and importing, local staging and publishing, remote staging and publishing, scheduling and messaging, and caching and clustering.

In the next chapter, we will introduce indexing, search, and workflow.

9
Indexing, Search, and Workflow

Search Engine Optimization (SEO) is the process of improving the volume of traffic to websites from search engines via natural search results. The portal is used to build public websites. It provides a wide range of features to help make SEO-friendly websites showing up at top of search results.

The portal provides indexing-search capabilities to search for web content in any websites, both organization's and site's. The portlets, such as, Search, OpenSearch, and Web Content Search, by default, are powered by the Apache Lucene search engine. As an alternative to Lucene, the portal supports pluggable search engines.

The portal framework is widely open to integrating third-party workflow engines. And the portal itself provides a workflow engine called the **Kaleo** workflow, allowing the users to define any number of simple to complex business processes, to deploy them, and to manage them through the portal interface. These business processes have the knowledge of users, groups, and roles without writing a single line of code. The only required part is creation of a single XML document. Note that you might get an error when you try to start the portlet with an empty database.

This chapter will first introduce Webs plugins and build Webs plugins using the cas-web and solr-web plugins as examples. Then, we will address indexing and search capabilities. The solr-web plugin will be used as an example to integrate the Solr search engine. Finally, we will discuss workflow integration and the workflow designer, where the plugin kaleo-web will be used as an example.

By the end of this chapter, you will have learned how to:

- Leverage Webs plugins and WAI
- Build Webs plugins cas-web and solr-web

- Index and search assets—both portal core assets and plugin custom assets
- Set up the solr-web plugin
- Apply a workflow to any assets
- Employ the kaleo-web plugin

Webs plugins

Webs plugins are regular Java EE web modules designed to work with portals, such as ESB (Enterprise Service Bus), SSO (Single Sign-On), workflow engine, search engine, and so on. A web plugin provides the ability to integrate third-party applications, supporting embedding hook definition and service-builder services, which is different from plain web applications.

Web plugin project

Similar to the project name of a portlet or hook, a web plugin project should have the name ${web.name}-web, under the folder $PLUGIN_SDK_HOME/webs. For example, the name ${web.name}-web could be cas-web or solr-web . Since there isn't any template for web projects, you have to create a web project manually.

The web project is made up of build.xml, an application WAR file (if using web application WAR directly), and a folder called docroot. For example, the web plugin cas-web has the following definitions in the file build.xml:

```xml
<?xml version="1.0"?>
<!DOCTYPE project>
<project name="cas-web" basedir="." default="deploy">
    <import file="../build-common-web.xml" />
    <property name="original.war.file" value="cas-web.war" />
</project>
```

As you can see, the property original.war.file points to the real WAR file or real web application ZIP file.

The folder WEB-INF is included under the folder docroot. Under the folder WEB-INF, we have web application configuration files, Liferay plugin package properties, service.xml, liferay-hook.xml, the src folder, and so on.

Web deployer and listener

As you can see, the web application WAR file, or the web plugin WAR, will be deployed automatically when the WAR file is dropped into the folder `deploy`. What's happening? In fact, the portal provides deployers, such as `WebAutoDeployer` and `WebDeployer`, and deploy listeners such as `WebAutoDeployListener`, for the web plugin WAR deployment.

Web applications integrator

Integrating standalone web applications into the portal isn't an easy task. However, the portal makes it possible to achieve near-native integration with minimal effort, via the **Web Application Integrator** (**WAI**). In fact, the WAI will automatically deploy any standard Java servlet application as a portlet within the portal.

In order to use the WAI, you can simply copy an application WAR file into the autodeploy directory, and then add the portlet to your page. The portal transparently handles the rest.

The purpose of the WAI is to facilitate the task of integrating existing web applications into the portal. Initially, it allowed the direct deployment of any existing web application without modification to achieve a medium-level type of integration.

The deployment process will embed the web application as an iframe inside the portlet. The WAI will automatically resize the iframe to fit its contents and provide a bookmark-able link to the current page.

As you can see, the WAI has a few limitations, as follows:

- Refreshing your browser will return to the application's home page
- Login credentials can't be shared with the embedded application

In addition, the WAI is an iframe-based approach, thus if the user navigates away from the site, the automatic resizing and permanent link functionality will stop functioning.

What's happening?

The WAI framework involves the following aspects: plugin package, deployment, and portlet. The plugin package DTD is defined in the file `$PORTAL_SRC_HOME/ definitions/liferay-plugin-package_{version}.xml` — this is the Liferay plugins XML file that lists the plugins available in the plugin repository.

The plugin-package element contains the declarative data of a plugin:

```
<!ELEMENT plugin-package (
    name, module-id, recommended-deployment-context?,
    types, tags?, short-description, long-description?,
    change-log, page-url?, screenshots?, author,
    licenses, liferay-versions, deployment-settings?)>
```

As shown in the preceding code, the `name` element contains the name of the plugin package that will be shown to the users. The `module-id` element contains the full identifier of the plugin using the Maven-based syntax `groupId/artifactId/version/file-type`. The `deployment-settings` element contains a list of parameters that specifies how the package should be deployed.

```
<!ELEMENT deployment-settings (setting)+>
```

As shown in the preceding code, the `setting` element specifies a name-value pair that provides information on how the package should be deployed.

The portal defines an interface `PluginPackage`, a class deployer `WAIAutoDeployer` and its dependencies, a class request `WAIHttpServletRequest`, and a class portlet `WAIPortlet`.

Indexing and search

Search engine indexing collects, parses, and stores the data to facilitate fast and accurate information retrieval. A search index could be considered as a searchable database of words that points to the documents containing that word. The popular engines focus on the full-text indexing of online, documents. Media types, such as, video, audio, and graphics are also searchable. The portal-integrated search engine Lucene, which indexes full-text of online, documents, records, and media types, such as, video, audio, and graphics. And the portal is framework-ready to integrate other search engines, such as, Apache Solr, FAST, GSA, Coveo, and so on.

Overview

As shown in the following diagram, the portal supports the following:

- Autogeneration of database tables and indexes
- Hibernate first-level cache and second-level cache settings
- Ehcache settings
- Portal cache and portal indexer

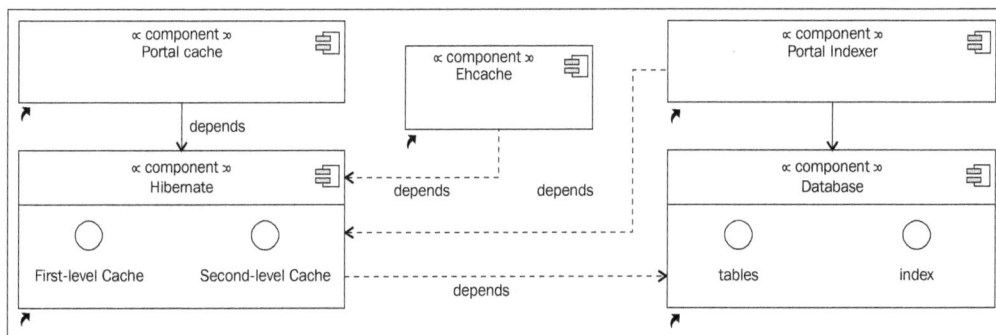

The service builder generates the database to create tables and indexes using SQL. A database index is a data structure that improves the speed of data retrieval operations on a database table. Remember to add a database index for plugins' database tables whenever in need. The following is service-builder generated code to create an index for the table `AssetCategory`:

```
create index IX_E639E2F6 on AssetCategory (groupId);
create index IX_2008FACB on AssetCategory (groupId, vocabularyId);
```

Hibernate uses two different caches for objects: first-level cache and second-level cache. The first-level cache always associates with the `Session` object. Hibernate uses this cache by default. The second-level cache always associates with the `Session Factory` object.

Ehcache (Easy Hibernate Cache) supports read-only and read/write caching, and memory-based and disk-based caching. As mentioned in the previous chapter, the portal supports different cache classes/interfaces, such as, `MultiVMPool`, `SingleVMPool`, `PortalCache`, and `ThreadLocalCache`. Leverage these cache classes in your plugins whenever required. We will address the portal `Indexer` in the next section.

Indexer

The purpose of using an index is to optimize speed and performance in finding relevant documents for a search query. The portal provides an indexer framework that almost any asset can index. This section is going to address the interface `Indexer` and its implementation in the portal.

Interface

The portal provides an indexer interface called `com.liferay.portal.kernel.`
`search.Indexer`. The following is a snippet of the interface `Indexer`:

```
public interface Indexer {
    public void delete(Object object) throws SearchException;
    public Document getDocument(Object object);
    public Summary getSummary();
    // see details in Indexer.java
}
```

As shown in the preceding code, the interface `Indexer` specifies a set of signatures, such as, `delete`, `getClassNames`, `getDocument`, `getIndexerPostProcessors`, `getSearchEngineId`, `getSortField`, `getSummary`, `hasPermission`, `isFilterSearch`, `isStagingAware`, `postProcesssContextQuery`, `postprocessSearchQuery`, `registerIndexerPostProcessor`, `index`, `search`, and `unregisterIndexerPostProcessor`.

More related interfaces include `IndexerPostProcessor`, `IndexerRegistry`, `IndexSearcher`, and `IndexWriter`. The following table shows an overview of these interfaces:

Interface	Implementation	Wrapper / Utility	Description
`Indexer`	`BaseIndexer`	`IndexerWrapper`	Interface Indexer
`Indexer PostProcessor`	`BaseIndexer PostProcessor`	none	Interface Indexer Post processor
`IndexerRegistry`	`Indexer RegistryImpl`	`Indexer RegistryUtil`	Interface Index registry
`IndexSearcher`	`IndexSearcher ProxyBean`	none	Interface Indexer searcher
	`LuceneIndex SearcherImpl`		
`IndexWriter`	`IndexWriter ProxyBean`	none	Interface Index writer
	`LuceneIndex WriterImpl`		

As you can see, the abstract class `BaseIndexer` implements the interface `Indexer`. First of all, the class `BaseIndexer` implements most of the signatures of the interface `Indexer`. Meanwhile, it keeps some signatures as abstract, that is, these signatures need to be implemented in the final classes, such as, `doDelete`, `doGetDocument`, `doGetSummary`, `doIndex`, and `getPortletId`. In addition, the class `BaseIndexer` adds a few methods, such as, `addLocalizedSearchTerm`, `addSearchAssetCategoryIds`, `addSearchAssetTagNames`, `addSearchEntryClassNames`, `addSearchExpando`, `addSearchGroupId`, `addSearchKeywords`, `addSearchTerm`, `addStagingGroupKeyword`, and `createFullQuery`.

Indexing core assets

The most portal core assets are indexed properly in the portal. For example, the class `DLIndexer` extends the abstract class `BaseIndexer`, implementing the interface `Indexer`. By default, this class `DLIndexer` is registered through the tag `indexer-class`, which is in the XML file `$PORTAL_SRC_HOME/portal-web/docroot/WEB-INF/liferay-portlet.xml`.

In addition, an indexer implementation class could be registered in different ways. The following code shows how to register the indexer implementation class `DLStoreIndexer` in the construction of the class `DLIndexer`:

```
public DLIndexer() {
    IndexerRegistryUtil.register(new DLStoreIndexer());
}
```

As shown in the following table, the portal provides a set of indexer implementations for core assets, such as `BlogEntry`, `BookmarksEntry`, `CalEvent`, and so on.

Indexer class	Extension	Override	Model/Portlet ID	Description
Blogs Indexer	BaseIndexer implements Indexer	postProcess ContextQuery, doDelete, doGetDocument, doGetSummary, doReindex, getPortletId	BlogEntry PortletKeys. BLOGS	Blogs portlet
Bookmarks Indexer	BaseIndexer implements Indexer	postProcess ContextQuery, doDelete, doGetDocument, doGetSummary, doReindex, getPortletId	Bookmarks Entry PortletKeys. BOOKMARKS	Bookmarks portlet

Indexer class	Extension	Override	Model/Portlet ID	Description
CalIndexer	BaseIndexer implements Indexer	doDelete, doGetDocument, doGetSummary, doReindex, getPortletId	CalEvent PortletKeys. CALENDAR	Calendar portlet
DLStore Indexer	BaseIndexer implements Indexer	doDelete, doGetDocument, doGetSummary, doReindex, getPortletId	FileModel	Document Library store
DLIndexer	BaseIndexer implements Indexer	hasPermission, isFilterSearch, postProcess ContextQuery, postProcess SearchQuery, doDelete, doGetDocument, doGetSummary, doReindex, getPortletId	DLFileEntry PortletKeys. DOCUMENT_ LIBRARY	Document Library portlet
Journal Indexer	BaseIndexer implements Indexer	postProcess ContextQuery, postProcess SearchQuery, doDelete, doGetDocument, doGetSummary, doReindex, getPortletId	Journal Article PortletKeys. JOURNAL	Journal (Web Content) portlet
MBIndexer	BaseIndexer implements Indexer	hasPermission, isFilterSearch, postProcess ContextQuery, doDelete, doGetDocument, doGetSummary, doReindex, getPortletId	MBMessage PortletKeys. MESSAGE_ BOARDS	Message boards portlet

Indexer class	Extension	Override	Model/Portlet ID	Description

`SCIndexer`	`BaseIndexer implements Indexer`	`doDelete, doGetDocument, doGetSummary, doReindex, getPortletId`	`SCProduct Entry`
			
			`PortletKeys. SOFTWARE_ CATALOG`
				Software catalog portlet

`Wiki Indexer`	`BaseIndexer implements Indexer`	`postProcess ContextQuery, doDelete, doGetDocument, doGetSummary, doReindex, getPortletId`	`WikiPage`
			
			`PortletKeys. WIKI`
				Wiki portlet

Registering custom asset indexers in plugins

The portal provides a framework in order to provide plugin search capabilities. For example, the knowledge base portlet defines a class called `AdminIndexer`, extending the abstract class `BaseIndexer` directly, implementing the interface `Indexer` indirectly. The indexing model is the interface `KBArticle`, and portlet ID has the value `PortletKeys.KNOWLEDGE_BASE_ADMIN`.

Loosely speaking, the class `AdminIndexer` got registered through the tag `indexer-class` (which is in the XML file `/docroot/WEB-INF/liferay-portlet. xml`), as follows.

```
<indexer-class>
com.liferay.knowledgebase.admin.util.AdminIndexer
</indexer-class>
```

As you can see, the `indexer-class` value must be a class that implements `com. liferay.portal.kernel.search.Indexer`, either directly or indirectly, and it is called to create or update a search index for the portlet.

In brief, the class `AdminIndexer` overrides a set of methods, such as `postProcessSearchQuery`, `search`, `doDelete`, `doGetDocument`, `doGetSummary`, `doReindex`, and so on. In real use cases, you would be able to override the same set of methods in plugins, according to your own requirements.

In the following two steps, you would be able to add search capabilities to a custom portlet.

1. Prepare an indexer implementation class, and, furthermore, override a set of abstract methods, such as, doDelete, doGetDocument, doReindex, doGetSummary, and so on.

2. Specify this class as a value of the tag indexer-class in the XML file liferay-portlet.xml.

In general, the class AdminIndexer provides index for following main fields of the Knowledge Base article. Of course, you can add your own custom fields, such as *title* as text columns and/or keyword columns. Here, for text columns, the search is based on the **string-containing** process; while for keyword columns, the search is based on the **string-equal** process.

```
KBArticle kbArticle = (KBArticle)obj;
Document document =
    getBaseModelDocument(PORTLET_ID, kbArticle);
document.addText(Field.CONTENT,
    HtmlUtil.extractText(kbArticle.getContent()));
return document;
```

In fact, you can refer to the method getBaseModelDocument from the abstract class BaseIndexer, for detailed information. The following table shows an overview of these fields:

Column name	Field name	Data type	Description
addUID	Field.UID	Long — Portlet ID, classPK	Unique identifier of the document
addText	Field.CONTENT	String	Content, description
addFile	Field.CONTENT	String (for binary files, such as, .doc PDF, and so on)	using addText and FileUtil.extractText
addKeyword	Field.ASSET_CATEGORY_IDS	Long array	Asset category IDs keyword
addKeyword	Field.ASSET_CATEGORY_NAMES	String array	Asset category names keyword
addKeyword	Field.ASSET_TAG_NAMES	String array	Asset tag names keyword

Column name	Field name	Data type	Description
addkeyword	Field.ENTRY_CLASS_NAME	String	Class name keyword
addKeyword	Field.ENTRY_CLASS_PK	Long	Class PK keyword
addKeyword	Field.PORTLET_ID	Long	Portlet ID keyword
addKeyword	Field.ROOT_ENTRY_CLASS_PK	Long	Resource Primary Key
addKeyword	Field.CLASS_NAME_ID	Long	Attached model — class name ID and class PK
	Field.CLASS_PK		
addKeyword	Field.COMPANY_ID, Field.USER_ID, Field.USER_NAME	Long, String	Audited model: company ID, user ID, username, create-date, and modified date
addDate	Field.CREATE_DATE, Field.MODIFIED_DATE	Date	
addKeyword	Field.GROUP_ID	Long	Grouped model — parent group ID and scoped group ID
	Field.SCOPE_GROUP_ID		
addKeyword	Field.STATUS	Integer	workflow status
Custom Attributes	Custom Attributes	ExpandoBridge IndexerUtil. addAttributes	Custom attributes

Lucene

The portal integrates the Apache Lucene search engine as default. In general, the Lucene search engine has many useful features, such as ranked searching — best results are returned first. This includes many powerful query types — phrase queries, wildcard queries, proximity queries, range queries, and more.

It also allows fielded searching (for example, title, author, contents, and so on), date-range searching, sorting by any field, multiple-index searching with merged results, and simultaneous update and searching. Refer to `http://lucene.apache.org/`, for more details.

The portal provides the following properties to configure the index settings in the
`portal.properties`. Using these properties, you would be able to change the index
engine default behavior. Of course, you can override the same set of properties in
`portal-ext.properties`.

```
index.search.highlight.enabled=true
index.date.format.pattern=yyyyMMddHHmmss
index.dump.compression.enabled=true
```

As shown in the preceding code, you can enable highlighting of search results via the
property `index.search.highlight.enabled`. Set the fragment size returned from
the search-result highlighter and from the number of lines for the snippet returned
by search engine; set the limit for results used when performing index searches.

You can enable scoring of results via the property `index.search.scoring.enabled`;
set the limit for results used when performing index searches that are subsequently
filtered by permissions. You can also set the property `index.read.only` to `true`, if
you want to avoid any writes to the index. This is useful in clustering environments
where there is a shared index and only one node of the cluster updates it.

You can set the property `index.on.startup` to `true`, if you want to index your
entire library of files at startup. This property is available so that the portal will
index all at startup. Note that you should not set this property to `true` on production
systems or else your index will be indexed at each startup. In case the index is stored
in the database, it is acceptable to have more than one node to update the index.

The portal provides the following properties to configure the Lucene search engine
in `portal.properties`. Obviously, you can override these properties in `portal-ext.properties`.

```
lucene.store.type=file
lucene.dir=${liferay.home}/data/lucene/
lucene.optimize.interval=100
lucene.replicate.write=false
```

The preceding code shows that the property `lucene.store.type` designates
whether Lucene stores indexes in a database via JDBC, `file` system, or in RAM. The
type `file` would be used as the best practice. You can also set the directory where
Lucene indexes are stored, via the property `lucene.dir`. This is referenced only if
Lucene stores indexes in the file system.

You can set the property `lucene.replicate.write` to `true`, if you want the portal
to replicate an index-write across all members of the cluster. This is useful in some
clustered environments, where you wish each server instance to have its own copy
of the Lucene search index. This is only relevant when using the default Lucene
index engine.

What's happening on these properties? The portal provides a set of interfaces and their implementations for the Lucene search engine, reading these properties in runtime. The following table shows a summary of these interfaces, under the package `com.liferay.portal.search.lucene`:

Implementation	Interface	Utility/models	Description
`Boolean ClauseImpl`	`BooleanClause`	`BooleanClause OccurTranslator`	Boolean clause implementation
`BooleanQuery FactoryImpl`	`BooleanQuery Factory`	`BooleanQuery`	Boolean query factory implementation
`Boolean QueryImpl`	`BaseBoolean QueryImpl extends BaseQueryImpl implements BooleanQuery`	`BooleanClause, BooleanClause Occur, Query`	Boolean query implementation
`Lucene HelperImpl`	`LuceneHelper`	`Lucene HelperUtil`	Lucene helper implementation
`LuceneSearch EngineImpl`	`SearchEngine`	`IndexAccessor, FieldWeightSim ilarity,PerFiel dAnalyzerWrapp er, LuceneFields, LuceneFile Extractor, LuceneHelper, LuceneHelperUtil, LuceneIndexer`	Lucene search engine implementation
`LuceneIndex SearcherImpl`	`Index Searcher`	`Document, Field, Hits, Query, SearchContext, Sort, Facet`	Lucene index search implementation
`LuceneIndex WriterImpl`	`IndexWriter`	`Document, Field`	Lucene index writer implementation
`LuceneQueryImpl`	`BaseQueryImpl`	`Query`	Lucene query implementation

Furthermore, the portal specifies a set of services for the Lucene search engine dump, cluster, and messaging. The following table displays a summary of these services:

Package	Classes	Interfaces	Involved models
com.liferay.portal.search.lucene.cluster	Lucene ClusterUtil	none	Address, LuceneHelper
com.liferay.portal.search.lucene.dump	DumpIndex DeletionPolicy IndexCommit SerializationUtil	IndexDeletion Policy indexCommit MetaInfo	IndexCommit, IndexDeletion Policy, IndexWriter IndexCommit, Directory, IndexInpit, IndexOutput
com.liferay.portal.search.lucene.messaging	CleanUpMessage Listener SearchEngine DestinationEvent Listener	BaseMessage Listener BaseDestination EventListener	Message Listener Destination EventListener

Solr

The portal is open to integrating the Apache Solr search engine or other search engines, instead of the embedded Apache Lucene search engine. The following diagram depicts this integration. As you can see, the portal first provides the service interface index to index both core assets and custom assets against the search engine. Then the portal provides the service interface search, to search both core assets and custom assets against the search engine.

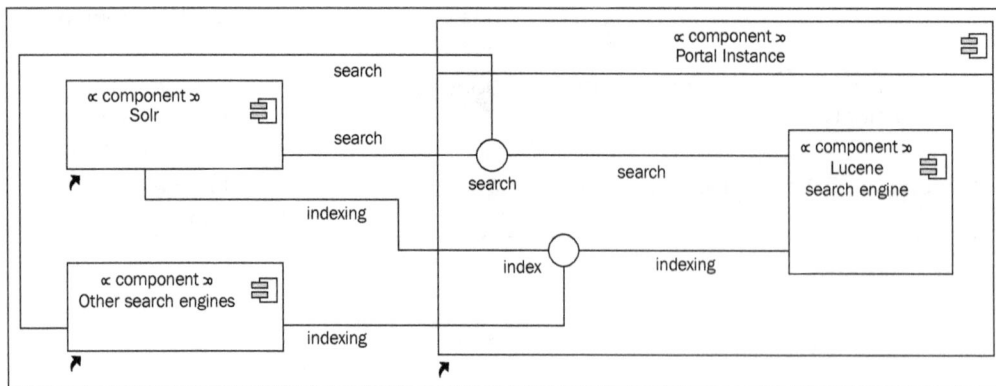

In addition, you can use a Tika and Solr combo to index various documents. **Apache Tika** detects and extracts metadata and structured text content from various documents (for example, Word, PDF, and so on) in a format that can be fed into the Solr or Lucene search engine combo. For more detailed information, refer to Apache Tika at `http://tika.apache.org/`.

Solr is the enterprise search platform with major features, including powerful full-text search, hit highlighting, faceted search, dynamic clustering, database integration, rich document (for example, Word, PDF, and so on) handling, and geospatial search. It is highly scalable, providing distributed search and index replication. Refer to `http://lucene.apache.org/solr/`.

In addition, Solr uses the Lucene Java search library at its core for full-text indexing and search, and has REST-like HTTP/XML and JSON APIs that make it easy to use from virtually any programming language.

Before using the Solr search engine in the portal, you need to install the Solr instance as the `$SOLR_HOME` variable first. Then, you should configure the `solr-web` plugin as well. As shown in the following table, you should update the domain name, port number, and schema XML:

XML files	Folder name	Parent folder	Configuration
`schema.xml`	`conf`	`/WEB-INF`	Copy the XML file to `$SOLR_HOME/example/solr/conf`
`messaging-spring.xml`, `solr-spring.xml`	`META-INF`	`/src`	Update the domain name and port number in the XML file `solr-spring.xml`

As configured in the XML files `messaging-spring.xml` and `solr-spring.xml`, the plugin `solr-web` provides a set of index and search implementations, shown in the following table:

Implementation	Interface	Involved models	Description
`SolrIndexSearcherImpl`	`IndexSearcher`	`Document, Field, Hits, Query, SearchContext, Sort, Facet`	Solr index searcher implementation
`SolrIndexWriterImpl`	`IndexWriter`	`Document, Field`	Solr index writer implementation
`SolrSearchEngineImpl`	`SearchEngine`	`IndexSearcher, IndexWriter`	Solr search engine implementation

Implementation	Interface	Involved models	Description
SolrFacet FieldCollector	FacetCollector	none	Solr facet
SolrFacet QueryCollector	TermCollector		
SolrTerm Collector			
BasicAuthSolr Server, BroadcastWriter SolrServer, LoadBalancer SolrServer	SolrServer	SolrRequest, UpdateRequest	Solr server

Search engine

The portal provides interfaces against search engines, such as `com.liferay.portal.kernel.search.SearchEngine`, `PortalSearchEngine`, and so on. The following is the code snippet of the interface `SearchEngine`:

```
public String getName();
public IndexSearcher getSearcher();
public IndexWriter getWriter();
```

The preceding code shows index writer `IndexWriter`, index searcher `IndexSearcher`, and the name in the interface `SearchEngine`.

```
public boolean isIndexReadOnly();
public void setIndexReadOnly(boolean indexReadOnly);
```

The preceding code is the code snippet of the interface `PortalSearchEngine`. As you can see, the interface `PortalSearchEngine` defines whether it is index-read-only or not. In fact, it provides the signatures `isIndexReadOnly` and `setIndexReadOnly`.

The main function `search` is specified in the abstract class `com.liferay.portal.kernel.search.BaseIndexer`. The following code snippet illustrates this:

```
searchContext.setSearchEngineId(getSearchEngineId());
// see details in BaseIndexer.java
Hits hits = SearchEngineUtil.search(
    searchContext, fullQuery);
if (isFilterSearch() && (permissionChecker != null)) {
    hits = filterSearch(
        hits, permissionChecker, searchContext);
}
return hits;
```

As shown in the preceding code, the function search requires the following steps:

1. Set the search engine ID in the search context.
2. Create a Boolean query and add asset categories, asset tags, entry class names, and group ID into the search content.
3. Set the query configuration.
4. Get permission checker, start number, and end number in the search context.
5. Call the search function from the class SearchEngineUtil.
6. Filter the search results with permission checker — filtering through the VIEW permission.

Interfaces

As shown in the following table, the portal has provided a set of search interfaces, such as, document and field, query, sort, string query, term query, wildcard query, and so on:

Interfaces	Implementation	Utility / Comparator	Description
Search Engine	Search EngineImpl	Search EngineUtil	Search engine interface
	LuceneSearch EngineImple		
PortalSearch Engine	PortalSearch EngineImpl	Search EngineUtil	Portal search engine interface
BooleanClause	Boolean ClauseImpl	BooleanClause FactoryUtil	Boolean clause
BooleanClause Occur	Boolean ClauseOccur Impl	none	Boolean clause occur
BooleanQuery extends Query	BaseBoolean QueryImpl	BooleanQuery FactoryUtil	Boolean query
Document	DocumentImpl	DocumentComparator, DocumentComparator OrderBy	Document interface
	Field		
Hits	HitsImpl	none	Search results hits

Interfaces	Implementation	Utility / Comparator	Description
Query, QueryTerm, Query Translator, StringQuery Factory	BaseQueryImpl, QueryConfig, QueryTermImpl, QueryTranslator Impl, StringQueryImpl	QueryTranslator Util, StringQuery FactoryUtil	Query, query terms, query translator, and string query
SortFactory	Sort SortFactory Impl	SortFactory Util	Sort and sort factory
TermQuery TermRange Query TermQuery Factory TermRange QueryFactory	TermQueryImpl, TermRange QueryImpl, TermQuery FactoryImpl, TermRange Query FactoryImpl	TermQuery FactoryUtil TermRangeQuery FactoryUtil	Term query and term range query
Wildcard Query	Wildcard QueryImpl	node	Wildcard query
Search Permission Checker	Search Permission CheckerImpl	none	Search permission checker and its implementation

As you can see, there are a few options to add the fields of both portal core assets and custom assets, such as, keywords, text, date, UID, and so on. These methods are defined in the interface com.liferay.portal.kernel.search.Document, implemented by the class DocumentImpl. The following table shows the details of these fields:

Name	Field name	Data type	Description
add	none	Field	Adds any field into the document
addUID	Field.UID	String, Long	Adds UID (portlet ID, String field, and Long field) into the document
addNumber	any	Double, Float, Integer, Long, String, Array	Adds a number into the document

Name	Field name	Data type	Description
`addText`	any	`String`, `String array`	Adds text into the document
`addKeyword`	any	`Boolean`, `Double`, `Float`, `Integer`, `Long`, `String`, `Array`	Adds a keyword into the document
`addLocalized Text`	any	`Map of Local` and `String`	Adds localized text into the document
`addLocalized Keyword`	any	`Map of Local` and `String`	Adds a localized keyword into the document
`addDate`	any	`Date`	Adds a formatted date into the document
`addFile`	any	`byte[]`, `File`, `InputStream`	Adds a file into the document

Search context

The class `com.liferay.portal.kernel.search.SearchContext` provides search context, such as, `facet`, `asset categories`, `asset tags`, `attributes`, `company Id`, `start number`, `end number`, `folder ids`, `group Ids`, `keywords`, `node ids`, `locale`, `query configuration`, `portlet ids`, `owner user ids`, `search engine id`, `sorts`, `time zone`, `user id`, `and-search`, and more.

In general, there are three steps to initiate the search process. They are, as follows:

1. Configure the search context, say, start, end, keywords, and so on.
2. Get the indexer via the specific model interface.
3. Use the indexer search method with the preceding search context.

For instance, you would be able to find the following sample code at `/knowledge-base-portlet/docroot/search/search.jsp`:

```
SearchContext searchContext =
    SearchContextFactory.getInstance(request);
Indexer indexer =
    IndexerRegistryUtil.getIndexer(KBArticle.class);
Hits hits = indexer.search(searchContext);
```

Faceted search

Loosely speaking, **faceted search** (also called **faceted navigation** or **faceted browsing**) allows the users to explore by filtering the available information, while a **faceted classification** system allows the assignment of multiple classifications to an object, enabling the classifications to be ordered in multiple ways, rather than in a single, predetermined, taxonomic order. The portal provides faceted search capabilities, for example, the faceted search portlet provides full-text search with the faceted classification based on the portal categories. This section will address them in detail.

In fact, the portal defines a class called `com.liferay.portal.kernel.search.FacetedSearcher`, extending the abstract class `BaseIndexer`, which implements the interface `Indexer`. The detailed implementation is displayed in the following table:

Method	Override	Returned data type	Description
`getInstance`	No	`Indexer`	Returns Faceted search instance
`getClassNames`	No	`String array`	Faceted search class names
`getIndexerPostProcessors`	Yes	`IndexerPostProcessor`	Indexer post processor
`search`	Yes	`Hits`	Faceted search
`unregisterIndexerPostProcessor`	Yes	`void`	Unregister indexer post processor
`addSearchExpandoKeywords`	No	`void`	Add search custom attribute keywords
`createFullQuery`	Yes	`BooleanQuery`	Create full query
`doDelete`	Yes	`Object`	Delete document
`doGetDocument`	Yes	`Object, Doucment`	Get document
`doGetSummary`	Yes	`Object, Summary`	Get summary
`doReindex`	Yes	`String, Long`	Reindex
`getPortletId`	Yes	`SearchContext`	Get portlet ID
`isFilterSearch`	No	`Boolean, SearchContext`	Check whether it is a filter search or not

More specifically, the portal provides the interface Facet, facet collector, facet configuration, facet validator, and so on. The following table shows an overview of these interfaces and their implementations.

Interface	Extension / Implementation	Utility	Description
Facet	BaseFacet, MultiValuefacet, RangeFacet, SimpleFacet, AssetEntriesFacet, ScopeFacet	None	Facet interface, its extension, and implementation
FacetCollector	BoboFacet Collector	None	Facet collector
TermCollector	Boboterm Collector	None	Facet collector
Facet Configuration	None	Facet Configuration Util	Facet configuration
FacetValue Validator	BaseFacet ValueValidator	FacetFactory Util, RangeParser Util	Facet value validator

Query parser syntax

Although Lucene provides the ability to create custom queries through its API, it also provides a rich query language through the **query parser**, a lexer that interprets a string into a **Lucene query**. The following table shows a summary of the Lucene query parser syntax:

Name	Sample	Description
Terms	"knowledge" Or "base" Or "knowledge base"	A query is broken up into terms and operators. There are two types of terms: single terms and phrases. A single term is a single word. A phrase is a group of words surrounded by double quotes.
Fields	Title: "knowledge base"	Fielded data. When performing a search, you can either specify a field or use the default field.
Term modifiers	None	Modifying the query terms to provide a wide range of searching options.

Name	Sample	Description
Wildcard	ba?e or ba*	Single and multiple character wildcard searches within single terms (not within phrase queries). To perform a single character wildcard search use the ? symbol. To perform a multiple character wildcard search use the * symbol.
Fuzzy	know~ or know~0.7	Fuzzy searches are based on the Levenshtein Distance or Edit Distance algorithm. To do a fuzzy search, use the tilde symbol (~) at the end of a single word term. The default that is used, if the parameter is not given, is 0.5.
Proximity	"knowledge base"~12	Finding words within a specific distance. To do a proximity search use the tilde symbol (~) at the end of a phrase.
Range	displayDate:[20110601 TO 2011101] or title:{Base TO Knowledge}	Range queries allow one to match the documents whose field(s) values are between the lower and upper bound specified by the Range query. Range queries can be inclusive or exclusive of the upper and lower bounds.
Boosting a term	knowledge^4 base or "knowledge base"^5 "liferay portal"	Lucene provides the relevance level of matching the documents based on the terms found. To boost a term use the caret symbol (^) with a boost factor (a number) at the end of the term you are searching for.
Boolean Operators	"knowledge" OR "base" "knowledge" AND "base" "knowledge" NOT "base"	Boolean operators allow the terms to be combined through logic operators, AND, +, OR, NOT, and -, as Boolean operators.
Grouping	{knowledge OR base} AND portal	Parentheses to group clauses to form sub queries.
Field Grouping	title:(+portal +"knowledge base")	Use parentheses to group multiple clauses to a single field.
Special Characters	+ - && | | ! ( ) { } [ ] ^ " ~ * ? : \	Escaping special characters is a part of the query syntax.

In the search input box of the search portlet, you would be able to leverage the preceding query syntax.

Look-ahead typing—auto complete

Look-ahead is a tool in algorithms for looking ahead a few more input items before making a cost-effective decision at one stage of the algorithm. In artificial intelligence, look-ahead is an important component of the combinatorial search that specifies, roughly, how deeply the graph representing the problem is explored. Look-ahead is also an important concept in parsers in compilers and establishes the maximum number of incoming input tokens the parser can look at to decide which rule it should use.

Look-ahead typing is very useful for searching assets by keywords. Moreover, it is nice that the system should remember the keywords that users input for the search. When users start typing, suggested keywords should be available.

For example, suppose that the users input a set of keywords to search the Knowledge Base article, such as, **liferay**, **life**, **live**, **look**, and **like**, and now they want to use these keywords in their keyword search. When a user types l, the system should list suggested keywords, such as, **liferay**, **life**, **live**, **look**, and **like**; when a user types li, the system should list the suggested keywords, such as, **liferay**, **life**, **live** and **like**.

The look-ahead typing should be everywhere in the portal. How to implement the same? In the following steps, you could build the look-ahead type feature everywhere in the portal and plugins:

1. Define the service XML and generate the related models and services via the service builder.

2. When a user enters a new keyword for search, if the search result is not empty, that keyword will be saved into the database. If the keyword exists (company-wise, group-wise, or asset-type-wise, through `classNameId`) in the database, then update the keyword modified date.

3. The suggested keywords will be retrieved from this table, ordered in descending order by the modified date. A number of keywords, such as 500 (configurable), will be retrieved.

Models and services

The service XML of the search keyword `SearchKeyword` could be defined as follows:

```
<!-- PK fields -->
  <column name="keywordId" type="long" primary="true" />
  <!-- Group instance -->
  <!-- Audit fields -->
  <!-- Other fields -->
```

```
<column name="classNameId" type="long" />
<column name="keyword" type="String" />
<!-- Order -->
<!-- Finder methods -->
```

The preceding code first defines a keyword ID, `keywordId`, for column as a primary key field. Then, it specifies a group instance by adding a column called `groupId`. Audited fields are added with a set of columns, such as `companyId`, `userId`, `userName`, `createDate`, and `modifiedDate`. Other fields include columns `classNameId` and `keyword`.

As you can see, the keywords can have different scopes: company-wise via the column `companyId`, group-wise via the column `groupId`, and asset-type-wise via the column `classNameId`, as shown in the following services:

```
public boolean updatekeyword(long companyId,
    long groupId, long classNameId, String keyword);
public List<String> getkeywords(long companyId,
    long groupId, long classNameId);
```

As shown in the preceding code, the keyword is saved by the primary key `keywordId` and a composed-key set (`companyId`, `groupId`, and `classNameId`). The keywords are retrieved by the composed-key set (`companyId`, `groupId`, and `classNameId`). If it was company-wise, ignore the inputs `groupId` and `classNameId`. If it was group-wise, ignore the input `classNameId`. Otherwise, it would be considered as asset-type-wise keywords.

In addition, it would be better to add the following properties to `portal.properties`:

```
look.ahead.typing.max.keywords=500
look.ahead.typing.scope.type=company
```

The property `look.ahead.typing.max.keywords` specifies the maximum number of look-ahead typing keywords, while the property `look.ahead.typing.scope.type` designates whether the look-ahead typing keyword scope type could be company, group, or asset-type.

AutoComplete

AutoComplete is effective when it is easy to predict the word being typed, based on those already typed, speeding up the human-computer interactions in environments to which it is well suited. The UI part will leverage the auto complete feature to implement the look-ahead typing function.

AUI (Alloy UI) provides a base class for `AutoComplete`, as follows: by widget lifecycle (for example, `initializer`, `renderUI`, `bindUI`, `syncUI`, and `destructor`), by presenting users' choices based on their input, by separating the selected items, and via keyboard interaction for the selected items.

```
var instance = new A.AutoComplete({
    dataSource: [
        ['liferay'],
        ['like']
    ],
    schema: {
        resultFields: ['key']
    },
    matchKey: 'key',
    delimChar: ',',
    typeAhead: true,
    contentBox: '#myAutoComplete'
}).render();
```

jQuery empowers `AutoComplete` as widgets, providing suggestions while you type into the field. `AutoComplete`, when added to an input field, enables the users to quickly find and select from a pre-populated list of values, such as `dataSource`, as they type, leveraging searching and filtering. **dataSource** is a simple JavaScript array, provided to the widget using the source option. Note that `AutoComplete` on jQuery is a part of the jQuery UI. `dataSource` is not limited to only JavaScript array, but it's possible to use the AJAX call `resultset` as `dataSource`. The following is some sample code:

```
$(function() {
    var dataSource = [
        "liferay",
        "like"
    ];
    $( #myAutoComplete" ).autocomplete({
        source: dataSource
    });
});
```

OpenSearch

OpenSearch is a collection of simple formats for the sharing of search results. The OpenSearch description document format can be used to describe a search engine, while the OpenSearch response elements can be used to extend the existing syndication formats, such as RSS and Atom, with the extra metadata needed to return the search results. Refer to http://www.opensearch.org, for more detailed information.

In brief, OpenSearch allows publishing the search results in a format suitable for syndication and aggregation. **Federated search** is a simultaneous search of multiple online databases or web resources, and it is an emerging feature of automated, web-based libraries and information retrieval systems. The portal implements federated search, based on the OpenSearch standard.

Interface and services

The portal provides the OpenSearch interface called com.liferay.portal. kernel.search.OpenSearch. The following are the methods defined in the interface OpenSearch:

```
public boolean isEnabled();
public String search(HttpServletRequest request,
    long groupId, long userId, String keywords,
    int startPage, int itemsPerPage, String format)
    throws SearchException;
```

The preceding code shows the interface OpenSearch. First, it specifies a method isEnabled to either enable or disable the OpenSearch capability. Then, it specifies three search methods with different parameters. Thus, we could use the search method either by the parameter URL or by parameters keywords, startPage, itemsPage, and format, based on different requirements.

As shown in the following table, the abstract class BaseOpenSearchImpl implements the interface OpenSearch, extended by the abstract class HitsOpenSearchImpl. The class DirectoryOpenSearchImpl goes further to extend the abstract class HitsOpenSearchImpl. For this reason, the Search portlet will include the search results from the portlet Directory.

Interface/ abstract class	Implementation/extension	Utility	Description
OpenSearch	BaseOpen SearchImpl	OpenSearch Util	Interface OpenSearch and its implementation
BaseOpen SearchImpl	PortalOpen SearchImpl; HitsOpen SearchImpl	none	Abstract class BaseOpen SearchImpl
HitsOpen SearchImpl	BlogsOpen SearchImpl, BookmarksOpen SearchImpl, CalendarOpen SearchImpl, DirectoryOpen SearchImpl, DLOpe nSearchImpl,Journ alOpenSearchImpl, MBOpenSearchImpl, WikiOpenSearchImpl	none	Abstract class HitsOpen SearchImpl and its implementations: Blogs, Bookmarks, Calendar, Directory, DL, Journal, MB, Wiki, and so on

Configuration

The portal provides many portlets to support the OpenSearch framework, such as, message boards, blogs, wikis, directory entries and document library documents, users, organizations, and so on. In addition, plugins such as the Knowledge Base portlet also support the OpenSearch framework. Normally, these portlets have the following OpenSearch framework configuration.

```
<open-search-class>class-name</open-search-class>
```

The Search portlet obtains an OpenSearch instance from each portlet that has the tag definition <open-search-class>. For example, the portlet Directory (portlet ID 11) allows users to search for other users, organizations, or user groups. The OpenSearch capability has been specified for the portlet Directory in the XML file $PORTAL_ SRC_HOME/portal-web/docroot/WEB-INF/liferay-portlet.xml, as follows:

```
<open-search-class>
com.liferay.portlet.directory.util.DirectoryOpenSearchImpl
</open-search-class>
```

As shown in the preceding code, the `open-search-class` value must be a class that implements `OpenSearch`, which is called to get the search results in the `OpenSearch` standard.

As mentioned previously, `OpenSearch` in the search portlet covers out-of-the-box portlets, such as, Blogs, Calendar, Bookmarks, Document Library, Message Boards, Wiki, Web Content, Directory, and so on. Fortunately, the portal adds the ability to remove these portlets from the list of portlets searched by the portlet `Search`, as follows:

```
com.liferay.portlet.blogs.util.BlogsOpenSearchImpl=true
# See details in portal.properties
com.liferay.portlet.wiki.util.WikiOpenSearchImpl=true
```

As shown in the preceding code, you can set any of the preceding properties to `false` to disable the portlet from being searched by the search portlet in `portal-ext.properties`.

What's happening?

In fact, the abstract class `BaseOpenSearchImpl` specifies the following code to read the properties, as mentioned previously. If the property is set to `false`, the portal will disable that portlet from being searched by the `Search` portlet.

```
// see details in BaseOpenSearchImpl.java
private boolean _enabled = GetterUtil.getBoolean(
    PropsUtil.get(getClass().getName()), true);
```

The `Search` portlet provides a federated search against both portal core portlets and custom plugins portlets. As shown in the following table, you will have the ability to specify the scope of search results, whether `Everything` or `This site`. `Everything` means search results will come from any groups in the current portal instance. `This site` means search results will come from the current group in the current portal instance.

Value	Group ID	UI Taglib	JSP sample
Everything	0	`<liferay-ui:search />`	`view.jsp, search.jsp`
This site	Current group ID	`<liferay-ui:search />`	`view.jsp, search.jsp`

Applying OpenSearch on plugin portlets

In general, the portal provides the OpenSearch framework, so that a user can create an OpenSearch implementation in the plugin environment. The portal will try to call this OpenSearch implementation when you hit the Search portlet. The Search portlet goes through all registered implementations and tries to create an instance.

For example, you could search for content in the Knowledge Base articles as well as the portal core portlets such as Blogs, Bookmarks, Calendar, Directory, and so on, via the OpenSearch framework in the portlet Search. How does it work? Eventually, you can apply OpenSearch on plugin portlets, as follows:

1. Create a class called AdminOpenSearchImpl, which extends the abstract class HitsOpenSearchImpl, and implements the interface OpenSearch indirectly:

```
public Indexer getIndexer() {
    return IndexerRegistryUtil.getIndexer(KBArticle.class);
// see details in AdminOpenSearchImpl.java
}
```

2. The preceding code is the snippet for the class AdminOpenSearchImpl. It defines constants such as SEARCH_PATH and TITLE, and a set of methods, such as, getIndexer, getURL, and so on.

3. Register OpenSearch implementation AdminOpenSearchImpl via the tag open-search-class in the file /WEB-INF/liferay-portlet.xml.

```
<open-search-class>
com.liferay.knowledgebase.admin.util.AdminOpenSearchImpl
</open-search-class>
```

As shown in the preceding code, the open-search-class value AdminOpenSearchImpl is a class that implements OpenSearch indirectly, called to get search results in the OpenSearch standard.

Workflow

A **workflow** consists of a sequence of connected steps. It is a depiction of a sequence of operations, declared as the work of a person, a group of persons, an organization of staff, or one or more simple or complex mechanisms. A workflow is a model to represent real work for further assessment, for example, for describing a reliably repeatable sequence of operations. More abstractly, a workflow is a pattern of activity enabled by a systematic organization of resources, defined roles and mass, energy and information flows, into a work process that can be documented and learned. Refer to Wikipedia for more details: http://en.wikipedia.org/wiki/Workflow.

While **Business Process Model and Notation (BPMN)**, developed by the **Object Management Group (OMG)**, provides a notation that is readily understandable by all business users, from the business analysts that create the initial drafts of the processes to the technical developers responsible for implementing the technology that will perform those processes, and finally, to the business people who will manage and monitor those processes. Thus, BPMN creates a standardized bridge for the gap between the business process design and process implementation. Refer to BPMN 2.0 at `http://www.omg.org/spec/BPMN/2.0/`.

The portal is able to integrate the workflow engines, such as jBPM, Kaleo, Activiti, Intalio (BPM) and to apply workflow on any assets. By this feature, users are able to manage the content creation process with a workflow. This feature especially helps the content creators collaborate and go through the necessary steps in order to produce better and more accurate content, say assets. Within a workflow, any type of asset, such as, document library documents, wiki entries, web content, blog entries, comments, and message board messages, can go through review-approval processes.

Liferay eats its own dog food. It uses its own products, such as hooks, webs, and services builder, to build the workflow engine Kaleo. Workflow-related portlets are My Submissions (portlet ID 158), My Workflow Tasks (portlet ID 153), Workflow Configuration (portlet ID 152), and Workflow Portlet (portlet ID 151). The workflow engine Kaleo is defined in the plugin `kaleo-web`.

Kaleo-web models

The portal has defined a set of entities in the plugin `kaleo-web`. These entities cover KaleoAction, KaleoCondition, KaleoDefinition, KaleoInstance, KaleoInstanceToken, KaleoLog, KaleoNode, KaleoNotification, KaleoNotificationRecipient, KaleoTask, KaleoTaskAssignment, KaleoTaskAssignmentInstance, KaleoTaskInstanceToken, KaleoTimer, KaleoTimerInstanceToken, and KaleoTransition. The following diagram depicts an overview of the workflow Kaleo models:

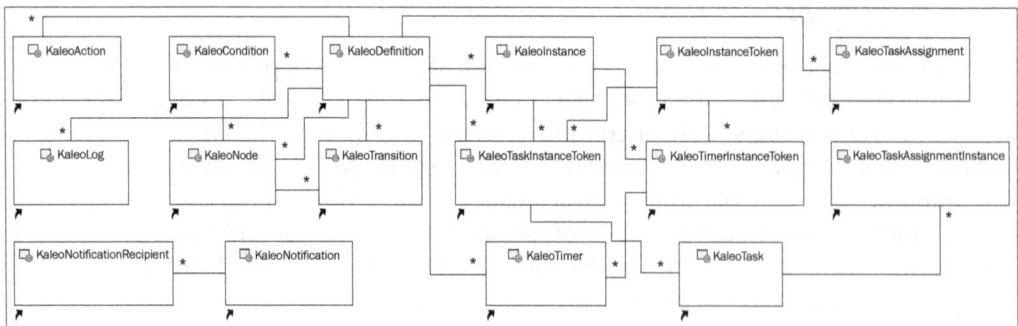

Obviously, these entities are defined in the XML file `svn://svn.liferay.com/repos/public/plugins/trunk/webs/kaleo-web/docroot/WEB-INF/service.xml`.

After using the service builder, a set of models and their implementations are generated. The following table shows these models and their implementations. The cache model class, implementing `CacheModel<Kaleo*>`, represents `Kaleo*` in entity cache.

Interface	Extension	Implementation	Wrapper/Clp/Soap
KaleoAction	KaleoActionModel, PersistedModel	KaleoAction BaseImpl extends KaleoAction ModelImpl KaleoAction CacheModel	KaleoActionWrapper, KaleoActionClp, KaleoActionSoap
Kaleo Condition	KaleoCondition Model, PersistedModel	KaleoCondition BaseImpl extends KaleoCondition ModelImpl KaleoCondition CacheModel	KaleoCondition Wrapper, KaleoConditionClp, KaleoConditionSoap
Kaleo Definition	KaleoDefinition Model, PersistedModel	KaleoDefinition BaseImpl extends KaleoDefinition ModelImpl, KaleoDefinition CacheModel	KaleoDefinition Wrapper, KaleoDefinitionClp, KaleoDefinitionSoap
Kaleo Instance	KaleoInstance Model, PersistedModel	KaleoInstance BaseImpl extends KaleoInstance ModelImpl, KaleoInstance CacheModel	KaleoInstance Wrapper, KaleoInstanceClp, KaleoInstanceSoap
KaleoLog	KaleoLogModel, PersistedModel	KaleoLog BaseImpl extends KaleoLog ModelImpl, KaleoLog CacheModel	KaleoLogWrapper, KaleoLogClp, KaleoLogSoap
KaleoNode	KaleoNodeModel, PersistedModel	KaleoNode BaseImpl extends KaleoNode ModelImpl, KaleoNode CacheModel	KaleoNodeWrapper, KaleoNodeClp, KaleoNodeSoap

Interface	Extension	Implementation	Wrapper/Clp/Soap
Kaleo Notification	Kaleo Notification Model, PersistedModel	KaleoNotification BaseImpl extends KaleoNotification ModelImpl, KaleoNotification CacheModel	KaleoNotification Wrapper, Kaleo NotificationClp, Kaleo NotificationSoap
KaleoTask	KaleoTaskModel, PersistedModel	KaleoTask BaseImpl extends KaleoTask ModelImpl, KaleoTask CacheModel	KaleoTask Wrapper, KaleoTaskClp, KaleoTaskSoap
KaleoTimer	KaleoTimerModel, PersistedModel	KaleoTimer BaseImpl extends KaleoTimer ModelImpl, KaleoTimer CacheModel	KaleoTimer Wrapper, KaleoTimerClp, KaleoTimerSoap
Kaleo Transition	KaleoTransition Model, PersistedModel	KaleoTransition BaseImpl extends KaleoTransition ModelImpl, KaleoTransition CacheModel	KaleoTransition Wrapper, KaleoTransition Clp, KaleoTransition Sopap

The portal adds a persist-related auditing interface class called `com.liferay.portal.model.PersistedModel`. The interface defines the following line, throwing `SystemException`, if a system exception occurrs:

```
public void persist() throws SystemException;
```

As shown in the preceding code, you should update this model instance in the database or add the same, if it doesn't yet exist. Also, you should notify the appropriate model listeners.

Kaleo-web services

The plugin `kaleo-web` uses Kaleo as the workflow engine. It provides the workflow services implementation, including deployer, comparators, parsers, and runtime services implementation.

The following table lists deployer, comparators, and parsers services, and their implementations:

Implementation	Interface/Abstract class	Involved models	Description
`DefaultWorkflow Deployer`	`Workflow Deployer`	`Condition, definition, Node, Task, Transition, KaleoDefinition, KaleoNode`	Default workflow deployer
`Workflow Comparator FactoryImpl`	`Workflow Comparator Factory`	`OrderByComparator Workflow Comparator FactoryUtil`	Workflow comparator
`Workflow Definition NameComparator`	`BaseWorkflow DefinitionName Comparator`	`Comparator`	Workflow definition name comparator
`Workflow Instance EndDate(State) Comparator`	`BaseWorkflow InstanceEndDate (State)Comparator`	`Comparator`	Workflow Instance End Date (or State) comparator
`WorkflowLog CreateDate (UserId) Comparator`	`BaseWorkflow LogCreateDate (UserId) Comparator`	`Comparator`	Workflow Log create date (or User ID) comparator
`WorkflowTask ompletionDate (CreateDate, DueDate, Name, UserId) Comparator`	`BaseWorkflow TaskCompletion Date(CreateDate, DueDate, Name, UserId)Comparator`	`Comparator`	Workflow task (Create Date, Due Date, Name, User ID) comparator
`DefaultWorkflow Validator`	`Workflow Validator`	`Definition`	Workflow validator
`XMLWorkflow ModelParser`	`Workflow ModelParser`	`Document, Element, Action, Condition, Definition, Fork, Join, Node, State, task, timer,` and so on.	Workflow model parser

The plugin `kaleo-web` also provides a workflow runtime implementation, as shown in the following table:

Class	Interface	Involved model	Description
`DefaultWorkflow EngineImpl`	`Workflow Engine`	`Workflow Definition; Workflow Instance;`	Workflow engine implementation
`Default KaleoSignaler`	`Kaleo Signaler`	`KaleoNode`	Kaleo workflow signaler
`DefaultTask ManagerImpl`	`TaskManager`	`WorkflowTask`	Workflow task manager
`DRLActionExecutor ScriptAction Executor Action ExecutorUtil`	`Action Executor`	`Fact, KaleoAction, Execution Context`	DRL and Script action executor
`BaseTask AssignmentSelector, CompositeTask AssignmentSelector, DefaultTask AssignmentSelector, GroupAwareRole TaskAssignment Selector, MultiLanguageTask AssignmentSelector, TaskAssignerUtil`	`Task Assignment Selector`	`KaleoTask Assignment; KaleoTask InstanceToken; ExecutionContext;`	Workflow assignment selector
`DefaultDueDate Calculator`	`DueDate Calculator`	`DelayDuration`	Workflow due-date calculator
`DRLCondition Evaluator Multi LanguageCondition Evaluator Scripting ConditionEvaluator`	`Condition Evaluator`	`KaleoCondition; Execution Context`	Workflow condition evaluator
`DefaultGraphWalker`	`GraphWalker`	`Kaleo, Execution Context`	Workflow graph walker
`PathElement MessageListener`	`Message Listener`	`Message, GraphWalker, PathElement`	Workflow path element message listener

Class	Interface	Involved model	Description
BaseNodeExecutor, ConditionNode Executor, ForkNodeExecutor, JoinNodeExecutor, StateNodeExecutor, TaskNodeExecutor	Node Executor	KaleoNode, Execution Context, PathElement	Workflow node executor, including Condition, Fork, Join, State, and Task
FreeMarker Notification MessageGenerator, TextNotification MessageGenerator, VelocityNotification MessageGenerator	Notification Message Generator	Execution Context	Workflow notification message generator
EmailNotification Sender, IMNotification Sender, PrivateNotification Sender, NotificationUtil	Notification Sender	Kaleo Notification Recipient; ExecutionContext	E-mail, IM, and private notification sender
TimerMessage Listener	Message Listener	Message, KaleoNode, Workflow engine	Workflow timer message listener

Custom SQL

The portal specifies the following custom SQL configurations in `portal.properties`:

```
custom.sql.configs=custom-sql/default.xml
```

As shown in the preceding code, you can provide a list of comma-delimited custom SQL configurations, in `portal-ext.properties`, as input.

The custom SQL scripts are provided at `/WEB-INF/src/custom-sql/default.xml`. Both service builder and `service.xml` will take care of the most basic needs in querying the database. The custom queries separate queries from the code—easy-to-find and easy-to-edit.

Obviously, you could override this XML file and add your own custom SQL to the plugins as well.

Hooks

The plugin `kaleo-web` defines two kinds of hooks — portal properties hook and service wrapper hook — in the XML file `/WEB-INF/liferay-hook.xml`:

```
<portal-properties>portal.properties</portal-properties>
<service>
    <service-type>
        com.liferay.portal.service.CompanyLocalService
    </service-type>
    <service-impl>
com.liferay.portal.workflow.kaleo.hook.service.impl.
CompanyLocalServiceImpl
    </service-impl>
</service>
```

As shown in the preceding code, the portal properties hook is specified with the tag `portal-properties`, and the service wrapper hook is defined with the tags `service`, `service-type`, and `service-impl`.

The portal properties hook overrides properties, such as, release info, upgrade process, and value object model, as shown in the following lines of code:

```
release.info.build.number=100
value.object.listener.com.liferay.portal.model.Company=com.liferay.
portal.workflow.kaleo.hook.listeners.CompanyModelListener
```

The following table shows a summary of these hooks:

Name	Interface / Abstract class	Implementation	Hook type
Service wrapper	`Company LocalService`	`CompanyLocal ServiceImpl`	Service wrapper
Release info	None	100, 0	Portal properties
Upgrade	`Upgrade Process`	`Upgrade Process_1_x_0`	Portal properties
Value object model	`BaseMode lListener <Company>`	`CompanyModel Listener`	Portal properties

Web

As a special web application, the plugin `kaleo-web` defines the portal context configuration in `web.xml`. To wire the XML files in a plugin from the portal's Spring, use `portalContextConfigLocation` as parameter name, while XML files `kaleo-spring.xml` and `messaging-spring.xml` are active as parameter value:

```
<context-param>
    <param-name>portalContextConfigLocation</param-name>
    <param-value>
    /WEB-INF/classes/META-INF/kaleo-spring.xml,
    /WEB-INF/classes/META-INF/messaging-spring.xml
    </param-value>
</context-param>
```

Spring beans and messaging

The following table displays a summary of Spring beans and messaging configuration. As you can see, there are a lot of general configuration files, such as `base-spring.xml`, `cluster-spring.xml`, and more. The plugin `kaleo-web` especially adds the special configuration files `kaleo-spring.xml` and `messaging-spring.xml`:

XML file	Folder	Sample bean	Description
base-spring.xml	/src/META-INF	ServiceMonitor Advice AsyncAdvice	Base Spring beans
cluster-spring.xml	/src/META-INF	ChainableMethod AdviceInjector	Cluster Spring beans
dynamic-data-source-spring.xml	/src/META-INF	DynamicDataSource TransactionInterceptor	Dynamic data source Spring beans
ext-spring.xml	/src/META-INF	bean(*TaskManager) || bean(*WorkflowEngine)	Extension of Spring beans
hibernate-spring.xml	/src/META-INF	PortletHibernate Configuration	Hibernate Spring beans
infrastructure-spring.xml	/src/META-INF	InfrastructureUtil	Infrastructure Spring beans
kaleo-spring.xml	/src/META-INF	WorkflowComparator FactoryUtil	Kaleo Sping beans

XML file	Folder	Sample bean	Description
messaging-spring.xml	/src/META-INF	ParallelDestination	Messaging Spring beans
portlet-hbm.xml	/src/META-INF	KaleoActionImpl	Portlet hibernate HBM file
portlet-model-hints.xml	/src/META-INF	KaleoAction	Portlet model hints
portlet-orm.xml	/src/META-INF	KaleoAction ModelImpl	Portlet ORM
portlet-spring.xml	/src/META-INF	KaleoActionLocal ServiceImpl, KaleoAction LocalServiceUtil	Portlet Spring beans
shard-data-source-spring.xml	/src/META-INF	ShardAdvice, ShardPersistence Advice	Sharding data source Spring beans

Portal workflow services

The portal itself is a workflow system, providing a set of workflow-related models and services. Furthermore, the workflow should work on an asset-permission basis. Therefore, the portal provides the workflow permission service in order to check workflow-related permissions.

Global models

The portal adds a workflow-related auditing interface class called com.liferay. portal.model.WorkflowedModel:

```
public int getStatus();
// see details in WorkflowedModel.java
public void setStatusDate(Date statusDate);
```

As you can see, the interface WorkflowedModel defines methods to get status, such as getStatus, isApproved, isDraft, isExpired, and isPending.

In fact, the workflow status could be any, approved, denied, draft, expired, inactive, incomplete, or pending, as shown in the constants class com.liferay. portal.kernel.workflow.WorkflowConstants:

```
public static final int STATUS_ANY = -1;
public static final int STATUS_APPROVED = 0;
// see details in WorkflowConstants.java
public static final int STATUS_PENDING = 1;
```

In addition, the portal defines models, such as `WorkflowDefinitionLink` and `WorkflowInstanceLink`. The following table shows an overview of these models:

Interface	Extension	Implementation	Wrapper/Soap
Workflow Definition Link	Workflow Instance LinkModel extends AttachedModel, BaseModel<Work flowInstanceLi nk>, GroupedModel, PersistedModel	WorkflowInstance LinkImpl extends WorkflowInstance LinkBaseImpl	Workflow Definition LinkWrapper, Workflow Definition LinkSoap
Workflow InstanceLink	Workflow Definition LinkModel extends AttachedModel, Ba seModel<Workflo wDefinitionLink >, GroupedModel, PersistedModel	WorkflowDefinition LinkImpl extends WorkflowDefinition LinkBaseImpl	Workflow Instance LinkWrapper, Workflow Instance LinkSoap

Global services

The portal provides a set of workflow-related services. The following table shows the workflow-related interface, their extensions and implementation, and utility classes:

Interface	Extension/Implementation	Utility	Description
Workflow Handler, Workflow Handler Registry	BaseWorkflow Handler, Workflow Handler RegistryImpl	Workflow Handler Registry Util	Interface Workflow handler and registry
Workflow Definition Workflow Definition Manager	DefaultWorkflow Definition, Workflow DefinitionManager ProxyBean	Workflow Definition ManagerUtil	Workflow definition and manager
Workflow Instance Workflow Instance Manager	Default Workflow Instance, Workflow InstanceManager ProxyBean	Workflow Instance ManagerUtil	Workflow instance and manager

Interface	Extension/Implementation	Utility	Description
`WorkflowLog` `Workflow` `LogManager`	`Default` `WorkflowLog,` `WorkflowLog` `ManagerProxyBean`	`WorkflowLog` `ManagerUtil`	Workflow Log and manager
`WorkflowTask` `Workflow` `TaskManager`	`DefaultWorkflow` `Task, WorkflowTask` `Manager` `ProxyBean, Workflow` `TaskAssignee`	`WorkflowTask` `ManagerUtil`	Workflow Task and manager
`Workflow` `EngineManager`	`Workflow` `EngineManager` `ProxyBean`	`WorkflowEngine` `ManagerUtil`	Workflow engine manager
`Workflow` `StatusManager`	`WorkflowStatus` `ManagerImpl` `WorkflowStatus` `ManagerProxyBean`	`WorkflowStatus` `ManagerUtil`	`Workflow` status manager

The portal especially defines a class related to `ThreadLocal`, called `WorkflowThreadLocal`, in the package `com.liferay.portal.kernel.workflow`. Besides this class, the portal defines a set of comparators (for example, `BaseWorkflowDefinitionNameComparator`, `BaseWorkflowInstanceEndDateComparator`, and so on) and listeners (for example, `DefaultWorkflowDestinationEventListener`, extending `BaseDestinationEventListener`, and implementing `DestinationEventListener`). These comparators are defined in a centralized way, in the package `com.liferay.portal.kernel.workflow.comparator`, while the listener is defined in the package `com.liferay.portal.kernel.workflow.messaging`.

Workflow permissions

The workflow permissions checker is defined in an interface called `WorkflowPermission`. As shown in the following code, the interface defines a method called `hasPermission`, with parameters `PermissionChecker`, `Long` `groupId`, `String className`, `Long classPK`, and `String actionId`:

```
public Boolean hasPermission(
    PermissionChecker permissionChecker, long groupId,
    String className, long classPK, String actionId);
```

The interface `WorkflowPermission` is implemented in the class `WorkflowPermissionImpl`, where you will be able to find out the detailed implementation. The utility class `WorkflowPermissionUtil` is available for end users to call services. For example, in order to check the workflow permission, you can call the following service:

```
Boolean hasPermission =
    WorkflowPermissionUtil.hasPermission(
    permissionChecker, groupId,
    className, classPK, actionId);
```

Workflow definition

The portal creates an XML schema (named `liferay-workflow-definition_6_1_0.xsd`) for the internal workflow engine. For more details on this XML schema, you can refer to the workflow definition XSD at `/definitions/liferay-workflow-definition_6_1_0.xsd`.

Workflow definition XSD

The XML schema XSD defines a set of complex types, elements, groups, and simple types. The following table shows an overview of these types, elements, and groups. It doesn't display the full list of all types, elements, and groups; instead, it tries to show the main items of the workflow XSD definition:

Name	Values	Type	Description
`abstract-timer-complex-type`	Name, description, delay, and recurrence	`complexType`	Abstract timer complex type
`abstract-workflow-node-complex-type`	Name and description	`complexType`	Abstract workflow node complex type
`action-complex-type`	Name, description, script, script-language, and priority	`complexType`	Action complex type
`condition, fork, join, state, task`	`abstract-workflow-node-complex-type`	`element`	Elements `condition`, `fork`, `join`, `state`, and `task`
`actions-group`	Action and notification	`group`	Group actions

Name	Values	Type	Description
assignments-group	Resource-actions, roles, scribed-assignment, and user	group	Group assignments
nodes-group	condition, fork, join, state, task	group	Group nodes
execution-type	onEntry, onExit	String, Enumeration	Execution type
notification-transport-type	email, im, private-message	String, Enumeration	Notification transport type
role-type	regular, organization, site	String, Enumeration	Role type
script-language-type	beanshell, drl, groovy, javascript, python, ruby	String, Enumeration	Script language type
task-execution-type	onAssignement, onEntry, onExit	String, Enumeration	Task execution type
template-language-type	fremarker, text, velocity	String	Template language type
timer-execution-type	onTimer	String	Timer execution type
time-scale-type	second, minute, hour, day, week, month, year	String, Enumeration	Type scale type

Kaleo workflow definition

The plugin `kaleo-web` defines a set of classes and interfaces to implement the workflow schema XSD. The following table shows the details of these classes and interfaces, where you would see how the plugin `kaleo-web` implements the workflow XSD definition:

Class	Interface/Extension	Type	Description
Action	ActionAware	none	Model Action
AddressRecipient, RoleRecipient, UserRecipient	Recipient	RecipientType	Model Recipient of address, role, and user

Class	Interface/Extension	Type	Description
`Resource Assignment, RoleAssignment, ScriptAssignment, UserAssignment`	`Assignment`	`AssignmentType, ScriptLanguage`	Model Assignment and its extensions
`Condition, Definition, Fork, Join, State, Task`	`Node` implements `ActionAware, Notification Aware`	`NodeType`	Model Node and its extensions
`DelayDuration`	none	`DurationScale`	Model delay duration
`Notification`	`Notification Aware`	`ExecutionType, TemplateLanguage`	Model notification
`Timer`	`ActionAware, Notification Aware`	none	Model Timer

Sample workflow

The plugin `kaleo-web` provides a few sample workflows, for example, `Category Specific Approval`, `Legal and Marketing Approval`, `Scripted Single Approver`, and `Single Approver`, as shown in the following table. Of course, you should be able to specify your own workflow, based on the preceding workflow definition.

Name	Tasks	Conditions	Description
Category-Specific Approval	update, content review, legal review, approve, and reject	Determine-branch, script language groovy, e-mail notification	A single approver can approve the workflow content. `category-specific-definitions.xml`
Legal and Marketing Approval	update, marketing review, legal review, and approve	Script language JavaScript, e-mail notification	Workflow assets must be approved first by Marketing and then by Legal. `legal-marketing-definitions.xml`

Name	Tasks	Conditions	Description
Scripted Single Approver	update and review, approve and reject	Script language groovy, e-mail notification	A single approver can approve the workflow content. `single-approver-definition-scripted-assignment.xml`
Single Approver	update, review, approve, and reject	E-mail notification	A single approver can approve the workflow content. `single-approver-definition.xml`

You can find more workflow samples at `/WEB-INF/src/META-INF/definitions`.

BPMN 2

Business Process Model and Notation (BPMN) is a graphical representation for specifying the business processes in a business process model. BPMN 2.0 contains several additional elements and new types of diagrams, especially for the improved modeling of processes that span several independent organizations. The workflow engine Kaleo should support BPMN 2.0.

In brief, BPMN provides businesses with the ability to understand their internal business procedures in a graphical notation, giving organizations the ability to communicate these procedures in a standard manner. Refer to its definition XML schema at `http://www.omg.org/spec/BPMN/2.0/PDF/` and `http://issues.liferay.com/browse/LPS-18980`.

Workflow designers

To facilitate use of the workflow engine Kaleo by non-developers, the portal must provide an easy-to-use graphical designer. The designer tool will enable the users to drag-and-drop the workflow components to form a process definition.

Workflow designer should leverage throughout the portal as the common UI for designing workflows support assets, such as, WCM content creation, approval and publishing, document workflows, workflow forms, and more. In general, the workflow designer, intended for a business user audience, should support drag-and-drop for workflow components.

This section will introduce a set of available workflow designers. Based on these workflow designers, the portal workflow designer should be able to provide support for BPMN 2.0. Currently, the Kaleo Workflow Designer is yet to be developed (refer to `http://issues.liferay.com/browse/LPS-13509`).

BPMN2 Visual Editor for Eclipse

BPMN2 Visual Editor for Eclipse is built on top of the Graphiti modeling framework and uses the BPMN2 EMF metamodel, behind the scenes. Refer to `https://github.com/imeikas/BPMN2-Editor-for-Eclipse`.

jBPM and Drools

Drools 5 has introduced the business logic integration platform, which provides a unified and integrated platform for rules, workflow, and event processing. Refer to `http://www.jboss.org/drools`.

jBPM 5, the de facto Java standard for workflows, is a flexible Business Process Management (BPM) suite, making the bridge between business analysts and developers. A business process allows us to model our business goals by describing the steps that need to be executed to achieve that goal and the order, using a flow chart. The core of jBPM 5 is a light-weight, extensible workflow engine, allowing us to execute business processes using the BPMN 2 specification. Refer to `http://www.jboss.org/jbpm`, for more details.

jBMP provides an Eclipse-based, and web-based, editor (that is, workflow designer) to support the graphical creation of business processes (such as drag-and-drop).

Activiti

Activiti is a light-weight workflow and BPM platform targeted at business people, developers, and system administrators. Its core is a super-fast and rock-solid BPMN 2 process engine for Java. Activiti runs on any Java application, on a server, on a cluster, or in the cloud. Refer to `http://www.activiti.org/`, for more details.

The **Activiti Modeler** is a web-based process editor that can be used to author the BPMN 2.0 process graphically in web browsers. The process files are stored by the server, a file system, so that they are easily accessible and can be imported without hassles into any Java IDE, while the **Activiti Eclipse Designer** can be used to graphically model, test, and deploy BPMN 2.0 processes.

Applying workflow to assets

The out-of-the-box workflow capability is applied, by default, to the portal core assets: blogs entries, comments, users, document library documents, layout revisions, DDL (Dynamic Data Lists) records, message board messages, web content, and wiki pages. Furthermore, the workflow is available for any custom assets such as Knowledge Base articles.

Portal core assets

The following table displays the out-of-the-box workflow capability of the portal core assets:

Workflow handler	Model	Interface/ Abstract class	Status columns	JSP files
LayoutRevision Workflow Handler	Layout Revision	BaseWorkflow Handler implements Workflow Handler	Status, by UserId, by UserName, Date	Not applicable
BlogsEntry Workflow Handler	Blogs Entry	BaseWorkflow Handler implements Workflow Handler	Status, by UserId, by UserName, Date	/blogs/view. jsp, edit_ entry.jsp
User Workflow Handler	User	BaseWorkflow Handler implements Workflow Handler	Status, by UserId, by UserName, Date	/users_admin/ view.jsp, edit_ user.jsp
DLFileEntry Workflow Handler	DLFile Entry	BaseWorkflow Handler implements Workflow Handler	Status, by UserId, by UserName, Date	/document_ library/view_ file_entry. jsp, edit_file_ entry.jsp
DDLRecord Workflow Handler	DDLRecord	BaseWorkflow Handler implements Workflow Handler	Status, by UserId, by UserName, Date	/dynamic_ data_lists/ view_record. jsp, edit_ record.jsp

Workflow handler	Model	Interface/ Abstract class	Status columns	JSP files
`JournalArticle Workflow Handler`	`Journal Article`	`BaseWorkflow Handler` implements `Workflow Handler`	`Status,` by `UserId,` by `UserName,` `Date`	`/journal/view_ article.jsp,` `edit_article. jsp, /article/ content.jsp`
`MBMessage Workflow Handler`	`MBMessage`	`BaseWorkflow Handler` implements `Workflow Handler`	`Status,` by `UserId,` by `UserName,` `Date`	`/message_ boards/ view.jsp,` `edit_message. jsp, edit_ discussion. jsp`
`WikiPage Workflow Handler`	`WikiPage`	`BaseWorkflow Handler` implements `Workflow Handler`	`Status,` by `UserId,` by `UserName,` `Date`	`/wiki/Edit_ page.jsp, View_ draft_page. jsp`

Plugin custom assets

This section will introduce how to add the workflow capability to any custom assets in plugins. Note that this can only be done for plugins using the service builder. Knowledge Base articles will be used as an example, one of the custom assets. The workflow can be added to custom assets in the following steps:

1. First of all, you should add the workflow instance link and its related columns and finder to `service.xml` (for example, knowledge base service XML `/knowledge-base-portlet/docroot/WEB-INF/service.xml`), as follows:

```
<column name="status" type="int" />
<column name="statusByUserId" type="long" />
<column name="statusByUserName" type="String" />
<column name="statusDate" type="Date" />
<reference package-path="com.liferay.portal"
    entity="WorkflowInstanceLink" />
```

As shown in the preceding code, the column element represents a column in the database; here, the four columns `status`, `statusByUserId`, `statusByUserName`, and `statusDate`, are required for the Knowledge Base workflow. The finder element represents a generated finder method; here, the method finder `R_S` is defined as `Collection` for return type with two columns, `resourcePrimkey` and `status`, where the reference element allows you to inject services from another `service.xml` within the same class loader. For example, if you inject the `WorkflowInstanceLink` entity, then you'll be able to reference the `WorkflowInstanceLink` service, from your service implementation, via the methods `getWorkflowInstanceLinkLocalService` and `get WorkflowInstanceLinkService`. You'll also be able to reference the `WorkflowInstanceLink` service, via the variables `workflowInstanceLinkLocalService` and `workflowInstanceLinkService`.

2. Add the workflow handler implementation.

   The portal provides pluggable workflow implementations, where developers can register their own workflow handler implementation for any entity they build. It will appear automatically in the workflow admin portlet so users can associate workflow entities with available permissions.

   To make this happen, we need to add a workflow handler to `$PLUGIN_SDK_HOME/knowledge-base-portlet/docroot/WEB-INF/liferay-portlet.xml`, as follows:

```
<workflow-handler>
com.liferay.knowledgebase.admin.workflow.ArticleWorkflowHandler
</workflow-handler>
```

   As shown in the preceding code, the workflow-handler value must be a class that implements `com.liferay.portal.kernel.workflow.BaseWorkflowHandler`, and it is called when the workflow is run. Of course, you need to specify `ArticleWorkflowHandler` under the package `com.liferay.knowledgebase.admin.workflow`. The following is the snippet:

```
public class ArticleWorkflowHandler
    extends BaseWorkflowHandler {
    public Article updateStatus( int status,
        Map<String, Serializable> workflowContext)
        {/* ignore details */};
}
```

   As you can see, `ArticleWorkflowHandler` extends `BaseWorkflowHandler` and overrides the methods `getClassName`, `getType`, `updateStatus`, and `getIconPath`.

3. Add the method `updateStatus`.

   As mentioned previously, we have added the method `updateStatus` in `ArticleWorkflowHandler`. It is time to provide implementation of the method `updateStatus` in the implementation class `ArticleLocalService-Impl`. The following is the sample code:

   ```
   public Article updateStatus(long userId, long resourcePrimKey,
       int status, ServiceContext serviceContext)
   {// see details in ArticleLocalServiceImpl.java
   }
   ```

   As shown in the preceding code, it first gets the latest article by `resourcePrimKey` and `WorkflowConstants.STATUS_ANY`. Then, it updates the article, based on the workflow status. Moreover, it updates article display order, asset tags and categories, social activities, indexer, attachments, subscriptions, and so on.

4. Last but not least, add the workflow-related AUI tags.

   First of all, add AUI input workflow action with the value `WorkflowConstants.ACTION_SAVE_DRAFT`.

   ```
   <aui:input name="workflowAction" type="hidden" value="<%=
   WorkflowConstants.ACTION_SAVE_DRAFT %>" />
   ```

   As shown in the preceding code, the default value of the AUI input `workflowAction` was set to `SAVE DRAFT`, with type hidden. That is, this AUI input is invisible to the end users.

   Afterwards, it would be better to add workflow messages by the UI tag `liferay-ui:message`, such as, `a-new-version-will-be-created-auto-matically-if-this-content-is-modified` for `WorkflowConstants.STA-TUS_APPROVED` and `there-is-a-publication-workflow-in-process` for `WorkflowConstants.STATUS_PENDING`.

   And then, add the AUI workflow status tag `aui:workflow-status` in `/admin/edit_article.jsp`. Finally, you should add JavaScript to implement the function `publishArticle`.

Summary

In this chapter, you learned how to leverage webs plugins and WAI, to build webs plugins, using cas-web and solr-web plugins as examples, to index and search assets (both portal core assets and plugins custom assets), to set up a solr-web plugin, to apply workflow to assets, and to employ the `kaleo-web` plugin.

In the next chapter, we're going to introduce WAP and portlets bridges.

10
Mobile Devices and Portlet Bridges

Websites or WAP sites are made up of many pages. Each page consists of a set of portlets with a specific look-and-feel, specified by themes. Moreover, all of the portlets in a page are arranged using layout templates. The websites could be viewed in Web or WAP browsers (mobile devices, such as Smartphones and tablets). The mobile device detectors provide mobile device support and detection within portal infrastructure.

Generally speaking, a theme is a user interface design that makes the portal more user-friendly and visually pleasing. The portal provides layout templates in order to describe how various columns and rows are arranged to display portlets. It also provides themes that can be used to customize the overall look-and-feel of websites, WAP sites, and pages. Basically, themes control the whole look-and-feel of the pages generated in the portal, using CSS, images, JavaScript, HTML tags, Velocity, and/or FreeMarker templates.

In addition, the portal provides a set of portlet bridges, such as, MVC, Struts, JSF, Spring MVC, and more, where diversities of portlet plugins could be built on top of these portlet bridges.

This chapter will first introduce layout template plugins and theme plugins. Then, it will address WAP mobile site-building. Portlet bridges will get introduced with different frameworks: Struts, JSF, and Spring MVC.

By the end of this chapter, you will have learned how to build:

- Layout template plugins
- Theme plugins
- WAP mobile themes and mobile device detectors
- Portlet bridges

- Struts 2 portlets
- JSF 2 portlets
- Spring 3 MVC portlets

Layout template plugins

As mentioned earlier, Liferay Plugins SDK provides a set of default templates, such as, **EAR, Ext, hook, layout template, portlet, theme**, and so on. The previous chapter has introduced portlet, ext, hook, and web projects templates. This section is going to introduce layout template project's default template. The theme project's default template will be introduced in the next section.

Layout template

Liferay Plugins SDK provides layout template project's default template. This default template has the following structure. The layout template project's folder name is represented as `@layouttpl.name@-layouttpl`. For example, `@layouttpl.name@` has the value `1-2-1-columns` for `1-2-1` layout templates. Under the folder `@layouttpl.name@-layouttpl`, there is a folder named `docroot` and an XML file called `build.xml`. As you can see, `build.xml` has the following code:

```
<!DOCTYPE project>
    <project name="@layouttpl.name@-layouttpl"
        basedir="." default="deploy">
    <import file="../build-common-layouttpl.xml" />
</project>
```

As shown in the code, `@layouttpl.name@` represents a real layout template name. When using Ant target `create`, it will create a new layout template project. Under the folder `docroot`, it includes a thumbnail file `blank_columns.png`, a web browser template file `blank_columns.tpl`, a WAP browser template file `blank_columns.wap.tpl`, and the `WEB-INF` folder.

The subfolder `WEB-INF` especially covers XML files, such as, `liferay-plugin-package.properties` and `liferay-layout-templates.xml`. Inside these XML files, you would have noticed that template variables `@layouttpl.template.name@` and `@layouttpl.template.name@` are in use. For instance, the content of the XML file `liferay-layout-templates.xml` is listed as follows:

```
<layout-templates>
    <custom>
        <layout-template id="@layouttpl.template.name@" name="@
layouttpl.display.name@">
```

```
<template-path>/@layouttpl.template.name@.tpl</template-path>
<wap-template-path>/@layouttpl.template.name@.wap.tpl</wap-
template-path>
</custom>
</layout-templates>
```

This code shows registration of the product-home layout template under the custom XML tag, with id as `@layouttpl.template.name@`, name as `@layouttpl.display. name@`, template-path as `/@layouttpl.template.name@.tpl`, wap-template-path as `/@layouttpl.template.name@.wap.tpl`, and thumbnail-path as `/@layouttpl. template.name@.png`.

Layout template DTD

As you can see, there are at least two kinds of XML files that are involved: `liferay-layout-templates.xml` and `liferay-plugin-package.xml`. The DTDs of these XML files are defined as at `$PORTAL-SRC_HOME/definitions`: `liferay-layout-templates_6_1_0.dtd` and `liferay-plugin-package_6_1_0.dtd`.

The layout template XSD is the XML Schema for layout templates deployment descriptor. The `layout-templates` element is the root of the deployment descriptor for Liferay layout templates. It can have zero or one `standard` and `custom` values. The `layout-templates` element contains the declarative data of a portlet, as follows:

```
<!ELEMENT layout-templates (standard?, custom?)>
<!ELEMENT standard (layout-template*)>
<!ELEMENT custom (layout-template*)>
<!ELEMENT layout-template (template-path, wap-template-path,
    thumbnail-path?, roles?)>
<!ELEMENT roles (role-name)>
```

The * sign, in this example, declares that the child element `layout-template` can occur zero or more times inside the `custom` and `standard` elements. The `layout-template` element has many child elements, such as, `template-path`, `wap-template-path`, `thumbnail-path`, and `roles`. As you can see, the `template-path` and `wap-template-path` elements can occur only one time, forming the key of the layout template for WEB and WAP, respectively, while the `thumbnail-path` and `roles` elements can occur zero or one time inside the element `layout-template`.

The `roles` element contains a list of role names. Users who have any of these roles will be able to use this layout template for their layouts. Anyone can use this layout template if no role names are set. `role-name` designates the name of a security role.

Sample layout template

Optionally, you could run a script to create a blank layout template project (of course, you can use **Liferay IDE** to build it). For example, for the preceding project, we have a project named `3-2-3-columns` and layout template display named `3-2-3 columns`. On Linux or Mac, you would change the directory to `$PLUGINS_SDK_HOME/layouttpl` and then type the following command:

```
./create.sh 3-2-3-columns "3-2-3 Columns"
```

On Windows, you would change the directory to `$PLUGINS_SDK_HOME/layouttp` and then type the following command:

```
create.bat 3-2-3-columns "3-2-3 Columns"
```

This command will create a blank layout template in the folder `$PLUGINS_SDK_HOME/layouttpl`. In fact, the script uses default template to create a blank layout template with the following Ant command:

```
ant -Dlayouttpl.name=$1 -Dlayouttpl.display.name=\"$2\" create
```

The portal has defined default standard layout templates. The following table shows a summary of these layout templates. Obviously, you can use these layout templates as references.

Name	Type	Files and Icons	Description
pop up	standard	`pop_up.png`, `pop_up.tpl`, `pop_up.wap.tpl`	Popup layout template
max	standard	`max.png`, `max.tpl`, `max.wap.tpl`	Maximized layout template
exclusive	standard	`exclusive.png`, `exclusive.tpl`, `exclusive.wap.tpl`	Exclusive layout template

Although you can define custom layout templates in plugins, the portal also defined a set of custom layout templates as default. The following table shows a summary of these layout templates:

Name	Type	Files and Icons	Description
Free form	custom	`freeform.png`, `freeform.tpl`, `freeform.wap.tpl`	Free form layout template
3 columns	custom	`3_columns.png`, `3_columns.tpl`, `3_columns.wap.tpl`	3 columns (1/3:1/3:1/3) layout template

Name	Type	Files and Icons	Description
2 columns	custom	`2_columns_i(or ii or iii).png`, `2_columns_i(or ii or iii).tpl`, `2_columns_i(or ii or iii).wap.tpl`	2 columns (alternatives – 50%:50%; 30%:70%; 70%:30%) layout template
2-2 columns	custom	`2_2_columns.png`, `2_2_columns.tpl`, `2_2_columns.wap.tpl`	2-2 columns (70%:30%, 30%:70%) layout template
1-2 columns	custom	`1_2_columns_i(or ii).png`, `1_2_columns_i(or ii).tpl`, `1_2_columns_i(or ii).wap.tpl`	1-2 columns (alternatives – 100%, 30%:70%; 100%, 70%:30%) layout template
1-2-1 columns	custom	`1_2_1_columns.png`, `1_2_1_columns.tpl`, `1_2_1_columns.wap.tpl`	1-2-1 columns (100%, 50%:50%, 100%) layout template

Layout template services

The portal provided the interface `LayoutTemplate`, extending `Comparable<LayoutTemplate>`, `Plugin`, and `Serializable`. It is implemented by the class `LayoutTemplateImpl` extending the class `PluginBaseImpl`. The following is the code snippet of the interface `LayoutTemplate`:

```
public String getLayoutTemplateId();
// see details in LayoutTemplate.java
public List<String> getColumns();
```

Of course, you would be able to leverage the service class `LayoutTemplateLocalService` and the utility class `LayoutTemplateLocalServiceUtil`.

As mentioned earlier, there are two kinds of layout templates: `custom` and `standard`. These layout templates got defined in the constants class `LayoutTemplateConstants`.

Theme plugins

We have discussed the layout template plugins in the previous section. This section is going to address theme plugins.

Theme default template

Liferay Plugins SDK provides theme project's default template. This default template has the following structure. The theme project folder name is represented as `@theme.name@-theme`. For example, `@theme.name@` has value so for `social office` theme. Under the folder `@theme.name@-theme`, there is a folder named `docroot` and an XML file called `build.xml`. As you can see, `build.xml` contains the following code:

```
<project name="@theme.name@-theme" basedir="." default="deploy">
    <import file="../build-common-theme.xml" />
    <property name="theme.parent" value="_styled" />
</project>
```

This means that when your newly created theme is built, it will copy all the files from the `_styled` folder in the `${PORTAL_SRC_HOME}/html/themes/` directory, to the `docroot` folder of your theme. The default `_styled` folder doesn't have enough files to create a completely working theme, and that is why you would see a messed-up page when the theme is applied to a page. The reason why this default `_styled` folder doesn't include enough files is that some Liferay users prefer to have a minimal set of files to start with.

As shown in the preceding code, `@theme.name@` represents a real theme name. When using Ant target `create`, it will create a new layout template project with a specific theme name and project title as parameters.

You can modify the `build.xml` file for your theme in the `${PLUGINS_SDK_HOME}/themes/@theme.name@-theme/` folder, by changing the value of the `theme.parent` property from `_styled` to `classic`, if you prefer to use the **Classic theme** as the basis for your theme modification:

```
<property name="theme.parent" value="classic" />
```

The folder `docroot` includes folders `WEB-INF` and `_diff`.

Default themes

The portal has defined default themes: _styled, _unstyled, classic, and control_panel, as shown in the following table:

Name	location	Folders	Files
_styled	/portal-web/ docroot/html/ themes/_styled	css; images	application.css, base.css, custom.css, dockbar.css, extra.css, forms.css, layout.css, main.css, navigation. css, portlet.css. screenshot.png
_unstyled	/portal-web/ docroot/html/ themes/_ unstyled	css; images (and sub folders); js; templates	application.css, and so on. favicon.ico, /add_ content/portlet_item. png, and so on. main.js; portal_normal.vm (ftl)
classic	/portal-web/ docroot/html/ themes/_classic	_diff/css; _ diff/images; _diff/ js; _diff/ templates	custom.css, and so on. screenshot.png, and so on. main.js; portal_ normal.vm (ftl)
control_panel	/portal-web/ docroot/html/ themes/control_ panel	_diff/css; _ diff/images; _diff/ js; _diff/ templates	custom.css, and so on. screenshot.png, and so on. main.js; portal_ normal.vm

Building themes

As much as we can say, the best practice of building a customized theme is to put only the differences of customized themes into the ${theme-name}/docroot/_diffs folder. Here, ${theme-name} refers to any theme project name, for example, so-theme. Using the best practice, we need to put customized CSS, images, JavaScript, and templates in the /_diffs folder only.

In the /_diffs/css folder, create a CSS file custom.css. We should place all of the CSS that is different from the other files. By placing custom CSS in this file, and not touching the other files, we can be assured that the upgrading of their theme, later on, will be much smoother. In the /_diffs/images folder, put all customized images with subfolders. For example, create at least two images — screenshot. png and thumbnail.png — to show what a page with the current theme looks like. Further, create a subfolder searchbar, and put all search-related images in a folder called /searchbar.

Create a JavaScript file main.js in the folder /_diffs/javascript. The portal includes the Alloy UI JavaScript library. Thus, we can include any plugin (note that plugin here refers to Alloy UI plugins or YUI plugins) that Alloy UI supports in the theme. In the /_diffs/templates folder, create customized template files such as, init_custom.vm (.ftl), navigation.vm (.ftl), portal_normal.vm (.ftl), portal_pop_up.vm (.ftl), and portlet.vm (.ftl).

look-and-feel DTD

For a specific theme plugin such as so-theme, there are at least two kinds of files in the folder /docroot/WEB-INF/, they are liferay-look-and-feel.xml and liferay-plugin-package.properties. The DTD of the XML file is defined as at /definitions/liferay-look-and-feel_6_1_0.dtd.

The look-and-feel element is the root of the deployment descriptor for a Liferay look-and-feel archive. The **look-and-feel archive** will hereafter be referred to as an **LAF** archive:

```
<!ELEMENT look-and-feel (compatibility, company-limit?, group-limit?,
theme*)>
```

The compatibility element specifies a list of Liferay Portal versions that will properly deploy the themes in this LAF archive:

```
<!ELEMENT compatibility (version+)>
```

The version element specifies a specific Liferay Portal version number. For example, if its value is 6.1.x, that means the themes in this LAF archive will deploy correctly in Liferay Portal 6.1.x. The portal will not deploy themes from an LAF archive, unless the version numbers match.

The company-limit element specifies a list of company IDs that can access the themes in this LAF archive. If company-limit is not set, then every company in the portal has access to all of the themes in this LAF archive. If company-limit is set, then the company IDs will be included or excluded, based on the company-includes and company-excludes elements. Note that if there is a disagreement between company-includes and company-excludes, company-excludes will take precedence:

```
<!ELEMENT company-limit (
    company-includes?, company-excludes?)>
<!ELEMENT company-includes (company-id*)>
<!ELEMENT company-excludes (company-id*)>
```

The company-includes element specifies a list of company IDs that will have access to the themes in this LAF archive. The company-excludes element specifies a list of company IDs that will not have access to the themes in this LAF archive.

The company-id element must have either the name or pattern attributes specified. If the name attribute is specified, then the exact company ID is either included or excluded, depending on whether the company-id element is inside the company-includes element or the company-excludes element. If the pattern attribute is specified, then a regular expression match is applied to the pattern, which will determine whether a company ID is included or excluded.

The group-limit element specifies a list of group IDs that can access the themes in this LAF archive. If group-limit is not set, then every group in the portal has access to all of the themes in this LAF archive. If group-limit is set, then the group IDs will be included or excluded based on the group-includes and group-excludes elements. If there is a disagreement between group-includes and group-excludes, group-excludes takes precedence:

```
<!ELEMENT group-limit (group-includes?, group-excludes?)>
<!ELEMENT group-includes (group-id*)>
<!ELEMENT group-excludes (group-id*)>
```

The group-includes element specifies a list of group IDs that will have access to the themes in this LAF archive. The group-excludes element specifies a list of group IDs that will not have access to the themes in this LAF archive.

The group-id element must have either the name or pattern attributes specified. If the name attribute is specified, then the exact group ID is either included or excluded, depending on whether the group-id element is inside the group-includes element or the group-excludes element. If the pattern attribute is specified, then a regular expression match is applied to the pattern, which will determine whether a group ID is included or excluded.

The theme element contains the declarative data of a theme.

```
<!ELEMENT theme (root-path?, templates-path?, css-path?, images-path?,
javascript-path?, virtual-path?, template-extension?, settings?, wap-
theme?, roles?, color-scheme*, layout-templates?)>
```

As shown in the following declaration, the id attribute specifies the unique key for a theme. For convenience, the id attribute can be referenced in the rest of the theme element as ${theme-id}. The name attribute specifies the friendly name of a theme that is displayed to the user:

```
<!ATTLIST theme
    id CDATA #REQUIRED
    name CDATA #REQUIRED
>
```

As shown in the theme element definition, the root-path value sets the location of the root path for the theme. For example, the root path for the Classic theme is /html/themes/classic. This means you can find the files for the Classic theme in /docroot/html/themes/classic. For convenience, the root-path attribute can be referenced in the rest of the theme element as ${root-path}. The default value is "/".

The templates-path value sets the location of the templates path for the theme. For example, the templates path for the Classic theme is /html/themes/classic/templates. This means you can find the FTL or VM templates for the Classic theme in /docroot/html/themes/classic/templates. For convenience, the templates-path attribute can be referenced in the rest of the theme element as ${templates-path}. The default value is ${root-path}/templates.

The images-path value sets the location of the images path for the theme. For example, the images path for the Classic theme is /html/themes/classic/images. This means you can find images for the Classic theme in /docroot/html/themes/classic/images. For convenience, the images-path attribute can be referenced in the rest of the theme element as ${images-path}. The default value is ${root-path}/images.

Meanwhile, the javascript-path value sets the location of the JavaScript path for the theme. For example, the JavaScript path for the Classic theme is /html/themes/classic/js. This means you can find JavaScript for the Classic theme in /docroot/html/themes/classic/js. For convenience, the javascript-path attribute can be referenced in the rest of the theme element as ${javascript-path}. The default value is ${root-path}/js.

The virtual-path value sets the virtual path used to fetch the CSS, images, and JavaScript files. By default, the portal returns the theme's servlet path. This setting allows you to override it. The default value is empty, which means this is not used.

You could set the `wap-theme` value to `true`, if the theme is designed for cellular phones or other mobile devices such as smartphones. The default value is `false`.

The `roles` element contains a list of role names. Users who have any of these roles will be able to use this theme for their layouts and layout sets. Anyone can use this theme, if no role names are set.

A theme can have many `color` schemes. Each color scheme references a `css` class name and defines an image path for the location of the color scheme's images:

```
<!ELEMENT color-scheme (default-cs?, css-class, color-scheme-images-
path?)>
```

The `id` attribute specifies the key for a color scheme that is unique for its parent theme. For convenience, the `id` attribute can be referenced in the rest of the `color-scheme` element as `${color-scheme-id}`. The `name` attribute specifies the friendly name of a color scheme that is displayed to the user:

```
<!ATTLIST color-scheme
    id CDATA #REQUIRED
    name CDATA #REQUIRED
>
```

You may set the `default-css` value to `true` if this is the default color scheme. The default value is `false`. The `css-class` value is a CSS class name that represents the color scheme. For convenience, the `css-class` attribute can be referenced in the rest of the `color-scheme` element as `${css-class}`.

The `color-scheme-images-path` value sets the location of the images path for the color scheme. For convenience, the `color-scheme-images-path` attribute can be referenced in the rest of the theme element as `${color-scheme-images-path}`. The default value is `${root-path}/images/color_schemes/${css-class}`.

What's happening after deploying themes?

In general, when you double-click on the Ant target `deploy`, under the theme of the Ant view, it will first copy all of the files from the folder `${app.server.portal.dir}/html/themes/_unstyled/` to the folder `$PLUGINS_SDK_HOME/themes/${theme.name}/docroot/`. Then, it will copy all of the files from the folder `${app. server.portal.dir}/html/themes/_styled/` to the folder `${theme.name}/docroot/`, too. Afterwards, it will copy all of the files from the folder `${theme.name}/docroot/_diffs/` to the folder `${theme.name}/docroot/`. It means that you will place all of your new and changed files into the folder `${theme.name}/docroot`. Here, `${theme.name}` refers to a real theme project name, for example, `so-theme`.

Afterwards, you will see folders css, images, js, and templates, under the folder ${theme.name}/docroot. Each of these folders will contain all merged files and subfolders from folders _unstyled, _styled, and _diffs. As mentioned earlier, the theme.parent property is specified with the _styled value in the ${theme.name}/ build.xml file. Of course, you can configure this property with the _unstyled value or the classic value. Fortunately, you can find details from the XML file build-common-theme.xml, as follows:

```
<if>
   <equals arg1="${theme.parent}" arg2="_unstyled" />
   <then>
      <copy todir="docroot" overwrite="true">
         <fileset dir="${app.server.portal.dir}/
            html/themes/_unstyled"
            excludes="templates/**"/>
      </copy>
         <!- see details in build-common-theme.xml -->
</elseif>
```

This code shows the process to deploy themes. For _unstyled, it just copies all files from the theme _unstyled to the folder /docroot. For _styled, it first copies all of the files from the theme _unstyled to the folder /docroot, and then it copies all of the files from the theme _styled to the folder /docroot and overwrites all the changes under the folder /docroot from the folder _styled.

Theme services

Similar to the interface LayoutTemplate, the portal provided the interface Theme, extending Comparable<Theme>, Plugin, and Serializable. It is implemented by the class ThemeImpl extending the class PluginBaseImpl. The following is a code snippet from the Theme interface:

```
public List<ColorScheme> getColorSchemes();
// see details in theme.javapublic String getName
```

Obviously, you would be able to leverage the service classes ThemeLocalService and ThemeService, and the utility classes ThemeLocalServiceUtil and ThemeServiceUtil. The following table shows these services, utilities, and interfaces:

Interface	Utility/Wrapper	Implementation	Main methods
Theme	None	ThemeImpl extends PluginBaseImpl	get*, has*, is*, resourceExists, set*
ThemeSetting	None	ThemeSettingImpl	get*, is*, set*

Interface	Utility/Wrapper	Implementation	Main methods

`Theme(Local)`
`Service`
	`Theme(Local)`
	`ServiceUtil`
	
	`Theme(Local)`
	`ServiceWrapper`
		`Theme(Local)`
		`ServiceImpl`
		`extends`
		`Theme(Local)`
		`ServiceBaseImpl`
			`getThemes,`
			`getWARThemes`

`Action`	None	`ThemeService` `PreAction`	`run, servicePre`

In addition, the portal provides a set of classes to display the theme in the package `com.liferay.portal.theme`, such as, `NaItem`, `PortletDisplay`, `ThemeDisplay`, and so on. The following table lists these classes and their involved models:

Class name	Interface	Involved models	Description
`NavItem`	`Serializable`	`RequestVars, Layout,` `List<NavItem>`	Layout navigation items in the theme
`PortletDisplay`	`Serializable`	`Writer,` `PortletPreferences`	Portlet display in the theme
`ThemeCompanyId`	`Serializable`	`String _value,` `boolean _pattern;`	Company ID in the theme

`ThemeCompany`
`Limit`
	`Serializable`	`List<ThemeCompanyId>`
		`_includes,`
		
		`List<ThemeCompanyId>`
		`_excludes;`
			Company limit in the theme

`ThemeGroupId`	`Serializable`	`String _value,` `boolean _pattern;`	Group ID in the theme

`ThemeGroup`
`Limit`
	`Serializable`	`List<Theme`
		`GroupId> _includes,`
		
		`List<ThemeGroupId>`
		`_excludes;`
			Group limit in the theme

`ThemeDisplay`	`Serializable`	`Account, ColorScheme,`
		`Company, Contact,`
		`Group, Layout,`
		`LayoutSet,`
		`LayoutTypePortlet,`
		`Theme, ThemeSetting,`
		`User;`
			Theme display

Theme factories

The portal implemented a set of theme-related factories, such as, `PortletDisplayFactory`, `ThemeDisplayFactory`, and `ThemeLoaderFactory`, as shown in the following table:

Factory	Model	Involved models	Description
PortletDisplay Factory	PortletDisplay	None	Portlet display factory
ThemeDisplay Factory	ThemeDisplay	None	Theme display factory
ThemeLoader Factory	ThemeLoader	ServletContext, ServletContextPool	Theme loader factory

Template engines

The portal integrated template engines **Apache Velocity** and **FreeMarker**, by default. FreeMarker is a Java-based template engine for servlet-based web application development and any other kind of text output, such as generating CSS, Java source code, and so on. Unlike JSP, it isn't dependent on the servlet architecture or on HTTP. Refer to `http://freemarker.org/`.

The portal has specified the following properties for the FreeMarker template engine in `portal.properties`:

```
freemarker.engine.cache.storage=
    com.liferay.portal.freemarker.LiferayCacheStoragefreemarker.engine.
macro.library=FTL_liferay.ftl as Liferay
```

As shown in the code, the portal provided the abstract class `com.liferay.portal.freemarker.FreeMarkerTemplateLoader` and its extension classes `ServletTemplateLoader` and `ThemeLoaderTemplateLoader`, extending `URLTemplateLoader` and `JournalTemplateLoader`. The following table shows details of these classes:

Abstract class/Interface	Abstract class/Utility	Extension/ Implementation	Description
FreeMarker TemplateLoader	URLTemplate Loader	JournalTemplate Loader	FreeMarker template loader
	LiferayTemplate Source	ServletTemplate Loader	
	URLTemplate Source	ThemeLoader TemplateLoader	

Abstract class/Interface	Abstract class/Utility	Extension/ Implementation	Description
Concurrent CacheStorage	None	LiferayCache Storage	Liferay cache storage
TemplateLoader	None	StringTemplate Loader	String template loader
SimpleHash	None	LiferayTemplate Model	Liferay template model
DefaultObject Wrapper	None	LiferayObject Wrapper	Liferay object wrapper
Configuration DefaultObject Wrapper Template;	FreeMarkUtil	None	FreeMarker Utility

As you can see, the template loader could be used in different domains: `servlet`, `Journal`, and `theme loader`.

Apache Velocity is a Java-based template engine, providing a simple yet powerful template language to reference objects defined in Java code. It permits anyone to use template language to reference objects defined in Java code. Refer to `http://velocity.apache.org/`.

The portal has specified the following properties for the Apache Velocity template engine in `portal.properties`:

```
velocity.engine.resource.listeners=com.liferay.portal.velocity.
ServletVelocityResourceListenervelocity.engine.logger.category=org.
apache.velocity
```

As shown in the code, you can set the Velocity resource managers. The portal extends the Velocity's default resource managers for better scalability. Note that the modification check interval is not respected because the resource loader implementation does not know the last modified date of a resource. This means you will need to turn off caching if you want to be able to modify VM templates in themes and see the changes right away.

In addition, the portal provided the abstract class `classcom.liferay.` `util.velocity.VelocityResourceListener` and its extension classes `ClassLoaderVelocityResourceListener`, `ServletVelocityResourceListener`, `ThemeLoaderTemplateLoader`, and `JournalTemplateVelocityResourceListener`, as shown the following table. These classes will run in sequence to allow you to find the applicable `ResourceLoader` to load a Velocity template. The following table lists a summary of these classes:

Abstract class/Interface	Abstract class/Utility	Extension/ Implementation	Description
StringResource Repository	Serializable StringResource	StringResource RepositoryImpl	Velocity String resource repository
ResourceManager Impl	LiferayResource Manager	None	Liferay Velocity resource manager
ResourceCache	LiferayResource CacheUtil	LiferayResource Cache	Liferay Velocity resource cache
VelocityPortlet	GenericPortlet	None	Velocity Portlet
ResourceLoader, ServiceLocator	None	LiferayResource Loader	Velocity Resource
VelocityResource Listener	None	ClassLoader VelocityResource Listener, JournalTemplate VelocityResource Listener, ServletVelocity ResourceListener, ThemeLoader VelocityResource Listener	Velocity Resource Listener
PortletPreferences	VelocityPortlet Preferences	None	Velocity Portlet Preferences
Velocity	VelocityUtil	UtilLocator	Velocity Utility

As you can see, the template loader could be used in different domains: `class loader`, `servlet`, `Journal template`, and `theme loader`.

Template engine services

The portal defines Velocity engine interfaces `VelocityEngine`, `VelocityContext`, and `VelocityVariables`, as shown in the following table:

Interface	Utility/Extension	Implementation	Main methods
Velocity Engine	Velocity EngineUtil	Velocity EngineImpl	get*, init, mergeTemplate, flushTemplate
Velocity Context	Template Context	Velocity ContextImpl	get, put
Velocity Variables	Velocity VariablesUtil	Velocity VariablesImpl	insertHelperUtilities, insertVariables

Similarly, the portal defined Velocity engine interfaces `FreeMarkerEngine`, `FreeMarkerContext`, and `FreeMarkerVariables`, as shown in the following table:

Interface	Utility/Extension	Implementation	Main methods
FreeMarker Engine	FreeMarker EngineUtil	FreeMarker EngineImpl	get*, init, merge*, resourceExists
FreeMarker Context	Template Context	FreeMarker ContextImpl	get, put
FreeMarker Variables	FreeMarker VariablesUtil	FreeMarker VariablesImpl	insertHelperUtilities, insertVariables

Template services

The portal provides template parser interface and implementation. The following table shows the template parser, transformer interface, and transformer listeners:

Interface	Utility/Abstract class	Implementation	Description
Template Parser	BaseTemplate Parser	VelocityTemplate Parser	Template parser interface and its implementation
Transformer	BaseTransformer	DDLTransformer Journal Transformer	Transformer interface and its implementation

Interface	Utility/Abstract class	Implementation	Description
Transformer Listener	BaseTransformer Listener	ContentTransformer Listener; LocaleTransformer Listener; RegexTransformer Listener; TokensTransformer Listener; ViewCounter TransformerListener	Transformer listener and its implementation

Template variables

The portal provides template files to control the look-and-feel of websites. These templates include both **VM** (Velocity) format and **FTL** (FreeMarker) format, such as, init, init_custom, navigation, portal_normal, portal_pop_up, and portlet. The following table shows a summary of these template files:

Template file	VM	FTL	Variables
init_custom	init_custom. vm	init_custom. ftl	This file allows you to override and define new FreeMarker/Velocity variables
init	init.vm	init.ftl	Common variables: theme, theme_display, theme_ settings, and so on
navigation	navigation. vm	navigation. ftl	Variables in Navigation: nav_ items, nav_item
portal_ normal	portal_ normal.vm	portal_ normal.ftl	Variables in the portal normal: theme, theme_display, theme_ settings, and so on
portal_pop_ up	portal_pop_ up.vm	portal_pop_ up.ftl	Variables in the portal pop up: theme
portlet	portlet.vm	portlet.ftl	Variables in the portlet: theme, portlet_display

Where are these variables declared? Eventually, these variables got defined in the classes `VelocityVariablesImpl` and `FreeMarkerVariablesImpl`, as shown in the following table:

Methods	Classes	Variables	Mapped classes
`insertHelper Utilities`	`Velocity VariablesImpl` `FreeMarker VariablesImpl`	`arrayUtil,` `auditMessage FactoryUtil,` `auditRouterUtil,` `BrowserSniffer,` `dateFormatFactory,` `dateTool,` and so on	`ArrayUtil_IW,` `AuditMessage Factory,` `AuditRouter.` `BrowserSniffer,` `FastDateFormat Factory,` `DateTool,` and so on
`insert Variables`	`Velocity VariablesImpl` `FreeMarker VariablesImpl`	`request,` `portletConfigImpl,` `portletRequest,` `portletResponse,` `xmlRequest` `themeDisplay,` `company, user,` `realUser, layout,` `layouts` `plid, scopedGroupId,` `permissionChecker,` `locale, timeZone` `portletDisplay,` `navItems` `init, theme,` and so on	`Request,` `portletConfigImpl,` `PortletRequest,` `portletResponse,` `String, themeDisplay,` `Company, User, Layout,` `List<Layout>,` `Long,` `PermissionChecker,` `Locale, TimeZone;` `PortletDisplay,` `List<NavItem>` `Init.vm, Theme,` and so on

As you can see, the variables, such as, `theme`, `themeDisplay`, `portletDislay`, `navItems`, and so on, got defined in both `VelocityVariablesImpl` and `FreeMarkerVariablesImpl`. The custom velocity variables could be added by overriding the class `VelocityVariablesImpl`.

Alloy UI

Alloy UI is a user interface meta-framework, providing a consistent and simple API for building web applications across all three levels of the browser: structure, style, and behavior. In brief, Alloy UI is a user interface web application framework, a unified UI library on top of the revolutionary YUI3, and a library of tools. Its purpose is to help make building and designing web applications an enjoyable experience. Refer to `http://alloy.liferay.com/`.

Structure—HTML 5

Alloy UI is based on HTML5's structure, providing reusable markup patterns. HTML5 is being developed as the next major revision of HTML (HyperText Markup Language), the core markup language of the World Wide Web.

HTML5 introduces a number of new elements and attributes that reflect typical usage on modern websites. Some of them are semantic replacements for common uses of generic block `<div>` and inline `<span>` elements, for example, `<nav>` website navigation block and `<footer>` representing bottom of web page or last lines of HTML code. Other elements provide new functionality through a standardized interface, for example, `<article>`, `<section>`, `<figure>`, `<summary>`, `<progress>`, `<canvas>`, `<audio>`, and `<video>` elements.

Style—CSS 3

Cascading Style Sheets (CSS) is a stylesheet language used to describe the presentation semantics (that is, the look and formatting) of a document written in a markup language. It's the most common application to style web pages written in HTML and XHTML, but the language can also be applied to any kind of XML document, including SVG and XUL.

CSS level 3 (CSS3) is modularized. It is both more compact and richer in semantics. The markup in the published texts of CSS is also not exactly the same as the markup that the authors used when writing the text.

Behavior—YUI 3

The Yahoo! User Interface Library (YUI) is an open source JavaScript library for building richly interactive web applications, using techniques such as Ajax, DHTML, and DOM scripting. In addition, YUI includes several core CSS resources.

YUI 3 is Yahoo!'s next-generation JavaScript and CSS library. The YUI 3 Library has grown to include the core components, a full suite of utilities, the widget infrastructure, and a few widgets.

Mobile device detectors

The portal provides mobile device support and detection with portal infrastructure. This framework will use information gathered on the device being used to view the portal to change various aspects of the request. For example, if the user is using an Android or an iPhone device, change the theme to a mobile theme; if the user is using a Tablet, redirect the request to an information page.

As shown in the following diagram, the portal has defined a set of entities for mobile device detection: `MDRAction`, `MDRRule`, `MDRRuleGroup`, and `MDRRuleGroupInstance`:

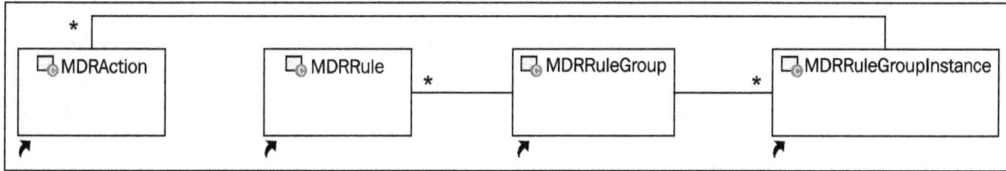

The following table shows an overview of mobile device detection-related interfaces and their implementation:

Interface	Implementation	Extension/Utility	Main methods
RuleHandler	SimpleRuleHandler	None	evaluateRule, get*
ActionHandler	BaseRedirect ActionHandler, LayoutTemplate Modification ActionHandler, ThemeModification ActionHandler	BaseRedirect ActionHandler, SimpleRedirect ActionHandler, SiteRedirect ActionHandler,	applyAction, get*
Device	AbstractDevice	UnknownDevice	get*, has*, is*
KnownDevices	NoKnownDevices	None	get*, reload
RuleGroup Processor	DefaultRuleGroup ProcessorImpl	RuleGroup ProcessorUtil	get*, register*, unregister*
ActionHandler Manager	DefaultAction HandlerManagerImpl	ActionHandler ManagerUtil	get*, register*, unregister*

WURFL

WURFL (stands for **Wireless Universal Resource FiLe**) is a **Device Description Repository (DDR)**, a set of proprietary APIs and an XML configuration file that contains information about device capabilities and features for a variety of mobile devices. The `wurfl-web` plugin delivers device recognition based on WURFL (using the `wurfl.jar` JAR file). Refer to `svn://svn.liferay.com/repos/public/plugins/trunk/webs/wurfl-web`.

WAP theme

Wireless Application Protocol (WAP) is a technical standard for accessing information over a mobile wireless network. A WAP browser is a web browser for mobile devices. The portal does not only run on web browsers, but also on WAP browsers. Now, most browsers support HTML 5. That is, these browsers support both web devices and mobile devices. Thus, building mobile themes means building HTML5-based look-and-feel; working on the vast majority of all modern desktops, smartphones (such as, **iPhone**, **iPad**, and so on), tablets, and e-reader platforms (such as, **Apple iOS**, **Android**, **Windows Phone 7**, **Blackberry 6**, **Palm WebOS**, **Firefox Mobile**, **Opera Mobile**, **Kindle 3**, and so on).

In general, the mobile theme should support a fully enhanced experience with **Ajax-based animated page transitions**, including, slide, slideup, slidedown, pop, fade, and flip. This section is going to address how to build a WAP theme for the portal.

WAP layout template

As mentioned earlier, any layout template has two types of tpl files—one for normal browsers (named *.tpl) and one for WAP browsers (named *.wap.tpl). In most cases, the layout template 1-column would be useful for WAP sites.

The file 1-column.wap.tpl has specified the following code:

```
<div class="columns-1" id="main-content" role="main">
    <div class="portlet-layout">
        <div class="portlet-column portlet-column-only"
            id="column-1">
                $processor.processColumn("column-1",
                    "portlet-column-content
                    portlet-column-content-only")
        </div>
    </div>
</div>
```

As shown in the code, only tag <div> is involved. In HTML, the <div> tag defines a division or a section in an HTML document, often used to group block-elements to format them with styles.

The tag <div> has defined attributes id and class. ID values (for example, main-content) are unique. Each element can have only one ID, and each page can have only one element with that ID. Classes' values (for example, columns-1) are not unique. You can use the same class on multiple elements; you can also use multiple classes on the same element.

You can also find the attribute `role` and its value (for example, `main`) using the `role` attribute as a class name. Use this method when individual elements need a different class name.

You will see the template variable `$processor.processColumn`, which processes portlet content of a given column. Eventually, the portlet layout-configuration provides the interface `ColumnProcessor`.

The abstract class `RuntimeLogic` has the following specification:

```
public abstract String processContent(
    Map<String, String> attributes) throws Exception;
```

The following table shows related interfaces and their implementation:

Interface/Abstract class	Implementation	Related models/classes	Description
ColumnProcessor	TemplateProcessor Customization SettingsProcessor	Layout, CustomizedPages, LayoutType PortletImpl	Column processor
RuntimeLogic	PortletLogic, Portlet ColumnLogic	LayoutTypePortlet, Portlet, ThemeDisplay	Runtime logic
None	InitColumn Processor	LayoutTemplate LocalServiceImpl	Initiate column processor

jQuery and UI

jQuery is a cross-browser JavaScript library designed to simplify the client-side scripting of HTML. It is a fast and concise JavaScript Library that simplifies HTML document traversing, event handling, animating, and Ajax interactions for rapid web development. Refer to `http://jquery.com/`.

jQuery UI provides abstractions for low-level interaction and animation, advanced effects and high-level, theme-able widgets, built on top of the jQuery JavaScript Library. Refer to `http://jqueryui.com/`.

jQuery mobile

jQuery Mobile, Touch-Optimized Web Framework for Smartphones and Tablets, is a unified user interface system across all popular mobile device platforms, built on the rock-solid jQuery and jQuery UI foundation. Refer to `http://jquerymobile.com/` for more information.

Building a WAP theme

Here, using jQuery and jQuery Mobile as an example, we're going to build a WAP theme. Loosely speaking, in the following steps, you can build this WAP theme as well:

1. Create a folder named `wap-theme`, for example.

    You can use Liferay IDE or Ant target. At the end, you will see the XML file `build.xml` and a folder called `docroot`. Under the folder `docroot`, you will see folders `WEB-INF` and `_diffs`. Under the folder, you will see the `liferay-plugin-package.properties` file.

    Under the folder `_diffs`, you will see folders `css`, `images`, `js`, and `templates`.

2. Put your custom images into the `images` folder, say, `screenshot.png`, `favicon.ico`, and `apple-touch-icon.png`.

    You can put more custom images within specific folders in the `images` folder.

3. Put your custom JavaScript files into the `js` folder, say, `jquery-x.x.x.min.js` and `jquery.mobile.min.js`.

4. Copy your custom CSS file to the folder `css` and rename it as `custom.css`, say, `jquery.mobile.min.css`. Copy the custom folder `images` and all files under this folder to the folder `css`.

    Note that both the custom CSS file `jquery.mobile.min.css` and the custom folder `images` should be in the same parent folder.

5. Create template a file under the `template` folder—`portal_normal.vm` if using Velocity engine, or `portal_normal.ftl` if using FreeMarker engine. Add the following lines:

```
<!DOCTYPE html>
<html>
<head>
    <link rel="stylesheet" href="$css_folder/main.css"
        type="text/css" title="$company_name style" />
    <script src="$javascript_folder/jquery-x.x.x.min.js"
        type="text/javascript"></script>
    <script src="$javascript_folder/jquery.mobile.min.js"
        type="text/javascript"></script>
</head>
<body>
    $theme.include($content_include)
</body>
</html>
```

- ° As shown in the code, HTML5 declaration is specified as `<!DOCTYPE html>`. For leveraging HTML5, all you need is `<!doctype html>`.

- ° Then, it parses `init` and defines template variables. Afterwards, it starts with HTML tag `<html>` and ends with HTML tag `</html>`. The `<html>` tag tells the browser that this is an HTML document. The `html` element is the outermost element in HTML documents, known as the root element. It contains a `head` element and a `body` element, as usual.

- ° The `head` element is a container for all the head elements. Elements inside `<head>` can include scripts, instruct the browser where to find style sheets, provide meta-information, and more. The following tags can be added to the head section: `<base>`, `<link>`, `<meta>`, `<script>`, `<style>`, and `<title>`.

- ° The `<title>` tag defines the title of the document and is the only required element in the head section. The `<script>` tag is used to define a client-side script, such as a JavaScript. The `<link>` tag defines the relationship between a document and an external resource and is most used to link to the style sheets.

- ° The `<meta>` tag provides metadata about the HTML document. Metadata will not be displayed on the page, but it will be machine-parsable. Meta elements are typically used to specify page description, keywords, author of the document, last modified date, and other metadata.

- ° The `<base>` tag specifies a default URL and/or a default target, for all elements with a URL (for example, hyperlinks, images, forms, and so on).

Furthermore, it starts with the HTML `<body>` tag and ends with HTML `</body>` tag. The `<body>` tag defines the document's body. The `body` element contains all the contents of an HTML document, such as text, hyperlinks, images, tables, lists, and so on. Here, the body element contains all the content, presented as a template variable such as `$theme.include($content_include)`.

Sample WAP page and page transitions

Once a WAP theme is ready (and a WAP layout template is ready, too), we can build a WAP page `view.jsp` in a portlet plugin, and furthermore, add the page transitions capabilities.

The following is a code snippet from the `view.jsp` JSP file:

```
<div data-role="page" id="home">
  <div data-role="header" data-theme="b">
    <h2><a data-ajax="false" href="#"></a>
      Action List</h2></div>
  <div data-role="content">
   <ul data-role="listview">
   <li class="view-home"><a href="#view-home"
      data-transition="pop">Map</a></li>
   <li><a href="#details-home">Details</a></li>
   <li><a href="#q-and-a-home">Questions and Answers</a></li>
   </ul>
  </div>
</div>
```

As shown in the preceding code, the jQuery Mobile tag `page` supports either single page, or local internal linked `page` within a given page. The immediate children of tag `page` are tags `div`, with `data-role` of `header`, `content`, and `footer`.

Lists are used for data display, navigation, result lists, and data entry. Any page can be presented as a modal **dialog** by adding the `data-rel="dialog"` attribute to the page anchor link. When the `"dialog"` attribute is applied, the framework adds styles to add rounded corners, margins around the page, and a dark background to make the tag "dialog" being suspended above the page. **Buttons** are core widgets used within a wide range of other plugins, while **toolbars** are used for headers, footers and utility bars.

Each **theme** includes several global settings, including font family, drop shadows for overlays, and corner radius values for buttons and boxes. In addition, the theme can include multiple color "swatches", each with color values for bars, content blocks, buttons and list items, and font text-shadow. jQuery Mobile's default theme includes five swatches that are given letters a, b, c, d, and e.

The jQuery Mobile framework includes a set of six CSS-based **transition effects** (such as, `slide`, `slideup`, `slidedown`, `pop`, `fade`, and `flip`), applied to any object- or page-change event, which applies the chosen transition when navigating to a new page and the reverse transition on hitting the **Back** button.

Portlet bridges

The **Portlet Bridge** is an implementation of the multiple-standard specification (for example, **JSR-301**) with added enhancements to support other web frameworks (such as, JSF, Struts, or Spring MVC), allowing any developer to get started quickly with their web application running in a portal environment. The good thing is that the developer no longer needs to worry about the underlying portlet development, portlet concepts, or the API.

This section is going to address a set of portlet bridges built into the portal. Spring 3 MVC, Struts 2, and JSF 2 will be addressed in the coming sections.

An overview of built-in portlet bridges

The portal supports multiple portlet bridges. The following table shows an overview of these portlet bridges:

Bridge name	Portlet name	Base extension	Description
alloy	AlloyPortlet	GenericPortlet	Alloy UI portlet bridge
BSF	BaseBSFPortlet	GenericPortlet	Base BSF portlet bridge
scripting	ScriptingPortlet	GenericPortlet	Scripting portlet bridge
groovy	GroovyPortlet	ScriptingPortlet	Groovy portlet bridge
javascript	JavaScriptPortlet	ScriptingPortlet	JavaScript portlet bridge
python	PythonPortlet	ScriptingPortlet	Python portlet bridge
ruby	RubyPortlet	ScriptingPortlet	Ruby portlet bridge
MVC	MVCPortlet	LiferayPortlet extends GenericPortlet	MVC portlet bridge
WAI	WAIPortlet	LiferayPortlet extends GenericPortlet	MVC portlet bridge
PHP	PHPPortlet	GenericPortlet	PHP portlet bridge

Alloy portlet

The Alloy portlet defines an interface called `AlloyController`. It defines a set of methods, such as, `afterProperties`, `execute`, and `setPageContext`.

The Alloy portlet also specifies a friendly URL. The following table shows a summary of alloy portlet, controller, and friendly URL:

Class	Interface/Extension	Involved models/ XML file	Description
BaseAlloy ControllerImpl	AlloyController	ActionRequest ActionResponse	Alloy controller and implementation
AlloyFriendlyURL Mapper	DefaultFriendly URLMapper	Alloy- friendly-url- routes.xml	Alloy friendly URL mapper
AlloyPortlet	GenericPortlet	ActionRequest ActionResponse	Alloy portlet

Base BSF portlet

Bean Scripting Framework (BSF) is a method of allowing the use of scripting in Java code, providing a set of Java classes that provide support within Java applications for scripting languages, and also allowing access to Java objects and methods. Refer to `http://jakarta.apache.org/bsf/`.

The portal predefines `base-BSF-portlet`. The following table depicts details of the `base-BSF-portlet`:

Portlet	Extension	Methods	Views	Involved model
BaseBSF Portlet	Generic Portlet	doView, doHelp, doEdit doDispatch, init processAction serviceResource	edit-file; help-file; view-file; action-file; resource-file; global-files	org. apache. bsf. BSFManager

Scripting portlet

A scripting language is a programming language that allows control of one or more applications. **Scripts** are distinct from the core code of the application, interpreted from source code or byte-code. The portal has a defined scripting portlet bridge called `ScriptingPortlet` and supports developing scripting portlets in **Ruby**, **Groovy**, **Python**, and **JavaScript**, in the plugins environment. The following table shows details of the portlet bridge `ScriptingPortlet`:

Portlet	Extension	Methods	Views	Involved models
Scripting Portlet	Generic Portlet	doView, doHelp, doEdit doDispatch, init process Action service Resource	edit-file; help-file; view-file; action-file; resource-file; scripting-language; global-files	ActionRequest, ActionResponse, RenderRequest, RenderResponse, ResourceRequest, ResourceRespons, PortletRequest, PortletResponse, PortletConfig, PortletContext

Ruby portlet

Ruby is a dynamic, reflective, general-purpose, object-oriented programming language that combines syntax inspired by **Perl** with **Smalltalk**-like features, supporting multiple programming paradigms. It has a dynamic type system and automatic memory management, similar in varying respects to **Python**, **Perl**, **Lisp**, **Dylan**, **Pike**, and **CLU**. Refer to `http://www.ruby-lang.org/en/`.

Ruby on Rails (short form, **Rails**) is an open source web application framework for the Ruby programming language. Refer to `http://rubyonrails.org/`.

JRuby is a Java implementation of the Ruby programming language, tightly integrated with Java to allow the embedding of the interpreter into any Java application with full two-way access between the Java and the Ruby code. Refer to `http://www.jruby.org/`.

The portal has defined the JRuby-based Ruby portlet-bridge, as shown in the following table:

Portlet	Extension	Methods	Language	Involved JAR file
RubyPortlet	ScriptingPortlet	init, getFileName	Ruby	jruby.jar

Python portlet

Python is an interpreted, general-purpose, high-level programming scripting language, supporting multiple programming paradigms, such as, object-oriented and functional programming styles, with a fully dynamic type system and automatic memory management, similar to that of Scheme, Ruby, Perl, and Tcl. Refer to http://www.python.org/.

Jython is an implementation of the Python programming language written in Java. Refer to http://www.jython.org/. The portal has defined the Jython-based Python portlet-bridge, as shown in the following table.

Portlet	Extension	Methods	Language	Involved JAR file
PythonPortlet	Scripting Portlet	init, getFileName	Python	jython.jar

Groovy portlet

Groovy is an object-oriented programming, dynamic-scripting, domain-specific language for the Java platform with features similar to those of Python, Ruby, Perl, and Smalltalk. Refer to http://groovy.codehaus.org/.

The portal has defined the Groovy portlet-bridge as shown in the following table:

Portlet	Extension	Methods	Language	Involved JAR file
GroovyPortlet	Scripting Portlet	init, getFileName	groovy	groovy.jar

JavaScript portlet

JavaScript is a prototype-based, object-oriented scripting language that is dynamic, weakly typed, and has first-class functions. JavaScript is the scripting language of the Web. The portal has defined the JavaScript portlet-bridge as shown in the following table:

Portlet	Extension	Methods	Language	Involved JAR file
`JavaScriptPortlet`	`Scripting Portlet`	`init, getFileName`	JavaScript	None

PHP portlet

PHP is a general-purpose scripting language, embedded into the HTML source document and interpreted by a web server with a PHP processor module, which generates the web page document. Refer to `http://www.php.net/`.

The **PHP/Java Bridge** is an implementation of a streaming, XML-based network protocol, connecting a native script engine (for example, PHP, Scheme, or Python) with a Java virtual machine. **J2EE backend clustering** and **Apache load balancing** are supported as well as running PHP scripts within JSP, JSF, or other frameworks. Refer to `http://php-java-bridge.sourceforge.net/pjb/`.

Quercus is a 100 percent open source Java implementation of the PHP language. Refer to `http://www.caucho.com/resin-4.0/examples/quercus.xtp`. The portal has defined the PHP portlet-bridge, as shown in the following table:

Portlet	Extension	Methods	Views	Involved models
`PHPPortlet`	`Generic Portlet`	`doView, doHelp, doEdit` `doDispatch, init` `processAction,` `destroy`	`edit-uri;` `help-uri;` `view-uri;com.caucho.quercus.servlet.QuercusServlet`	`ActionRequest,` `ActionResponse,` `RenderRequest,` `RenderResponse,` `PortletRequest,` `PortletResponse,` `PortletConfig,` `PortletContext`
`PHPServletRequest`	`HttpServletRequestWrapper`	`getContextPath,` `getParameter,` `getPathInfo,` `getQueryString,` `getRequest,` `getServletPath`	None	`RenderRequest,` `RenderResponse,` `PortletConfig`

MVC portlet

Model-view-controller (**MVC**) is software architecture, isolating the application logic for the user from the user interface, permitting independent development, testing, and maintenance of each. The **model** manages the behavior and data of the application domain, responds to requests for information about its state, usually from the **view**, and responds to instructions to change state, usually from the **controller**. The view renders the model into a form suitable for interaction, typically a user interface element. Multiple views can exist for a single model for different purposes. The controller receives user input and initiates a response by making calls on model objects. The portal has defined the MVC portlet-bridge, as shown in the following table:

Portlet/request	Extension/ Interface	Methods	Views	Involved models
MVCPortlet	Liferay Portlet	doAbout, doConfig, doView, doHelp, doEditDefaults, doEditGuest, doPreview, doPrint, doDispatch, init, invokeTaglib Discussion, processAction, serveResource, callActionMethod, checkJSPPath, include,	about-jsp, config-jsp, edit-jsp, edit-defualts. jsp, edit-guest.jsp, help-jsp, preview-jsp, view-jsp	ActionRequest, ActionResponse, RenderRequest, RenderResponse, PortletRequest, PortletResponse, PortletConfig, PortletContext
Liferay Portlet	Generic Portlet	doAbout, doConfig, doDispatch, doEditDefaults, doEditGuest, doPreview, doPrint,	None	ActionRequest, ActionResponse, MimeResponse, RenderRequest, RenderResponse,
Action CommandCache	Action Command	processCommand	None	PortletRequest, PortletResponse

WAI portlet

As mentioned in the previous chapter, the **Web Application Integrator** (**WAI**) will automatically deploy any standard Java servlet application as a portlet within the portal. The portal predefines the WAI portlet. It also specifies a WAI portlet-friendly URL. The following table shows a summary of WAI portlets and friendly URLs:

Class	Interface/Extension	Involved models/XML file	Description
`WAIPortlet`	`LiferayPortlet`	`RenderRequest,` `RenderResponse,` `PortletContext`	WAI portlet
`WAIFriendly` `URLMapper`	`FriendlyURLMapper`	`wai-friendly-url-` `routes.xml`	WAI friendly URL mapper

Vaadin widgets

Vaadin is a web application framework for rich Internet applications. In contrast to JavaScript libraries and browser plugin-based solutions it features server-side architecture—the majority of the logic runs on the servers. Ajax technology is used at the browser end, to ensure a rich and interactive user experience. Refer to `http://vaadin.com/`.

Vaadin has been integrated in the portal by default. The integration is done by performing the following steps:

1. Copy the `vaadin-${version}.jar` JAR file into the `$PORTAL_SRC_HOME/lib` folder with the new filename `vaadin.jar`.

2. Update the Vaadin version in `version.html` and `versions.xml`, in the `$PORTAL_SRC_HOME/lib` folder.

3. Build Ant target `build-vaadin` in `$PORTAL_SRC_HOME/portal-web/build.xml` and build Vaadin. For more details, you can refer to `build.xml`.

The following table shows a summary of Vaadin themes and widgets:

Name	Folder	Sample	Description
`base`	`/html/` `VAADIN/` `themes/base`	`absolutelayout`, `accordion`, `button`, `caption`, `common`, `csslayout`, `customlayout`, and so on	Base theme
`default`	`/html/` `VAADIN/` `themes/` `default`	`images` `favicon.ico`, `styles.css`	Default theme
`liferay`	`/html/` `VAADIN/` `themes/` `liferay`	`formlayout`, `panel`, `popupview`, `processindicator`, and so on	Liferay theme

Name	Folder	Sample	Description
reindeer	/html/ VAADIN/ themes/ reindeer	a-sprite-definitions, label, link, menubar, notification, and so on	Reindeer theme
Runo	/html/ VAADIN/ themes/runno	Absolutelayout, slider, table, tabsheet, textfield, tree, and so on	Runo theme
com.vaadin. portal.gwt. PortalDefault WidgetSet	html/VAADIN/ widgetsets/	Prettify	Portal default widget set

Sample portlets

The portal has specified a set of sample portlets. This section is going to introduce some of them. In addition, you could find many sample plugins (webs, hooks, layout templates, themes, and portlets) at svn://svn.liferay.com/repos/public/ plugins/trunk/.

OpenLaszlo

OpenLaszlo is a platform for the development and delivery of rich Internet applications. The OpenLaszlo platform consists of the **LZX** programming language and the **OpenLaszlo Server**. LZX is an XML and JavaScript description language, similar in spirit to XUL, MXML, and XAML, while the OpenLaszlo Server is a Java servlet that compiles LZX applications into executable binaries for targeted runtime environments. Refer to http://www.openlaszlo.org/.

JSON

JSON, an acronym for **JavaScript Object Notation**, is a lightweight, text-based open standard designed for human-readable data interchange, derived from the JavaScript scripting language for representing simple data structures and associative arrays, called objects. JSON is built on two structures: a collection of name/value pairs and an ordered list of values. Refer to http://json.org/.

You can use JSON in your plugin by performing the following steps:

1. Prepare a servlet in a portlet plugin, for example, SampleJSONServlet extending HttpServlet class. Register the servlet in the web.xml file.

2. Apply JSON object JSONObject in the method service and export the JSON object as a string.

YUI

YUI is an open source JavaScript library for building richly interactive web applications using techniques such as Ajax, DHTML, and DOM scripting, including several core CSS resources. **YUI 3** is Yahoo!'s next-generation JavaScript and CSS library. Refer to `http://developer.yahoo.com/yui/`.

Although the AUI has integrated YUI 3, you would also be able to use your own YUI 3 (for example, the latest version) in custom plugins. The following steps would help you bring YUI 3 into a custom portlet:

1. Copy the CSS file, say, `yui.css`, and related images into the `css` folder.

2. Copy the JavaScript file `yui.min.js` into the `js` folder.

3. Configure the portlet with custom CSS and JavaScript, such as, `header-portlet-css` and `header-portlet-javascript`, in the `liferay-portlet.xml` file.

Ext JS

Ext JS is a JavaScript library for building interactive web applications, using techniques such as Ajax, DHTML, and DOM scripting, with data stores for accessing the data. Refer to `http://www.sencha.com/products/extjs`.

Ext JS includes a set of GUI-based form controls, called widgets, for use within web applications: text field and text-area input controls, date fields with a pop-up date-picker, numeric fields, list box and combo boxes, radio and checkbox controls, HTML editor control, grid control (with both read-only and edit modes, sortable data, lockable and draggable columns, and a variety of other features), tree control, tab panels, toolbars, desktop application-style menus, region panels to allow a form to be divided into multiple sub-sections, sliders, and so on.

Dojo Toolkit

Dojo Toolkit is an open source modular JavaScript library (JavaScript toolkit) designed to ease the rapid development of cross-platform, JavaScript-/Ajax-based applications and websites. Refer to `http://dojotoolkit.org`.

Dojo widgets are components comprising of JavaScript code, HTML mark up, and CSS style declarations that provide cross-browser, interactive features: menus, tabs, tooltips, sortable tables, dynamic charts, and 2D vector drawings and 3D animated effects (fades, wipes and slides), facilities for custom animation effects, tree widgets that support drag-and-drop, various forms and routines for validating form input, calendar-based date selectors, time selectors, clocks, core widgets, and so on.

DWR—Direct web remoting

Direct Web Remoting (DWR) is an RPC library that enables the Java on a server and the JavaScript in a browser to interact and call each other. It generates the JavaScript to allow web browsers to securely call into Java code almost as if it was running locally, marshalling virtually any data, including collections, POJOs, XML, and binary data such as images and PDF files (refer to `http://directwebremoting.org/dwr/index.html`).

In general, you can bring DWR into the portal by performing the two following steps:

1. Configuring the portal: The `WEB-INF/web.xml` configuration options will be useful to all DWR users, or you can declare what to export using `dwr.xml`.

2. Scripting the browser: You can simply bring JavaScript libraries (more specifically, `engine.js` and `util.js`) into your portlets:

    ○ `engine.js`: Handles all server communication

    ○ `util.js`: Helps you alter web pages with the data you got from the portal

jWebSocket

jWebSocket is a pure Java/JavaScript high-speed, bi-directional communication solution for the Web. It provides a wide range of functionality from a basic token exchange up to powerful data and GUI synchronization, remote procedure calls, and much more. Refer to `http://jwebsocket.org/`

Apache Wicket

Apache Wicket (short form, **Wicket**) is a lightweight, component-based web application framework for the Java programming language, conceptually similar to **JavaServer Faces** and **Tapestry**. With proper mark-up/logic separation, a POJO data model, and a refreshing lack of XML, Wicket makes developing web apps simple and enjoyable. Refer to `http://wicket.apache.org/`.

Struts 2 portlet

Apache Struts is a web application framework for developing Java EE web applications, and using and extending the Java Servlet API to encourage developers to adopt an MVC architecture. **Apache Struts 2** is an elegant, extensible framework for creating enterprise-ready Java web applications, designed to streamline the full development cycle, from building to deploying, to maintaining applications over time. Refer to `http://struts.apache.org/`.

Strut 2 especially leverages **Object-Graph Navigation Language** (OGNL). OGNL is an **Expression Language** (EL) for Java, allowing getting and setting properties through defined `setProperty` and `getProperty` methods, found in JavaBeans, and execution of methods of Java classes. Refer to `http://incubator.apache.org/ognl/`.

Struts 2 portlet-bridge

Struts 2 provides a **JSR-168** portlet framework, using `org.apache.struts2.portlet.dispatcher.Jsr168Dispatcher` as the portlet class in the `portlet.xml` file. The Struts 2 **JSR-286** portlet framework is expected to be ready in the near future. The following table shows details of the **JSR-168** portlet framework `Jsr168Dispatcher`. The advantage of using Struts portlet-bridge is that it is an easier way to convert Struts-based web applications into portlets.

Key	Sample value	Default value	Description
portletNamespace	/portlet	Default namespace	The namespace for the portlet in the action configuration, appended to all action lookups, making it possible to host multiple portlets in the same portlet application.
viewNamespace	/view	Default namespace	The namespace in the xwork config for the view portlet mode.
editNamespace	/edit	Default namespace	The namespace in the xwork config for the edit portlet mode.
helpNamespace	/help	Default namespace	The namespace in the xwork config for the help portlet mode.
defaultViewAction	/viewAction	Default	Name of the action to use as default for the view portlet mode, when no action name is present.
defaultEditAction	/editAction	Default	Name of the action to use as default for the edit portlet mode, when no action name is present.
defaultHelpAction	/helpAction	Default	Name of the action to use as default for the help portlet mode, when no action name is present.

These are the `init-param` elements that you can set up in `portlet.xml` for configuring the portlet mode. Basically, you can think of the different portlet modes as different web applications, so that you can set up the `struts.xml` configuration with different namespaces for the different portlets and portlet modes.

In addition, a base configuration file named `struts-default.xml` is included in the `struts2-core-${version}.jar` file. This file is automatically included in the `struts.xml` file to provide the standard configuration settings without having to copy them.

A Struts 2 plugin (called `struts2-portlet-plugin-${version}.jar`) extends and replaces existing Struts framework functionality. To configure the plugin, the JAR may contain a `struts-plugin.xml`, which follows the same format as an ordinary `struts.xml` file. As a plugin can contain the `struts-plugin.xml` file, it has the ability to define new packages with results, interceptors, and/or actions to override framework constants and to introduce new extension point implementation classes.

Sample Struts 2 portlet

Struts 2 could be running in the portal. It leverages the Struts 2 portlet bridge `Jsr168Dispatcher` and the standard configuration settings `struts.xml`.

How can we achieve this Struts 2 portlet in the portal? In general, you can bring Struts 2 into the portal using the following steps:

1. Prepare Struts 2-action called `com.bookpub.portlet.struts.action.Struts2Action` which extends `org.apache.struts2.dispatcher.DefaultActionSupport`. Note that you can have a different package name and class name.

2. Set up the `struts.xml` configuration in the folder `/src`. Note that you may have different configuration settings according to your own requirements.

3. Configure portlets, such as `portlet-class` and `init-param`, in the `portlet.xml` file.

4. Prepare JSP files `view.jsp` and `results.jsp`. You would have many JSP files and add your own logics inside these JSP files according to your own expectation.

Of course, you can refer to the attached code for more information.

JSF 2 portlet

JavaServer Faces (JSF) is a request-driven MVC web framework based on the component-driven UI design model, using XML files called view templates or Facelets views. Basically, requests are processed by the `FacesServlet`, which loads the appropriate view template, builds a component tree, processes events, and renders the response, typically in HTML, to the client. Refer to `http://javaserverfaces.java.net/`.

JavaServer Faces 2.x (JSR-314) has enhanced functionality and performance. Core features cover managed beans, a template-based component system, built-in Ajax support using `<f:ajax />`, built-in support for bookmarking and page-load actions, integration with the unified expression language (EL), a default set of HTML- and web application-specific UI components, a server-side event model, state management, two XML-based tag libraries, and so on.

For instance, **PrimeFaces** is a lightweight, open source component suite for Java Server Faces 2, featuring a rich set of JSF components, while the Mobile module features a UI kit for developing mobile web applications. For more information, refer to `http://www.primefaces.org/`.

Portlet faces bridge

The following projects offer Ajax-based JSF frameworks:

- **jBoss RichFaces (Ajax4jsf)**: Ajax-enabled JSF components for layout, file upload, forms, inputs, and many other features. For more information, refer to `http://www.jboss.org/richfaces`.

- **ICEfaces**: Java JSF extension framework and rich components; Ajax without JavaScript. For more information, refer to `http://www.icefaces.org`.

- **MyFaces**: JavaServer Faces implementation, along with several libraries of JSF components that can be deployed on the core implementation. For more information, refer to `http://myfaces.apache.org/`.

The following table depicts a summary of these JSF frameworks and their portlet-bridges:

JSF Implementation	Portlet bridge	URL	Description
jBoss Richfaces	jBoss portlet bridge	`http://www.jboss.org/portletbridge`	Implementation of the JSR-301 and JSR-329 specifications to support JSF within a portlet. Currently, the bridge supports any combination of JSF, Seam, and RichFaces, with running inside a portlet.
ICEfaces	Portletfaces portlet bride	`http://www.portletfaces.org/projects/portletfaces-bridge`	Enabling development of JSF 2 applications that run inside a Portlet 2.0-compliant portlet container. In addition, the bridge facilitates the deployment of ICEfaces 2 applications.
MyFaces	MyFaces portlet bridge	`http://myfaces.apache.org/portlet-bridge/`	Implementations of the technology needed to expose a JSF application as a portlet within a Portlet 2.0 or Portlet 1.0 environment.

JBoss portlet bridge

The JBoss portlet bridge is an implementation of the **JSR-301** and **JSR-329** specifications to support JSF within a portlet and with added enhancements to support other web frameworks, such as, Seam and RichFaces, with running inside a portlet.

The class `javax.portlet.faces.GenericFacesPortlet`, extending the class `GenericPortlet`, provides JSR-301 generic faces portlet.

The following table shows `GenericFacesPortlet` initialization parameters:

Parameter	Sample value	Default value	Description
javax.portlet.faces. defaultViewId	/welcome. xhtml /error. xhtml	View Edit help	It defines the default ViewId that should be used when the request doesn't otherwise convey the target. There must be one initialization parameter for each supported mode. Each parameter is named DEFAULT_ VIEWID.mode, where mode is the name of the corresponding PortletMode.
javax.portlet.faces. autoDispatchEvents	None	True	It contains the setting for whether the GenericFacesPortlet overrides event processing by dispatching all events to the bridge or delegates all events processing to the GenericPortlet.
javax.portlet.faces. preserveActionParams	true	empty	It specifies, on a per-portlet basis, whether the bridge should preserve parameters received in an action request and restore them for use during subsequent renders.
javax.portlet.faces. defaultContentType	text/html	Empty	It defines the render response ContentType, that the bridge sets prior to rendering. If not set, the bridge uses the request's preferred content type.
javax.portlet.faces. defaultCharacter SetEncoding	None	UTF-8	It defines the render response CharacterSetEncoding, that the bridge sets prior to rendering. Typically, only set when the JSP outputs an encoding other then the portlet containers' and the portlet container supports response encoding transformation.

Parameter	Sample value	Default value	Description
`javax.portlet.faces.BridgeImplClass`	None	Empty	It names the bridge class used by this application. Typically, not used unless more than one bridge is configured in an environment.

As shown in the following table, jBoss portlet bridge provides the `GenericFacesPortlet` portlet classes:

Class	Extension	Involved interfaces	Description
`GenericFaces Portlet`	`Generaic Portlet`	`ActionRequest; ActionResponse;` `EventRequest; EventResponse;` `PortletConfig, PortletContext;` `PortletRequest;` `PortletResponse; PortletMode;` `PortletRequestDispatcher;` `RenderRequest; RenderResponse;` `ResourceRequest;` `ResourceResponse;` `StateAwareResponse; WindowState`	jBoss portlet-bridge

MyFaces portlet bridge

The **MyFaces portlet bridge** project provides implementations of the technology needed to expose a JSF application as a portlet within a Portlet 2.0 (**JSR-286**) or Portlet 1.0 (**JSR-168**) environment, defined by the portlet bridge for JavaServer Faces standards.

The class `javax.portlet.faces.GenericFacesPortlet`, extending the class `GenericPortlet`, is provided to simplify development of a portlet that, in whole or part, relies on the Faces Bridge to process requests. If all requests are to be handled by the bridge, `GenericFacesPortlet` is a turnkey implementation. Developers don't need to subclass it. However, if there are some situations where the portlet doesn't require bridge services, `GenericFacesPortlet` can be sub-classed and overridden.

The following table shows `GenericFacesPortlet` initialization parameters and default values which are similar to that of jBoss portlet bridge `GenericFacesPortlet`:

Parameter	Sample value	Default value	Description
`javax.portlet.faces.defaultViewId`	`/guess.xhtml`	`View` `Edit` `help`	It specifies, on a per-mode basis, the default `viewId` the Bridge executes when not already encoded in the incoming request.
`javax.portlet.faces.excludedRequest Attributes`	None	`Empty`	It specifies, on a per-portlet basis, the set of request attributes the bridge is to exclude from its request scope.
`javax.portlet.faces.preserveAction Params`	None	`Empty`	It specifies, on a per-portlet basis, whether the bridge should preserve parameters received in an action request and restore them for use during subsequent renders.
`javax.portlet.faces.defaultContentType`	`text/html`	`Empty`	It specifies, on a per-mode basis, the content type the bridge should set for all render requests it processes.
`javax.portlet.faces.defaultCharacter SetEncoding`	None	`UTF-8`	It specifies, on a per-mode basis, the default character set encoding the bridge should set for all render requests it processes
`javax.portlet.faces.BridgeImplClass`	None	`Empty`	It specifies the `Bridgeimplementation` class used by this portlet.

As shown in the following table, the MyFaces portlet bridge provides the portlet class `GenericFacesPortlet`. As you can see, both MyFaces portlet bridge and jBoss portlet bridge have a similar implementation of the `GenericFacesPortlet` class.

Class	Extension	Involved interfaces	Description
GenericFaces Portlet	Generaic Portlet	ActionRequest; ActionResponse; EventRequest; EventResponse; PortletConfig, PortletContext; PortletRequest; PortletResponse; PortletMode; PortletRequestDispatcher; RenderRequest; RenderResponse; ResourceRequest; ResourceResponse; StateAwareResponse; WindowState	MyFaces portlet-bridge

PortletFaces

PortletFaces Bridge enables development of JSF 2 applications that run inside a Portlet 2-compliant portlet container, such as the one provided by Liferay Portal. In addition, the bridge facilitates the deployment of ICEfaces 2 applications. For more information, refer to `http://www.portletfaces.org/`.

AlloyFaces provides JSF 2 UI components and Facelet composite components for use with Alloy UI, JSF equivalents of the `aui:` JSP tag library, provided by Liferay Portal.

LiferayFaces provides JSF 2 UI components and Facelet composite components for use with Liferay Portal, JSF equivalents of the `liferay-ui:` and `liferay-security:` JSP tag library, provided by Liferay Portal.

PortletFaces Bridge provides a portlet class called `org.portletfaces.bridge.GenericFacesPortlet` extending `GenericFacesPortlet`. The following table shows `GenericFacesPortlet` initialization parameters, similar to that of jBoss portlet bridge `GenericFacesPortlet`, and MyFaces':

Parameter	Sample value	Default value	Description
javax.portlet. faces. defaultViewId	/xhtml/ portlet ViewMode. xhtml	View Edit help	It specifies, on a per-mode basis, the default viewId the Bridge executes when not already encoded in the incoming request.
javax.portlet. faces. BridgeImplClass	none	Empty	It specifies the Bridge implementation class used by this portlet.

As shown in the following table, the jBoss portlet bridge provides the portlet class GenericFacesPortlet:

Class	Extension	Involved interfaces	Main methods
GenericFaces Portlet	Generaic Portlet	ActionRequest; ActionResponse; EventRequest; EventResponse; PortletConfig, PortletContext; PortletRequest; PortletResponse; PortletMode; RenderRequest; RenderResponse; ResourceRequest; ResourceResponse	init; processAction; processEvent; serveResource; doEdit, doHeaders, doHelp, doView; getFacesBridge

Sample ICEfaces 2 portlet

ICEfaces 2 **IPC Ajax-push** could be running in the portal. It leverages the PortletFaces portlet bridge GenericFacesPortlet, **IPC (inter-portlet communication)**, **AJAX push**, **Multistep form**, and the standard configuration settings faces-config.xml.

How to achieve the ICEfaces 2 portlet in the portal? You can bring the ICEfaces 2 portlet in the following steps, using the portlet sample-icefaces-2-portlet as an example:

1. Prepare models and services. You can use the service builder to generate models and related services.

2. Prepare web configuration web.xml and faces configuration settings faces-config.xml.

3. Prepare ICEfaces UI files, for example, `booking.xhtml`, `customers.xhtml`, and `styling.xhtml`. **XHTML** is short for **eXtensible HyperText Markup Language**.

4. Configure portlets, such as `portlet-class` and `init-param`, in `portlet.xml`.

Sample MyFaces 2 portlet

Using the MyFaces portlet bridge, we would be able to bring MyFaces 2 into the portal. The following is a sample scenario. Fortunately, MyFaces portlet bridge allows us to add more detailed features. To build a specific MyFaces 2 portlet named `sample-myfaces-2-portlet`, you may take the following steps:

1. Prepare models, services, web configuration `web.xml`, and faces configuration settings `faces-config.xml`.

2. Prepare MyFaces UI files, for example, `index.html`, `guest.xhtml`, `response.xhtml`, and `template.xhtml`.

3. Configure portlets, for example, `portlet-class` and `init-param`, in the `portlet.xml`.

Sample RichFaces 4 portlet

As with the Myfaces 2 portlet, we would be able to bring RichFaces 4 into the portal via the jBoss Portlet Bridge. Suppose that we are going to build a plugin called `sample-richfaces-4-portlet`, we could take the following steps into account:

1. Prepare models, services, web configuration `web.xml`, and faces configuration settings `faces-config.xml`, `pages.xml`, `compoments.xml`.

2. Prepare RichFaces UI files, for example, `index.jsp`, `error.xhtml`, `welcome.xhtml`, and `welcome-content.xhtml`.

3. Configure portlets, for example, `portlet-class` and `init-param`, in `portlet.xml`. This step is the same or almost the same as that of the MyFaces 2 portlet bridge.

Spring 3 MVC portlet

Like Struts, **Spring MVC** is a request-based framework. The **Spring Framework** comprises several modules that provide a range of services: inversion of control container, aspect-oriented programming, data access, transaction management, model-view-controller, remote access framework, convention-over-configuration, batch processing, authentication and authorization, remote management, messaging, testing, and so on. Refer to `http://www.springsource.org/` for more information.

Spring MVC portlet bridge

The Spring MVC portlet bridge is a request-driven web MVC framework, designed around a portlet that dispatches requests to controllers and offers other functionality facilitating the development of portlet applications. The class `DispatcherPortlet`, however, is integrated with the Spring `ApplicationContext` and allows us to use every other feature that Spring framework has. The following table shows the `DispatcherPortlet` initialization parameters:

Parameter	Sample value	Default value	Description
contextClass	application Context.xml	XmlPortlet Application Context	Class that implements WebApplicationContext, which will be used to instantiate the context used by this portlet.
contextConfig Location	kb-display-portlet.xml	Empty	String that is passed to the context instance to indicate where context(s) can be found. The String is potentially split up into multiple Strings to support multiple contexts.
namespace	kb-list-portlet	${portlet. name}-portlet	The namespace of the WebApplicationContext.
viewRenderer Url	None	Empty	The URL where DispatcherPortlet can access an instance of ViewRendererServlet

As shown in the following table, Spring 3 MVC provides two portlet classes: `DispatcherPortlet` and `FrameworkPortlet`:

Class	Interface/Extension	Involved interfaces	Description
Dispatcher Portlet	FrameworkPortlet	ActionRequest; ActionResponse; EventRequest; EventResponse; MimeResponse; PortletException; PortletRequest; PortletResponse; PortletSession; RenderRequest; RenderResponse; ResourceRequest; ResourceResponse; StateAwareResponse;	Spring MVC portlet-bridge

Class	Interface/Extension	Involved interfaces	Description
Framework Portlet	GenericPortlet Beanmplements Application Listener<Context RefreshedEvent>	ActionRequest; ActionResponse; EventRequest; EventResponse; PortletException; PortletRequest; PortletResponse; RenderRequest; RenderResponse; ResourceRequest; ResourceResponse;	Abstract class

Sample Spring 3 MVC portlet

The Spring 3 MVC IPC portlet could be running in the portal. It leverages the Spring 3 MVC portlet bridge `DispatcherPortlet`, IPC (inter-portlet communication), and the standard configuration settings `applicationContext.xml`.

How to achieve the Spring 3 MVC portlet in the portal? In general, you can bring Spring 3 MVC into the portal in the following steps:

1. Prepare models and controllers. You can use the service builder to generate models and related services. Controllers must implement the interfaces `org.springframework.stereotype.Controller`, `org.springframework.web.bind.annotation.RequestMapping`, `EventMapping`, and `ActionMapping`.

2. Prepare context XML files, for example, `kb-display-portlet.xml` and `kb-list-portlet.xml`, and the application context called `applicationContext.xml` under the folder `/docroot/WEB-INF`.

3. Prepare view resolver JSP files. The prefix and suffix of view resolvers got specified in the context XML files, as mentioned in the previous step.

4. Configure portlets, such as `portlet-class` and `init-param`, in `portlet.xml`.

Summary

In this chapter, you first learnt how to build layout template plugins, theme plugins, and WAP mobile themes. The mobile device detectors and WURFL were addressed too. Then you learnt how to leverage portlet bridges, Struts 2 portlets, JSF 2 portlets, and Spring 3 MVC portlets.

In the forthcoming chapter, we're going to address the common API.

Index

M

[PACKT] PUBLISHING   open source*
community experience distilled

Thank you for buying
Liferay Portal Systems Development

About Packt Publishing

Packt, pronounced 'packed', published its first book "*Mastering phpMyAdmin for Effective MySQL Management*" in April 2004 and subsequently continued to specialize in publishing highly focused books on specific technologies and solutions.

Our books and publications share the experiences of your fellow IT professionals in adapting and customizing today's systems, applications, and frameworks. Our solution based books give you the knowledge and power to customize the software and technologies you're using to get the job done. Packt books are more specific and less general than the IT books you have seen in the past. Our unique business model allows us to bring you more focused information, giving you more of what you need to know, and less of what you don't.

Packt is a modern, yet unique publishing company, which focuses on producing quality, cutting-edge books for communities of developers, administrators, and newbies alike. For more information, please visit our website: www.packtpub.com.

About Packt Open Source

In 2010, Packt launched two new brands, Packt Open Source and Packt Enterprise, in order to continue its focus on specialization. This book is part of the Packt Open Source brand, home to books published on software built around Open Source licences, and offering information to anybody from advanced developers to budding web designers. The Open Source brand also runs Packt's Open Source Royalty Scheme, by which Packt gives a royalty to each Open Source project about whose software a book is sold.

Writing for Packt

We welcome all inquiries from people who are interested in authoring. Book proposals should be sent to author@packtpub.com. If your book idea is still at an early stage and you would like to discuss it first before writing a formal book proposal, contact us; one of our commissioning editors will get in touch with you.

We're not just looking for published authors; if you have strong technical skills but no writing experience, our experienced editors can help you develop a writing career, or simply get some additional reward for your expertise.

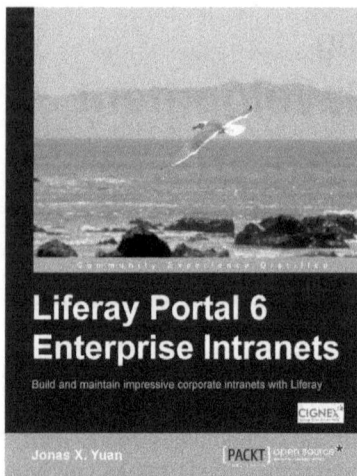

Liferay Portal 6 Enterprise Intranets

ISBN: 978-1-849510-38-7   Paperback: 692 pages

Build and maintain impressive corporate intranets with Liferay

1. Develop a professional Intranet using Liferay's practical functionality, usability, and technical innovation

2. Enhance your Intranet using your innovation and Liferay Portal's out-of-the-box portlets

3. Maximize your existing and future IT investments by optimizing your usage of Liferay Portal

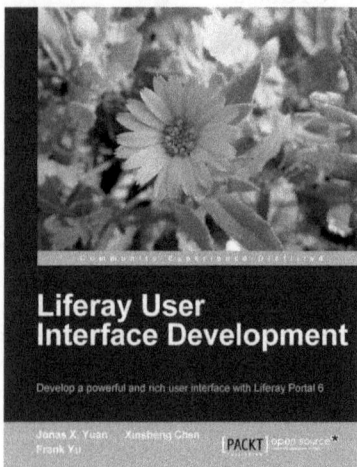

Liferay User Interface Development

ISBN: 978-1-84951-262-6   Paperback: 388 pages

Develop a powerful and rich user interface with Liferay Portal 6.0

1. Design usable and great-looking user interfaces for Liferay portals

2. Get familiar with major theme development tools to help you create a striking new look for your Liferay portal

3. Learn the techniques and tools to help you improve the look and feel of any Liferay portal

4. A practical guide with lots of sample code included from real Liferay Portal Projects free for use for developing your own projects

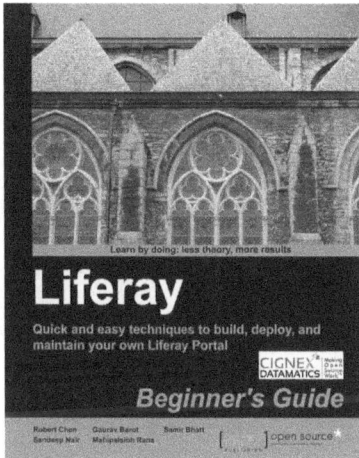

Liferay Beginner's Guide

ISBN: 978-1-84951-700-3   Paperback: 396 pages

Quick and easy techniques to build, deploy, and maintain your own Liferay portal

1. Detailed steps for installing Liferay portal and getting it running, for people with no prior experience of building portals

2. Follow the example of building a neighbourhood site with pre-installed portlets and custom portlets

3. Create your own communities, organizations and user groups, and learn how to add users to them

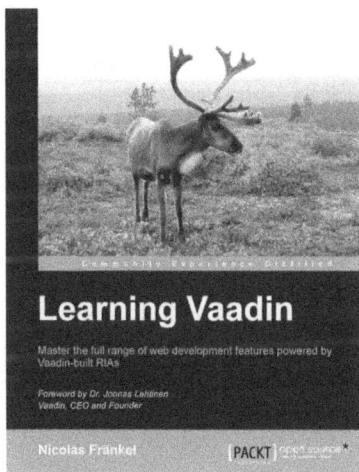

Learning Vaadin

ISBN: 978-1-84951-522-1   Paperback: 412 pages

Read this book or eBook to master the full range of Web Development features powered

1. Discover the Vaadin framework in a progressive and structured way

2. Learn about components, events, layouts, containers, and bindings

3. Create outstanding new components by yourself

4. Integrate with your existing frameworks and infrastructure

Please check **www.PacktPub.com** for information on our titles

www.ingramcontent.com/pod-product-compliance
Lightning Source LLC
Chambersburg PA
CBHW060952210326
41598CB00031B/4799